# Arrival

Also by Nick Mount

*When Canadian Literature Moved to New York*

# Arrival

## The Story of CanLit

## Nick Mount

Ⓐ

ANANSI

Published in Canada in 2017 and the USA in 2017 by House of Anansi Press Inc.
www.houseofanansi.com

House of Anansi Press is committed to protecting our natural environment. As part
of our efforts, the interior of this book is printed on paper that contains 100% post-
consumer recycled fibres, is acid-free, and is processed chlorine-free.

21  20  19  18  17     1  2  3  4  5

Library and Archives Canada Cataloguing in Publication

Mount, Nick, 1963–, author
Arrival : the story of CanLit / Nick Mount.

Includes bibliographical references and index.
Issued in print and electronic formats.
ISBN 978-1-77089-221-7 (hardcover).—ISBN 978-1-77089-222-4
(EPUB).—ISBN 978-1-4870-0218-3 (Kindle)

1. Canadian literature—20th century—History and
criticism.  I. Title.

PS8061.M68 2017          C810.9'0054          C2017-901117-0
                          C2017-901118-

Book design: Alysia Shewchuk

We acknowledge for their financial support of our publishing program the Canada
Council for the Arts, the Ontario Arts Council, and the Government of Canada through
the Canada Book Fund.

Printed and bound in Canada

*for David and Tegan*
*who have never known a time I wasn't working on*
*"that stupid book"*

# Contents

You, historian, looking back at us.
Do you think I'm not trying to be helpful?
— Margaret Avison, "To Professor X, Year Y"

# Preface

**I WROTE THIS BOOK BECAUSE IT DIDN'T EXIST.** We have many excellent biographies of the writers who emerged during what came to be called the CanLit boom. We also have some good histories of the publishing side of the story in both English and French Canada, and a great many books about the time itself. What we don't have is a book that puts all those stories together. This is the first book to try to do that, to tell the whole story, for both those who know parts of it and those who know none of it. I'm an academic, and this book builds on existing scholarship as well as many new interviews and many hours in many archives. But it's not an academic book. I just wanted to tell a story, or bring together many stories between a single set of covers.

Several people with whom I spoke for this book hoped it would also evaluate the writing left behind by the CanLit boom, that the time had come to separate great books from honest work. I didn't want to write that book — time and readers generally do a better job than critics of preserving the books that matter, and I didn't want criticism to get in the way of an already large story. But for those people, and because I am a reader too, I have placed throughout this book brief assessments of the most popular, acclaimed, or otherwise remarkable books from the period.

No doubt foolishly, I have rated each of these books using the following system:

| | |
|---|---|
| ★ | got published |
| ★★ | occasionally interesting |
| ★★★ | very good |
| ★★★★ | excellent; among the best of its kind |
| ★★★★★ | world classic |

I had hoped a digital version of this book would allow readers to disagree with my ratings and modify them over time — that, as they say, there would be an app for that. This hasn't turned out to be possible, so you'll just have to disagree the old-fashioned way, by writing your own ranking in the margin. (Or by telling me I'm wrong on Twitter, if it's still around: @profnickmount.) I have tried to place these reviews where they will be helpful to the main story, but they're not essential to that story — you can read or skip them as you like.

By chance as much as planning — mostly because it took over ten years to write — *Arrival* has arrived in the sesquicentennial year, Canada's 150th birthday. That's appropriate, because much of it's about Canada's last big birthday, the energies that coalesced around the Centennial of 1967. But it's not for that Canada, or those people (partly because I'm not one of them — I wasn't alive when much of this story takes place, and I'm not old enough to have read any of its writers at that time). This book is about the past, but like all such books, it's for the present, a book that I hope helps explain how we got from there to here, from a country without a literature to a literature without a country.

— N.M.

## Chapter 1

# Surfacing

**HE HAD A SMALL CROSS** tattooed on his chest and a significant scar on his throat. He told different stories about how he got them. In one version, the tattoo was a grateful reminder of his education in a Canadian church mission school and the scar the remains of a childhood surgery. At another time, for another audience, he might say he picked up the tattoo while drunk on shore leave, the scar in a knife fight.

Harold Sonny Ladoo emigrated from Trinidad to Canada in 1968, an early arrival in a wave of immigration made possible by a new points system that made Canada more open than ever before to immigration from non-European countries. Like most such immigrants, he came to Toronto. He came in his early twenties, already married, with children. And he came determined. You might doubt his stories, but no one who met Harold — never Harry — ever doubted he would tell them.

Two years and a lot of dishwashing later, he met the new writer-in-residence of the new Erindale College at the new Islington subway station. As Peter Such tells it, he noticed a young man in a cheap coat several sizes too large for him, a man "staring straight ahead, looking at somewhere else completely." Whatever he saw out there, he wrote it down on the back of a TTC transfer. On a hunch,

Such asked the young man if he was a writer; he said, yes, I am. Such invited him to see Erindale, and with the help of an equally impressed registrar, Harold Ladoo found himself enrolled as a mature student at the new Mississauga campus of the University of Toronto.

The calendar said 1970 but it was still the sixties, and the talk in his corner of the student cafeteria was of Marx and Fanon, Lenin and Mao, Che Guevara and Angela Davis. Ladoo joined the battle as if he had been waiting for it his whole life (because he had), arguing about anything and everything, vigorously, intensely, to win. The other students called him Plato, partly out of respect, partly to mock him. He liked it. He was of them but apart from them, disdainful even, caring more for the words he was forever writing than the words and worries of others. A writer.

At first, of course, his words were borrowed. He wrote carefully measured poems, finger exercises from the Empire's song book. Peter Such told him about a Toronto publisher named after an African god; he sent the poems to them. Their editor rejected them and told Ladoo to write about what he knew. Ladoo wrote a spiteful letter back, but he also burned everything he had written to that point, two suitcases full of manuscripts. And a week later he showed up in Such's office with a half-dozen stories about the village near which he had grown up. By the end of his first year at Erindale, he had the draft of a novel. He submitted it to the editor who had rejected his poems; they met at the Red Lion pub on Jarvis, the manuscript on the table between them. Again the editor said no, not yet.

That summer, Ladoo learned on the day of his father's death — August 12, 1971 — that the people of Canada wanted to give him money to write a book. He used $300 of his $500 grant from the Canada Council for the Arts to return to Trinidad, where he found his mother drunk, his brother a confirmed lunatic, and his sisters and neighbours fighting over the property. When he came back to Toronto in September, he had no money, his wife was unemployed, his son was sick, and they were about to be evicted. A relative let the family move into the basement of her bungalow on Victoria

Park Avenue. Ladoo borrowed enough money to go back to school for his second year, making the long commute from the edge of Scarborough to the middle of Mississauga. And he wrote the book he was paid to write, the book he had learned to write, the book he was born to write:

> In my long hours of aloneness, in my frustration and sorrow, in my sleeplessness and the painful awareness of impotence and doom, even during the illness of my wife and my son, I took to my typewriter to write a book.... For fifty days I heard only the groaning of my son as the keys of the typewriter went still. But I could not stop.

This time the editor said yes. In the fall of 1972, Harold Sonny Ladoo from Trinidad became a published Canadian author. His first novel, *No Pain Like This Body*, edited by Dennis Lee, was published by House of Anansi Press in Toronto for $8.50 cloth, $2.95 paper. On the back, a photograph by Graeme Gibson shows Ladoo smoking, staring straight ahead.

HAROLD LADOO WAS part and product of a literary explosion unlike anything Canada has ever experienced, before or since. The long decade between the late 1950s and the mid-1970s saw the emergence of the best-known names in Canadian literature, writers to whom time (never mind subsequent events) has so far been kinder than it has to Ladoo. These are the names most people still think of when they think of Canadian writing, names like Margaret Atwood, Marie-Claire Blais, George Bowering, Leonard Cohen, Mavis Gallant, Margaret Laurence, Dennis Lee, Alistair MacLeod, Alice Munro, bpNichol, Michael Ondaatje, Al Purdy, Mordecai Richler, and Michel Tremblay.

It wasn't just literary. Canada awoke in the 1960s, shaken by the excitement leading up to the party in Montreal. But the explosion was loudest and echoed longest in print. By the 1950s, Canadian art had a "distinct canon of images": the lonely pine, the snow-covered village church, the canoe, the mountain. No such set of literary images existed in the national psyche until after the sixties — no double hooks, no stone angels, no beautiful beasts or beautiful losers. That's partly the problem addressed by the Massey Report, the government's 1951 inquiry into Canadian culture: the realization that, as a means of national expression, literature had "fallen far behind painting."

This book tells the story of when all that changed. It's a story about writers, publishers, and readers, people who in one way or another played leading roles. It's also the story of the culture that created and sustained them, a society finally comfortable enough to think about something besides trees and wheat. Postwar prosperity created both an existential backlash — the nagging sense that this can't be all there is — and the means to buy what was missing or the leisure to produce it. Few realized it at the time, but that's what the hippies of Yorkville shared with their parents, and with the politicians in Ottawa: the desire to redirect affluence into immaterial rewards, the "intangibles" that the Massey Report said make up a nation. You can't get much more intangible than barefoot in the park.

**IN 1959, SGT. PEPPER** had not yet taught the band to play. Instead, from the top of the charts, smoke got in your eyes. Frank Sinatra had high hopes, but Miles Davis was kind of blue. Roman chariots crashed on the big screen, American stagecoaches on TV. Buddy Holly fell from the sky and Maurice Duplessis died on the job. Canada opened a seaway while Vietnam opened a trail. Khrushchev and Nixon debated communism versus capitalism in Moscow; a doll named Barbie spread her plastic legs in New York and settled the argument. Western Electric launched its Princess telephone in five colours ("It's little, it's lovely, it lights"), Buick rolled out the Electra, and Xerox became a verb.

It was, in retrospect, a big year for Canadian literature, the start of something not yet visible. In the west, the University of British Columbia began publishing the scholarly journal *Canadian*

*Literature*, the first in the field. The *Toronto Daily Star* created the country's first daily book column. *Le Devoir* called the language of French schoolchildren *joual*, launching an argument and a literature. Al Purdy gave his first public reading, at Av Isaacs' gallery on Bay Street in Toronto. A short walk away, Peter and Carol Martin established the Readers' Club of Canada; their first selection was *The Apprenticeship of Duddy Kravitz*, published earlier that year. Mavis Gallant, Marie-Claire Blais, and Sheila Watson published their first novels; Margaret Atwood had her first professional publication, a poem in *Canadian Forum* under the byline M. E. Atwood. The recently created Canada Council for the Arts took over the Governor General's Literary Awards, awarding its first prizes to Irving Layton's *A Red Carpet for the Sun* and Hugh MacLennan's *The Watch That Ends the Night*, a bestseller all that summer.

The boom that followed lasted into the seventies, ending around 1974 — after Margaret Laurence ran out of novels, after Victor Coleman quit Coach House, after Hubert Aquin wrote his last book. Its culmination is most visible in its achievements. When the Writers' Union of Canada formed in 1973, it limited membership to writers who had published a real book with a real publisher, because — unlike its predecessor, the Canadian Authors' Association — it could. When John Metcalf took over editing *New Canadian Stories* in 1975, he retitled it *Best Canadian Stories*, because he could. All-Canadian bookstores opened, because they could. The Harbourfront reading series began in Toronto, its authors and audiences made possible by the dozens of small reading series that came before it at campuses and coffee shops across the country. In Ottawa, after years of debate and commissions, the federal government finally moved to protect Canadian publishers by prohibiting foreign takeovers.

In the fall of 1973, the *Times Literary Supplement* of London gave over its cover and much of one issue to "Canadian Writing Today." Michael Snow's walking women grace a cover concealing a half-dozen generally grim poems: Margaret Atwood hides a rifle under her shawl, Gwendolyn MacEwen tracks God's sperm, Patrick Lane looks for a dead man in the snow, Michael Ondaatje watches stars from a graveyard, and Tom Wayman wonders (as I do now), "Why is there so much here about death?" Inside are essays on Canadian books and advertisements for Canadian publishers, including a full-page ad for something called Books Canada at 19 Cockspur Street, London, a store that promised three thousand Canadian titles for sale. The lead essay, by University of Sherbrooke professor Ronald Sutherland, told England that "in terms of dynamic activity, excitement, experimentation, even spirit of discovery and chauvinistic pride, Canadian writing is now going through what might best be described as its 'Elizabethan' period." Another essay by "Miss Margaret Atwood" called it "a literary expansion of Malthusian proportions." "One fact is indisputable," she said. "Things are very different now than they were fifteen years ago."

ONE STRIKING DIFFERENCE between the Canadian literary scenes of the 1950s and the 1970s was the sheer number of books. Books from home, books from away. Books for the shelf, as always, but now also books for the coffee table and books for the pocket. Books in small stores, chain stores, drug stores, and department stores; books on newsstands, books in the mail, books by the pound. Counting the CanLit boom is hard; then, as now, government statistics on publishing revenues were incomplete, irregular, and often hugely wrong, partly because the only people who exaggerate book sales more than authors are their publishers.

In 1973 a small group of students and faculty in the English departments of York University and its Glendon campus became frustrated by the lack of information. On the suggestion of Michael Ondaatje, they decided to do something about it. For the next two years, CanLit's original freaks and geeks laboured mightily to assemble a statistical portrait of literary publishing in Canada. They used correspondence and interviews with Canadian publishers, counting titles and sales from the publishers who agreed to provide them and guessing as best they could for those who wouldn't or couldn't. What they found was, well, remarkable. From 1963 to 1972, the number of Canadian-authored, Canadian-published

English-language literary books (fiction, poetry, drama, children's literature, and literary criticism) in print had increased by 250 percent, to at least 1,700 titles. New titles had increased by 300 percent. Sales had increased by 320 percent, to at least one and a half million copies in 1972.

To put those numbers in context, the Canadian population increased over those same years by just 17 percent. South of the border, American literary titles also increased over the decade, also in excess of population growth, but by only 45 percent — nothing compared to Canada. And, as carefully assembled as they were, the numbers in *The Lumber Jack Report* (yes, really) don't tell the whole story. For starters, they leave out books published in French Canada, itself experiencing a publishing boom driven by and driving the changes in Quebec. Even more of an omission, most of the books Canadians read in those years weren't published in Canada: they were imported, mostly from America. And just to make things really complicated, some of those imported American books were by Canadian authors, repeating a long history of Canadian writers publishing and sometimes living outside the country.

The CanLit boom took place during and partly because of the paperback revolution, what UNESCO called the entry of the book into the "mass distribution and consumption system." The number of book titles published worldwide almost tripled between 1950 and 1980. But the Canadian publishing boom was much larger than the world's, with new titles increasing at something like eight times the global rate. Ours was also a markedly *literary* boom: book sales increased in the order of 130 percent in Canada between 1963 and 1972, while literary book sales increased by 320 percent.

Those numbers drove other numbers. Like the number of bookstores, which grew at twice the rate of the population. Or the number of little magazines, a mimeographed revolution that was both effect and cause of the boom. "There must be a million of them," said Ondaatje in 1969. "They multiply like the Green Slime." The number of mainstream magazines stayed roughly flat over the decade, as did the overall number of publishers of all kinds (books, periodicals, newspapers, maps, etc.). But the value of the goods they produced more than doubled over the decade, even while losing three-quarters of the market to imported books and periodicals. The CanLit boom didn't come from a sudden proliferation of Canadian publishers; it came from a few existing publishers, a handful of new small presses, and many new little magazines, all printing more Canadian writing than ever before.

Despite how it looks, it also didn't come from a sudden proliferation of writers. Looking back, Margaret Atwood compares it to opening a floodgate or the eruption of a volcano: forces building for years and finally breaking out. "It looks as if there's this sudden, intense burst of creativity, but actually, there was suddenly an outlet, places you could publish and read. It looked as if all of a sudden people were creating, but they had been creating all along." Dennis Lee remembers his time holding the tap of one of those new outlets:

> When people began to send manuscripts to Anansi, I had this image of people crawling up from a basement flat with manuscripts under their arms, or falling down from an attic room, blinking their eyes, looking up and down the street, and discovering that four doors over, somebody was coming up from the basement with a manuscript of their own, and somebody else was lowering a manuscript from a third-storey attic, and they had no idea that this was going on around them.

The number of Canadians who claimed to write for a living increased only modestly over the 1960s, not much over 10 percent. The largest increase to date came in the *next* decade, with writers doubling in number between 1971 and 1981 — partly as an effect of the boom, as the amateurs of the sixties became the professionals of the seventies and others jumped on the now well-lit CanLit bandwagon. And their number has continued to increase, steadily and significantly. Today Canada has more writers per capita than ever (about one writer for every 600 Canadians, versus one for every 1,500 in 1971 and one for every 3,000 in 1931). If the trend holds, tomorrow there will be more still. One reason the writers of the

1960s were so well noticed then, and are so well remembered today, is not that they were so many, but that they were so few.

THE CANLIT BOOM echoed across the country. In Vancouver, visiting American poets lit the fire that ignited the most storied little magazine in Canadian history, a free newsletter called *Tish*. Out east, the Newfoundland Renaissance swept through St. John's a half-hour later, washing up painters and actors and poets. The prairies grew Margaret Laurence, Rudy Wiebe, and Maria Campbell, all three in their own way heralds of a coming Native renaissance. English Montreal let loose Mordecai Richler, Mavis Gallant, and Leonard Cohen on the world; French Quebec produced Hubert Aquin, Michel Tremblay, and Marie-Claire Blais in a "golden age of Québécois expression."

Mostly it came from Toronto, from places like the alley that housed Coach House Press, or McClelland & Stewart in the wilderness of East York. Before the 1960s, nobody but an anthropologist would have used the words *culture* and *Toronto* in the same sentence. Culture was elsewhere, in London or New York, even Montreal, cities with restaurants and bars and theatres, cities where you didn't have to fill out a form to buy a bottle of whisky. In 1960, a novel serialized in *Chatelaine* told a by then familiar joke: "the one about the Montreal contest where the first prize was one week in Toronto, and the second prize was two weeks in Toronto." In the decade that followed, both the reputation and the reality of Toronto changed, and they changed with and partly because of the CanLit boom. This isn't something Canadians are comfortable admitting, because we still love to hate Toronto, and we now hate to leave out anywhere else. But in good measure, the story of the CanLit boom is also the story of how Toronto finally became the cultural capital English Canada never had.

Again the painters got there first. Painters Eleven formed in 1953 and picked up modern Canadian art where the Montreal Automatistes had left it: about five years behind New York. Toronto the Good wasn't quite ready for the lines and blobs of abstract

expressionism and "generally ignored" the group's first exhib-
ition in a real gallery, but warmed up after they won the praise
of American reviewers. More important than their paintings, the
group's post-show parties made Canadian art and Toronto something neither had been before: sexy. The Group of Seven painted a
mean maple tree, sure, but their shows never offered fruit and cold
cuts served on a model's naked body.

Painters Eleven disbanded just as the fifties swung into the
sixties, mission accomplished. Toronto's newly acquired modern
taste moved to Av Isaacs' new gallery on Yonge, across the street
from where the reference library now sits. Isaacs sold the next generation of Canadian artists, some of them customers when they
were students buying supplies at his framing shop in the Gerrard
Street Village: Michael Snow, Joyce Wieland, William Kurelek, Jack
Chambers, and Greg Curnoe, among others. Like Painters Eleven,
Isaacs helped make Toronto exciting, cosmopolitan, showing new
Canadian art alongside Japanese prints, French lithographs, African
and Inuit sculpture. He added martinis and jazz to his exhibits,
hosted poetry readings, and organized mixed-media shows, like a
chess match between John Cage and Marcel Duchamp with each
move wired into a live electronic soundtrack. And he made art
accessible beyond his symbolic location at Rosedale's border, selling
art on the instalment plan, "like TV sets."

Further downtown, Jack Pollock gave Norval Morrisseau the
first exhibit devoted to indigenous art by a Toronto art gallery.
Memorial University hired native son Christopher Pratt to cur-
ate its new gallery, the future "crossroads and command post for
Newfoundland's cultural revolution." Charlottetown opened the
Confederation Centre, Saskatoon the Mendel, Calgary the Glenbow.
As the sixties became the Sixties, a vibrant art scene emerged in
London, for a moment "the swingingest city in Canada." Younger
artists for whom the Isaacs group were "wall painters" started artist-
run interdisciplinary cultural centres like Intermedia in Vancouver
and A Space in Toronto. In July 1968, performance art came to
Canada when Glenn Lewis walked into the Vancouver Art Gallery
and dumped an umbrella full of flour over his head.

On the stage, the main story of the sixties is the opening of large, well-equipped professional theatres across the country. In Stratford's footsteps came the Vancouver Playhouse, the Neptune Theatre in Halifax, the Fredericton Playhouse, the Confederation Centre in Charlottetown, the Citadel Theatre in Edmonton, the National Arts Centre in Ottawa, the St. Lawrence Centre in Toronto, and Manitoba Theatre Centre's Mainstage Theatre. Also following Stratford's example, most staged few, if any, Canadian plays. There weren't many to be had, and even fewer that could fill a theatre. On the eve of the Centennial, the country's leading drama critic, Nathan Cohen, pointed out that for all the new spaces and new money for theatres, Canada still couldn't claim a single full-time playwright in either language, no one good enough or popular enough to make a living writing plays. Smaller theatre companies did begin to devote themselves to Canadian content in the early seventies, notably Factory Theatre Lab in Toronto, Théâtre d'Aujourd'hui in Montreal, and CODCO in St. John's (by way of Toronto). But the most successful play of Canadian literature's boom years was first staged in New York after Stratford refused to put it on: John Herbert's men-in-prison play *Fortune and Men's Eyes*, since produced more than four hundred times in pretty much every language the theatre uses.

Something of the same story played out on television, with the best-known Canadian actors of the sixties appearing on American networks (Wayne and Shuster on *Ed Sullivan*, Lorne Greene on *Bonanza*, Barry Morse on *The Fugitive*, William Shatner on *Star Trek*) and Canadian broadcasters preferring American programs. In the fall of 1967, with the lights still on at Expo, the Association of Canadian Television and Radio Artists complained that the CBC — the network officially devoted to all things Canadian — had committed just 3 percent of its total expenditures that year to English-language writers and actors.

Meanwhile, pop music was winning Canada its largest international audience since Palmer Cox's Brownies took over American childhood in the 1880s. Denny Doherty from Halifax earned enough with the Mamas and the Papas to buy Mary Astor's

Hollywood mansion (the smaller one, but still). Ian and Sylvia's folk songs bought an elegant house in Toronto and a two-hundred-acre ranch east of the city. Steppenwolf sold two million albums in the U.S. in 1968, becoming the most successful rock band in Canadian history. By the summer of '69, not just a few acts but a whole "new sound" storming American charts seemed to be coming from the north, a fusion of sixties rock with country and folk music. The Band broke away from Dylan's shadow with their performance of "The Weight" in *Easy Rider* in July and at Woodstock in August. The Guess Who's "These Eyes" sold over 700,000 copies that summer, most of them in the States. Twenty-five-year-old Joni Mitchell played colleges and clubs forty weeks of the year, earning up to $3,000 a night. Two years her junior, Neil Young had already appeared on the *Tonight Show* and bought himself a Bentley. Leonard Cohen's first album was still selling several thousand copies a week, a year and a half after its release. Their successes helped fuel the CanLit boom, directly in Cohen's case and indirectly for others, by showing Canadian audiences that Canadian artists were making art worth hearing — defined, as always, as art that America found worth hearing.

FROM BEFORE CONFEDERATION through the Second World War, Canadian nationalism was mostly about political autonomy from Britain. After the war, it became mostly about cultural autonomy from the United States. The definition and focus shifted partly because of America's emergence as the major power in the postwar world, but also because of both countries' postwar growth and prosperity. With oil in Leduc, iron in Ungava, uranium in Blind River, aluminum in Kitimat, salt in Goderich, and the construction of a national pipeline and an international seaway, more Canadians than ever before had more disposable income than ever before, and they spent much of it on America's new resource: mass-market consumer products, from Barbie dolls to paperback novels. By 1949, over 80 percent of all manufactured goods imported into Canada came from America. In the decade that followed, trade with the United States doubled and American investment in Canada tripled. America wanted what Canada had, and Canada wanted what America made. For Canada, the result wasn't just an "unprecedented rise in the standard of living." It was also a large though not unprecedented rise in anxiety about the source of that rise, America and its stuff.

This is the economic context that put televisions in Canadian homes and then built a theatre in Stratford. It's the context that sold whole Canadian industries to American investors while giving John Diefenbaker's vision of a new "Canada of the North" the largest majority of any government in the country's history. It's the context that produced the economic continentalism and the cultural nationalism of the 1960s, both Canadian and Québécois, including the literary explosion in both languages.

It took many different forces coming together at the same time and place to turn Harold Ladoo's *No Pain Like This Body* from an ambition into a book. Federal forces, like the Canada Council's mandate to give money directly to writers, and the new immigration policy that let Ladoo into the country. A provincial government had to build a new university campus, that university had to hire a writer, and that writer had to decide to help a stranger at a subway station. People become artists for reasons as individual as their art. "For most of us," Atwood says, "nationalism didn't start out as something ideological. We were just writers and wanted to publish our books." Irving Layton became a poet because his high school teacher read Tennyson's *The Revenge* aloud in class. Matt Cohen became a writer because of Bob Dylan and a woman. Like them all, Harold Ladoo became a writer because he had no choice. My question isn't so much why Layton or Cohen or Ladoo became a writer; it's why they all did at the same time and in the same place.

In 1972, House of Anansi published a book about Canadian literature aimed mostly at high school teachers: a guide with lists of recommended books, suggestions for further reading, and contact information for magazines, publishers, and readings. Mostly written by Margaret Atwood, the book was a collective effort by Anansi staff. They called it *Survival* — because the book was a last-ditch attempt to keep Anansi alive, because survival was the main theme it found in Canadian writing, and because surviving was what Canadian literature did.

*Survival* sold 50,000 copies in three years. It saved Anansi and demonstrated a literature whose existence its title doubted. Canadian literature hadn't just survived; it had arrived. This is the story of how.

Chapter 2

# Beautiful Losers

**A dull people**
**enamoured of childish games,**
**but food is easily come by**
**and plentiful**
> **—Irving Layton, "From Colony to Nation"**

HUGH MACLENNAN'S MOTHER was a Glace Bay girl, Highland Scottish, the kind who writes poems in her spare time. His father was a doctor, Highland Scottish, the kind who studies the classics in his spare time and enforces the Sabbath and drives his daughter to a breakdown and his son to a Rhodes Scholarship and when the telegram arrives tells the boy the walk needs shovelling. In 1915 the MacLennans moved from Cape Breton to Halifax, where eight-year-old Hugh fell in love with the war, the battleships in the harbour and the campaigns in the *Boy's Own Paper*.

He spent his twenties quarrelling with his father's Calvinist god. Freud helped. He studied classics at Oxford, struggling to keep up while dreaming of becoming Keats 2.0 and proving the first of his substitute gods right by sublimating rebellion and sex into tennis, rugger, cycling, and running — running every afternoon around Christ Church Meadow, running in circles. After graduation he ground through a Princeton Ph.D., flirted with Marx, convinced himself bohemian, and wrote pastiches of Hemingway, Joyce, and Lawrence to which twenty-eight publishers mercifully said no thanks, been there, done that. Running in circles.

He returned to Canada in the middle of the Depression and took the only teaching job he could find, at a private boys' school in Montreal. A year later he married a Chicago woman with a B.Sc. in botany and a heart damaged in childhood. Dorothy had her own authorial ambitions; in fact she beat Hugh to the bookstores, publishing the lifestyle book *You Can Live in an Apartment* the year Hitler invaded Poland. Of more lasting importance, she persuaded her husband to set his third attempt at a novel at home: *Barometer Rising*, the story of the explosion that shook Halifax when Hugh was ten, washing his knees for school in the bathroom of his home on South Park, behind Citadel Hill (the home survived the explosion but was torn down in 1993 for a new CBC building).

MacLennan's first published novel received excellent reviews, sold out three printings in a month, and earned its author less than $600. He kept his teaching job.

In the fall of 1943 he won a fellowship from an American foundation that let him take a leave from teaching and begin his next novel. Published, like his first book, in New York, the novel that America paid for and published became one of Canada's best-known novels, a book whose title alone has shaped how this country speaks and thinks.* *Two Solitudes* won the Governor General's Literary Award for fiction and made MacLennan $12,000 after taxes, enough to live on for three years. He quit his job and bought himself and Dorothy a summer cottage in North Hatley, a small resort community in Quebec's Eastern Townships.

Two less successful novels followed. In 1951 MacLennan decided he couldn't pay the bills as a writer and took a teaching position in the English department of McGill University. He worked on his fifth novel for the next eight years, while his wife was slowly dying.

---

* Misshaped, apparently. MacLennan's biographer Elspeth Cameron insists that the title is regularly misread as about division when it's really about unity, a definition of love from a letter by poet Rainer Maria Rilke. In love, said Rilke, "two solitudes protect, and touch, and greet each other."

Eight months after her death, he finished his best novel, an elegy for his wife and his country. *The Watch That Ends the Night* arrived at number one on *Quill & Quire*'s bestseller list in June 1959 and stayed there until September. In New York, Scribner's bookstore on Fifth Avenue gave the novel its window. Ottawa sent another GG, and Hollywood came knocking. The movie was never made, but with $70,000 for the film rights plus walking-around money from book sales, the boy from Cape Breton finally didn't have to care.

**THE PREVIOUS SPRING,** another child of Scottish immigrants had published a book that explained the society MacLennan lamented. John Kenneth Galbraith was born on a farm southwest of St. Thomas, Ontario. After graduating from the Ontario Agricultural College, he did a Ph.D. in agricultural economics at Berkeley and postdoctoral work at Cambridge. His CV after that is kind of absurd. Contributing editor at *Fortune* magazine. Harvard professor. Host and writer of his own BBC TV series. Personal advisor to five Democratic presidents, from Roosevelt to Clinton. In charge of controlling inflation at the Office of Price Administration in the early years of the Second World War, and a director of the Strategic Bombing Survey at its end. Ambassador to India. Chairman of Americans for Democratic Action. The man who popularized the phrase "conventional wisdom" and spent a lifetime trying to change it. Awarded the Medal of Freedom, the Order of Canada, and fifty honorary degrees. The author of four dozen books, including one published in May 1958 by Houghton Mifflin in Boston called *The Affluent Society* that is generally regarded as the second most important book on

**THE WATCH THAT ENDS THE NIGHT**
Hugh MacLennan (1959)

*The Watch That Ends the Night* is told by McGill professor George Stewart, whose wife is dying of heart disease. Her first husband has returned to Montreal; believed killed by the Nazis in France, he is very much alive. If George doesn't lose his wife to death, he might lose her to love.

It's a conservative book, a desperate and in MacLennan's mind revolutionary attempt to restore morality to the modern novel. But it also captures the anxieties of its time and place better than most of the more *au courant* novels of its day. By the end of 1959 it had sold 18,000 copies in Canada. MacLennan wasn't alone in his old tastes, or his new worries.

macroeconomics of the twentieth century, right after John Maynard Keynes's *General Theory of Employment, Interest and Money*.

Classic economics — "conventional wisdom" — says free markets produce inequality and insecurity, poverty and wealth in unequal and unstable portions. For those on the right or in the liberal middle, the market and its winners and victims should be left alone, because peril is its virtue; for those on the left, markets require intervention, such as Henry George's land taxes or Karl Marx's revolution. But conservative, liberal, and socialist economists alike all accept a "tradition of despair." For Galbraith, the problem with this particular wisdom was that there didn't seem much left to despair of in postwar America. Inequality was not increasing, as classic economics said it would. In fact, he said, the gap between the rich and poor was narrowing. Wealth envy was declining, because economic power had shifted from famous wealthy families to anonymous corporate executives, and because wealth was becoming more common, so new tastes dictated that it be less visible: there was no glory for the rich in owning a Rolls-Royce when pop stars could. Governments had legislated equality through a scaled income tax to push the top down and a social safety net to hold the bottom up. Unions had won security and benefits for workers. Corporations had reduced risk by using advertising to ensure predictable markets for their products. Poverty, inequality, and instability had all been, if not eliminated, ameliorated, and were seen by both specialists and the public as solved problems.

The affluent society was not without drawbacks. In a way, its affluence was its problem. Because of outdated priorities, the main economic barometer continued to be production, even though America now produced more than enough goods to meet its needs and could probably even afford to take Fridays off, as the Republican candidate for the vice-presidency, Richard M. Nixon, proposed in 1956. To keep production increasing, consumers would have to be persuaded to buy things they didn't need with money they didn't have. Advertising solved the first problem, and credit cards (introduced in 1958) solved the second. Consumer debt began its long climb, and dumps filled with last year's delights.

**GALBRAITH FOCUSED ON** the country to the south, but the political border was as irrelevant to the affluent society as it was to the money and goods that flowed across it in record quantities. Postwar Canadians and Americans shared the highest standard of living in the world — or they believed they did, which in economics amounts to much the same thing. In Canada, new resources like oil, aluminum, and uranium increased production and attracted foreign investors. Manufacturing wages doubled in the first decade after the war, with minimal inflation. Taxi drivers in Edmonton complained that oil workers were hiring cabs just to cross the street. In Toronto, where oil and mining did their banking, the Cadillacs per capita outstripped Detroit. French Canadians left coldwater flats for modern kitchens and a charge account at Dupuis Frères. Home ownership increased across the country, and with it the purchase of everything it took to furnish, decorate, and drive to those homes. "At some point," Robert Fulford remembers, "people just began speaking of Canada as a rich country. The war left us richer, but it was still a puritan country. It didn't have that expansive feeling that you have when you believe you're well-to-do. That changed in the '50s, and that's prosperity."

One of the best windows on this time is Doug Wright's *Nipper* (*Fiston* in French Canada), a weekly comic strip that by the early sixties reached two million subscribers in forty-one newspapers across the country, capturing the arrival and rise of the baby boomers in real time. When its hero first appeared in the Montreal *Standard* in 1949, he was a toddler living in a sparsely illustrated urban flat (the first strip shows him banging on the floor with a mallet, driving the downstairs neighbour crazy).

**THE JOURNALS OF
SUSANNA MOODIE (1970)**
Margaret Atwood

★★★★★

*The Journals of Susanna Moodie* is Atwood's masterpiece. The book has never been out of print, and we will still be reading it a century from now (if we still read, if there is still a *we*). This is the book in which Atwood applied New American poetic tools — lean language, short lines, using the space on the page, dedication to the local — to the Canadian story of immigration. It's the book in which she made the European Gothic her own by internalizing it, moving the uncanny inside instead of outside, in the castle or the forest. And it's the book in which she put confessional poetry to her own use — the true confessions of someone else. It's the book in which she conquered her influences and planted them in this country like a flag.

By the summer of 1953, Nipper had moved with his creator to a new house in the flourishing Montreal suburb of Lachine, and the panels around him filled with backyard pools, asphalt driveways, TV sets and hi-fis, toboggans and pedal cars. In one strip, Nipper sands the new car with the sandpaper his dad is using to build a new picket fence. In others, he destroys an aluminum window for go-kart parts and spray-paints the TV.

A province west and a rung or two up the economic ladder from Nipper's family, the same society found itself pinned and wriggling in Phyllis Brett Young's novel *The Torontonians*, published in *Chatelaine* over the early winter of 1960. Told through the eyes of a suburban housewife, *The Torontonians* recounts better than a shelf of social history the swift prosperity of a large swath of postwar Toronto, from the financial district up through the university to the leafy enclaves north of Bloor: the chrome vacuum cleaner, the dishwasher, the Mixmaster, the Frigidaire, the Bendix washing machine and dryer, the TVs and the TV dinners. A new Buick every two years. Power mowers and garden furniture, summer camps and summer cottages. Jaeger shirts for the men, Dior dresses and pearls for the women.

In the early sixties the drive to the cottage hit a few bumps. As Peter C. Newman explained to confused Canadians in the book that launched his career, his 1963 account of recently deposed prime minister John Diefenbaker, "The massive development projects that powered Canada's postwar growth — the oil of Leduc, the iron ore of Ungava, the uranium of Blind River, the aluminum smelter of Kitimat, the building of the St. Lawrence Seaway, the construction of the Trans-Canada, Trans Mountain, and Westcoast Transmission pipelines — all happened to slow down at about the same time." At the same time, the baby boomers were becoming teenagers and looking for work, along with many of their suddenly free and suddenly indebted mothers. The net result was rising unemployment and a shrinking dollar, neither of which slowed the spending spree of the Canadian consumer. In 1960, with unemployment hitting a postwar peak of 8 percent, retail sales per capita were at record heights and still climbing. The first fully enclosed, climate-controlled mall in Canada opened that year in London, not twenty-five miles from where Galbraith was born. Paying the bills got a bit harder in the sixties, but the shopping was easy.

By 1967, employment had returned to postwar levels and Canadians were again telling themselves they had one of the highest standards of living in the world. Thirty years later, Pierre Berton was still saying it, writing in *1967: The Last Good Year* that Canadians had reason to feel good about their country in its centennial year, because "the Organization for Economic Cooperation and Development had just named Canada the second most affluent country in the world (after the United States)." They hadn't, actually. The OECD doesn't rank countries by affluence, and it didn't then; it ranks them by a purely economic measure, GDP per capita at purchasing power parity. By that measure, Canada ranked eighth in 1967, behind Qatar, the United Arab Emirates, Kuwait, Switzerland, the U.S., Denmark, and Sweden. If you remove the mathematical obscenities of the top three (many dollars, few people), Canada hovered around the fifth highest per capita GDP in the world throughout the 1950s, '60s, and '70s.

Still, fifth in the world is pretty good, and as with any ideology, belief jacked reality. Canada felt rich again because it was rich, and because it wanted to look and feel its best for the party. One Monday morning, on February 13, 1967, readers across the country opened their newspapers to find a free seventy-page magazine aimed at kick-starting the centennial celebrations. MacLennan, the nation's best-known novelist, led off *Century, 1867–1967: The Canadian Saga* by declaring that a land once considered by most Europeans to be worse than Siberia had become "one of the richest and most envied countries on earth." Novelist and broadcaster W. O. Mitchell underlined the changes on the prairies since the war, "the country skeined with oil and gas pipe lines, the cities' perimeters opulent with ranch style, Cape Cod, modern functional suburbia." Literary angler Roderick Haig-Brown reported on B.C.'s easy lifestyle, "elegant houses on the rocks in West Vancouver, retirement in Victoria, pleasure boats, year around golf." In Halifax, novelist Thomas Raddall found smart suburban streets where he'd once shot rabbits. Playwright John Gray wrote about Toronto, a city become a metropolis, with "new buildings, new suburbs, a new subway, acres of factories, men who can corner the market in Krieghoffs" (a reference to newspaper publisher Ken Thomson, whose collection of more paintings by Cornelius Krieghoff than should be allowed to exist on any one planet is now the Art Gallery of Ontario's problem). When Mordecai Richler returned to Montreal that summer to cover Expo 67, he was, to use his word, overwhelmed:

> All the ambitious building of twelve years, the high-rise apartments, the downtown skyscrapers, the slum clearance projects, the elegant new metro, the Place Ville Marie, the Place des Arts, the new network of express highways, the new hotels, have added up to another city. Home, suddenly, is terrifyingly affluent.

THE MARTYROLOGY:
BOOKS 1 & 2 (1972)
bpNichol

★★★★★

The Martyrology is an epic poem about the lives of saints written by a poet who loved comic books. As Nichol said, myth is only relevant if it's relevant to our own time, so he threw out the old saints and made up some new ones. His magnum opus simultaneously mocks Christian mythology and gives it new life, knocks down the whole silly structure and then builds it up again, for fun and because he must.

It's also a dream, a prayer, a love letter, "an act of desperation," and a diary that lasted the rest of his life, nine books published in six volumes. There is nothing quite like it in Canadian or any other literature.

THIS IS THE SOCIETY that established the Stratford Festival, dozens of new university and college campuses, the National Library, the National Ballet, a national television network, and a national arts council. It's the society that made the CanLit boom possible. *The Torontonians* and *Nipper* weren't just windows on the affluent society; they were also products of that society, goods whose production and consumption were made possible by a society that after several centuries of cutting trees and swatting bugs suddenly found itself with time and money on its hands. The writers who emerged during the CanLit boom were not themselves baby boomers; most were born in the thirties or early forties and are more likely to have been fans of Beckett than of the Beatles. They were the generation who became writers just as the largest, most affluent generation in Canadian history became readers.

Canada's postwar affluence paid for new spaces in which its artists could perform and exhibit. It paid for new universities with departments devoted to studying and fostering music, drama, literature, and the visual arts; for new campuses with their own galleries, theatres, radio stations, magazines, publishers, and bookstores. It built new houses with new hi-fis that needed playing and new bookshelves that needed filling, and then it built new shopping malls in which to buy the new records and new books. The proliferation of coffee-table books was driven by the proliferation of coffee tables, the sudden interest in large, colourful canvases by the sudden acquisition of large living rooms with large white walls. (The first exhibit of the artists who would become Painters Eleven was called *Abstracts at Home*, set amid the furniture displays at Simpson's department store in downtown Toronto.) Affluence paid for the salaries that bought the homes that filled with the babies that filled the universities, both creating and conditioning the first generation for whom culture was a mass-market product. "We have moved," said Marshall McLuhan as the sixties dawned, "from an era when business was our culture to one in which culture is our business." He meant in the West, but he learned it in Canada.

Affluence gave Canadians not just the means but also the time to consume and produce goods that are unnecessary to life. In 1951, the commissioners of a two-year investigation into Canada's cultural activities presented their report, *Royal Commission on National Development in the Arts, Letters and Sciences, 1949–1951*, better known as the Massey Report. "Our task," they told the Governor General, "was opportune by reason of certain characteristics of modern life."

> One of these is the increase in leisure. The work of artists, writers and musicians is now of importance to a far larger number of people than ever before. Most persons today have more leisure than had their parents; and this development, along with compulsory education and modern

communications, enables them to enjoy those things which had previously been available only to a small minority.

So it was, and so they told themselves. Twenty years after the Massey Report, the first national survey of leisure opened by announcing, again, that "We have reached the threshold of a major and rapid expansion in leisure-time activities." Which didn't, of course, make it any truer in 1972 than it had been in 1951. It just meant that people still believed it to be true — which made it true, sort of.

Many of the people with whom I spoke for this book resisted (to put it politely) the suggestion that they were affluent. Stan Bevington recalled bartering printing work for food. "Unless you got a university job teaching," said Daphne Marlatt, "writers didn't have money. Sure, we bought books, but we gave a lot of books away, among ourselves. When a book came out, you made sure you had copies to give to your friends who couldn't afford to buy copies. When *Tish* began, it was free."

For most writers and some publishers in the sixties, affluence took the form it still takes for most writers and some publishers today, a form it acquired in and thanks to the affluent society: not money but time, the leisure to forsake profit or payment, to give their labour away, and ultimately to imagine something their parents could not — a life without a job. Marlatt's classmate Frank Davey remembers it as "the luxury of larger aspirations." Around the middle of the nineteenth century, the writer became a paid professional; around the middle of the twentieth she became an artist again, able and determined to put art ahead of commerce, precisely because commerce had got ahead of art.

Good thing too, because for all the new GNP, it was still tough to make a living from literature in Canada in the 1960s. The publisher of the most commercially successful Canadian writers of the period, McClelland & Stewart, flirted with bankruptcy throughout and after the CanLit boom. The premier literary magazine of the time, the *Tamarack Review*, never had more than two thousand subscribers. Most writers lived cheaply and at times precariously, surviving on small grants, the occasional teaching or writer-in-residence contract, sometimes even their writing. In the introduction to his 1970 high school anthology *Sixteen by Twelve*, John Metcalf noted that a good printing in Canada for a collection of short stories might run to three thousand copies and take five years to sell, earning the writer — for, say, a five-dollar book with 10 percent royalties — just $1,500 over five years, or a little under six dollars a week. Canadians had more spending money than ever before, but most of them spent their entertainment dollars on entertainment, especially American entertainment. The redirection of material affluence into national culture recommended by the Massey Report was more symbolic than substantial. But as its authors knew, symbols matter more than facts to nations. Maybe, they hoped, they could also matter more than dollars.

**MORDECAI RICHLER SAID** he found the new affluence of his old home terrifying and overwhelming. I have a hard time imagining Richler terrified or overwhelmed by anything. But he wasn't alone. Running beneath and often beside the celebration of prosperity in the centennial magazine *Century* is genuine anxiety about that same prosperity. "Too rich too fast, we knew in our hearts," says MacLennan in his opening essay. Virtually all the contributors note the wealth around them, but often nervously. Most spend more time on the country's past than its present, a time when Canada was slower, quieter, simpler. *Century* is more 1867 than 1967, more schooners than skyscrapers.*

Some of the sources of that anxiety are not hard to find. *Century* names them openly. Modern machinery and modern technology. In the Atlantic provinces, the children leaving; in Toronto, the world's children arriving. An increasingly loud Quebec. The Bomb. Bombs in Quebec. An American war in Vietnam and American companies in Canada. Mostly, though, the uneasiness that many otherwise

---

* Predictably, the only real exception is Max Braithwaite, working the working-class genre of comedy. Braithwaite spends more time on the Red River carts of 1867 than the airplanes of 1967, but only to make the point that the carts took more time too, never mind their lack of seats. Affluence didn't make all Canadians anxious. As C. P. Snow pointed out in 1959, it's rarely manual labourers who miss the good old days of manual labour.

comfortable Canadians felt in their prosperity was less certain of its causes, sure only of the symptom — a nagging dissatisfaction with satisfaction itself, with their own success.

**THE CRUISING AUK (1959)**
George Johnston

George Johnston taught Old English at Carleton University and wrote poetry when time allowed or circumstances occasioned. "I am not so much a poet," he said, "as a teacher and a family man who has been lucky enough to write some acceptable poems." *The Cruising Auk* is his first and best book, written during the war but not published until 1959. Most of the poems are set in an Ottawa neighbourhood populated by recurring characters, middle-aged Prufrocks with "Two little children and a wife / Living a small suburban life." They're not like any Canadian poems of their time (partly because they're not of their time): witty, bittersweet snapshots in regular rhyme that flirt with being sentimental and get away with it. If Philip Larkin had been a happy man, these are poems he would have written.

Their worries are everywhere evident in the books they wrote and read. MacLennan's *The Watch That Ends the Night* and Galbraith's *The Affluent Society* both document a society that has lived through the Depression and the Second World War and has come out materially comfortable and politically secure, but existentially bankrupt, with nothing bigger to believe in than the shiny new cars in the driveways of its shiny new homes. Young's *The Torontonians* opens with Karen Whitney considering suicide while awaiting delivery of a beautiful carpet that is the final touch on her beautiful house. "When they could afford a carpet like that," she remembers thinking, "they would have 'arrived'." But now, on delivery day, she asks herself, "arrived where, and why, and what in hell does it do for us?"

With material prosperity came the human backlash, the alienation from comfortable conformity that turned the toddlers of the fifties into the hippies of the sixties and left their hungover parents wondering if happiness really was just a new carpet. The arts flourished because they provided an answer, assuring those Canadians who cared that some things mattered more than carpets, things like taste, education, and a national culture. For some, the arts were ornaments — the right painting above the sofa, the right music on the hi-fi, the right book on the coffee table. For others, the arts were more of a remedy than a complement to prosperity. If they couldn't have authentic experiences, they'd take the next best thing, experiencing somebody else's authentic experiences in a book or a movie or a song. Either way, the arts gained customers.

In literary historian Richard Ohmann's superb account, postwar America looks much like Galbraith's affluent society: middle-class, professional, and prosperous, an age in which the only remaining problems are "happy problems" like having to replace your suit because lapels are narrower this year. The problem, of course, was that — people being what they are, and capitalism and America being what they are — many people were not happy. Their unhappiness produced not only black rebellion, student revolts, and antiwar protests but also an entire literature of lost, sad, and outright crazy characters: Salinger's *Catcher in the Rye*, Plath's *The Bell Jar*, Bellow's *Herzog*, Updike's *Rabbit*, Kesey's *One Flew Over the Cuckoo's Nest*, Pynchon's *The Crying of Lot 49*, Roth's *Portnoy's Complaint*, Vonnegut's *Breakfast of Champions*, etc., etc.

Much the same thing happened in Canada and for much the same reasons, with the additional reason of America itself. In the moment of our success, we read and rewarded books about failures. Hugh MacLennan's war-shattered heroes. Mordecai Richler's Duddy Kravitz, a failure as a businessman and as a man. Michael Ondaatje's ill-fated cowboys and Rudy Wiebe's ill-fated Indians. Women

**THE FIRE-DWELLERS (1969)**
**Margaret Laurence**

A year in the life of a lonely, scared Vancouver housewife, *The Fire-Dwellers* was one of the books the affluent society took to bed at night to tell them they weren't alone. Some such books offered the consolation of faith, like *The Watch That Ends the Night* and *Beautiful Losers*. Laurence was too much the realist for those answers. The point of books like *The Fire-Dwellers* wasn't to offer another life but to reconcile readers to this life, to the marriage and the house and the kids and the diet. Everything's fine. And if not, there's a gin and tonic hidden in the Mixmaster bowl.

writing alone in an Alice Munro story, dying alone in a Margaret Laurence novel. Leonard Cohen's beautiful losers, bpNichol's martyred saints, George Bowering's lost explorers. Marie-Claire Blais's tormented children and Hubert Aquin's tortured men. Daphne Marlatt's and Dennis Lee's failed communities. George Grant's *Lament for a Nation* and Pierre Vallières's *White Niggers of America*. Margaret Atwood's victims, both those she found in older Canadian literature and those she added to the list as a writer. Atwood wasn't wrong about CanLit's obsessions; she just made the human mistake of projecting the worries of her time into her past, and the equally human mistake of assuming that those worries were unique to her place.

**BEAUTIFUL LOSERS (1966)**
Leonard Cohen

★★★

Like Jack McClelland, I'm damned if I know if *Beautiful Losers* is a great book or not. I know it's a great (if morally difficult) book to teach, but I have a hard time imagining anybody but the very young, the very stoned, or the very overeducated actually enjoying it, and I'm still naive enough to think enjoyment is part of art.

It's a book about wanting to fuck a saint, a seventeenth-century Mohawk woman named Catherine Tekakwitha. It's got it all: masturbation, cheerleader fantasies, paraphilia, pedophilia, adultery, torture, gay sex, straight sex, telephone sex, machine-assisted sex, and a post-sex bath with Hitler. Alongside the passages of degradation are passages of great beauty, which is of course the point. In 1970 Michael Ondaatje called it "the most vivid, fascinating, and brave modern novel I have read."

It's hard to imagine two novels more different than MacLennan's *The Watch That Ends the Night* and Leonard Cohen's *Beautiful Losers*. One, a deeply conservative bestseller that won the country's highest literary award. The other, a wildly experimental, amphetamine-fuelled pornographic prayer that its own publisher called revolting ("I've had to wash my mind," said Toronto columnist Gladys Taylor after reading it). And yet both lament the same world, a world that has become plastic, graceless, meaningless. "Canada was rich now," says MacLennan's narrator. "But I wondered whether she was finding herself or losing herself." "I wanted to confront the machines of Broadway," says Cohen's. "I wanted Fifth Avenue to remember its Indian trails. . . . I want the world to be mystical and good." And so both go looking for something real, something to believe in, a hero to follow or a woman to love. Both find a kind of consolation in God, the old trick of renaming mortal confusion as divine mystery. The final lesson of *Beautiful Losers* is that, appearances notwithstanding, "God is alive. Magic is afoot." The final lesson of *The Watch That Ends the Night* is that appearances don't matter, because God is always watching.

For readers, the vehicle of that consolation was books. Not God or magic, but stories in which such things could be alive and afoot for a few hours. Affluent North Americans of the 1960s were no more messed up than you and me. But they were the first to be messed up in their way and it confused and scared them, so they turned to art for comfort. Books especially, because they're easy to hold in bed.

Affluence didn't just make the CanLit boom possible: it made it necessary, the therapist and companion to a society. It couldn't cure what ailed them, but it could tell them they were not alone.

**Chapter 3**

# Fifth Business

They have named a royal commission
    To ask itself what for,
Which is a really deadly serious question,
    Never been asked before.
        —George Johnston, "The Royal Commission"

MORDECAI RICHLER WAS the second son of an unhappy marriage between a junk dealer and a rabbi's daughter. He grew up in a Jewish ghetto, on a street *Time* magazine called the Hell's Kitchen of Montreal. Raised Orthodox, he announced himself an atheist at age thirteen after reading Charles Darwin. His father hit him, and Mordecai hit him back.

Mordy went to Baron Byng High School down the street, Jews taught by Gentiles. He followed the Habs in the *Herald* and the liberation of Europe on his bedroom wall. He joined a Zionist youth group, favoured black, smoked Sweet Caps, and wrote his first short stories, G. A. Henty read-alikes in which English fops start their sentences with "I say, Marmaduke." On graduation his marks were too low for McGill but good enough for Sir George Williams College (now Concordia University), where he joined the literature club, wrote for the school paper, and hustled freelance work at the *Herald*. He had by now moved up from Henty to Hemingway and the *New Yorker*. Once he snuck into a ballet.

In the early fall of 1950, now nineteen, Richler dropped out of

college and boarded the Cunard Line's RMS *Franconia*, bound for
Paris, bound and determined to become a writer. He spent the
next two years in France and on the Spanish island of Ibiza, living
the writer's life in cafés, bars, and brothels. The Sweet Caps gave
way to Gauloises, beer to brandy, shoes to sandals. He acquired a
taste for Sartre and what he hoped was a dose of syphilis (more
likely scurvy). Within a month he had his first acceptance letter,
from *Points*, a Paris magazine for new writers backed by American
heiress Peggy Guggenheim and barely edited by her bored son.
The *New Yorker, Harper's, Mademoiselle,* and *Atlantic Monthly* all
said no, as did the publishers to whom he sent his first attempt at
a novel, described by his biographers as cribbed from Hemingway
and Céline and by his friend and fellow expatriate Mavis Gallant
as a juvenile exercise in revenge.

Broke and mostly beat, Richler sailed for home in September
1952. On the way, he stopped in London to press the manuscript of
a second novel on an agent, Joyce Weiner. Weiner didn't much like
the novel but she did like Richler, and she found a publisher who
also didn't much like the novel but did like Richler. After a year in
Montreal, Richler returned to Europe with his first book contract in
hand, this time to London, his home base for the next twenty years.

In a Hampstead flat he lived the writer's life again, typing by day and
drinking by night with other émigrés, including one he had brought
with him and married, a French-Canadian divorcée in her early thirties. They survived on typing jobs, loans and care packages from family
and friends, and a regular "London Letter" for a Montreal magazine
that paid fifty dollars. Increasingly, money came from the movies:
screenplay and script-doctoring work picked up through friends in
the business. Richler's London publisher brought out three of his novels
in four years, about which the kindest that can be said is that each got a
little less hateful. None sold well or attracted much interest, other than
hurt and anger from his family and the Jewish community back home.*

---

* The Canadian Jewish Congress called Richler's second novel self-hate literature, "a caricature of Jewish life one might expect in *Der Stürmer*" (a Nazi tabloid). Richler later tried
to keep his first two novels out of print and rarely spoke of the third.

Meanwhile in Ottawa, the new Canada Council for the Arts embarked on its first year. On the strength of a reference from Hugh MacLennan, the Council agreed to support a novel by Mr. Mordecai Richler of 61 Hallowell Street, Montreal (his mother's rooming house). In the spring of 1958, the Council informed Richler that he had won a $2,000 Junior Arts Fellowship. He put the money toward renting a villa on the French Riviera for himself, his wife, and their friends Stanley and Florence Mann.

That June in Roquebrune, two marriages ended and another began. And Richler wrote his fourth and first successful novel, the novel in which his biographers agree he found his voice. When *The Apprenticeship of Duddy Kravitz* was published in the fall of 1959, Richler dedicated it to Florence, his new and forever love. On the next page he thanked the Canada Council for allowing him "to write this novel free from the usual financial pressures."

"I am," he said, "most grateful."

**THE USUAL STORY** is that Canadian literature was legislated into being. In 1949 the federal government established a royal commission on the state of Canadian culture, which begat the Canada Council, which begat Mordecai Richler. "No other Canadian commission," says the biographer of its chair, "has had such an immediate and transforming effect." As a more recent historian puts it, "The history of Canadian literature after the Massey Commission is largely the history of how economic policies and forms of government intervention created a vibrant literary culture, but one founded on the idea that literature and subsidy go hand in hand."

It's a good story, that one. But it's not the whole story, or the only way to tell it. Here's another way. In early 1958, around the same time that the Canada Council gave Richler $2,000 for a novel it would take him a year to write, a British production company paid him £1,400 ($3,760 Canadian) for three weeks of screenplay work. By the time *Duddy Kravitz* was published, Richler was making enough money in the movie business to joke that "next year I will give a grant to the Canada Council."

Or this way—a story from the other end of fortune. In June 1975, three months before her husband beat her to death with a hammer while their children slept, Vancouver poet Pat Lowther told the arts newspaper *Performance* that the Canada Council's maximum grant for junior artists "will keep one person at or near the poverty line. For a person with dependants, it is totally unrealistic."

The Canada Council certainly played a part in the making of Canadian literature, both that portion that came to be known and taught by the mid-1970s as "CanLit" and much now lost in its dim reaches. But especially outside French Quebec, where the Council uniquely supported publishers as well as writers, its role was small. As in most stories in our time, the main character was the economy. Cultural nationalism flourished at the same time and because of economic continentalism. Patriotism arrived in the same package as affluence, a new flag for your new home. As Robert Bourassa put it for the Québécois, "American technology, French culture."

**THE APPRENTICESHIP OF
DUDDY KRAVITZ (1959)**
Mordecai Richler

★★

Like Philip Roth's *Goodbye, Columbus*, published the same year, *The Apprenticeship of Duddy Kravitz* is about Jewish North Americans leaving the urban ghettos for college and the suburbs. But while Roth's Neil Klugman isn't entirely sure about moving on up, Richler's Duddy Kravitz is completely sure, and he'll sell anything and anybody to get there.

The best novel Richler had yet written, *Duddy Kravitz* is still too much life and too little art. The writing is still hasty, the story still too often an opportunity to retell unfiltered memories and rehearse old grievances. You could take the author out of St. Urbain Street, but taking the street out of the author would take a little longer yet.

**GOVERNMENT SUPPORT FOR** the arts exists in Canada because private support does not. With a few exceptions, such as the Chalmers Fund for the performing arts, wealthy Canadian families have preferred to amass and bequeath private collections rather than support living artists. Most philanthropic support for the arts and sciences in Canada in the first half of the past century came from wealthy American families, especially the Carnegie Corporation and the Rockefeller Foundation, which together spent almost $20 million in Canada between the First World War and the 1950s. Even today, when tax and marketing benefits have made corporate sponsorship of the arts *de rigueur*, the Scotiabanks and Rogers of the country prefer to reward art rather than invest in artists. Corporations brand the winners now, but the citizen still funds the field.

At the federal level, the notion of the Canadian public becoming the patron of its own arts dates to a proposal in 1948 by, of all people, the minister of national defence, former sergeant major Brooke Claxton. Claxton's goal seems to have been pretty much exactly what the Massey Report finally yielded a decade later — direct government support for artists — but he hid his core proposal amid a laundry list of less contentious items, from improving national parks to building the long-promised national library. With the support of fellow cabinet member Lester Pearson, Claxton persuaded Prime Minister Louis St. Laurent that a public inquiry into Canada's cultural institutions would appeal to the growing number of educated and affluent Canadians among the postwar electorate. For the new prime minister, the idea had the added benefit of letting somebody else sort out several pressing issues, including rumours of communist sympathizers over at the National Film Board and the looming arrival of the new kid on the block, television.

In January 1949, the Governor General announced the Royal Commission on National Development in the Arts, Letters and Sciences. Public hearings began in Ottawa in August and ended in St. John's the following July. In between, the Commission received 462 briefs and heard more than 1,200 witnesses at 114 hearings in sixteen cities and in every province: not quite a "complete cross section of the Canadian population," but certainly an excellent representation of its interested

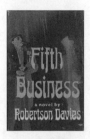

**FIFTH BUSINESS (1970)**
Robertson Davies

★★★★

A prolific writer and editor in the 1940s and '50s, Robertson Davies spent most of his energies in the sixties as Master of Massey College. His first novel in twelve years became his best-known book and one of the most successful Canadian novels ever. He had found a voice that suited him perfectly, because it was his own: a witty, erudite scholar and teacher obsessed with magic and melodrama. I can see the Harry Potter generation picking up Davies when they're older.

For me, the story bogs down toward the end (and even more in the next two volumes of the trilogy), becoming a paint-by-numbers fictionalization of Carl Jung's mythologies. But it spent forty-two weeks on the *Toronto Daily Star*'s bestseller list, so obviously Davies wasn't the only one longing for marvels.

portion. It's hard to imagine anyone doing better in the time the commissioners had, or working harder.

One task on which the Commission worked hard from the start was to defuse concerns that it would impose highbrow tastes on Canadians, the kind of culture the newspapers liked to call "cultcha." Fun fact: the word *culture* does not appear in the Commission of Appointment for this country's largest cultural inquiry. Instead, the Commission's marching orders spoke of "national interest," "national life," and "national feeling," terms more likely to win welcome in a country proud of its own recent achievements and increasingly apprehensive about international influences, both Soviet and American. At the first press conference, commission chair Vincent Massey tried to get ahead of the story by confiding to reporters that he was himself "a bit shy about the word 'culture.' It has a sort of highbrow ring about it." Vincent Massey was a charter member of Toronto's social elite, an Oxford-educated anglophile of whom the leader of the British House of Lords once remarked that he was "a fine chap, but he does make one feel a bit of a savage." For Massey to pass himself off as a man of common tastes was absurd, as absurd (and as necessary) as when his fellow commissioner Professor Hilda Neatby stressed to reporters her ability to milk a cow. There may have been more culturally inclined Canadians among the electorate than ever before, but this was still North America, and the commissioners knew their constituents.

**THE NEW ANCESTORS
(1970)
Dave Godfrey**

It's a good thing Godfrey published his only novel himself — both because it's doubtful anyone else would have, and because it became a best-seller and won the Governor General's Literary Award for fiction, notoriously beating out *Fifth Business*.

*The New Ancestors* is the least enjoyable novel I have ever read. There's no plot to follow, no style to admire, no characters to feel for. Aside from the many sex scenes, for most of its four hundred pages I had very little idea what was even happening. All I can say about it with confidence is that it takes place somewhere in Africa, and that Margaret Laurence thought it was the work of a genius. I'd say a madman, but the line between them is sometimes thin.

According to Paul Litt's excellent history of the Massey Commission, most of the individual Canadians who took the time to appear before it proved the commissioners right. As one indignant citizen put it, "the trouble with the intelligéntsia is that they are not willing to pay for their own pleasures." For the cultural organizations that dominated the public hearings, though, their main worry was the pleasures of the many. The Vancouver branch of the Canadian Authors' Association told the Commission that "For years we Canadians have been flooded with American moving pictures, American radio programs, American magazines, American books. Something should be done before the Canadian viewpoint is lost entirely." In Quebec City, the Canadian Association of French Language Educators warned about "*le danger d'américanisation par le cinéma de notre vie et de notre culture*," the loss of "our life and our culture."*

Although the Massey Commission is remembered as an inquiry into the arts, the most contentious part of its mandate was broadcasting, radio and television. The Commission believed the new mass media could improve public taste, opera on the CBC. But the broadcasting industry didn't want public interference in private profits. The arts were a small part of the real battle because they were a small part of the potential gains, cultural or financial. They were, however, a large part of the Commission's final report, which is partly why its interests are misremembered today. Tabled in the House of Commons on June 1, 1951, the Massey Report spoke stirringly, if vaguely, of "important things in the life of a nation which cannot be weighed or measured," and "the intangibles which give a nation not only its essential character but its vitality as well" (avoiding *culture* wasn't easy). To foster these intangible somethings, the report recommended a national arts council at arm's length from the government: state support, without state control.

Aside from predictable grumbling in predictable places about taxing the common man to support "longhairs," the report was well received by the press. *Le Devoir* found evidence of a conspiracy to

---

* Canada's lonely communists developed their own Massey report at party conferences in the late 1940s and early '50s, calling for "organized resistance to the inundation of Canada by Hollywood movies, US radio programs, and pulp magazines." On this issue, if no other, Vincent Massey and Communist Party of Canada leader Tim Buck could agree.

undermine French culture, *bien sûr*, but the response from French Quebec was mostly positive: partly because the Commission had operated fluently in French while there, and partly because French Canadians were happy with any support for French culture. In English Canada, editorials were typically supportive of the report's loftier ideals of developing the "spiritual resources" of the nation, lukewarm about a federal arts council that might actually do anything about it, and enthusiastic about recommendations for federal aid to universities, constitutionally a provincial responsibility. As Hilda Neatby noted privately, Canadians might say no to culture, but never to education.

Within a year, the government had granted $7.1 million in aid to universities. It amended the Broadcasting Act to better support public broadcasting, and then it made the Act obsolete by licensing private television stations.

And that's about it.

Most of the Massey Report's recommendations were never implemented. Others, such as the National Library (1967) and the National Gallery (1988), happened under different governments and so many years later that it's difficult to credit the report with more than early support.

As for the arts council that the commissioners considered key to the report, Litt says it was still too novel an idea for political comfort. It may simply have gotten lost in the work of running a country. But it also seems likely that the Massey Commission made it easy to ignore its own proposals by providing abundant evidence of the health of the very culture it was supposed to develop: the hundreds of cultural organizations it heard from across Canada. By the time the government got around to asking about them, the arts were already flowering in Canada, nurtured by a postwar society with money and time to spare. The Massey Commission was a symptom of this society, not its cause — a travelling version of the Hamilton Discussion Group or the Fredericton Art Club or the Ladies' Morning Music Club of Montreal, equally enthusiastic and with only slightly more impact.

**THEN A BUTTERFLY** flapped its wings in Brazil and two wealthy men died in Canada.

On August 5, 1955, the richest man in the country made his last cast on the Cascapédia River. Five months later, a steel baron's heart gave out behind the nine-foot fence of his New Brunswick manor. Between the two of them, they left the federal government with inheritance taxes of almost $100 million.

That fall in Ottawa, the prime minister found himself with nothing to say for a speech he had to give to the National Conference of Canadian Universities. His advisors pointed out the recent windfall and suggested that he use the money to give $50 million to the universities for capital expansion and $50 million to endow the Massey Report's nearly forgotten arts council, which would also help the universities with grants to their scholars.

Louis St. Laurent, says Litt, could think of no reason to say no. He announced the funding in his speech to the universities and appointed Brooke Claxton, now retired, as the council's first chair. On April 30, 1957, nine years after he suggested it, Claxton chaired the first meeting of a national council with royal authority to "foster and promote the study and enjoyment of, and the production of works in, the arts, humanities and social sciences."

In August, the Canada Council invited applications for its first awards. Uncertain how best to achieve its mandate, it tried something of everything. Capital grants for universities. Operating grants for orchestras, theatres, opera and ballet companies, art schools, historical societies, arts festivals, a film institute. A literary history of Canada. A Newfoundland bibliography. Folk song collecting. Scholarships for graduate students and grants for high school teachers, journalists, and broadcasters. And fellowships for "practitioners and teachers of the arts." Junior arts fellowships provided $2,000 for one year plus a travel allowance; senior fellowships averaged $4,000 plus travel, plus two-thirds of the travel allowance "for wife."*

---

* The Council announced its grants as open to both men and women but made no mention of a travel allowance "for husband."

Writers were not a priority for the early Canada Council. In its first fiscal year, while still awaiting applications, the Council managed to approve $4.1 million in grants. The only grant for a writer was $1,000 for E. J. Pratt, a Newfoundland poet who happily was also a Toronto professor, for "recognition on 75th birthday." The following year, its first in full operation, the Council approved $11.4 million in grants, of which about $44,000 went to writers. Richler was one of four writers to receive forty-seven inaugural junior arts fellowships in 1958–59, along with Leonard Cohen, Daryl Hine, and Gaston Miron. Established writers did better, winning nine of twenty-seven senior fellowships. But junior or senior, creative writers were well down the Council's list, below universities, musical and theatrical companies, graduate students and professors, and even foreign grad students and professors. If you wanted support from the Canada Council in the early 1960s and you weren't a university or an academic, your best bet was to be an opera singer.

Literature wondered what happened to its invitation to the party. In 1964, the *Canadian Author & Bookman* accused the Canada Council of failing many of the arts and all of the letters in its mandate. Editor H. R. Percy noted that although the Council said it supported the creation of novels, poems, paintings, and music "to hand on to our children," its annual report showed the vast bulk of its arts budget going to academics, theatre companies, symphony orchestras, opera, and ballet. The Winnipeg Symphony Orchestra had received the same amount as all the writers in the country combined (about $30,000), and the Canadian Opera Company twice as much. Instead of encouraging the creation of Canadian culture, the Council was subsidizing the performance of European culture.

In its defence, the Council reasoned that it took more people and therefore cost more to perform a symphony than to paint or write. Which was true, but didn't address the problem Percy had pointed out. The Council's funding priorities were partly a consequence of the class and tastes of those doing most of the asking and the giving. The greater cause was what Percy almost recognized: a government predilection for funding organizations over individuals. The Council was comfortable with supporting large cultural institutions; governments, and before them monarchs, had done so for centuries. The idea of giving taxpayer money to Leonard Cohen so he could get high in Greece took some getting used to.

At first the Council relied on scholarly councils and a charitable organization called the Canada Foundation to rank applications. In the mid-sixties, it began assessing arts awards on its own, with advice from other artists and art professionals. It also began to look more at the art than the application. Twenty-eight-year-old David Silcox went to work for the Council in September 1965.

> We did whatever we wanted to do. It wasn't bureaucratic. If somebody wanted to do something, and it seemed like a good idea, we put up the money for it. I got the application form down to one page. We listened to them if they were musicians, or auditioned them if they were in theatre, or read them if they were writers. It was a pretty informal process. It had to be. We were supporting writers, painters, choreographers, composers — creative people.

The Council also made an even more radical change. From the start, the main purpose of its grants for individuals had been to help talented Canadians leave Canada. Senior arts fellowships were tenable only abroad; junior fellows could hold their awards in Canada or abroad, but the extra money for travel pointedly encouraged the latter. As Silcox explains, the idea was that "you would go somewhere where there *was* culture, so you could find out something about it." Starting in the mid-sixties, the Council let artists go abroad or stay home, whatever they thought best for their art.

Funding for writing slowly increased, both in total and relative to the big-budget performance companies. In 1967–68 the Council spent $461,000 on writing across the country, including literary publishers and magazines, poetry readings, writers-in-residence programs, and grants for writers. It still wasn't much — about 6 percent of the Council's arts budget — but it was more. And much more than writers got from the Ontario Council for the Arts, which spent almost $600,000 on the arts that year, $2,420 of it on writing.

Literature, clearly, made much of what it got. The Canada Council was a minor player in the CanLit boom, neither hero nor villain but a help to many. Council money let Al Purdy find *North of Summer* on Baffin Island. It helped Graeme Gibson finish *Five Legs*, and it helped Anansi publish it. It helped Mordecai Richler write *Duddy Kravitz* in France and Dennis Lee write *Civil Elegies* in Nathan Phillips Square. It brought Margaret Laurence back to Canada to promote *A Jest of God* and sent Leonard Cohen to London and, yes, Hydra. The Council's choices were not all so prescient, in both those it picked and those it did not, like Nobel laureate Alice Munro, whose application for babysitting money in 1958 was turned down. But sometimes the little it spent went a long way. Margaret Atwood received one Canada Council grant, for $6,000 in 1969. It helped her write three books that confirmed her career and defined Canadian literature: *Surfacing, Survival*, and *Power Politics*. As Atwood points out with a wry smile, measured in her subsequent income taxes alone, that just might be the best $6,000 the people of Canada ever spent.

**NORTH OF SUMMER: POEMS FROM BAFFIN ISLAND (1967)**
Alfred Purdy

★★★★

In the summer of 1965, Al Purdy flew from Montreal to Baffin Island to find some poems. He found the first while still in the air, a French-Canadian stewardess named Suzanne (no, not that Suzanne). He found others on the ground: stubborn trees, hungry huskies, singing "You Are My Sunshine" with Inuit women, watching a Gary Cooper western in a Nissen hut.

It's a thoughtful, entertaining book, a close look at a remarkable place. Purdy had an old Inuk in Pangnirtung do some drawings to accompany it, but his publisher went with oil sketches by Group of Seven painter A. Y. Jackson, courtesy of the Hudson's Bay Company. Purdy hated them. They look like "geriatric vomit done from habit," he wrote to Margaret Laurence. They're not that bad, but you can see what he means.

**ON SEPTEMBER 26, 1959,** *Maclean's* in Toronto published the first installment of a lavishly illustrated 20,000-word excerpt from *The Apprenticeship of Duddy Kravitz*. The magazine paid Richler $2,000 for it, the same amount the Canada Council had given him to write the novel, and more than twice the advance from his publisher. The book sold about two thousand copies in Canada. *Maclean's* brought Richler to half a million readers.

Richler earned more money and far more readers freelancing than he did as a novelist. *Maclean's* cared little about fiction by then, but they loved Richler, especially in the early sixties. It bought articles from him about his first girlfriends, about professional wrestling and bodybuilding, about the Jews and the French and the English. It sent him to Israel for three weeks in 1962 and flew him to Stockholm for the world hockey championships in 1963. He wrote about London for the *Montrealer*, about Canada for the London *Spectator*, and about why he had left Canada for everybody. He covered Expo 67 for the *New York Review of Books*, the FLQ crisis for *Life*, and the Cannes Film Festival for *Harper's*. He sold excerpts from *St. Urbain's Horseman* to a half-dozen magazines, including a Christmas scene to *Chatelaine* and a seventeen-page excerpt to the American women's magazine *McCall's* for $3,500. "The thing to remember when writing a novel," he told a friend, "is to include a chapter with a recipe."

Richler spent most of 1960 in Montreal and Toronto. He and Florence wanted to get married in Montreal, and since he saw *Duddy* as the first in a trilogy about "Montreal jew-ville," he decided he needed some time at home. They were married in July; Florence went into labour with their first son, Noah, the next night.*

In the fall of 1963, the Richler family, now including two-year-old Emma, moved from London to a large old country home in Surrey, in the village of Kingston Hill. Don Owen's 1971 interview with Richler for the CBC walks the viewer up the stone path, past three of now five children,

**ST. URBAIN'S HORSEMAN
(1971)**
Mordecai Richler

Richler's seventh novel revisits the characters and at times the setting of *The Apprenticeship of Duddy Kravitz*. But it's a very different and far better book, because Jake Hersh is a very different and far better man than Duddy, and because Richler had himself become a better man (thanks to Florence) and a better writer. Unlike Duddy, Jake is happy, a success, so he expects not to be. He's scared of dying, scared his kids will die, scared the Nazis will come back, scared, mostly, of his own success — so he tries to destroy it.

"What a rich pleasure this novel is," raved the *New York Times*. It was short-listed for the Booker Prize and earned Richler his second Governor General's Award.

---

* Daniel Richler is Florence's son by her first husband, Stanley Mann.

to the front door and up the stairs to his office. "It's a very pleasant life," Richler tells the camera. "Happy is the man who can do the work he wants to do and earn a living out of it."

He came back to Canada increasingly often: for his father's funeral and for Expo in 1967, for a writer-in-residence position at his alma mater in 1968, for a western tour of the "campus vaudeville circuit" in 1970. In 1971 he talked Carleton University into paying for his family to move home for a writer-in-residence job. The Richlers returned to Canada permanently on Dominion Day 1972, on the Soviet ocean liner *Aleksandr Pushkin*. They put the kids in private schools and bought two four-bedroom homes, one in Westmount and a summer home on Lake Memphremagog in the Eastern Townships. Richler sat down and started typing. He stopped in 2001.

# Chapter 4

# The National Dream

It was a "good" life:
you did not find
everything you wanted
but you learned to accept
everything you found.
　　　　　—Dorothy Livesay, "Centennial People"

PIERRE FRANCIS DE MARIGNY BERTON was six foot three, with
red hair hidden by black-and-white television from the generation
that knew him best. Born in the Yukon to a prospector and a kin-
dergarten teacher, he grew up in Dawson City two decades after
the gold rush that birthed the city and, in 1920, him. Twelve years
later, his family moved to Victoria, British Columbia, where Berton
joined the Boy Scouts and became a teenager before teenagers were
invented. At the University of British Columbia he was an indif-
ferent history major and an outstanding student reporter. The first
words of the first piece credited to the best-known journalist this
country has ever produced were: "The following six books were
purchased this week by the library."

Berton graduated in the spring of 1941 and went to work for the
*Vancouver News-Herald*. With much of the editorial staff gone to
war, he briefly became the youngest city editor on any Canadian
daily before himself enlisting. Like many, he spent the war training
for war and never saw active service. After his discharge he worked

for the *Vancouver Sun*, interviewing celebrities in the mornings and covering the waterfront in the afternoons. He married Janet Walker, a fellow editor on UBC's student paper *The Ubyssey*.

In 1947 Berton wrote a popular series of travel articles for the *Sun* debunking a legend about a tropical valley hidden in the Canadian northwest. The International News Service picked up the series, and *Maclean's* magazine offered Berton a job in Toronto. Berton took the job as a stepping stone to New York, to *Life* or the *Saturday Evening Post*. If that didn't work out, at least Buffalo was close.

The young couple rented a bachelor flat on the northwest corner of Bloor and Spadina before finding an apartment above a hardware store in East York. The following year, they bought a lot on the Humber River near Kleinburg and had the first of the seven children who would fill its home. Berton cranked out seven feature articles in his first four months with *Maclean's*, fifteen in the next year: stories on the internment of Japanese Canadians, anti-Semitic employment practices in Toronto, mental health and drug addiction; profiles of powerful Canadian families; three articles on his boyhood home Dawson City and the North.

It took ten more years and a couple million words written or recycled for anyone who would buy them for Pierre Berton to become Pierre Berton Enterprises. In 1957 he won his first Governor General's Award for *The Mysterious North*, his third book, fourth if you count the memoir he all but ghostwrote for his mother, *I Married the Klondike*. He made his first appearances as a regular panellist on *Close-Up* and *Front Page Challenge*, public affairs shows both launched that year on CBC TV. Print journalism paid Berton's bills but TV made him famous, the kind of fame that compelled magazines to ask what he ate for breakfast.

When *Maclean's* asked him to choose his loyalties, Berton left the magazine to start the most popular daily column in Canadian newspaper history. "By Pierre Berton" began in the *Toronto Daily Star* in September 1958 and ran for the next four years, 1,200 words a day for $15,000 a year. He wrote whatever he wanted: opinion pieces, celebrity profiles, the changing city, Berton family holidays. One of his most frequent and popular roles was as what he

called a "one-man Consumers' Report": the solver of the affluent
society's happier problems, sending his "operatives" undercover to
help expose bogus real estate promotions, hard sells at your door,
fraud in the funeral industry, used car deal-
ers, TV repairmen, and Arthur Murray Dance
Studios. One column might be an open letter to
Trans-Canada Airlines about their poor food,
another a letter to the president of Eaton's saying it took a Ph.D. to assemble the store's Ranch
Wagon Pedal Auto. "What's a knurled centre
pin?" fumed the baffled father.

The 1960s were Berton's busiest years, the
peak of his productivity and fame. Besides his
regular role on *Front Page Challenge*, he hosted
*The Pierre Berton Show* on CTV, a required-
Canadian-content answer to *The Tonight
Show*. W. O. Mitchell made him the journalist protagonist of his second novel, *The Kite*;
Richler satirized him in *The Incomparable Atuk*
as female columnist "Jean-Paul McEwen," the
gender change a slur on Berton's column and
a safeguard against libel. He voiced a character
on *Rocket Robin Hood* and wrote the lyrics for a
Klondike musical. He published the bestselling
book of his career, a commissioned critique of
the Anglican Church that sold over 300,000
copies.

By 1968 his name was on seventeen books.
His best was still to come, a two-volume history of the Canadian Pacific Railway that he
drafted in seven weeks. In September 1972,
Pierre Berton set a record that has never been
equalled, four books on the *Star*'s national bestseller list at the
same time: *The National Dream* (by then almost two years on the
list) at number three, its sequel *The Last Spike* (fifty-two weeks) at
number one, an illustrated companion volume at number nine,

**THE INCOMPARABLE ATUK
(1963)
Mordecai Richler**

Richler's fifth novel recounts
the rise and fall of an Inuit poet
from Baffin Bay who becomes
the darling of the Toronto literary world. Besides its running
satire of Canadian nationalism and Toronto pretension,
the novel is a grab bag of par-
odies of contemporary individuals and institutions: the CBC,
the Hudson's Bay Company
(changed to the "Twentyman
Fur Company" to avoid a lawsuit), drama critic Nathan
Cohen (the corpulent "Seymour
Bone"), Pierre Berton, the Inuit
art craze, John Diefenbaker
and Lester Pearson, Jews and
Protestants, Americans and an-
ti-Americans.

A silly book then, it's mostly
unreadable today. The humour
is juvenile, the writing sloppy,
the story slapped together. Jack
McClelland told Richler that "I
am absolutely convinced it is
your worst work to date," but he
published it anyway.

and an expanded edition of *Klondike* at number seven. As Berton knew better than anyone, he had shown up at the right time in the right place.

**FORTY-ONE DAYS AFTER** the first meeting of the Canada Council, the Liberals lost the government they had held since the Depression to John Diefenbaker and his Progressive Conservatives.

The Massey Report's version of culture played no part in Diefenbaker's version of nationalism, either his vision of the North that never happened or his extension of the welfare state that did. The thirteenth prime minister's recreational tastes ran more to fishing and professional wrestling than the arts. His private library at his official residence was mostly political history and biography, especially books about or owned by his idol Sir John A. Macdonald and most of Churchill's works, along with scattered titles from other fields, like *How to Stop Worrying and Start Living*, *Tom Brown's School Days*, *The Red Fog Over America*, a lonely copy of *Crime and Punishment*. His minister of justice, Davie Fulton, enjoyed the Stratford Festival but was discouraged from attending to avoid lending credence to his political image as an intellectual, a reputation Diefenbaker's government worked hard and for the most part successfully to avoid.

As for the Massey Report's concerns about the influence of American culture, Diefenbaker worried more about keeping out American nuclear warheads than keeping out American movies or magazines. In fact, after *Time* magazine ran a favourable cover story on the new leader and presented him with the oil portrait used on the cover, the Conservatives removed the Liberals' tax on advertising in Canadian editions of foreign magazines. Under pressure, Diefenbaker did appoint a royal commission in September 1960 to look into American competition in the Canadian magazine market. The resulting report recommended tax measures to support Canadian magazines, but Diefenbaker did nothing besides the usual Senate appointment for the commission's chair.

If publishing historian Eli MacLaren is right, the government initiative of the Diefenbaker years most significant for literature was Canada's ratification of the Universal Copyright Convention in 1962, which gave American copyright to Canadian books. New York publishers weren't exactly lining up to pirate the latest literary sensation from Etobicoke, but even so, knowing that their property would still be their property south of the border was good news for Canadian publishers. Also under Diefenbaker's watch, the Canada Council took over the Governor General's Literary Awards from the Canadian Authors' Association, adding categories for French literature and increasing the profile and value of the awards, from $1,000 in 1959 to $5,000 by 1975.

Nineteen fifty-nine saw the first significant changes to obscenity law in Canadian history, changes that were as much a consequence of concerns about American cultural influence as the Massey Report was. Obscenity law in Canada and the United States was based on the so-called Hicklin test, named after an 1868 British decision that measured obscenity by its effects on the supposedly more corruptible minds of children, women, and the working classes. In America the Hicklin test finally fell apart with *Roth v. United States*, which shifted the test for obscenity to its effect on the average person. In Canada the test wasn't much needed because there wasn't much matter to matter, obscene or not. But in the late 1940s public alarm began to grow about American pulp novels, crime comics, and "girlie" magazines on Canadian newsstands. In 1952 the government struck a committee on Salacious and Indecent Literature that caught the interest of opposition MP Davie Fulton, a Kamloops lawyer who had already piloted legislation to ban crime comics. Six years later, now the justice minister in a majority government, Fulton attempted what neither Hicklin nor the Criminal Code had dared: a definition of obscenity, not just a test for its presence. Passed on July 18, 1959, the new (and still current) legislation defined as obscene "any publication a dominant characteristic of which is the undue exploitation of sex, or of sex and any one or more of the following subjects, namely, crime, horror, cruelty and violence."

Opponents of the new law cast Fulton as a puritan on a crusade. Maybe he was, but he was also a nationalist. Repeatedly, Fulton stressed that the new definition wasn't aimed at works of "genuine literary or artistic merit," to which the Hicklin test would continue to apply. Its only target, he said, was a "certain type of objectionable material that now appears on the newsstands in Canada and is being sold to young people of our country with impunity." Fulton's law was the stick to the Canada Council's carrot: one to promote Canadian high culture, the other to proscribe American popular culture.

And, as a glance at today's digital newsstands will tell you, about as effective. A few bookstores paid a few fines, but pornography survived Bill C-58 and Canadian bookstores remained dominated by American books and magazines. When a reader wrote publisher Jack McClelland seven years later to complain about the "orgy of filth" in Leonard Cohen's *Beautiful Losers*, McClelland suggested "looking at the 'pulps' on the local newsstand instead of attacking the work of a serious writer."

Many stores refused to sell *Beautiful Losers*, including Simpson's department stores and the W. H. Smith chain of bookstores. But perhaps because few people read it, the first and so far only Canadian novel to feature vaginal, anal, and armpit penetration by a self-propelled flying vibrator somehow escaped obscenity charges. At number two on the Canadian bestseller lists, D. H. Lawrence's *Lady Chatterley's Lover*, newly legal in Britain and America, did not. In November 1959 a police morality squad seized copies of the novel during a raid on three Montreal news dealers. Fulton said his new law applied only to "newsstand trash," and he probably meant it — but his law didn't say that, so the Quebec courts had little choice but to declare the book obscene and ban it in the province. The Supreme Court did have a choice, and in March 1962

**THE TRUE EVENTUAL STORY OF BILLY THE KID** (1970)
bpNichol

★★

Turns out, Billy the Kid became fast with a gun because he had a little dick. He killed his first man because that man had a bigger dick than Billy. The sheriff let Billy keep shooting the dicks off people because he had a little dick too. When Billy died, God said Billy why'd you do what you did and Billy said because I had a little dick.

And that's the story of Billy the Kid, as told by bpNichol in a four-page pamphlet that won a Governor General's Literary Award. This made Conservative MP Thomas "Mac" McCutcheon very angry. He stood up one day in the House of Commons and called Nichol's story "an affront to decency and a discouragement to serious literary efforts." Which is of course exactly what it was meant to be, so points to Mac.

it decided that whatever the law might or might not say, obscenity could not be decided without considering artistic merit and contemporary community standards. The *Lady*, it said, was free to go.

Toronto art dealer Dorothy Cameron wasn't so fortunate. In the spring of 1965, Cameron curated an exhibit of erotic art called *Eros 65* at her Yonge Street gallery. Pierre Berton spoke at the opening about romantic love finally coming of age in Toronto the Good. "We've come a long way in this city, as a country and as a people," he said, "to have a show of this nature." Two days later, morality squad detectives seized seven drawings of nude women from the show, including several that depicted "lesbian activity." Despite defence testimony by art experts,* Cameron was convicted of exposing obscene matter to the public. She lost her appeals in both the Ontario and Supreme Courts, and then she lost her gallery to legal costs. Ironically, a law created to keep out American pulp fiction proved more effective at taking down Canadian art. Cultural nationalism had opened Cameron's show, and cultural nationalism shut it down.


**"MIKE'S ARTISTIC INTEREST** was not keen." So says John English, biographer of Canada's prime minister from 1963 to 1968. Outside classes as a university student, Lester Pearson preferred baseball diamonds and hockey rinks to theatres or art galleries. At home as prime minister, he was more likely to disappear behind a newspaper than a book. As secretary of state under St. Laurent, Pearson had supported what became the Massey Commission and suggested its chair. But the only mention of any interest or involvement in

---

* Robert Fulford, who covered the exhibit and the trial for the *Toronto Daily Star*, says those experts got Cameron convicted. Instead of defending the works on the basis of, say, a long tradition of nudity in European painting, each of the art experts called (including William Withrow, director of the Art Gallery of Toronto) said they didn't see nude women, only interesting plays of light and shadow, abstract patterns, and the like. "In 1965 all high thinking in art was formalist.... They had become so caught up in abstract theory that content had literally become invisible to them. What everyone else in the world could see, they could not." Without a credible defence, the magistrate had no choice but to find Cameron guilty.

the arts, official or personal, in English's biography of Pearson's subsequent political career is a reference to the Prime Minister disappointing whisky smuggler Sam Bronfman's hopes for gentility with an appointment not to the Senate but to "the lowly board of the Canada Council."

More within his job description, though, Pearson and his government took the most significant steps since Confederation toward defining a country that could define its arts, the Canada that was a corequisite for CanLit. Deeply influenced by John Kenneth Galbraith, especially *The Affluent Society*, they redirected private prosperity into public services, including a national student loan program, a national health-care service, and a national pension plan. They ended capital punishment, giving Canadians another way to see themselves as not-American. They created a Canadian flag, and they gave Canadians reasons to wave it. They also happened to be in charge the year Canadians most wanted to wave it, the year their country turned one hundred.

Canada's biggest party was not a government idea. Starting as early as 1959, organizations such as the YMCA and the Canadian Citizenship Council began lobbying the federal government for a celebration to mark the hundredth anniversary of Confederation. In 1961 the government established the Centennial Commission; two years later, Diefenbaker appointed its chair, John "Mr. Canada" Fisher, a former CBC broadcaster known for his fifteen-minute talks on all things Canadian. Fisher was a poor administrator and couldn't speak French (though English Canada thought he could) but was otherwise the perfect person for the job, as popular as he was patriotic. He also had about $80 million to give away, which helped make him popular and others patriotic. The Commission organized its own centennial projects, including the Confederation Train ("a moving panorama of Canada from pre-historic times to the present") and a voyageur canoe race from Rocky Mountain House to Montreal. It also subsidized hundreds of community projects, from building or updating community centres, parks, and libraries to racing bathtubs across the Georgia Strait and constructing a landing pad to welcome aliens to Canada's birthday in St.

Paul, Alberta. Of them all, I'm most sorry I missed the Centennial
Barge that travelled the Mackenzie River north to Inuvik, equipped
with a Ferris wheel.

The main event was, of course, in Montreal.
Neither Diefenbaker nor Pearson was enthusiastic about hosting a World's Fair, but after
Russia gave up its winning bid, Mayor Jean
Drapeau convinced first Ottawa and then the
Bureau International des Expositions that its
next big show should come to Quebec. With
less than five years to get ready, Drapeau's
tough guys ("*les durs*") moved heaven and, literally, earth to prepare the site, using twenty-
five million tons of landfill to double the size
of one island and make another from scratch.
The cost was equally colossal, $439 million by
the time Expo opened — almost what the St.
Lawrence Seaway had cost, and five times what
Ottawa spent on the Centennial for the whole
country. But Expo was for the world, and the
world came: sixty-one nations set up shop and
more than fifty million people passed through
the gates, the most successful world's fair of
the century. Even Richler liked it, and Richler
didn't like much. "Expo is, as they say, awfully
good fun and in the best possible taste," he con-
ceded in the *New York Review of Books*.

The Centennial Commission ended
up spending some $25 million on the arts,
money the Canada Council worried would
create expectations of continued support at
Centennial levels. As with the Council, the lion's share went to
the performing arts, especially a national program called Festival
Canada that was the Commission's largest single expense after the
Confederation Train. Fisher's team bought a centennial anthem
and a centennial hymn that few heard, and a centennial song that

**THE MODERN CENTURY**
**(1967)**
**Northrop Frye**

★★★

The Modern Century is a lecture series that Frye gave at
McMaster University in January 1967, the first in the series'
history by a born Canadian.
The lectures were supposed
to be about Canadian culture,
but Frye spent most of his time
talking instead about modern
art, modern advertising, and the
role of universities in teaching
the difference between them.
As for Canada, he says that
while much would surely be
said that year about its matura-
tion from colony to nation, to
him the country had skipped
nationhood for a post-national
society — and good thing too.
The fact that we keep wondering about Canadian identity is
evidence of an open society,
not the closed shop of nationalism. The Canadian identity
*is* "the identity we have failed
to achieve."

few escaped. They commissioned centennial plays in French and English, of which the centrepiece was a collaborative revue by region that did as well as could be expected for "a play commissioned by a commission, written by a committee, and backed by the public treasury." They helped develop centennial exhibits, including what was then the largest show of Canadian art ever assembled: *300 Years of Canadian Art*, at the still homeless National Gallery of Canada. (The gallery tried to promote the exhibit internationally by sending a slide library of the collection to major galleries, but some of the artists involved objected to their work being reproduced without compensation. So the show went to Toronto for a month.)

To help fill the libraries it paid for, the Commission bought Canadian books and let libraries choose the titles they wanted, so long as half the books they took had Canadian content and a fifth were in French. In co-operation with the Canada Council, it spent a quarter of a million dollars helping authors and associations publish books to mark the Centennial, mostly local histories. *History of the Huxley Area* and *The Lansdowne Story: Grain, Gravel & Growth* joined coffee-table books like *Canada: A Year of the Land* in what Richler called Centennial's "mountain of non-books." For writers of a more literary bent, the Commission held a contest for short stories, essays, and poetry with "Canadian subjects or subjects of particular interest to Canadians." Atwood won the poetry prize; the essay prize went to May Cutler of Montreal, founder earlier that year of Tundra Books, Canada's first children's book publisher.

Expo was substantially about art, a summer-long program of concerts and shows held inside a 900-acre gallery of every kind of art ever imagined anywhere, from carpets in the Iran pavilion to pop art in the American pavilion. But because Expo was an international event that just happened to take place in Canada, only a small portion of its art was Canadian. Even less was *new* Canadian art, produced for or because of Expo. Leonard Cohen read his poems to a jazz background at the Youth Pavilion. Richler put in enough of an appearance at the Canadian Authors' Association conference to collect his fee. Paintings by Harold Town and Jack Chambers hung among older Canadian works in the Canada pavilion, next door to Norval Morrisseau's mural for the Indians of Canada pavilion. At the Ontario pavilion, stainless steel versions of Michael Snow's *Walking Woman* strolled the grounds. The most prominent and ambitious new Canadian art at Expo was the many experimental films, especially the National Film Board's $4.5 million *In the Labyrinth*, a multi-screen allegory of "the essential Story of Man" for which Northrop Frye served as a consultant.

Expo's greatest work of art was Expo itself. Its official theme, "Man and His World," was as much a response to the affluent society as the Massey Report was. Urban planner Claude Robillard was one of the men and women who chose the theme at a Quebec resort in May 1963. "I thought the time was over," he said, "when we could have world exhibitions showing gadgets, mechanical devices, the latest automobiles and the latest screwdriver, and that it was time the accent was placed on man rather than his inventions." Previous exhibitions had celebrated technical advances that promised a better life; with that better life now at hand, the celebration could turn to creative achievements. As Robert Fulford wrote after it ended, Expo's real subject was that humanity had moved beyond scarcity.

Neither Expo nor the Centennial left much art behind. The Centennial Commission did more lasting good for the arts than Expo, helping to build or remodel some two hundred galleries, theatres, and public libraries across the country. Expo's main art object disappeared when it ended, leaving behind an amusement park now leased to an American company and a failed experiment in affordable urban housing. Ironically, given its decision to eschew gadgets, the main artistic legacy of Expo is a gadget: IMAX film technology, developed by Expo filmmakers and now thriving after forty years of delivering nothing more memorable on its massive screens than whales singing and Rolling Stones aging.

The most lasting cultural influence of the Centennial was the interest it created in the *past*, in Canadian history, local or national. Canada's Centennial, said a grateful Pierre Berton thirty years later, "turned many Canadians into history buffs." In the short term, its most powerful by-product was pride. Expo, especially, generated unqualified, boisterous pleasure in Canadian achievement — mostly for the same reason postwar Canadians usually take pride in themselves, because America liked it. Neither the government nor the rest of the country was sure until Expo's opening day. But when the American press gushed its praise — *Time*, for instance, called Expo "the greatest international exposition ever" in an eleven-page cover story — Canadians looked, and lo, it was good.

That new-found nationalism gave Canadian artists new-found confidence. Ontario writer David Helwig, whose first book bears a copyright of that year, says in his memoir that "Nationalism has its limits, of course, as a source of artistic values, but writing is easier if you no longer believe that all the action is somewhere else." In the late 1960s, the energies of the centennial year told Canadian writers and — just as important — Canadian readers that some of the action was here. Expo didn't create those energies; it rode them, cultural nationalism atop economic continentalism, the affluence that made a half-billion-dollar birthday party both financially possible and existentially necessary.

**PEARSON'S SUCCESSOR WAS** an extremely focused man. As a student, Pierre Elliott Trudeau cared about the arts, especially poetry. He even wrote a play in high school, albeit an ethnic nationalist, anti-Semitic play. But like most everything else in his life, the arts got set aside after Trudeau took office in the spring of 1968, trotted out only as a reference to impress a woman or the press. His nighttime reading at 24 Sussex Drive was government briefs; his main interest in the arts was in female artists, mostly young actors and musicians. As a politician, he had as little interest in your bookshelves as he had in your bedroom. Trudeau was a federalist but not a nationalist, not after he grew up.

He associated with some Canadian artists besides those he dated. He was a fan and correspondent of Marshall McLuhan (mostly because McLuhan was his fan and correspondent) and read and admired John Kenneth Galbraith. He was the occasional lunch or dinner companion of Mordecai Richler and family friends with the Mowats, who gave the Trudeaus a Lab they called Farley.

Leonard Cohen was an honorary pallbearer at his funeral. He met the artists Michael Snow and Joyce Wieland at a party in New York and inspired Wieland to make a quilt of his motto, *Reason over Passion,* which saw more passion than reason when his young wife Margaret ripped the words from it in one of their fights.

In 1971 Trudeau announced two new programs to combat unemployment in an economy struggling to find work for its postwar babies. Opportunities for Youth (OFY) paid for summer jobs for high school and university students with community organizations; the Local Initiatives Program (LIP) kicked in during the winter months, with funding for projects like daycares and Meals on Wheels. In Trudeau's mind, both programs would help realize his vision of a just society while also creating jobs that helped the disadvantaged. What he perhaps didn't see coming was how adept the country's arts administrators — by now well trained on Canada Council applications — would prove at putting a socially responsible spin on applications to the new programs. In Vancouver, for example, the grants funded a season by John Gray's experimental Tamahnous Theatre. Toronto Free Theatre was created by and because of a $100,000 LIP Grant (that's how it was free). A LIP grant let James Reaney, his director, and the entire cast workshop the second part of *The Donnellys* for a month at Halifax's Neptune Theatre.* Coach House Press in

**POWER POLITICS (1971)**
**Margaret Atwood**

It was likely a good thing for Atwood's soon-to-be ex-husband Jim Polk that her fifth book of poems had no dedication. Like *The Journals of Susanna Moodie, Power Politics* is a series of linked confessional poems, but this time poems most readers would assume are spoken by the author about a current relationship.

Atwood complained to her biographer that readers missed the humour in the book's opening lines ("you fit into me / like a hook into an eye / a fish hook / an open eye"), and so the humour in the book. Maybe. But when Margaret Laurence wrote to her that the lines "expressed in hardly any words the whole man-woman thing in its painful essence," Atwood didn't rush to tell her it was all just in fun.

---

* The Canada Council's Theatre Officer at the time, David Gardner, complained that Trudeau's programs spent as much on theatre in 1971–72 as the Council did, nearly $4 million. From the Council's point of view, the OFY and LIP theatre grants were makework projects awarded by amateurs to amateurs and, like Centennial arts funding, set a worrying precedent for continued support.

Toronto received enough OFY aid to give everyone a raise and hire
the editor's mother as house cook.

The official bilingualism initiated by Pearson's government
and pushed through by Trudeau never translated from Ottawa's
management of the arts into the arts themselves. Trudeau made
Canada bilingual politically but not culturally, where it matters.
(In fact, a last-minute revision to the Constitution he repatriated
during his second term allowed the provinces to opt out of federal
initiatives in education and culture, eliminating one possible support for a bicultural if not a bilingual literature.) That said, his
defeat of Quebec separatism meant there was still a country to
have a literature.

Most Canadians supported Trudeau's response to the FLQ kid-
nappings. For others, including many of the country's writers and
artists, October 1970 extinguished the pride lit by the Centennial
flame. Berton demanded a royal commission. Journalist and
activist June Callwood said she no longer knew what Canada was.
"What collapsed when my countrymen loved the War Measures
Act, *loved it*, was my conceit that I was something special because
I am a Canadian," she wrote in *Maclean's*. For novelist Graeme
Gibson, seeing the troops in the same streets that had hosted Expo
destroyed the national optimism that produced the CanLit boom.
Joyce Wieland called Trudeau a psychopath and said she had made
her quilt as a joke.

Trudeaumania turned easily from attraction to anger because
there was something there to turn, a nationalist if not completely
national enthusiasm unlike anything Canadians had ever experienced before, especially young Canadians. Trudeau helped Canada
itself feel youthful, exciting, his cape and convertible ministerial
versions of Expo's leap from scarcity into style. He made us sexy
for a while, and sexy begets progeny of all kinds.

# Chapter 5

# The Diviners

since universities started paying money
for old worksheets I preserve them carefully
in fireproof boxes
                              —Al Purdy, "Japanese Painter"

**THE TWO MOST** influential Canadian intellectuals of the 1960s
grew up in small Canadian cities that were not Toronto, Marshall
McLuhan in Winnipeg and Northrop Frye in Moncton. Both
came from Methodist homes; Frye was ordained in Methodism's
gentler descendant, the United Church, and McLuhan converted
to Catholicism. They received their undergraduate degrees in the
same year, Frye from Victoria College in Toronto and McLuhan
from the University of Manitoba. Both went to England for further
studies, Frye earning an M.A. from Oxford and McLuhan a Ph.D.
from Cambridge.

Frye started teaching at Victoria College in September 1939, hired
as a lecturer at $1,600 a year less 5 percent to remind him it was still
the Depression. He had studied for the Church and worked as a student minister in rural Saskatchewan for a few months. But theology
bored him and he couldn't talk with people, so he quit preaching for
another pulpit, one from which he could invent his own theology
and do more writing than talking. McLuhan arrived seven years
after Frye for a position with St. Michael's College, one block and five
sacraments away from Frye's corner of the University of Toronto. In

public, their relationship was polite, collegial. In private, Frye called McLuhan's ideas "blithering nonsense" and McLuhan dismissed Frye's thinking as "Protestant."

Both were fundamentally religious thinkers, but McLuhan had the Catholic's affection for mysteries that stay mysteries, Frye the Protestant's rebellious desire for answers. One thought about the effects of technology on society, the other about the effects of myth on literature. McLuhan taught his students that no technology is neutral, that every tool changes our lives and our world. The telephone, he told them, created the call girl. Frye taught that all stories are part of a single story, told in pieces, over and over. Poets create more than they know, he said; study the form to reveal its content, the Big Story we keep telling. No, said his colleague down the street, the form *is* the content, the medium the message.

As a teacher, Frye was best known for his undergraduate course on the Bible, "considered *de rigueur* for any serious literature student" by the time young Peggy Atwood arrived at Vic in 1957. The centrepiece of McLuhan's entire intellectual life was a Monday night seminar called "Media and Society," technically a graduate course but in practice open to anyone who showed up and could field McLuhan's bad jokes and strange ideas. Where Frye liked the distance of the lecture (a "hot" medium, in McLuhan's terms), McLuhan preferred the intimacy of the seminar ("cool") in which he could demand a response or nap while others talked.

From their classrooms came the books that made them famous. Frye's *Anatomy of Criticism*, born like all his subsequent books as lectures, is the only book of literary criticism by a Canadian to become required reading for the discipline. By the mid-1970s it was the most cited work of humanities scholarship by a twentieth-century author, and Frye was the humanities' eighth most cited scholar, behind Marx, Aristotle, Shakespeare, Lenin, Plato, Freud, and Roland Barthes. His conclusion to the *Literary History of Canada* (1965) became the most influential essay ever published on Canadian literature, launching a slew of theses on the country's "garrison mentality" and changing the perennial Canadian question from "Who am I?" to "Where is here?"

McLuhan's *Understanding Media* made him essential reading for anyone with intellectual pretensions, not just English professors. *Life, Playboy, Vogue,* the *New York Times Magazine,* and many other magazines (Pierre Berton says ninety-seven in 1967 alone) ran articles about him. The *New Yorker* printed cartoons about him; *Newsweek, Saturday Review,* and *Maclean's* put him on their cover; NBC aired a one-hour documentary called *This Is Marshall McLuhan.* Just when Canada was celebrating itself, by chance the world was celebrating a Canadian, the man *Life* magazine called "the oracle of the electric age."

**UNDERSTANDING MEDIA:
THE EXTENSIONS OF MAN
(1964)
Marshall McLuhan**

IN *THE AFFLUENT SOCIETY,* John Kenneth Galbraith had argued that the way to restore the balance between private and public wealth was to spend more public money on public goods. On education especially, because it moves society away from the false grail of production by increasing the number of citizens whose employment isn't tied to production: writers, professors, doctors, scientists, and the like, what Galbraith called the "New Class" of the affluent society. In a society that can see the end of toil as an economic institution, the index of progress is not production but education. "The future of work," said McLuhan, "consists of learning a living."

McLuhan's ideas were easy to make fun of: "As extension of man the chair is a specialist ablation of the posterior, a sort of ablative absolute of the backside, whereas the couch extends the integral being." But at least he *had* ideas, more per book (and in *Understanding Media,* more per chapter) than most of us have in a lifetime. The speed and range of his thinking is dizzying. In two pages he can move from TV being bad for baseball to the trend for small European cars, to patio furniture, to why the Twist is the dance of the teenager. In McLuhan's mind, if nowhere else, it all fit together. He died of a stroke in 1980, after celebrating Mass and watching a Marx Brothers movie.

The arrival of the baby boomers at university age was a more pressing cause than economic theory, but even so, Canada's Liberal governments of the 1950s, '60s, and '70s could have been working from Galbraith's playbook (and by the sixties often were). Universities became an unexpectedly large part of the Massey Commission's work — no doubt partly because all five members held postgraduate degrees, three were professors, and one was a university president, but also because the Commission heard repeatedly from universities already struggling to deal with rising enrolment. When the Canada Council was finally established six years later, half its endowment and by far the largest share of its annual grants went to universities and academics.

Federal spending on universities paled beside the provincial binge-building to come. Between 1960 and 1975, the number of Canadian universities and colleges almost quadrupled, from twenty-eight to nearly a hundred. Twenty-two universities were established, including the University of Victoria, Simon Fraser, Calgary, Moncton, UPEI, and the ten-school Université du Québec. The University of Toronto opened two new campuses, scrambling like everyone else to accommodate enrolments that had more than tripled in a decade. In the five years between 1963 and 1968, university enrolments in Canada increased as much as they had in the previous half-century.

North America reinvented itself in the 1960s because of and for the baby boomers, achieving in a very short time what one of the decade's many historians calls a "full scale societal, cultural, and political shift towards accommodating young people." One of the smaller consequences of this massive transformation was the boost it gave to literature, including Canadian literature. More universities meant more university libraries and bookstores, even if they bought most of their books from American publishers. It meant more literature departments, even if staffed by mostly British- and American-educated professors teaching mostly British and American books. And it meant more Canadians with more education, some of whom would want to read and even write Canadian books.

CANADIAN WRITING HAS never been essential to Canadian classrooms. Individual teachers, schools, and provinces have from time to time taught the writers of their place, out of affection or duty. But because education is constitutionally a provincial responsibility (pragmatically, because of Quebec), Canadian schools have never had a Canadian curriculum. Instead, each province bases its curriculum and trains its teachers on the best of international pedagogy, and imports its content with its methods. When Frye's future student Margaret Atwood went to high school, English class was "British, Shakespeare and after."

> The general impression was that to be a poet you had to be English and dead. You could also be American and dead but this was less frequent. There was, to be sure, E. J. Pratt, who was Canadian and at the time still alive, but I despaired of ever being able to write long poems about shipwrecks.... Novels by Canadians were almost unheard of, for once a faithful reflection on the part of the high school curriculum of conditions in the outside world.

(Thirty years later, Atwood got her revenge by turning Leaside High into a women's prison in her dystopian novel *The Handmaid's Tale*.)

In the 1960s, a few older Canadian novels became high school standards as postwar students became teachers and superintendents. W. O. Mitchell's 1947 novel about a boy growing up and finding God in Saskatchewan, *Who Has Seen the Wind*, was (and still is) a popular choice, especially in western classrooms. Eastern schools liked Ernest Buckler's *The Mountain and the Valley* (1952), about a boy growing up and finding God in Nova Scotia. Quebec schools favoured Gabrielle Roy's *Bonheur d'occasion* (1945) if French and MacLennan's *Two Solitudes* (1945) if English. Younger writers surfaced in *Sixteen by Twelve* (1970), the first anthology of Canadian short stories for high schools. Edited by John Metcalf, the popular collection included stories and comments by a dozen Canadian writers, including Margaret Laurence, Hugh Hood, Alice Munro, George Bowering, and Metcalf himself.

The largest single beneficiary of classroom interest was likely Richler's *Duddy Kravitz*. *Duddy* sold modestly in Canada and the U.S., maybe three thousand copies all told.* But after Penguin

---

* In February 1963, Britnell's bookstore in Toronto offered its remaining stock of *Duddy Kravitz* at ninety-eight cents each.

Books in Britain and the Paperback Library in New York reprinted the novel in cheap paper editions in the mid-sixties, it became a regular high school and college text, selling a steady two to three thousand copies a year. By 1959 Richler had been away from home for a decade, and it showed: the city in *Duddy Kravitz* is more Montreal of the forties than of the sixties, more coldwater flats than Cadillacs. But if the book's setting was behind the times, its satire was by chance on time and on target, reaching Canadians just when they were ready to enjoy a shot at someone who valued only material success — especially if that someone wasn't them. Duddy gave Canada a good example of a bad example, "a conniving little yid," and in exchange Canada gave Duddy a seat in its schools.

Like the centennial celebration, CanLit in the classroom wasn't a government idea. No province required students to read Canadian literature until Ontario in 1977, by then a consequence rather than a cause of the CanLit boom. And even then, Ontario's Ministry of Education might never have acted were it not for the extraordinary efforts of one teacher, Jim Foley from Port Colborne High.

Foley was himself extraordinary, a soft spoken man in his early fifties whose mild manner hid a dedication to Canadian literature that Dennis Lee remembers as almost evangelical. Orphaned at three by the death of his parents, Foley ran away from Children's Aid in Toronto when he was nine. He wanted to work on a farm but got no farther than the streets of Cabbagetown, where three prostitutes who shared a house at 269 Carlton found him and took him in. The women enrolled him in school, and when he finished, paid his way to St. Michael's College. After Foley won a

**TÊTE BLANCHE (1960)**
**Marie-Claire Blais**

Marie-Claire Blais's second novel is about a young boy sent away to boarding school who is more attracted to evil than good. "Today, I hurt Felderik with a lasso, I made fun of Pierre, and I didn't pray at mass," he writes his mother. "What about you, Mama? What did you do?"

It gets worse. Tête Blanche — nicknamed for his bleached blond hair — is one of Blais's child monsters, a lost boy with an abusive drunk for a father and a mother who ignores her son's cries for help. "Come quickly before I get too bad," he writes to her, but she doesn't. It's a chilling book, a window on the mind of a disturbed child who will become a disturbed man.

Critics turned Blais's first novel into a more important book, the book Quebec wanted. Her second is a better book.

scholarship to Columbia University in New York, they wrote him to say that now he had amounted to something, it would be best if they didn't see each other again. Foley came back to the house on Carlton, but his patrons were gone, and he never saw them again.

He spent nine years in the States, earning a Ph.D. in philosophy from Columbia while supporting himself with odd jobs and small business ventures, including investments in the first Silicon Valley companies (later rumoured to have made him very rich). He returned to Canada in the mid-1960s and began teaching high school, first in Rivers, Manitoba, and then in Ontario, ending up at Port Colborne on Lake Erie.

According to Foley, his interest in Canadian literature began with his realization that "Canada must be the only country in the world where high school kids aren't taught their own literature." In 1968, now head of English at Port Colborne High, Foley and his students wrote to almost two hundred high schools across Canada, asking for outlines of their Canadian literature courses. When those who responded said they had no such course, Foley and his principal invited all the Canadian writers they knew of — twelve, including Hugh Garner, Miriam Waddington, Margaret Laurence, and Milton Acorn — to their school to help design a Canadian literature course. The meeting became an annual event, registered by Foley under the name Canada Day.

Garner and Waddington returned for the first Canada Day, on February 28, 1971, along with humorist Max Braithwaite, poet John Newlove, and Ontario Premier Bill Davis. By 1973 the program listed twenty-two authors, editors, and publishers,

**GOING DOWN SLOW (1972)**
John Metcalf

Metcalf based his first novel on his first teaching job in Canada and his affair with Grade 11 student Gale Courey, later his wife. He changed the school's name from Rosemount to Merrymount, kept Gale Lebanese but renamed her Susan, called himself David Appleby, and moved history ahead a few years, to sometime after Expo 67.

*Going Down Slow* is glancingly a love story, more a stranger-in-a-strange land satire of Canadian weather, Canadian spelling, French Canadians, and especially Canadian schools, the glaring gap between the lives of David's students and their doddering teachers and bowdlerized books. It's a gleefully written, witty novel that at times overdoes it, a young man's book. Metcalf's best work as a writer was still to come, like the fearless essays in *Kicking Against the Pricks* and the thoroughly grown-up stories in *Adult Entertainment.*

including Pierre Berton, Farley Mowat, Margaret Atwood, and Jack McClelland. More than two thousand high school students and teachers attended from across Ontario and as far away as Saskatchewan and Nova Scotia. In 1975, with historians and geographers now added to the guest list and funding from the Ontario Arts Council and the Department of Education, Canada Day outgrew its high school home and moved, with Foley, to Mohawk College in Hamilton.

The Canada Day model spread to schools across and beyond the province. Russell Brown, a Texan who joined Lakehead University's English department in 1969 and later became co-editor of the *Oxford Anthology of Canadian Literature*, still remembers the excitement of a Canada Day at a Thunder Bay high school that featured Michael Ondaatje, Sylvia Fraser, Eli Mandel, and George Jonas. Graeme Gibson recalls flying to a school in Sudbury in a winter storm with Jonas and the playwright John Herbert. Atwood wrote in *Maclean's* about arriving by Greyhound bus in Renfrew, Ontario, for her first high school reading, lugging two suitcases full of her books along Highway 17 in six inches of early snow. In Montreal, John Metcalf, Hugh Hood, Doug Jones, and John Newlove read for a Canada Day at the Selwyn House private school in Westmount.*

Besides organizing Canada Day, Foley and his wife assembled a database and a resource library of Canadian literature. They answered thousands of phone calls and letters from teachers about what Canadian books to teach and how to teach them. They wrote repeatedly to Ontario's minister of education, urging him to add CanLit to the high school curriculum. Together with press coverage of Canada Days, their prodding likely pushed the ministry into

---

* With Hood, Clark Blaise, Ray Smith, and Ray Fraser, Metcalf ran his own reading series in the city's Catholic high schools and CÉGEPS. (The Protestant school board declined after Hood became enraged when a post-FLQ security guard at the board's office asked him to provide identification.) Launched the same month as Foley's Canada Day, the Montreal Story Teller Fiction Performance Group was the first fiction-reading series in the country, consciously created to retake some of the attention and the "loot" from poets. Unlike Canada Day authors, who received only expenses, the group charged $200 for a two-hour performance — forty dollars each. They gave more than fifty readings between 1971 and their last reading in 1976, in most years earning more than they made from their writing.

requiring high school graduates to take classes in Canadian studies in 1974 and Canadian literature in 1977. As Pierre Berton said, it was easier to say yes to Jim Foley than to answer all his letters.

In 1977, Trudeau's secretary of state, John Roberts, quietly negotiated with Foley for the use of the name "Canada Day," which was already being used in the press and debated in Parliament as a replacement for "Dominion Day." The debate wouldn't end until 1982, but long before then Foley's creation had faded in the shadow of its national namesake, until even its memory disappeared. Foley returned to full-time teaching, and CanLit in the classroom lost its greatest advocate and its moment in the sun.

**ABOUT A DOZEN** universities were teaching some Canadian literature by the 1920s, mostly as an elective. French Quebec included a text or two of *littérature canadienne* among the primarily French and classical literatures of its pre-university *baccalauréat* program; English-Canadian universities tacked a few Canadian poems or a novel onto the end of courses in American literature. Even when such courses were called "American and Canadian Literature," the content was largely American. In the University of Toronto's AmCan course, Canadian literature took up less than 10 percent of the syllabus for thirty years, from the mid-thirties to the mid-sixties.

In the 1940s and '50s a growing number of professors began teaching courses devoted to Canadian literature, including Roy Daniells at UBC, Carlyle King at the University of Saskatchewan, Arthur Phelps at McGill, and Léopold LeBlanc at the Université de Montréal. By 1959 about a quarter of all English-Canadian universities offered dedicated Canadian literature courses.

By 1974, they all did.

French Quebec saw a similar explosion, especially in the new pre-university CÉGEPs, created in 1967 and specifically charged with teaching more works by Québécois writers. For the same main reason — nationalism, if for the sake of different nations — Canadian literature moved in both English- and French-Canadian post-secondary schools from a nuisance to a necessity. As York University's Clara Thomas remembered, "We who had been teaching it under adverse circumstances were suddenly in demand — crowds of students were signing up for courses and asking for more."

The expanding post-secondary market contributed to the global publishing boom, in Canada as around the world. Unfortunately for Canadian publishers, university bookstores bought almost all their books elsewhere: from England or the States if English-speaking, from Belgium or France if French. Publishers of Canadian literature fared better, especially with books that foreign publishers no longer owned or had forgotten they owned, issuing paperback reprint series aimed at the education market, like Éditions Fides' Classiques Canadiens and McClelland & Stewart's New Canadian Library. And foreign publishers gladly supplied some of the most popular texts by living writers, like the CÉGEP favourite *Kamouraska* (published in Paris by Éditions du Seuil) and the prairie perennial *Who Has Seen the Wind* (published by the Canadian branch of Macmillan of London and reprinted in their own paperback series, the Laurentian Library).

University libraries jumped into the game, playing catch-up. Simon Fraser and Dalhousie began collecting avant-garde and small-press Canadian literature. The University of Toronto gave bookseller David Mason a copy of Reginald Watters' eight-hundred-page *Check List of Canadian Literature* and told him to buy them everything they didn't have. By 1970 U of T had bought manuscripts from Hugh MacLennan (McGill wasn't interested), John Newlove (who used the money to buy himself a new set of teeth), Earle Birney, Gwendolyn

**SURVIVAL: A THEMATIC GUIDE TO CANADIAN LITERATURE (1972)**
Margaret Atwood

At the time and for many years after, *Survival* was an incredibly important book, a book that gave courage, ammunition, and a ready-made syllabus to many teachers and professors. It's still the most ambitious book ever written on Canadian literature, the only one to attempt to define all of it — from start to date, English and French — in a single word. "Our stories are likely to be tales not of those who made it but of those who made it back," said Atwood, and generations of Canadians took note. As a bonus, she is a witty, engaging critic, rarely boring even when talking about boring books. Reviewing it in the *Vancouver Sun*, George Woodcock called *Survival* "a fine example of what happens when a first-rate intelligence takes on a task usually carried out by literary morons."

MacEwen, Margaret Atwood, and Leonard Cohen — including the manuscript of *Beautiful Losers* for $6,000, easily twice what the book earned him in sales. In the mid-seventies the University of Calgary became the country's big buyer, paying $15,000 for MacLennan's papers in 1973 and $50,000 for Richler's in 1974, plus $50,000 in tax receipts. University library budgets dried up by 1980, leaving universities able to offer only tax receipts that benefit only writers with substantial income, like professors. During the CanLit boom, in contrast, selling their papers helped writers be writers.

Not so long ago, it was possible and even common to teach at a university without a Ph.D., especially in the humanities. Canadian universities happily hired M.A.s and B.A.s, partly because their need for faculty exceeded the local supply, but also because the profession hadn't yet professionalized. Qualifications mattered more than credentials, with the result that many Canadian writers of the time found short-term or ongoing employment in a trade conducive to writing. Margaret Atwood wrote her first novel on exam booklets while teaching grammar to engineering students at UBC. Rudy Wiebe taught creative writing at the University of Alberta while writing *The Temptations of Big Bear*. Irving Layton published a dozen books during his nine years in York's English department, while also, said his dean, "excelling in the classroom and the pub." Robertson Davies wrote *Fifth Business* at the University of Toronto's Massey College. Michael Ondaatje won his first Governor General's Award while teaching for Western; the Université du Québec à Montréal hired Hubert Aquin after he became the first French-Canadian writer to refuse the award.

**THE TEMPTATIONS OF BIG BEAR (1973)**
Rudy Wiebe

Judging by the typos alone, Wiebe's editors had the same problem with his fourth novel that legions of undergraduates have had: staying awake while reading it. Part of the problem is focus, which the story doesn't find until Big Bear's trial near the end. Part of it is Wiebe's plodding style — obese, ungainly sentences that trudge across the pages like the story's vanishing buffalo.

Readers today will have other difficulties with the book, like its silent transformation of a Cree chief into a Christian martyr. But the main problem is how hard Wiebe made it to care about a man and a story clearly worth caring about. It's too bad we don't remake novels with the same freedom that we do movies.

Many literary magazines of the time got their start on university campuses, conceived and edited by professors and students. The *Malahat Review* at UVic, *Prism* and *Tish* at UBC, *Quarry* at Queen's, the bilingual *ellipse* at the Université de Sherbrooke, the *Fiddlehead* at UNB, and many others provided lots of places, if little payment, to publish. The University of British Columbia established the country's first creative writing program in 1965, the same year the Canada Council launched a writer-in-residence program. In its first fifteen years, the Council's program helped make ninety appointments at twenty-five institutions, mostly universities. The University of New Brunswick brought Norman Levine back from England in 1965 to be its first writer-in-residence. Montreal's Sir George Williams picked up George Bowering in 1967–68 for $11,000 (half came from the Council) and Mordecai Richler in 1968–69 for $12,000. The University of Ottawa's French department housed Gaston Miron and other francophone writers. Western started with poet Margaret Avison, followed by Margaret Laurence and alumna Alice Munro. The University of Toronto's new Mississauga campus hired Peter Such in time for him to meet Harold Ladoo at the subway station. The downtown campus began with Earle Birney, who liked the place so much he never left.

Like any cultural venture, the writer-in-residence program yielded mixed returns. The most cited legacy of Al Purdy's residency at Montreal's Loyola College is the term's worth of empty beer bottles that appeared under his office window when the snow melted in the

**A NORTH AMERICAN EDUCATION (1973)**
Clark Blaise

★★★★

Born in North Dakota to a schoolteacher and a sociopathic drifter, Clark Blaise has moved around a great deal. In 1966 he landed in Montreal for twelve years, which is how an American became a Canadian writer.

*A North American Education* began life as a novel written at the University of Iowa's Writers' Workshop in the early sixties and then destroyed and rewritten in Montreal. It's a collection of stories about its author under different names and in different places: a French-speaking boy in Florida, an American teacher in Montreal, a husband flying to India to meet his wife's family. The prose is outstanding, the work of a writer who revised much and published little. As a bonus, the stories are often exciting, menacing. Things happen in these stories. Usually bad things.

spring — "Purdy's crocuses," the students called them.* At George Williams, Richler told his students that writing couldn't be taught and told friends he had rented out his office to a bookie. A few years later, at Carleton, he prepared for class by drinking gin and tonics on the train, gave all his students a B, and when asked to give a public lecture, used it to call the faculty useless and the students ignorant. More typical was John Metcalf's experience, in which students and professors didn't seem to know he was there. "I played darts a lot," he says of his first residency, at UNB in Fredericton in 1972–73.

> During that entire year at UNB, I saw two students. When I was writer-in-residence at the University of Ottawa, one student came to see me; she was in the English Department and wanted to know if I thought she should quit. She seemed very intelligent so I advised her to quit forthwith. We still correspond. When I was writer-in-residence at Loyola of Montreal not a single student appeared. When I was writer-in-residence at Concordia one student did come to see me but he turned out to be an unpublished poet seeking my aid in securing a teaching position at a CEGEP.
>
> At four universities, then, at great cost to the universities themselves and to the Canada Council, I had dealings with three students. At these four universities I was asked only once to address a class. And honesty compels me to admit that the professor who *did* ask was one given to the bottle who regarded teaching as a chore disruptive of serious drinking.

Still, residencies gave writers time and money to write, more of either than the Canadian market could give them. Richler may not have believed writing could be taught, but he kept agreeing to teach it.

---

* Some versions of the story speak of beer cans rather than bottles. The difference is likely insignificant to literary history.

In 1955, the Canadian Writers' Conference at Queen's resolved
to make a home in the academy for Canadian literature. In 1973,
the University of Calgary's Conference of Writers and Critics celebrated its arrival. UBC hosted the Vancouver Poetry Conference in
the summer of 1963, uniting writers who had changed American
poetry with students who were changing Canadian poetry. Three
years later, some of that summer's participants and much of its spirit
helped launch a reading series at Sir George Williams University
that ran for eight years and hosted more than sixty North American
poets. The audiences were large, the parties long, the poets paid —
$100 (more than $700 in today's dollars), plus airfare and accom-
modation with room service at the Ritz-Carlton. It wasn't Newport
or Cannes, but for an English department it was something close.*

**OUTSIDE OF QUEBEC,** Canadian university administrations initiated very little direct support for Canadian literature and in fact
did much to slow its arrival. As in the high schools, change came
from individual teachers, mostly permanent faculty with the time
and autonomy to change the script, at this point mostly men. At the
University of Alberta, Frederick M. Salter convinced his department to accept a novel about Mennonites in Saskatchewan for an
M.A. instead of another thesis on Shakespeare. At the University of
Toronto, Shelley scholar Milton Wilson moonlighted at *Canadian
Forum* and supervised doctorates in Canadian literature. At UBC,
a committee suggested a journal devoted to Canadian literature,
Warren and Ellen Tallman brought poets into their classes and
their home, and Earle Birney insisted on first a course and then a
program in creative writing. Up the mountain at SFU, Robin Blaser
taught that poetry is not something you do but something you live.
In Montreal, McGill poet-professor Louis Dudek inspired two generations of Canadian poets. ("A sizeable number of his students,"
said one when his teacher died, "decided they were intended by fate

---

* Thanks to Jason Camlot and his students, you can hear these readings still, at http://
spokenweb.concordia.ca/sgw-poetry-readings.

to become Dante or at least Baudelaire.") Roy Kiyooka and others conceived and organized the Sir George Williams poetry series; Clark Blaise proposed Concordia's creative writing program.

Northrop Frye's influence on Canadian writers has been greatly exaggerated, both by supporters and by those who saw him as a Svengali silently pulling the strings of a Toronto or academic conspiracy to rule the literary world. But he did inspire some writers, especially James Reaney, and his influence on Canadian as well as international literary criticism continues to this day. Mostly, what Frye — and McLuhan — did for Canadian writers of all kinds and loyalties was to provide examples of international success, proof that you could be not just Canadian and a writer but Canadian and written about, argued over, read.

Universities did little to encourage Canadian literature, but they did create a record number of new spaces in which others could — all those new campuses and new classrooms and the theatres, galleries, bookstores, pubs, and cafés that followed them. More by accident than by design (which is pretty much how a university develops, because pretty much how knowledge develops), they greatly increased the opportunities for the kind of chance encounters that turn young people toward artistic lives. At the same time they also greatly increased the number of Canadians likely to care about art and able to pay for it. In the 1960s, a generation raised for the first time in relative comfort went to university. Not surprisingly, many embraced pursuits made possible by their leisure, like joining a protest, playing in a band, or reading a novel. Fortunately for the writers of their generation, the last habit proved easiest to keep.

## Chapter 6

# The Double Hook

We have moved to elaborate audiences now.
At midnight we open the curtains
    —Michael Ondaatje, "Postcard from Piccadilly Street"

**GWEN MACEWEN DROPPED** out of high school to become a writer
when she was eighteen. At the time, her mother was in a psychiatric hospital and her alcoholic father was sleeping where he could.
Gwendolyn lived with her aunt and uncle and a changing cast of
foster children in an old house on a hill in Toronto's west end and
worked part-time in a library.

Nights, she wrote. She had been writing poems since she was
twelve — she still had the pencil with which she had written her first,
sealed in a small white envelope. She taught herself Hebrew, then
modern Arabic and ancient Egyptian, all in the service of poetry.
She wrote fiction for poetry's sake, hoping to make enough money
as a novelist to live as a poet. In October 1963 a small New York
press published her first book, a short novel about Christ's return
to earth as a travelling magician. It earned her $400, plus another
$71.23 for a Canadian edition that spelled her name "MacEven" on
the title page.

She read her poems publicly for the first time in August 1960
at an upstairs jazz club, where cars now park at the Hudson's Bay
Centre. That summer, a coffee shop called the Bohemian Embassy
opened on St. Nicholas Street. Nineteen-year-old MacEwen became

an Embassy regular, meeting other young poets and reading her work for them and others. She read with confidence, pulling audiences together through the talk and the smoke. Most who heard her read were captivated, even those who didn't much care for the poems themselves — because she read well, because she believed in what she read.

In February 1962 she married another Embassy poet who believed his poems. Milton Acorn was from Charlottetown, a Second World War veteran with a metal plate in his head, a socialist chip on his shoulder, and a serious case of chronic depression. He came to Toronto in the summer of 1960 and soon became an Embassy idol, shouting poems at the rafters, scaring the college kids, helping lawyers and housewives imagine themselves part of the revolution for a night. He was nineteen years older than Gwen, a cigar-smoking caveman to her Isis reborn. The marriage lasted eight months, ending in Gwen's affair with the man to whom she dedicated her first book, a painter who conducted seances on Ward's Island and claimed to be from another planet.

MacEwen's first book of poems came out in the fall of 1963. She called it *The Rising Fire*, after the phoenix, a mythical bird reborn from the ashes of its old life. Reviewing it in UBC's *Canadian Literature*, George Bowering called it "an important book...evidence that a young woman with a marvellous talent is beginning to take charge." The Toronto *Telegram* ran a full-page profile of MacEwen with half a dozen photographs of pensive poses. America noticed, publishing one of her poems in a special Canadian supplement of the *Atlantic Monthly*. The Canada Council gave her a grant to write a novel about Akhenaton, the Egyptian pharaoh who gave up on his gods.

By the mid-sixties she had outgrown the Embassy and was making what she called a living from poetry readings at libraries and colleges and reading manuscripts for Macmillan. Good thing, because the books weren't earning much. Ryerson Press paid no advance on her second book of poems, *A Breakfast for Barbarians*, and her Egyptian novel did poorly in Canada and was rejected by eight American and eighteen British publishers before her agents gave up on it.

In the spring of 1970, by which time she had moved on to the Greek language and a Greek boyfriend, MacEwen's fourth book shared the Governor General's Literary Award for poetry with two books by her early champion George Bowering. Two years and two books later, on the evening of April 26, 1972, she gave a solo reading at Toronto's St. Lawrence Centre that drew over five hundred people, the largest audience of her career. She read by heart, a small woman alone on a stage, performing the poems she believed.

**JULIAN THE MAGICIAN**
**(1963)**
**Gwendolyn MacEwen**

Julian is a beautiful young magician, the bastard son of a gypsy. After he is mysteriously baptized by "the greatest Magician," he abandons his act for what looks increasingly like real magic: changing water into wine, walking on water, raising the dead.

Most people can see the affinity between magic and art; MacEwen actually believed it, both that magic was poetry and that poetry was magic. She was eighteen years old when she wrote *Julian the Magician*, and it's an eighteen-year-old's book, full of the first thrill of learning, seeing parallels in history and its stories, and feeling the power of making those stories come to life. MacEwen's novels were about magic; her poems made magic, which is a harder and a better thing to do.

**HISTORY HAS A** hard time with readers. Authors leave us their books, often their letters, journals, and reviews, clippings archived against their ruin. Publishers leave accounts of books bought and sold, internal memos, correspondence with the authors they published and those they didn't. But most readers leave nothing behind, no record of their existence other than a page turned down, maybe a name on a bookplate, a note in a margin, a digital footprint in a device bound for the nuisance grounds. We know how many people came out to hear Gwendolyn MacEwen read that night in 1972 at the St. Lawrence Centre, because a journalist reported that the 483-seat hall was "jammed to overflowing with her fans." We know that most enjoyed it, or were polite enough to go along with those who did, because the same journalist tells us the audience demanded curtain calls at the end. But we don't know how many of them actually read MacEwen's book, let alone what they thought about it.

Bestseller lists can tell us some things about some readers, if not much about poetry readers. Unfortunately, Canada had no national bestseller list between 1962, when *Quill & Quire* gave up on them, and 1970, when the *Toronto Daily Star* began compiling them for Canada and *La Presse* for Quebec (which didn't stop publishers from advertising their books as "bestselling" in the intervening years). We might at least learn something about how much readers spent from census records of the bookselling or publishing industries — if accurate records existed, which they mostly don't, and if they were comparable from census to census, which they mostly aren't. And even if we were able to find specific, precise numbers — like learning that Macmillan of Canada printed one thousand copies of MacEwen's *Armies of the Moon*, of which it shipped 750 copies in the first year — we still wouldn't know how many of those were later returned unsold, or how many that were bought were actually read, or how many were later owned, borrowed, or read by other readers.

We do know that the number of *potential* readers increased just in time for the CanLit boom. By the mid-1960s, the first of the baby boomers were leaving their teens, ready and generally able to become adult consumers and adult readers. Growing up beside them were the children of the 1.7 million mostly European immigrants who arrived in Canada between 1946 and 1962, so-called New Canadians with a particular interest in reading about their new home. Partly because there were more of them, and partly because more of them could afford it, more Canadians than ever before were going to school, to high school and beyond, acquiring the education and the interests to become and remain readers. To John Metcalf, newly arrived from England, Canada in the 1960s was "an intellectual and creative wasteland with a large percentage of its population functionally illiterate." Metcalf wasn't entirely wrong, and he was especially right about the part of the country where he happened to have landed. In 1961, just under half of all adult Canadians had less than a Grade 9 education. Quebec had the most illiterates of any province, and Montreal (where Metcalf arrived in 1962) the most of any city. But he was not as right as he would have been ten years before, and even less right ten years later.

In 1970 a consulting firm commissioned by the federal government told Canadians for the first time how much money they spent on books in a year: $222 million. Three years later, a study at York University reported that between 1963 and 1972, book sales had increased in Canada seven times faster than the population. Literary sales had increased nineteen times faster than the population. What *The Lumber Jack Report* neglected to point out was that the increases were so large because the numbers were so small to start with. Even in 1972, half the literary titles sold in Canada sold fewer than 250 copies each, and less than 4 percent sold more than five thousand copies. Two hundred and twenty-two million dollars a year to spend on books no doubt sounded like a lot of money to most Canadians (and all writers), but it was a third of what America or Britain spent on books per capita, and less than a sixth of what Canada's largest distillery made that year.

**THE RISING FIRE (1963)**
Gwendolyn MacEwen

MacEwen's first book of poetry is a youthful book for a youthful decade, one of the first books of poetry published in the sixties that is actually of the sixties. Because it's by MacEwen, it's also an ancient book, poems about gods and goddesses sprinkled with "electric roses" on "cosmic tablecloths."

The downside of MacEwen's affection for myth is her tendency toward the mystical, pseudo-statements like "The flower in the yellow vase / is questionable." But the best of these are beautiful, musical poems, Keats in *The Waste Land*. Milton Acorn — briefly MacEwen's husband during the writing of this book — played his poems on a banjo, while MacEwen sung to a lyre.

The first survey of Canadian readers as anything other than contributors to the GNP was conducted in 1972 by the Readers' Club of Canada, a national book-of-the-month club with just over two thousand members. According to the results, the club member who reported reading more than twelve books a year was most commonly a male university-educated professional over the age of thirty-five. He lived within three miles of a bookstore, which he claimed to visit at least monthly. Besides books, he read at least one or two newspapers a day and subscribed to *Maclean's*. If he watched TV at all, it was the CBC, also his choice on the radio. He preferred nonfiction to fiction, and despite his membership in an all-Canadian book club, read more foreign than Canadian authors.

Six years later, Statistics Canada conducted the government's first survey of reading habits, completed by 16,700 Canadians. Based on the data, the typical Canadian book reader in the winter of

1978 — the reader left behind by the CanLit boom — was a thirty-five-year-old woman who read more than six hours a week. She read at least one newspaper and subscribed to at least one magazine. She too had gone to university. She read books mostly for "relaxation and recreation." She got her most recent book from a bookstore. She read slightly more nonfiction than fiction, poetry rarely or never. She chose Canadian books "at least some of the time."

**THE SHADOW-MAKER**
**(1969)**
Gwendolyn MacEwen

★★★

MacEwen's third book departs from the more topical books that came before and after it, returning to her comfort zone of myth and mysticism. A handful of the poems take place in a recognizably real world, like a dramatic monologue ostensibly spoken by an illiterate man she met on a train between Fredericton and Halifax. But most are mystical, even occult — records of dreams, conversations with voices the rest of us can't hear, things unnamed and unsaid. The shadow-maker is God, perhaps also his Son, but the gods here are more often dark and frightening than loving or comforting, as much devils as gods.

The text is printed in green type throughout; her next book, also with Macmillan, used blue. Presumably it meant something to her.

**"IN NOT MORE** than twenty-five book shops in Canada, we are told, is it unnecessary to sell other merchandise in order to stay in business." So said the Massey Report in 1951, one of its rare acknowledgements that the problem with writing in Canada might be a problem with reading. Over the next twenty years, affluence, education, and urbanization increased the number of bookstores, as did new locations like shopping centres and new things to sell, like paperbacks and pornography. By 1971 Canada had 1,260 businesses that sold books, including a hundred or so college bookstores and about 150 trade bookstores — still just one real bookstore for every 140,000 Canadians, almost all in major cities. With "a few important exceptions," concluded yet another royal commission in 1973, "retail bookselling in Canada is in a pitifully underdeveloped condition in comparison with bookselling in most other countries."

In the fifties you could almost count those exceptions on one hand: Halifax's ancient Book Room, Classic Books and Libraire Tranquille in Montreal, Britnell's in Toronto, Calgary's Evelyn de Mille, Hurtig Books in Edmonton, Duthie Books in Vancouver. All faced the usual problems of running a bookstore in Canada — small markets, large distances, and competition from publishers selling directly to customers through the mail at a discount, the 1950s' version of losing to Amazon. But all survived into the sixties and even expanded, adding space and new locations. Mel Hurtig's seven-thousand-square-foot flagship store on Jasper Avenue was, according to Mel, the biggest bookstore in Canada; Bill Duthie added four more stores to his first, at Robson and Hornby. By 1967 Louis Melzack had built Classic Books up to twelve stores: six in Montreal, three in Toronto, and one each in Ottawa, Quebec City, and Saint John.

Jim and Alice Munro opened one of the best new bookstores of the 1960s. Duthie's was already in Vancouver, so the Munros moved to Victoria, a town with a new university and no good bookstore. Munro's Books opened at 753 Yates Street on September 19, 1963, with "Victoria's largest assortment of quality paperbacks on all subjects,"* the distinctively British Penguin and Pelican titles displayed face-out around the walls. Jim later claimed they were the first store in Canada to carry books from the San Francisco beat publisher City Lights. Increasingly, Munro's also carried Canadian authors, including its own: when the *Globe and Mail*'s William French visited the store in 1973, Alice Munro was one of the store's top-selling authors, "right behind Pierre Berton and Farley Mowat."

Other new stores appeared, like the socialist Vanguard Books at 1208 Granville in Vancouver, where Milton Acorn licked his wounds, and Montreal's tiny but mighty Argo Bookshop on Saint Catherine West. Renaud-Bray, now the largest chain of

**SOMETHING I'VE BEEN MEANING TO TELL YOU (1974)**
Alice Munro

★★★★

*Something I've Been Meaning to Tell You* marked Munro's first appearance on a Canadian bestseller list, but several reviewers had trouble with what we'd now call its metafictional passages — moments where the narrator disrupts the story to talk about the difficulty of making the story. What those reviewers couldn't yet see is that Munro's stories aren't stories at all, not to her; they are attempts to make sense of people, why they do the things they do, remember what they do. Writing for her isn't fiction, not really. It's the truth, and the truth is difficult.

---

* The quality of "quality paperbacks" had more to do with the content than the package, a way to distinguish high- and middlebrow tastes from newsstand and pulp fiction.

French-language bookstores in North America, opened its first store in Montreal's Côte-des-Neiges neighbourhood in 1965.

In September 1967 the first Rochdale College newsletter included a guide to Toronto's bookstores for students and other new arrivals in the city. Probably written in whole or in part by Dennis Lee, the tour began at the U of T Bookstore, "one of the two or three best in the city for selection." Next came Classic Books, in the Colonnade on Bloor, "a straight bookstore, but not bad for all that." Just south on Bay was the Book Cellar, a "swinging place" with a good poetry section upstairs. Next door was the SCM (Student Christian Movement) Book Room, best and cheapest in the city for scholarly books. One block east, at Charles and Yonge, was the main Coles, good for remainders and paperbacks. Two blocks up Yonge was Britnell's, "the most distinguished straight bookstore around," appropriately across the street from Toronto's Trotskyite bookstore. In 1968, too late to be included in Rochdale's guide, railway porter Leonard Johnston and his wife Gwendolyn opened Third World Books in the Gerrard Street Village, specializing in "Afro Asian Books and Crafts."

The guide's choice for "most amiable bookseller in town" was Marty Ahvenus, proprietor of the Village Book Store. Marty was Finnish Canadian, the son of a Forest Hill housekeeper and an absent father. After dropping out of school he worked as a farmhand, an office clerk, a circus gazoony (somewhere below a carny), a dancehall bouncer, and a salesman. By the mid-fifties he was selling photocopy machines for Eastman Kodak, successfully if not contentedly. Marty dreamed of opening a jazz club, but that took money. He also loved books, and compared to sound systems, books were cheap, especially used books. So he decided to open a second-hand bookstore and began buying books and storing them in his apartment. When that ran out of room, he rented a three-storey building at 29 Gerrard Street West for $125 a month. He hired a woman to mind the store during the day, from whom he would take over till ten. He took the second floor for himself and gave a "poor song lyricist" the third floor for helping out as needed. The most important bookstore in the history of Canadian poetry opened on Friday, September 15, 1961. It grossed $125 in its first full month of business. Marty kept his day job.

The Village Book Store was in the heart of the Gerrard Street Village, the closest that 1950s Toronto got to Bohemia. It was a ten-minute walk from the Bohemian Embassy, in the early sixties the gathering place for young poets living in or travelling through the city. It had the best selection of used books in Toronto. And it had an owner who liked books and liked talking about books, who liked to share a drink and who stayed open late.

In no time at all, the poets showed up.

Al Purdy came first and stayed longest. "If I could think of any way to do without both women and money," he wrote to Marty, "I guess I'd be living in Toronto and sleeping in your five foot shelf of books in the back room." Margaret Atwood and John Newlove stored their papers at the store; bpNichol used it as a mailing address. Milton Acorn came by after Gwen left him and wrote a dark poem on the wall. MacEwen's next lover, artist/magician Bob Mallory, set up a table in Marty's store from which he sold his magazine, *The Caligula Times*.

In 1967 Marty was finally able to quit his job and run the store during the day, keeping Thursdays as his evening open. Bookseller David Mason remembers Thursdays at Marty's as his university, a place where writers mixed with collectors, booksellers, art dealers, and librarians, including Sybille Pantazzi of the Art Gallery of Ontario and Richard Landon, future director of U of T's Thomas Fisher Rare Book Library.

> I went every Thursday. We would go into the back room, and whoever showed up would sit there having drinks, sliding books aside, sitting on top of cheques. Al Purdy would come in with a bottle of his homemade wine, Doug Fetherling, John Newlove. Acorn would come in with Purdy if he was in town. Booksellers, of course. A Bay Street lawyer, Bob Pepall, who loved books and art. The Group of Seven dealer Phil McCready. Tommy Tate, who had a little framing shop next door. Whoever came in could join in. A man

in the store would be listening to us yelling in the back, and he would interject a comment, and then he'd be there until three o'clock in the morning.

Affable with all, Marty was especially kind to poets. He cashed their cheques, gave them small loans, and sold them books at a discount and on credit. When they brought him their self-printed chapbooks, he displayed them face-out on their own shelf. When they published actual books with actual publishers, he bought those too, turning over an ever larger section of his store to new poetry from small presses like Hawkshead, Weed/Flower, Periwinkle, Talonbooks, and Very Stone House. In December 1966, Contact Press invoiced the Village Book Store for ten copies of Margaret Atwood's first book, five in cloth and five in paper. In July 1967, Marty bought five copies of bpNichol's first Canadian publication. Two months later, he bought five copies of Anansi's first book, Dennis Lee's *Kingdom of Absence*. The quantities weren't large, but at least he had them, which was more than Coles could claim.

Besides the Village Book Store, the best place to find new Canadian poetry was a five-minute drive north to Bruce and Vivienne Surtees's Book Cellar. Neither in a cellar nor mostly known for its books, the Book Cellar had the largest magazine selection in the country: some 850 titles, by Pierre Berton's count. Marshall McLuhan, Robertson Davies, and Robert Fulford were regulars. Upstairs was a poetry section that by 1967 had as many "scrubby little out-of-the-way books" as Marty's, including books by the beat poets that drew Victor Coleman and other young poets to the store. In 1965, when Dennis Lee published Edward Lacey's *Forms of Loss* — the first openly gay book of poetry published in Canada — he sold six copies to Marty. The Surteeses took eighty-two copies, presumably most of them after Fulford reviewed the book favourably in the *Star* and told his paper's 350,000 readers they could buy it at the Book Cellar for $1.25.

Published by larger publishers with better distribution, Canadian fiction and nonfiction was generally easier to buy than Canadian poetry. Britnell's couldn't be bothered with strange little books from strange little presses, but they could and did sell books for Macmillan and McClelland & Stewart. W. H. Smith refused to stock Mordecai Richler's *Cocksure* in England but had no qualms about selling the book in its Toronto store. Classic Books made a point of displaying Canadian books just inside the door of its stores, a precursor of the ubiquitous "Canadiana" section in English-Canadian bookstores of the seventies, with Pierre Berton and Charlie Farquharson shelved alongside canoeing manuals and picture books of the Rockies.

Still, one reason why Canadians read more foreign than Canadian books in the 1960s was simply that foreign books were easier to find, especially if you didn't happen to live within shopping distance of Yonge and Bloor. Finding Canadian books was even harder in French Canada, where bookstores finally escaped the monopoly of a foreign church only to have their books chosen for them by foreign wholesalers like the giant Parisian firm Librairie Hachette — which, *quelle surprise*, overwhelmingly preferred to sell French books.

Québécois publishers broke the straitjacket ("*carcan*") of the bookstores by selling their books in drugstores, corner stores, supermarkets, and train stations. By the early seventies, English Canada had enough books in print to open its own stores. Beth Appeldoorn, Susan Sandler, and June Waltho opened the first all-Canadian trade bookstore in the country at 630 Yonge in Toronto, in a small store just north of St. Joseph that they rented for $1,100 a month. Their motivations were avowedly political, a nationalist response to foreign dominance of the Canadian book market. The Longhouse Book Shop opened in late March 1972 with ten thousand titles and

**COCKSURE (1968)**
**Mordecai Richler**

"All I can tell about the new novel is that it is not set in Canada, but in Swinging London and is staggeringly filthy." So wrote Richler to Jack McClelland about his sixth novel, about a literary editor who finds himself working for a Hollywood tycoon. As in *The Incomparable Atuk*, the increasingly ridiculous plot is just an excuse for social satire, topical targets like the movie industry and the new "permissive" society. It's better focused than *Atuk*, a little more select in its satire. As promised, it's got a lot of sex and dirty words.

Bolstered by a puff from Anthony Burgess in *Life* ("I wish I'd written it myself"), *Cocksure* became Richler's first commercially successful novel. It shared a Governor General's Award with his first collection of essays, *Hunting Tigers under Glass*, a better book, if now just as dated.

a poster declaring, "Give a Damn, Think Canadian!" It sold textbooks, cookbooks, French- and English-Canadian plays, poetry,
and fiction — pretty much anything and everything Canadian* —
as well as an international children's section mischievously set up
at the back, where customers on that particular stretch of Yonge
were more accustomed to finding pornography. An increasing
part of the store's business was supplying books to international
universities. An apparently hurried Pennsylvania professor wrote
in 1974 requesting "10 Richlers, 10 Edibles, 10 Fryes" (Appeldoorn
guessed Atwood's *The Edible Woman* but had to call to confirm
*Duddy Kravitz* and *The Educated Imagination*). Longhouse also
hosted many book launches, including a packed party for Margaret
Laurence's *The Diviners* for which the owners calmed the nervous
author with Valium (they told her it was Aspirin).

Peggy Blackstock and Bill Roberts opened Books Canada in
Ottawa and Victoria. In Halifax, tourists bought local titles at A
Pair of Trindles, in a refurbished warehouse on the waterfront.
In London, Ontario, the Oxford Book Shop ran an all-Canadian
bookstore at Richmond and King called Oxford Canadiana Books,
which helped pay the rent by selling government publications and
Inuit carvings.

In Montreal, romance novelist Hélène Holden had a hard time
finding English-Canadian books to show her American neighbour,
journalist Joan Blake. So the two women brought in a third neighbour, Judy Mappin (daughter of Toronto multimillionaire E. P.
Taylor), and in October 1974 opened their own neighbourhood bookstore at 4174 Saint Catherine West, near their homes in the wealthy
anglophone suburb of Westmount. Named after Sheila Watson's
1959 novel, the Double Hook sold English- and French-Canadian
books. Its most popular authors were women: Gabrielle Roy, Anne
Hébert, and Marie-Claire Blais among the French, and Laurence,
Atwood, and Alice Munro among the English. An English store on

---

* Not quite everything. Appeldoorn had her own definition of "Canadian author" and
wouldn't stock books by the popular British-Canadian writer Arthur Hailey or the then
equally popular New York madam Xaviera Hollander, who lived in Toronto in the seventies.

a French island, it almost certainly would not have survived if its owners weren't able to work for nothing and if Mappin hadn't used family money to buy their next (and last) home, a building around the corner on Greene Avenue. But survive it did, for more than thirty years.

**ONE OF THE** things that makes literature different from writing is that for literature, the most important readers are other writers. The literary author writes first for other authors, the living and the dead; literature is the record of their conversation. Those who see a writer's work before anyone else are usually writers themselves, peers or mentors asked to respond to unpublished work. In the little magazines and small presses that became such a large part of Canadian literature in the 1960s, the editors were almost always writers themselves. For a writer, the reader who decides to publish your work is the most important reader of all, the reader without whom there can be no others. After the work is published, an encouraging review by another writer can (and often must) make up for an absence of many readers.

For poets, their most important readers are also pretty much their only readers. Sometime after the First World War, poetry decided to trade a large audience for a learned audience. Poets surrendered the accessible pleasures of their medium — rhyme, narrative, sentiment —

**THE DOUBLE HOOK (1959)**
Sheila Watson

★★★★★

She wanted to write a western that wasn't a western. *The Double Hook* is a lean book set in a lean land, the story of a small community in a dusty valley in British Columbia. There's action aplenty: murder, assault with a whip, robbery, a pregnant teenager, a house fire, and a ghost. Over it all watches Coyote, an ambivalent god in a land forgotten by God. Watson got help from Native Trickster stories and Samuel Beckett's pared-down language. But the result is all hers: a tragic, hopeful book that, despite the long list of writers it influenced, is utterly unlike anything before or after it. The *Globe and Mail* called it obscure, eccentric, and difficult, which is all true. It's also both the great western Canadian novel and the best candidate I know for the great Canadian novel.

to popular music, and focused on its difficult pleasures, on challenging rather than affirming what readers thought and felt. As poetry written for the page grew ever more sophisticated, its audience grew ever smaller, from the public to the academy and ultimately to its makers. In the 1960s all that almost changed: when singers became songwriters, poetry remembered its old place, and poets like Gwen MacEwen sought and caught a bit of the light from Dylan's stage. But in their hearts, poets believed what history had shown: that great poetry in their century came from writers that most people never read. Being Canadian, in other words, was no impediment to being a poet. "We wrote for ourselves," says Atwood.

In 1969 Milton Acorn was short-listed for the Governor General's Award for poetry for *I've Tasted My Blood*, a selection of his poems prepared by his friend Al Purdy. His ex-wife Gwen MacEwen was also on the short list. Milton had never forgiven Gwen for leaving him, and she was afraid enough of him to write to the judges that if there was any chance of her having to share the award with Acorn, she would rather withdraw her book from consideration. In the end, the judges split the award between MacEwen and British Columbia poet George Bowering.

Acorn hadn't been doing well since Gwen left him, wandering from coast to coast and couch to couch. He tried to kill himself at least once and was twice hospitalized for depression. His drinking had become legendary. His friends felt that *I've Tasted My Blood* was not only his best book but maybe his last book. Because one of the GG judges that year was Warren Tallman, an American-born UBC professor who had taught Bowering and others in the *Tish* circle, Acorn's supporters took his loss as evidence of the colonization of Canadian poetry by American poetics. They enlisted Irving Layton's support and circulated an appeal, signed by Layton and Eli Mandel.

**I'VE TASTED MY BLOOD: POEMS 1956 TO 1968 (1969)**
**Milton Acorn**

★★★

Poems old and new, *I've Tasted My Blood* ranges across the country with the years, from Charlottetown's harbour to the lawn of the B.C. Legislature. There are flashes of humour, but mostly these are serious and often angry poems, poems about those left behind by affluence or riding its coattails: homeless men, working men, convicts, prostitutes, poets.

Despite Acorn's reputation as a populist poet, his voice is less conversational than Purdy's, more self-consciously poetic. He was at his best when he remembered his own rule that "description isn't for poets" and just spoke from his heart. *I've Tasted My Blood* contains a few such poems and one great one, the sixties battle cry "I Shout Love," a fierce, wild thing that exceeds and redeems pretty much everything Acorn did, as a writer if not as a man.

We wish to register our protest that the Governor General's Awards Committee failed to include Milton Acorn's distinguished collection of poems *I've Tasted My Blood* among the winners of the Literary Awards this year.

We want to indicate to Milton that we admire and applaud his work; and we want to honor him for his contribution to Canadian poetry.

We propose, then, that a fund be raised and presented to Milton Acorn as the Canadian Poets Award.

You are invited to contribute whatever amount you feel appropriate. Please send the money or pledge of money as soon as possible.

Earle Birney, Leonard Cohen, Doug Fetherling, and John Glassco contributed, among others. On May 16, 1970, five days after Bowering and MacEwen picked up their awards at the Château Laurier in Ottawa, Mandel hosted a party for Acorn at Grossman's Tavern, on Spadina Avenue in Toronto. Layton came, and Atwood. Al Purdy came from Ameliasburgh, Dorothy Livesay from Edmonton. On behalf of the poets both absent and assembled, Mandel presented Acorn with a cheque for $1,000 and a medallion declaring that the winner of the Canadian Poets' Award was "Milton Acorn, The Peoples' Poet." The punctuation has since been fixed, but the People's Poet remains the title by which Acorn is remembered and the prize is known today — a title created and bestowed entirely by other poets, his people.

## Chapter 7

# The Torontonians

Yonge Street twelve o'clock Saturday night all the bars emptying
up and down the block...
　　　a little jazz still singing in our heads
as we greet the new day, Christ's day, but not yet our own.
　　　　　—Raymond Souster, "Colonial Saturday Night"

MARGARET ATWOOD GREW UP, as she likes to say, in the middle
of the middle class, in the middle of the century. By high school
she had decided to be a writer. On her English teacher's advice
she chose Victoria College, enrolling in the English language and
literature program. She read Canadian writers on her own at the
college library, in magazines like *Fiddlehead, Tamarack Review*, and
*Canadian Forum*, and in books from the shelves of poet and Vic
lecturer Jay Macpherson. At the end of her second year, the *Forum*
accepted one of her poems. In fourth year she gave her first reading at the Bohemian Embassy, one of "two young Toronto poets"
to open up for Milton Acorn on November 17, 1960.

Atwood's Milton professor, Northrop Frye, persuaded her
that a graduate degree from Harvard might be better for her
writing than drinking absinthe in Paris. Maybe so, but aside
from reading a lot of nineteenth-century British novels for a
Ph.D. thesis she never finished, the main legacy of Atwood's
time in America was to turn her into a Canadian. She also met
the man who would become her husband, Jim Polk, like her a

scholarship student amid the ivy, a boy from Montana with a girl from Canada.

**THE CIRCLE GAME (1966)**
**Margaret Atwood**

★★★★

Even now, or maybe especially now, it's easy to see why Atwood's first book vaulted her to the front of Canadian poetry. *The Circle Game* owes something to confessional poetry (Sylvia Plath's suicide became news while Atwood was writing it), but it's all Atwood, all her own: that measured voice, the startling images, the Gothic sensibility.

As her biographer Rosemary Sullivan says, Atwood's early poetry is preoccupied with things submerged, buried, hidden underwater or underground. What's underneath is sometimes psychological like Plath's poetry, sometimes mythical like MacEwen's, but mostly historical, ancestors lurking beneath the surface. For all that, though, *The Circle Game* is powerfully a book of its time and place, riddled with Cold War anxieties. The title poem is partly about being trapped in a relationship but also about being trapped in the times: "I want the circle / broken."

Atwood kept publishing while she was in graduate school — poems and the occasional review in the magazines she had read at Vic and in newer ventures like *Alphabet*, edited by Frye's former grad student James Reaney. She wrote a novel that at least three publishers asked to see and then rejected. "It was way ahead of its time," says Atwood. "It ended with the heroine deciding whether or not to push the leading man off a roof." She sent manuscripts of her poems to Contact Press, Macmillan of Canada, Ryerson Press, and McClelland & Stewart, all of which said no or never answered.

In August 1965, little Contact Press accepted a revised version of the poetry manuscript they had rejected in 1963. They suggested calling it *The Circle Game*, after its long central poem. Atwood designed the cover herself. They printed 290 copies, for which her pay was twelve free copies. The only newspaper to notice was the *Toronto Daily Star*, which made a brief mention in a survey of new poetry for the fall of 1966 by CBC Radio producer Robert Weaver. In January Atwood sold the manuscript to a Montreal rare book dealer because she needed the money.

Two months later, Weaver chaired the committee that awarded *The Circle Game* $2,500 and a Governor General's Award for poetry. Atwood was twenty-seven, the second-youngest person to win the GG for poetry (her mentor Jay Macpherson had won it when she was five months younger, in May of 1958). She borrowed a dress from a roommate for the ceremony, held at Government House in Ottawa on June 2, 1967.

Today Atwood is both the most famous writer to emerge from the CanLit boom and the writer most closely associated with Toronto. Which is odd, in a sense, because during the Boom she was away from Toronto more often than not, studying in Boston. In 1964–65 she was in Vancouver, teaching at UBC. After she left Harvard, she taught Victorian and American literature at Sir George Williams in Montreal for a year, then moved with her husband to Edmonton for jobs in the English department of the University of Alberta.

Atwood's first novel came out in September 1969. *Time* magazine singled out *The Edible Woman* as "the most interesting early offering of the season," calling it "a finely controlled fantasy about an articulate graduate student bewildered by the affluent society." UBC professor George Woodcock wrote the first review to appear, a rave in the *Toronto Daily Star* that said Atwood's venture into fantasy made Richler's *Cocksure* seem "crude and uncraftsmanly." Most newspapers assigned the novel to female reviewers, most of whom loved it. Eileen Johnson in the *Vancouver Sun* "couldn't put it down"; the *Ottawa Journal*'s Dorothy Bishop pronounced it "one of the wittiest and funniest books to come from a Canadian writer in a coon's age." They also had no trouble recognizing the unnamed city in which it takes place. As MariJo Amer said in the *Peterborough Examiner,* "Miss Atwood's Toronto IS Toronto." Like Richler, Atwood had become known for a novel about a city in which she no longer lived. She launched the book at the Hudson's Bay store in Edmonton, giving her first book-signing in the men's socks and underwear section. Up the aisle, you could hear the muses laughing.

Atwood sold the film rights to *The Edible Woman* for $15,000 and

**THE EDIBLE WOMAN (1969)**
Margaret Atwood

★★★

The story of a woman who finds herself engaged to be married and unable to eat, Atwood's first novel is what she called an "anti-comedy," a marriage novel that doesn't end in marriage. It's also a proto-feminist fable, a satire of the affluent society, and an all-too-real window on eating disorders. Marian McAlpin's growing disgust with the female body is palpable, at once comic and horrific, balanced on the knife edge of Atwood's irony.

The novel was based in part on Atwood's experiences working for a Toronto market research company, and on her breakup with fiancé Jay Ford. Atwood makes a self-mocking cameo appearance: she's the grad student in black stockings who shows up uninvited at Peter's party and talks about death symbols.

wrote the screenplay for a movie that was never made. With the film money and a Canada Council grant, she and her husband quit their jobs in Edmonton and spent the winter of 1970–71 in England, missing Jim Foley's first Canada Day and the FLQ crisis for writing trips to France and Italy. Atwood came home in August 1971 for a job at York University. The job ended a year later, around the same time as her marriage, but she stayed. She has lived in or near her city ever since.

**MODERN ENGLISH-CANADIAN POETRY** was born in Montreal, the cradle of A. J. M. Smith, F. R. Scott, A. M. Klein, and P. K. Page.* For McGill poet-professor Louis Dudek, the city had been the centre of poetry in Canada since the 1920s, and therefore — it went without saying — of all serious literature in Canada. Dudek thought Montreal's literary prominence owed something to the city's "odd, ugly vitality," something to its cosmopolitan diversity, and most to its poets' spawning of more poets. "Nothing stimulates a beginning poet more than the irritating activity of another poet in his vicinity," wrote Dudek in 1957. "And once this local decoction has been started, it perpetuates itself — it can hardly be stopped."

But, as Dudek later realized, what can't be stopped can also move on. Sometime after 1947, he said, modern poetry began to change from something made in Montreal to something made all over, but centred on Toronto.

Nineteen forty-seven is the year that Toronto became the first English-speaking city in Canada to allow hard liquor in bars and dining rooms.

Literary history is probably not quite that simple. But it's hard to avoid the conclusion that the end of Toronto the Good both marked and caused the start of Toronto as the cultural capital of English Canada. According to Dudek's calendar, English-Canadian poetry stayed in Montreal for just as long as it was the only place in the country to get a drink.

---

* T. S. Eliot has much to answer for.

Until 1947, the only place to buy hard liquor in Toronto was a government liquor store, where your name was recorded for each purchase. You could buy beer in a hotel or tavern, as long as you drank it from a glass, while sitting down, with no more than three other people at your table, and after noon and before midnight Monday to Saturday — except between 6:30 and 8:00 p.m., when the law quietly but firmly suggested that you should be home having dinner with your family. Even after '47, licensed establishments were few and far between. Pierre Berton counted five when he arrived in the city that summer. Living in still-dry North Toronto in the mid-fifties, Dave Mason couldn't find a single bar between Summerhill Avenue and the Jolly Miller in York Mills — four miles of Yonge Street with not so much as a restaurant that could serve a drink. Irish-raised Kildare Dobbs arrived in Toronto in 1953 and found a city in which "Calvinist misery reigned," where everyone went to church on Sunday because there was precious little else to do. "You remember Toronto," one joke went. "It's that big cemetery with lights."

It was a charade, of course. Alcohol was publicly prohibited and privately ubiquitous. People carried flasks in their pockets and purses, hid entire bars beneath the deliberately floor-length tablecloths in the dining room of the Royal York Hotel, and pre-drank at home or in hotel rooms (legally because deemed "in residence"). They had to sign their name to get it, but affluence brought home more and better booze along with everything else. "Say Seagram's," said the beautiful people in their magazines, "and be sure." Across the street from City Hall, a striptease show started at noon. Switchblades outsold squirt guns. Downtown police

**THE TORONTONIANS (1960)**
**Phyllis Brett Young**

★★★

"We have a beautiful house," Karen Whitney tells her husband, "but it's smothering us because it has become an end in itself, and because it epitomizes a way of life that is essentially trivial. As long as we go on living in it, we won't really be living at all."

Realism pulled toward romance, *The Torontonians* is a smart insider account of the affluent society, especially its women: housewives who have every new time-saving appliance but wonder, "For what? So that you could go back upstairs and bake another superb cake?" It didn't need to be, but at the end the novel seems almost ashamed of itself; Karen's vague thought that she must "do something" to help her city's previously invisible poor is the loudest of the book's few false notes. It should be better known than it is.

patrolled in pairs for their protection, not yours. Robbery, rape, and murder were commonplace.

After the province loosened the liquor laws, the next open assault on Old Toronto was the popularity in the late fifties and early sixties of after-hours jazz clubs like the First Floor Club, George's Spaghetti House, and the House of Hambourg. Initially popular among recent immigrants to the city, the smoky clubs were what jazz critic John Norris called "the first step toward the development of the new, swinging Toronto." Even more frightening to some than immigrants or progressive jazz, abstract art arrived at about the same time, brought to town by Painters Eleven. Av Isaacs opened his first gallery in 1955, providing a home and creating a market for exciting, colourful, assertive art — pretty much everything Toronto was not.

The jazz clubs and art galleries opened their doors to arts that were still homeless in the city. Gwen MacEwen gave her first reading at the First Floor Club. The House of Hambourg staged Jack Gelber's New York experimental play about heroin addicts waiting for their dealer, *The Connection*, with Vancouver jazz musician Don Francks as the host and Montrealer Percy Rodriguez as the dealer. Choreographer Garbut Roberts hosted an "exotic dance revue" at the Hambourg featuring African, Bengali, Japanese, West Indian, and German expressionist dances. The Canada Council's first grant for a poetry reading series went to the Isaacs Gallery in 1959, for a series started two years before by Ray Souster and U of T grad student Ken McRobbie. D. G. Jones was the first to read in the series, in April 1957, and James Reaney the last, in April 1962. "Our attendance varied from about thirty to a hundred," Av remembered. "There was always a modest charge, and the poets got paid. It wasn't until the third year that the Canada Council gave us a grant of $845, which we were grateful for, even though we had asked for more."

**TOWARD THE END** of 1960, a few coffee houses opened in a small downtown Toronto neighbourhood northeast of Bloor and Avenue Road. As Stuart Henderson explains in his history of what happened next, Yorkville became the place for the Canadian counterculture to see and be seen because of, not despite, its shopping. Drawn by hip clothing stores and restaurants, young professionals, artists, and students moved into the still-affordable flats around them. The coffee shops quickly followed, serving exotic drinks — espressos and cappuccinos — to a generation with the money to buy them and the time to enjoy them (and all they could drink if under twenty-one, then the legal drinking age in Ontario). In the early sixties, Yorkville was to Toronto "a world of little shops selling Finnish rugs, gold bathtub faucets, hand-dipped candles, nutmeg-flavored coffee and bearded guitar players."

Bearded guitar players were as much an artifact of affluence as nutmeg-flavoured coffee. So, of course, were poets, which is one reason why they regularly shared the bill at the jazz clubs and coffee houses, places like the First Floor, the Half Beat, the Purple Onion. For poets, the most important of these was the Bohemian Embassy, opened on June 1, 1960, in the loft of what had once been a police stable. The Embassy wasn't in Yorkville; it was on St. Nicholas, a small street west of Yonge and Wellesley, about halfway between the old Gerrard Street Village to the south and Yorkville to the north. It was created with $100 each by five CBC employees looking for something between a clubhouse and a salon, chief among them twenty-seven-year-old Don Cullen, then a copy clerk for CBC-TV news.

**THE LAST OF THE CRAZY PEOPLE (1967)**
Timothy Findley

Findley's first novel is a mash-up of Greek tragedy and American Gothic. From the Greeks it takes grief and madness driving ineluctably toward the fall of a noble house. From William Faulkner and many others it takes a long, hot summer, mentally ill white main characters, and minor black characters for comic relief and folk wisdom. Reviewers wondered what it was doing set in Toronto (actually just outside), but it's not hard to see it as a story about the end of Toronto the Good, the Family Compact on its last legs.

Its author came from the theatre and, not surprisingly, the novel feels stagy: melodramatic dialogue in a sparse setting, characters hard to feel for without an actor to give them life. Perhaps readers who haven't read its American predecessors might be more impressed.

The Embassy didn't serve anything stronger than coffee. There were several licensed options nearby, including its namesake, the Embassy Tavern on Bloor (where Harry Rosen now sits) and the King Cole Room in the basement of the Park Plaza Hotel, U of T's unofficial pub and occasional classroom. The CBC already had its own bar, the Celebrity Club on Jarvis. In Cullen's mind, the Embassy would be something else, what he described in its first flyers as a community "in aid of the almost lost causes of: Culture in Toronto, Intelligent Conversation, Informality, Inter-Galactic friendship, and General Subversion." He set it up as a private club and offered citizenship in bohemia for twenty-five cents a year.

Outside flew the Bohemian lion rampant, red on white. At the top of narrow stairs you entered a long room with whitewashed brick walls and a plank floor painted dark red. Round tables with the obligatory red-checked tablecloths. Chairs for a hundred people. A low stage at one end beneath a set of large wooden doors, from the room's former life as a hayloft, and a portable stage for solo acts, midway along one wall. A small concession behind a curtain sold coffee for fifteen cents, espresso for a quarter, cappuccino for thirty-five cents, and something called "café boheme" for forty cents (at the King Cole Room, students smashed their glasses in protest when beer went up to fifteen cents). Everyone smoked, but drugs weren't yet part of the scene. Any outliers were soon sniffed out and asked to leave by Cullen — "a sweet guy," says Victor Coleman. "Very funny, but strictly Upper Canada College."

The Embassy was open only at night, from around nine p.m. till whenever. Folk on Fridays, jazz on Saturdays. Other nights, anything and everything: acting lessons, fencing lessons, stand-up and improv comedy, drama, informal talks. Atwood's first reading followed an unannounced talk by American stripper Libby Jones, in town for a week's work at the Lux Burlesque Theatre. They tried a happening, but with no drugs, it didn't happen. Newfoundland playwright

**NO CLOUDS OF GLORY**
**(1968)**
**Marian Engel**

★★

University of Toronto English professor Dr. Sarah Porlock is having a mid-life crisis. She's had two affairs with married men, including her sister's husband. The *Star* has just published an article about her that made her look like a "bull dike." Literature bores her, especially Canadian literature. Teaching bores her. Toronto is driving her fucking crazy.

Engel's first novel is partly a feminist novel, but the cause of Sarah's unhappiness isn't being held back. It's having made it and then not knowing what else to do. Like *The Torontonians*, it's a novel about people unhappy with their own success. In the end, Sarah sells her books to Marty Ahvenus, takes the train to Montreal, and starts over.

David French staged a one-act play at the Embassy in December 1963, eight years before what's commonly regarded as his debut, *Leaving Home* at the Tarragon Theatre (according to Nathan Cohen it was a disaster, so perhaps best forgotten). Ian and Sylvia played on Wednesdays. Dylan dropped in and offered to play at a poetry reading in 1962, but the organizer said no thanks, we're good. Joni Mitchell did perform, as did Denny Doherty before the Mamas and the Papas, Zal Yanovsky before the Lovin' Spoonful, Bill Cosby before *I Spy*, and Lorne Lipowitz before he was Lorne Michaels.

U of T graduate student John Robert Colombo was the Embassy's first literary manager, paid five dollars a week to produce "literary and visual entertainment" on Thursday nights, typically poetry readings interspersed with 16 mm films and folk music by Sylvia Fricker. Colombo booked mostly local poets, including current and former U of T students like Atwood, Jay Macpherson, Phyllis Gotlieb, and James Reaney, high school dropouts Joe Rosenblatt and Gwen MacEwen, and banker Ray Souster, who ran a poetry workshop on Mondays. Milton Acorn all but lived in the place. Al Purdy read when he was in town. Cullen remembers a poet showing up one night in the rain, clutching his poems wrapped in plastic, saying he'd just hitchhiked in from Vancouver and could he read them and could Cullen spare five bucks.

When word got around in the summer of 1964 that the Embassy was broke and about to close, Victor Coleman and nine others came up with $100 each to keep it open. In exchange, Cullen let Coleman and his friend Don Black organize a literary series on Tuesday evenings. Coleman had more out-of-town connections than Colombo and different tastes. He brought in

**CABBAGETOWN DIARY: A DOCUMENTARY (1970)**
**Juan Butler**

Juan Butler's first novel sold some five thousand copies, mostly on the strength of rumours that printers had refused to print it. *Cabbagetown Diary* pretends to be a diary from the summer of 1967 of a bartender living in an eight-dollar-a-week room in Toronto's Cabbagetown. The heart of the novel — if that's the right word for a heartless book — is Allan Gardens, an even dirtier, drunker, more violent Allan Gardens than today, populated by stoned hippies, drunken Natives, pedophiles, delinquents, queers, and brutal cops. Written in a hyperrealist style known as naturalism, it's hard to tell if the novel is a deliberate window on the racism and sexism of its time or an example of it.

West Coast poets like Robert Hogg, Jamie Reid, Fred Wah, George Bowering, and Phyllis Webb (then living in Toronto), and American poets from New York, Buffalo, Detroit, and San Francisco. "We didn't have a budget," says Coleman. "We'd pay people the gate. But since the Embassy was the only game in town for poetry, it was pretty high-profile, and there would always be eighty people there."

In 1965 folk music found an amplifier and hipsters became hippies. At the Embassy, Coleman staged a second, more successful happening to welcome Andy Warhol to Toronto, and with his wife Elizabeth organized an underground film series that sold out over the controversy of its first announced film, the banned-in-America art porn *Flaming Creatures*.* But the main stage had moved to Yorkville. Cullen closed the Bohemian Embassy on June 1, 1966, six years to the day after it opened.

While it lasted, the Embassy meant a lot to many poets whose names we neither know nor need to know. "I never had a place like this," one self-described "beatnik housewife" and happy poet told the *Telegram*. "It gives young people an opportunity to display their work before others." It let Toronto rub shoulders with the avant-garde, like the couple who woke up to find Milton Acorn passed out in their fireplace. It made the names of its two best readers, the fiery Acorn and the magical Gwen MacEwen. Margaret Atwood gave her first public reading on its stage, and its literary manager printed her first chapbook. Today its literary evenings survive (uncredited) in the International Festival of Authors, founded by Greg Gatenby, the Embassy's literary manager during its brief return to life in the mid-seventies at Toronto's Harbourfront Centre. "Bohemian Embassy" is now the registered trademark of a real estate developer and the name of its condo complex on Queen Street West. Cullen filed an objection with the Canadian Intellectual Property Office. His objection was dismissed because, unlike the developer, he couldn't

---

* The film was never shown at the Embassy. On the series' opening night, with the police morality squad in the audience, the print didn't arrive from New York in time and Coleman replaced it at the last minute with a Michael Snow film borrowed from Av Isaacs. When the print showed up, Embassy staff prescreened it and decided, over Coleman's objections, not to show it. Today it's on YouTube.

provide evidence that he had spent any money to advertise the name or made any money from it.

**BY 1967 YORKVILLE** was a tourist attraction. People came from outside the city and even outside the province to see, to score, to hook up or pick up. Cars took two to three hours to drive between Bay and Avenue Road — two short blocks overflowing with hippies, bikers, greasers, runaways, hitchhikers, cops in pairs, and college kids holding hands. At nearby Queen's Park, the Yorkville Diggers organized a Victoria Day Love-In that drew some five thousand people. Hippies burned incense, blew soap bubbles at police, and gave flowers and bananas to the curious while Buffy Sainte-Marie and Leonard Cohen sang and the *Globe* took photographs of girls in miniskirts.

The Summer of Love no doubt contributed to the CanLit boom in ways that can't be easily measured: the sense that anything was possible, that everything could change. As U of T grad student and poet Andy Wainwright (twenty-one that summer) remembers, "You didn't think for a moment about crossing boundaries, whether it meant meeting people or breaking rules or starting a magazine or inhaling whatever you were inhaling."

In tangible terms, however, most of the art that Yorkville left behind is popular music, the folk-rock that came out of places like the Riverboat. Poetry readings continued in the coffee shops of Yorkville, but no well-known poets came out of Yorkville the way that Acorn, Atwood, and MacEwen emerged from the Bohemian Embassy. By the mid-sixties drugs were very much part of the scene, and drugs don't encourage arts that require sustained work or attention. Hippies wrote a great deal of poetry, but even the best of it needed musical support. The Canadian canon contains just one novel in which drugs are known to have played a substantial role in its composition, Cohen's *Beautiful Losers*. As several American winners of the Nobel Prize in Literature could attest, alcohol does not necessarily get in the way of writing stories that last. But the only good novel you can write while high is a novel about being high.

The arts had other places to commune in Toronto of the sixties besides Yorkville. Dashikis were rare on the rooftop of the Park Plaza, where *Maclean's* editors Robert Fulford and Peter Gzowski talked shop and Farley Mowat showed off his wolf howl while his publisher, Jack McClelland, did an interview for *Time* in a quieter corner. A few blocks away, Av Isaacs employed a high school kid on Saturdays to run messages between the gallery and his artists in residence at the Pilot Tavern.

At the corner of Bloor and Huron, 850 residents and many more crashers attempted to reinvent civilization in an eighteen-storey community called Rochdale College. Originally conceived as a student residence built by a student-owned housing co-operative, Rochdale became a college when Campus Co-op general manager Howard Adelman added an educational component to qualify for municipal tax grants and federal rebates on building materials. The college's "resource people" — Rochdale had no faculty, no entrance requirements, no curriculum, no degrees — included the poet Dennis Lee and fiction writers Judy Merril and Dave Godfrey. Independent publisher Nicky Drumbolis slept on the tenth floor in the summer of '68, before the windows went in. Stan Bevington lived on the top floor before the elevators worked. Victor Coleman and his second wife Sarah lived for two years in a two-bedroom apartment called a Kafka suite. Matt Cohen was writer-in-residence, "an appointment perfectly in tune with Rochdale's open-minded philosophy," he later said, "since I had published nothing." Reg Hartt showed foreign movies, the start of Cineforum. In the underground parking lot, Jim Garrard inaugurated Toronto's alternative theatre movement with a play about an American revolutionary.* In a garage out back, kids in their twenties ran the most exciting press the country had ever seen, magazines and books "Printed in Canada," as Coach House's early titles proudly declared, "by Mindless Acid Freaks."

Over on Church Street, the post-opera black-tie set went for

---

* Paul Foster's *Tom Paine*, suspended after one performance because Garrard didn't have the rights to perform it.

cultural slumming to the Pit, Tom Hodgson's studio at King and Church, known for encounters with visiting celebrities like blues musician Muddy Waters, naked models, and the illicit whiff of weed. Up the street, Liz Woods and illustrator Bill Kimber ran an open-door salon/crash pad for poets, musicians, speed freaks, and other misfits in their apartment over a shop at 489 Church, across the street from a parking lot for Maple Leaf Gardens. The anarchist novelist Juan Butler came by occasionally, draft-dodging poet Joe Nickell was a regular, and Doug Fetherling moved in. Fetherling (who now goes by his father's name, George) remembers Patrick Lane dropping in and telling stories about logging and hunting in British Columbia. Lane remembers Fetherling throwing himself down the stairs in a house on Beverley in a drunken display. The Church Streeters also rented a performance space in a nearby warehouse and a farm in Renfrew County. Fetherling leased the farm from Al and Eurithe Purdy for $600 a year as a place to write, but it was more often used by others for acid and sex.

There were other such places, especially on the West Coast. Vancouver's 4th Avenue became another Yorkville, as did Stanley Street in Montreal. Québécois *partipristes* hung out on Saint-Denis or at the Swiss Hut tavern on Rue Sherbrooke Ouest and the Asociación Española club across the street. In the second half of the decade, a vibrant arts scene flourished in London, Ontario, home to artists' studios, James Reaney's theatre workshop, and Monday-night performances at the York Hotel by the Nihilist Spasm Band.

But in Toronto, the literary community that emerged from the city's Calvinist closet had the advantage of proximity to the

**CIVIL ELEGIES AND OTHER POEMS (1972)**
**Dennis Lee**

Set in front of Toronto's new City Hall, *Civil Elegies* is a lament for a Canada that might have been. It's a poem about failure, about drowned painters and dead poets, criminal politicians and consenting citizens, about ideas unrealized and lives unlived. But it's also a hopeful poem, a poem that sees Canada's failure to become what it might have been as cause for celebration as well as regret. Without definition, Canada is always open to redefinition, always capable of being reimagined by current and new citizens. It's the same Canada that Frye saw in *The Modern Century*, a country with an "open mythology." *Civil Elegies* is the closest that Canadian literature has come to a founding epic — our Waste Land, but also our Aeneid.

greatest concentration of publishers, readers, and other writers in the country. Toronto had all the large English-language publishers and the most important small presses. It had the highest-circulation magazines and the most prestigious literary magazine. It had two long-term book reviewers with national clout, Robert Fulford at the *Star* and William French at the *Globe*. It had the only national newspaper — the only way for a book to hope for national notice on its release. It had the CBC, the only national television and radio network. By the early seventies it had the first and only theatres devoted to producing plays written by English Canadians.

Margaret Atwood didn't become Toronto's writer because she went to school in the city or came back to it. She became Toronto's writer because Toronto made her a writer, from the small presses that printed her first books through the branch-plant press that published her poetry to the national and ultimately multinational company that published her novels.

**AS ATWOOD TELLS** it, she decided to become a poet on her own, without any irritation from nearby poets. She says she made up her mind while walking across her high school's football field at age sixteen, well before she knew any other writers or publishers or anything about modern poetry, or that wearing black was compulsory.

I believe her, mostly. Dudek's model isn't the only way to make a poet, and she certainly wouldn't have read living rivals at Leaside High. But even if she decided on her own, she couldn't have done it on her own. Most writers need other writers, in print or in person,

**THE MEETING POINT** (1967)
Austin C. Clarke

The first novel in Clarke's Toronto trilogy takes place over the winter and summer of 1963–64. For Rachel Burrmann, a wealthy Jewish housewife in Forest Hill, it's a time of dinner parties, novels on the sofa, Canadian Club on ice, Beethoven on the stereo, pottery classes at the YWHA, summer camps for the kids. For her housemaid Bernice Leach and her West Indian friends, it's a very different Toronto: white as the snow, a routinely racist city where children point at her on the subway and her employers sing Negro spirituals while paying her less than the German housemaid across the street. As some reviewers objected, the Burrmanns are more caricatures than characters. But from Bernice's window they could hardly be anything else, and her story could hardly end other than it does.

whether to irritate or encourage. Graeme Gibson, who helped found
the Writers' Union of Canada:

> There's no substitute for spending an evening drinking with
> other writers, sitting together and talking. One of the most
> important things is what Margaret Laurence, perhaps senti-
> mentally but quite accurately, called "the tribe." It was very
> important for a great many writers in Canada to feel they
> were part of a community.

Even writers who prefer to drink alone need living company —
people to respond to their writing, people in related fields like editing, publishing, printing, and reviewing. They need a community,
no matter how far-flung.

In the late 1950s, young writers began to forge such a community in Toronto, at first under the shelter of other arts. Toronto
was not the first or the only place in which this happened. Earlier
generations of Canadian writers found and supported each other in
New York in the 1890s and in Montreal in the 1920s. In the fifties,
Montreal was still the core of the country's poetic universe. In the
sixties, Vancouver's poetry community was probably larger and
certainly louder than its counterparts in Montreal or Toronto. But
unlike New York, Montreal, or Vancouver, Toronto was the centre
for publishing in English Canada, head office for half a century to
foreign and Canadian textbook publishers drawn by the largest
educational market in the country. Add money to spend and places
to drink, and voilà — the CanLit cocktail.

It would be a mistake to remember these communities as
friendly. Like any social group, especially in a field that measures
success by reputation, they quarrelled both privately and publicly.
At different times and for different reasons, Leonard Cohen and
Austin Clarke both threatened in print to punch Mordecai Richler.
Matt Cohen left House of Anansi after an argument with Dennis
Lee; Anansi itself only barely survived internal battles. The feud that
heated up over the decade between western and eastern poets was
real, even if the differences were exaggerated. Winning the GG for

her first book while still in her twenties did not win Atwood friends among poets. When she, Gibson, Farley Mowat, Hugh Garner, and other writers appeared before the Ontario Royal Commission on Book Publishing, they fought among themselves about things irrelevant to the hearing. "There is a moral in this, surely," wrote the nonplussed commissioners in their report.

As Alice Munro wrote of another extended family, "It was a clan that didn't always enjoy each other's company but who made sure they got plenty of it." What mattered, in that family as in hers, was that it came together at all.

Chapter 8

# Understanding Media

**Something, something in the air.**
**—Gwendolyn MacEwen, "Icarus"**

**"HE WAS A BIG MAN,"** says David Helwig, "affectionate, malicious, opinionated, widely read in an eccentric way, and what he cared about most was poetry."

Before all that, Alfred Purdy was the only child of a doting widow in the small town of Trenton, Ontario, in a red-brick house next door to a tombstone works, on a street that electricity had not yet reached. His mother paid him five cents a book to read Dickens; he preferred pulp magazines and Saturday afternoon serials, *Doc Savage* and *The Jade Box*. At thirteen he began writing poems after discovering that it impressed girls. He also liked football, especially the knocking-people-over part. Otherwise he did poorly in high school and ended his formal education by failing Grade 9.

By 1936 Purdy was seventeen and bored. He decided to go west, less for work, as many others were doing, than for something to do. He hitchhiked to north of Sault Ste. Marie, where the highway ran out, then hopped a freight train and rode the rails through the prairies and the mountains to the sea. In Vancouver he saw a movie, visited Stanley Park, and jumped on a train headed back east.

He summered on the rails until Germany gave him something else to do. Purdy's war passed at air force bases in Ontario and

British Columbia, mostly on guard duty, because his blood pressure kept him out of the sky. He was promoted to corporal, then demoted soon and often for insubordination and various derelictions of duty. In 1941 he married one such dereliction, seventeen-year-old Eurithe Parkhurst, a farmer's daughter from the country north of Belleville, whom he met and dated while stationed in Picton. Their son Jimmy was born two weeks before the bombs fell on Hiroshima and Nagasaki. After the war Purdy ran a taxi/bootlegging business with his father-in-law in Belleville that dodged the police but not, eventually, the bank.

The Purdys moved to Vancouver in 1950. Eurithe found work in a hospital, Al at a mattress factory. They lived in a small house on Vanness Avenue in the east end, beside the tram tracks. When he wasn't brewing the homemade beer it took to get him through a day at the factory, Purdy read Eliot, Yeats, Pound, and especially Dylan Thomas. He wrote Irving Layton a fan letter; Layton sent him his books to sell. Purdy had been publishing his own poems since before the war, including a slim book called *The Enchanted Echo* that he paid $200 to publish himself (a single copy costs many times that today, partly because Purdy didn't pay the bill, so the printer destroyed most of the copies). In 1955 Ryerson Press published a second chapbook and the CBC bought a radio play, his first sale to the CBC and his largest literary paycheque yet.

Purdy decided he was a poet and that he could make beer just as easily in Montreal, where there were more poets per square mile to help him drink it. He and Eurithe left Vancouver in the summer of 1956 and rented an apartment in Côte-des-Neiges. "It was an intoxicating and euphoric period to be a writer in Montreal," he wrote four decades later in his autobiography. "We were all great writers, or would be soon." They drank with the Laytons and the Scotts, met Louis Dudek and Hugh MacLennan. With Milton Acorn, Al started a literary magazine and argued poetry and politics and the best way to cook eggs. He published poems in Dudek's *Delta* and Ray Souster's *Combustion* and sold two more plays to the CBC. Eurithe worked as a secretary for CP Rail.

In the spring of 1957 the Purdys left Montreal to look after

Al's aging mother in Trenton, living with her in Al's boyhood home on Front Street.* Using money from the CBC, they put $300 down on an $800 lot a half-hour away on the shore of a small lake, across from the village of Ameliasburgh. Eurithe found a plan for an A-frame cottage in *House Beautiful*, her father provided advice and a truck, and Al bought a load of used lumber and other building supplies from a building being demolished in Belleville. They had no electricity, no plumbing, and little money. Some food came from a neighbour's garden, some from the lake, and some diverted from the A&P supermarket's dumpster. Al made wine from wild grapes, oranges, dandelions, rhubarb, and pineapples — whatever he could find growing or in the A&P's garbage. They were poor, hungry, and, when winter came, cold. They fought a lot. In the fall of '59 they went back to Montreal to find enough work to eat and finish the house.

Purdy won his first Canada Council grant in 1960 and used the money to leave Roblin Lake the next summer, travelling on his own to Tsimshian territory in northern British Columbia. In 1962 he published his first real book, with Contact Press. *Poems for All the Annettes* was Purdy's turning point, the book that announced the man and the poet that David Helwig and everyone who ever met him remembers. It did well, selling out and winning the praise of poets. Its success encouraged him to submit the manuscript of his next book to McClelland & Stewart in Toronto. *The Cariboo Horses* received the Governor General's Literary Award for

**POEMS FOR ALL THE ANNETTES (1962)**
**Alfred Purdy**

Purdy's first full-length book is a mixed bag: nature poems and city poems, poems that use the space on the page the way the cool kids were doing it and poems that line up politely on the left, poems that say "forsooth" and poems that say "fuck." This is the book in which Purdy figured out what kind of poet he was not, but not yet the poet he was.

In 1968 House of Anansi printed a book under the same title that was actually a selection of Purdy's poems to date, including a half-dozen new poems backdated to hide them from his new publisher, Jack McClelland. It's a better book than Contact's, more consistent, even though it includes both older and newer work. By then Purdy knew who he was.

---

* Now an empty lot beside a liquor store — surely a metaphor for something.

poetry for 1965. Like Margaret Atwood a year later, Purdy attended the ceremony wearing borrowed clothes.

THE COUNTRY THAT produced Marshall McLuhan is also the country that proved him wrong, if only temporarily. According to McLuhan and everyone after, electric media like radio and TV replaced (he liked to say "imploded") print culture. But in Canada, the so-called golden ages of radio and television both preceded the so-called golden age of Canadian literature. They also helped make it happen.

Radio's golden years came to Canada in the 1940s and '50s. Under its first head of drama, U of T graduate Andrew Allan, the CBC commissioned hundreds of original plays and adaptations for the programs *Stage* and *Wednesday Night*. By the late forties, CBC Radio was producing more fictional Canadian stories for a larger audience than any publisher or magazine in the country. Most Canadians heard their first Canadian plays at home, from scripts by playwrights such as Lister Sinclair and Mavor Moore.

The CBC was especially important to W. O. Mitchell's career and reputation. Mitchell's first contribution to the CBC was a fifteen-minute short story that aired in 1949; his last came a half-century later, an appearance on the final episode of Peter Gzowski's *Morningside*. In between, he wrote hundreds of radio plays and television scripts and appeared as a guest on many shows. By far his best-known CBC production was *Jake and the Kid*, a radio serial about a hired hand in the fictional Saskatchewan town of Crocus that ran for some two hundred episodes between 1950 and 1956. The show was so popular that Mitchell grew sick of hearing about it. It also reawakened interest in his first and up to that point only book, a novel most Canadians hadn't noticed. *Who Has Seen the Wind* had done well when it was published in 1947, selling some four thousand copies in its first six months (all told, the book earned $1,100 a year for the seven years it took to write it, which is why Mitchell started writing for the CBC in the first place). But after the success of *Jake* on the radio, Mitchell's novel was reprinted in school and paperback editions and is now said to have sold close to a million copies.

Two years after Alfred Purdy won the Governor General's Award for poetry, he introduced himself on CBC Radio as a CBC writer first and a poet second. "My name is Al Purdy," he began. "I write plays for CBC, which they buy at the rate of one for every twelve written. And I write poems. It used to be I couldn't sell the poems at all, but things are a little better now." Purdy's first CBC piece was a verse play he wrote while living in Vancouver, a fantasy based on his childhood, partly derived from Dylan Thomas's verse play *Under Milk Wood*. It took several years, many rejections, and much patient advice from two women in the CBC's script department, Alice Frick and Doris Hedges, to make his next sale, two plays sold to *Stage* in 1957 for $1,000. Over the next ten years he sold a dozen more plays to the CBC, including an adaptation of Earle Birney's poem "David" read by John Drainie (also the voice of Jake on *Jake and the Kid*). Between 1959 and 1968, Purdy earned about $4,000 from the CBC. That's not a great deal of money over nine years, but it was more than any publisher paid, and it looked good to a guy making wine from weeds and last week's fruit.

The CBC bought original radio dramas for its national network from some two dozen poets and novelists in the 1960s besides Purdy, including Timothy Findley, Maurice Gagnon, Daryl Hine, Gwen MacEwen, and Mordecai Richler. More important for Canadian literature, it also produced adaptations of a handful of contemporary Canadian novels and short stories. George Ryga's adaptation of *The Stone Angel* first aired on CBC *Sunday Night* in August 1965. In October, CBC *Stage* dramatized two of Mavis Gallant's now best-known stories, "Bernadette" and "The Ice Wagon Going Down the Street." Margaret Laurence's "A Bird in the House" came to radio in 1966, Alden Nowlan's "Miracle at Indian River" in 1971, and Margaret Atwood's *Surfacing* in 1973. As in the bricks-and-mortar theatres, most of the CBC's adapted drama was by non-Canadians, with Shakespeare and Belgian detective novelist Georges Simenon topping the list. But for a few Canadian stories, public radio provided a second life and a larger audience.

Many writers worked for the CBC, especially in Quebec. Radio-Canada provided positions as editors, directors, and producers to poets Jean-Guy Pilon, Paul-Marie Lapointe, and Fernand Ouellette, and novelists Gilles Archambault, André Langevin, Hubert Aquin, and Wilfrid Lemoine. Michel Tremblay's last full-time job was in Radio-Canada's costume department.

George Jonas began working for the CBC in 1960, as a freelancer reading submissions for radio and television at three dollars a script. Jonas had left Hungary in the 1956 uprising, choosing Canada over America because of a childhood affection for the *Jalna* novels and because the lineup at the Canadian embassy was shorter. He came to Toronto and drove a taxi the first few years, making extra money running customers to floating crap games. "I went to the CBC and asked for work," he told me shortly before he died, in an accent still more Budapest than Bloor Street. "Unlike in Europe, or in Canada today, in 1960 you could just walk into an office unintroduced and say, 'I want to work here.'" The CBC took him on full-time two years later as a staff editor for $5,000 a year. Besides editing and producing, he wrote a dozen radio plays in the sixties, including adaptations of Rudy Wiebe's *First and Vital Candle* and John Steinbeck's *Of Mice and Men*.

Phyllis Webb joined the CBC in 1964. Born in Victoria, Webb had majored in English and philosophy at UBC. In 1949, the year she graduated, she ran in the provincial election for the CCF (later the NDP) in a Victoria riding. She lost, and the party's national chair, McGill law professor and poet Frank Scott, convinced her to move to Montreal. She worked at McGill as a secretary, survived a year of graduate school, and met Layton, Dudek, Purdy, and other poets in the city.

**THE HAPPY HUNGRY MAN**
**(1970)**
George Jonas

The title of Jonas's second collection comes from an Arabian proverb about the hungry man being happy because free of passions. Jonas flipped the proverb and the man, writing poems about a Canadian everyman of the late sixties who has food and shelter but is starving existentially. There's lots for him to do, but little that matters. He goes to meetings, pays his taxes, considers suicide, has sex with strangers. He spends much time alone with his modern coffee table, his modern rug, and his modern books.

*The Happy Hungry Man* did very well in its day, selling upwards of two thousand copies, more per capita than almost any books of poetry sell today. It is difficult for poems that are utterly of their time to outlive their time, poems like these.

McClelland & Stewart published her first book of poems when she was twenty-nine, in 1956. After spending eighteen months in Paris on a Canadian Government Overseas Award—the precursor of Canada Council travel grants, and like them intended to send Canadians elsewhere for culture—she decided the climate in Montreal was "a form of natural madness" and returned to Vancouver, teaching at UBC and copy-editing manuscripts for M&S.

Webb had freelanced for CBC Radio since the early 1950s, writing book reviews and essays for the shows *Critically Speaking* and *Anthology*. In the spring of 1964 she moved to Toronto for a full-time job as organizer of a CBC educational program called *University of the Air*. Soon after she arrived, she suggested to the producer of another adult education program, *The Learning Stage*, that they merge their shows and aim at a general audience. As the website of that new show still says, the first three episodes of *Ideas* included a discussion of evolutionary theory, classical music from Brazil, and a poetry lecture by Webb's UBC professor Earle Birney. Subsequent guests during Webb's tenure included Northrop Frye, Marshall McLuhan, and bpNichol, talking about subjects from structuralism and experimental theatre to anarchism and the United Nations.

In 1967, the year she became executive producer, *Ideas* had Austin Clarke interviewing Black Power activist Stokely Carmichael, Martin Luther King giving the Massey Lectures, and a "contrapuntal radio documentary" for the Centennial called *The Idea of North*, produced by Glenn Gould. That same year, she wrote and hosted a thirteen-episode series for CBC TV called *Modern Canadian Poetry* that started with F. R. Scott, Irving Layton, and

**THE SEA IS ALSO A GARDEN (1962)**
Phyllis Webb

Webb's early work reads like a mashup of T. S. Eliot and John Donne, which is to say like Eliot. They're poems of grief and despair expressed through dense, repeating images. In this, her second book, Eliot still dominates, but now Webb talks back. "Breaking," for instance, begins with a cry from the heart of *The Waste Land*: "Give us wholeness, for we are broken." But it continues, "What are we whole or beautiful or good for / but to be absolutely broken?"

"Breaking" is a real poem, one of several whose power comes from Webb's willingness to think through despair, like "To Friends Who Have Also Considered Suicide." Admittedly the despair feels more learned than earned, more poetry than experience, but so does the midlife crisis of the twenty-two-year-old author of "The Love Song of J. Alfred Prufrock."

Miriam Waddington talking about poetry in the forties and ending with a live reading at the Parliament Street library in Toronto by six poets, including Margaret Atwood, Roy Kiyooka, and Michael Ondaatje.

Exhausted, Webb left the CBC in 1969 after winning a Canada Council grant. She moved — temporarily, she thought — to Salt Spring Island on the West Coast. She's still there.

**THE FIRST CBC** programs to air Webb's work had the same executive producer, a tall, pipe-smoking University of Toronto graduate in his early thirties. A phenomenon as large and complex as a national literature cannot be attributed to any one person. But at the time, no one gave more Canadian writers more of an audience than Robert Weaver. From his office at 372 Jarvis and a café across the street, Weaver ran radio CanLit for more than forty years. His biographer, Elaine Naves, subtitled her book *Godfather of Canadian Literature*. It's a title only Jack McClelland could have disputed, and only because books last longer than radio waves.

Weaver's own father had died when he was ten, leaving him to grow up in a house with his mother, sister, and four spinster aunts. After high school he worked at a bank a block from home. He enlisted when it could no longer be escaped, in 1942. Discharged without getting farther than Kingston, he nonetheless qualified for Veterans Aid and enrolled at U of T's University College. He was an avid reader, and his affections were socialized by college. He joined a literary club, wrote for the university newspaper, and edited his college magazine. He contributed to *Canadian Forum*, for which his professor Northrop Frye was then managing editor. He also wrote about Canada for the American weeklies *The Nation* and the *New Republic*, bylines that caught the attention of the CBC and led to a job offer after he graduated in 1948.

He said he liked books, so they put him in charge of a fifteen-minute weekly show called *Canadian Short Stories*. Soon after, the CBC launched a new arts magazine program called *Critically Speaking* and gave him that one too. When another producer suggested a half-hour show devoted to the literary arts, Weaver persuaded management to let him have that one as well. He called it *Anthology*. It aired for the first time on November 9, 1954, at eleven p.m. Eastern Time on CBC's national AM network, just before *Ragtime Rhythm*.

Like any weekly magazine, *Anthology* included a lot of forgettable material by many now forgotten writers. It also aired, and often introduced, almost every Canadian writer of its time whom we do remember. On its first episode, listeners heard a short story by an unpublished Montrealer living in London: "The Secret of the Kugel" by twenty-three-year-old Mordecai Richler. On October 29, 1957, the show included a reading of five poems by another twenty-three-year-old, Leonard Cohen, then back in Montreal opening rejection letters from American publishers and graduate schools. Weaver or his producers bought work from Alice Munro, Margaret Atwood, and George Bowering when they were still university students. Munro's "Dance of the Happy Shades" aired on *Anthology* in October 1960, eight years before it became the title story in her first book.

Weaver's tastes were not as eclectic as those he accepted have said. He was open to new writers but not necessarily to new writing. Other than Bowering, poets from the West Coast *Tish* circle and Toronto's Coach House appeared rarely on his programs. In 1964 he vetoed the broadcast of a series of interviews Phyllis Webb had conducted with American Black Mountain poets, calling the results "fatuous nonsense." But unlike many in the cultural sector, he wasn't anti-American; he chose the writing that he did not because it was Canadian but because he thought it was good. He was also unusually open to women writers, certainly

**MY HEART IS BROKEN**
**(1964)**
Mavis Gallant

★★★★★

Gallant wrote stories, not books, so it's hard to say which is her best book. Her second collection is a good candidate, with three outstanding stories ("Bernadette," "My Heart Is Broken," and "The Ice Wagon Going Down the Street") and a novella that's as close to perfect as art gets. These are her people in her places — men and women, the comfortable and the poor (mostly the latter in this collection), living assumed lives in borrowed homes, hotels, and *pensions* and apartments in Europe and Canada. This is her voice at its ironic, realistic best, nailing whoever she saw to fiction's wall. "He must have learned to smile, and glance, and give his full attention, when he was still very young," she says of a part-time actor and full-time flirt in Paris. "Perhaps he charmed his mother that way."

more than *Tish* or Coach House. Margaret Atwood told Naves that "Bob was absolutely and completely not sexist. He didn't care." His CBC colleague Eric Friesen went further, saying Weaver had "a special affection and understanding" for women writers. Maybe it came from growing up in a houseful of women.

The CBC broadcasted in Weaver's time from an old girls' school at 354 Jarvis, north of Carlton. Weaver's office was in an adjacent Georgian-style home reserved for CBC executives, known as "the Kremlin." Across and up the street a bit was the Celebrity Club, the CBC watering hole for which the Bohemian Embassy was created as a dry alternative. In 1961 the first Four Seasons Motor Hotel opened across the street from Weaver's office, three storeys wrapped around a pool, with patio furniture by Canadian designer Court Noxon and waiters in white dinner jackets. In its café, coffee with Bob became what Gwen MacEwen called a cultural institution. Matt Cohen describes the ritual:

> He said I would recognize him by the fact that he would be wearing a tweed jacket and smoking a pipe. When I arrived at the café entrance at eleven in the morning, I saw a man answering Weaver's self-description sitting across from a young woman I took to be another supplicant. He was in the midst of lighting his pipe — a gesture he repeated about a hundred times an hour — and in the same motion he recognized me and gave a wave that I translated as, "Don't worry, your turn will come."

When your turn did come, says George Fetherling,

> He would clean and re-clean his pipe and tell you his latest warm and affectionate story about Morley Callaghan or Margaret Laurence and behave in a generally circumlocutory way until the end of the meeting. Then, sometimes while rising to find his coat, he would let drop that he would buy a batch of poems or this or that short story for broadcast.

Occasionally the meeting moved from the café to the restaurant, to suit the time of day or the writer. *Anthology* regular Al Purdy remembers not coffee but lunches over martinis with beer chasers. "Those lunches with Bob almost did for me," he confesses in his autobiography.

Weaver didn't wait for writers to come to him. He went looking for them, by mail or in person. John Metcalf, who wrote his first short story for a CBC contest (he won, $200), still remembers Weaver coming to Montreal and taking him and Ray Smith out for drinks at the Ritz-Carlton. Metcalf showed up without a jacket, so Weaver lent him one to get him into the bar. Alice Munro remembers Weaver walking up Grouse Mountain to meet her in person for the first time. He loved meeting writers, talking with writers, and especially talking about writers. Atwood calls him "one of the world's greatest gossips."

His importance to many individual Canadian writers was massive. For starters, he had money. In 1968, when it grew to an hour and moved to Saturday nights at ten, *Anthology* had a budget of $48,000 a season. Weaver seems to have spent what he could of the money as much to support writers as to buy writing — a one-man Canada Council with a built-in audience. He often bought work he knew he couldn't use, just to keep the writer writing. He couldn't pay much for most of it, but he paid more than anybody else in the country. "He kept me eating and working during dark and difficult times," said George Ryga. The $75 for Richler's first story arrived when he was living on loans from family and friends and about to get married. Alice Munro bought her honeymoon outfit with a piece for *Canadian Short Stories*. Years later, Weaver apologized to Gwen MacEwen for only being able

**THE CARIBOO HORSES**
**(1965)**
**Alfred Purdy**

★★★

As Doug Jones said, you can usually locate Purdy's poems on a map. In *The Cariboo Horses* you'll find them mostly in Canada, from his home on Roblin Lake, past railway towns like Piapot, Saskatchewan, to 100 Mile House and Stanley Park. He loved poems about real people in real places. His poems are all "Music on a Tombstone," the title of one. They want to "Say the Names" — the title of another — to record what's passed and what's passing, like the roll call of Ontario townships in his best-known poem, "The Country North of Belleville." Speaking of which, Purdy admits in his autobiography that he could never tell north from south. "I can get lost in a telephone booth," he says. Maybe that's why he needed poems.

to pay her $150 for a batch of her poetry in the mid-sixties. "That would have kept me in Kraft Dinners for three or four months," she said, patting his arm.

More than money, Weaver's recognition meant acknowledgement. For a generation that had grown up on radio, hearing your own work on the radio was, as Atwood says, "big." Someone had taken your words seriously enough to broadcast them across the country. Your parents knew you were a writer now. Your neighbours knew. That teacher who said you couldn't write knew. And most important, you knew. That was Weaver's gift to writers — not the CBC's money or airtime, but his encouragement, his belief in you as a writer. Purdy said you left lunch with Bob with "something important...a warmth, community of some kind." Too far away for lunch, Munro says Weaver's letters "reminded me that I was a writer."

> The most precious encouragement was not in what they said, but in what they took for granted.... All over the country, unknown writers, and writers beginning to be known, and writers who hadn't written anything for a while, were getting these letters. They were being prodded into writing when they thought they had no time to write, when they were sick of sending things off to impossible markets and unresponsive editors, when their ideas of what and why they wanted to write seemed to be getting muddied and mislaid. He was keeping us going, not making any rash promises, getting the best he could out of us, not coddling, but giving us what we needed most — his serious attention, his reasonable hopes, a real market.

Munro dedicated a book to Weaver. So did Austin Clarke, Hugh Garner, Hugh Hood, Alden Nowlan, Al Purdy, and Mordecai Richler. He was literally CanLit's most dedicated employee.

Much of his labour was charity work, work that helps many but changes nothing. And as Atwood says, *Anthology* could only have become as important as it did in "in a landscape that was otherwise pretty sparse." In the 1950s and '60s, Weaver was almost the only game in town for creative writers in Canada, one of very few literary publishers in any medium with a real budget and a real audience. Especially at first, he didn't have many writers to choose from (which is why he could meet or write to them all), and he bought work from almost all of them. It's not surprising that he picked some writers we remember along with many we don't.

But that said, it's possible, even likely, that the first Canadian to win the Nobel Prize in Literature would not have kept writing without him. In 1973 Munro told *Performing Arts* magazine that Weaver "did more than anyone else to keep me believing in myself as a writer for many, many years." Weaver supported Richler before the Canada Council did. He bought Atwood's poems before she had a book, and when her first book did come out, he wrote its only large-circulation review and chaired the committee that gave it the Governor General's Literary Award for poetry (though that was confidential at the time).

Like any artistic community, Weaver World was incestuous, but it was also a family in good ways. With his gossipy anecdotes, Weaver made solitary writers feel connected to other writers, to people they might never meet but who in his stories were all part of one big, mostly happy family. *Anthology* was the family's sitting room, a place for the growing CanLit clan to gather, entertain guests, and admire its offspring. Robert Fulford sums it up:

**THE EDUCATED IMAGINATION (1963)**
**Northrop Frye**

Broadcast on CBC Radio in November 1962, Frye's contribution to the Massey Lectures (inaugurated the year before) sold out and by 1970 was in its seventh printing. It's his most popular book, because of its introduction on the radio and because it's a short, accessible introduction to the main ideas of a prolific thinker — the sort of thing that fit nicely on the coffee tables and the consciences of the affluent society, that told them books mattered more than toasters. His tone works well, a combination of fireside chat, sermon, and mostly, as he says, the classroom. Frye's most important contribution to Canadian literature wasn't his often exaggerated influence on Canadian writers: it was the encouragement he gave tens of thousands of readers in his actual and virtual classrooms, the reasons he gave them to read.

There had been books published in Canada for a long time. There had been writers for a long time, many writers. But in terms of a national — that is national in English-speaking Canada — literary community, it didn't exist, and it was the CBC that helped call it to existence. And I think it was Weaver who did more than anyone else to call into existence this national community.

Even more important in the long run, the CBC provided a national audience for that literary community. *Anthology* alone had a weekly audience of somewhere between thirty thousand and fifty thousand people, easily more than the combined circulation of every literary magazine in the country. More writers found more of their first fans on CBC Radio than in any print publication, from the 1950s audiences that made *Who Has Seen the Wind* a classic to the listeners who pushed Frye's *The Educated Imagination* into a second printing after hearing it on *Ideas* in 1962. CanLit's core market is a community of listeners that became a community of readers. As Alice Munro said, Weaver took that market for granted long before it was fashionable to do so. He simply assumed that an audience existed for Canadian writing.

When he arrived at Munro's door in West Vancouver, she said, "You don't look right."

"How should I look?" he asked.

"More fatherly," she said.

**IN ENGLISH CANADA,** most of the gold of TV's golden age came from America. Required from the start to broadcast Canadian content (55 percent by 1962), television stations voided the spirit of the regulations by airing domestic programming outside of prime time and by counting news, World Series games, late-night organ music, and even test patterns toward the quota. In the centennial year, the Association of Canadian Television and Radio Artists pointed out that the country's official network spent just 3 percent of its money on English-Canadian writers and performers.

Still, 3 percent of the CBC's budget in 1967 was five million dollars — a larger pie than actors were going to find anywhere else in the country. Playwrights had even fewer options, verging on none. Centennial funding stimulated some forgettable new plays and one success, George Ryga's *The Ecstasy of Rita Joe* at the Vancouver Playhouse. Trudeau's Opportunities for Youth and Local Initiatives Projects bankrolled some local theatre, some of which was also locally written. But without specific government incentives, artistic directors preferred plays by dead foreign playwrights or, at the alternative theatres, by living foreign playwrights. The first theatre devoted to English-Canadian plays didn't open until 1970, in a former candle factory above an auto-body shop in midtown Toronto. Factory Theatre Lab had a few early successes — notably David Freeman's *Creeps* in February 1971 — but no one made what you'd call a living from it, least of all its writers. In its third season, the company lost its $40,000 LIP grant for failing to pay minimum wage.

With nowhere else to turn, aspiring playwrights sent work written for the stage to the CBC, usually with predictable results. According to Robert Fulford, all the one-hour dramas the CBC produced in the 1950s yielded just one successful writer, a first-generation British immigrant to Toronto whose most substantial writing experience had been editing a trade journal called *Bus and Truck Transport*. In 1955 Arthur Hailey came up with an idea for a play while flying home from Vancouver. He wrote *Flight into Danger* in two weeks and sent it to the CBC. They bought it for $600. It aired live on *General Motors Theatre* in April 1956, starring James Doohan (later chief engineer of the starship *Enterprise*) as an ex–fighter pilot forced to land a commercial airliner after its pilots get food poisoning.

The show was hugely popular, the CBC's biggest hit to date. NBC bought the script for America and BBC for the British. It spawned a Hollywood movie, a novelization, a satirical comedy (*Airplane!*), and an endless string of disaster-movie copies. It made Hailey the highest-paid TV playwright in the country, bought him and his family a new house overlooking Lake Ontario beside the Toronto Hunt Club, and turned him into Canada's most commercially successful novelist ever. His next book, a novel about hospital politics set in Pennsylvania and published in New York in 1959, was selected for the Literary Guild of America's book club and the *Reader's Digest* Condensed Books series. Three more novels in the 1960s all made the American and Canadian bestseller lists. After *Hotel* (novel, movie, TV series), he moved to California, and then to an estate in the Bahamas.*

Like CBC Radio, CBC TV bought scripts from working Canadian writers in the 1960s, half- or one-hour dramas for shows like the low-budget *Shoestring Theatre* and occasionally the mostly foreign-authored *Festival*, estimated to reach some 900,000 homes. None of the resulting productions led anywhere near oceanfront in the Bahamas, but they did provide income and experience for some playwrights, poets, and novelists, including Hugh Garner, David French, Al Purdy, George Bowering, and George Ryga. James Reaney's first play *The Killdeer* reached far more Canadians on *Festival* than it ever did on stage.

On March 1, 1967, *Festival* aired Marie-Claire Blais's *The Puppet Caravan*, the first CBC drama in colour and the first produced in both English and French versions. The *Toronto Daily Star*'s television columnist, Roy Shields, attended a much publicized advance screening at CBC's Studio 2. He thought it "the silliest, artsy-craftiest nonsense produced by *Festival* in many a year." Television historian Mary Jane Miller was unable to find a surviving copy, so for now we're left with Shields's judgement. (Blais herself said at the French advance screening in Montreal that she had written the play back in 1960 and felt it was "childish, a young work.")

For Miller, the CBC's best author-written drama of the time was Timothy Findley's *The Paper People*, a ninety-minute film that aired on *Festival* about an artist who makes and burns life-size papier-mâché people. She is much less enthusiastic about *The Play's the Thing*, a short-lived 1974 series of one-hour plays by notable Canadian writers, produced by George Jonas and hosted by Gordon Pinsent. As

---

* To Lyford Cay, a private community built in the 1950s by Toronto beer tycoon E. P. Taylor for the same reasons that the Haileys, Sean Connery, Ted Rogers, the Aga Khan, and others of the world's wealthiest bought there: the climate, the golf, and to avoid paying taxes at home.

far as Miller could discover, the writers' reputations scared off anyone from editing the scripts. Whatever the cause, the series had more than its share of duds, including a clumsy melodrama by Robertson Davies, a "really pretty bad" historical play by Margaret Atwood (much later the basis of her novel *Alias Grace*), and a sophomoric satire about a midlife crisis by Mordecai Richler.

The big winners were those lucky enough to have their work adapted for television or, better yet, the big screen. Timothy Findley's largest television success was adapting Pierre Berton's history of the CPR for the CBC with his partner, William Whitehead, but the miniseries — which reached three million viewers, still a record for CBC drama — sold many more books for Berton than it did for Findley. Film and television adaptations of Arthur Hailey's novels helped sell more than 150 million copies of his books worldwide, in thirty-five languages. Paul Newman's Oscar-nominated adaptation of Margaret Laurence's *A Jest of God* moved Manawaka to New England, but it also bought Laurence a five-bedroom home in the English countryside and led to paperback reprints in Britain, the States, and Canada. The most successful Canadian film adaptation of the time was *The Apprenticeship of Duddy Kravitz*, which was nominated for an Academy Award (best screenplay adaptation) and a Golden Globe (best foreign film) and won the Canadian Film Award for film of the year. McClelland & Stewart printed a new hardcover edition of the novel and an illustrated paperback movie edition; together they sold 25,000 copies in two months.

Richler was also well served by the CBC, better than any novelist of his generation. The CBC bought his first story for radio, and

**THE ANIMALS IN THAT COUNTRY (1968)**
Margaret Atwood

★★★★

Atwood's second book is mostly confessional poetry, dedicated to and sometimes about the man she married in Montana the summer before. But her confessions have become more often about the world, both because she has become more confident and because the world has left her little choice:

Each time I hit a key
on my electric typewriter,
speaking of peaceful trees

another village explodes.

Written in America, *The Animals in That Country* is a more overtly Canadian book than *The Circle Game*. It's Atwood's answer to the map of Canada she finds in "At the Tourist Centre in Boston," a mirage of empty lakes and uninhabited forests. "I seem to remember people," she says, "at least in the cities."

his first novel for television. In May 1961, its new experimental TV show *Q for Quest* aired a special one-hour episode that mixed dramatizations of the then largely unread *Duddy Kravitz* with the thirty-year-old author talking about his life. In November the popular broadcaster Elaine Grand (like Richler, a Canadian expat in England) interviewed him in London for CBC TV's *Close-Up*. Richler had just published a series of articles about Canada in a London magazine, in which he said young people were leaving Canada because it was boring ("I like the bowling alleys," he tells Grand when pressed to say what he does like about Canada). He appeared as an interviewer and a guest on *This Hour Has Seven Days*, the CBC's best-known talk show of the 1960s. When *St. Urbain's Horseman* came out, director Don Owen filmed Richler driving his children to school for the CBC documentary series *Telescope*. As his biographer Charles Foran says, Richler's cynical wit appealed to the generation that took over the CBC in the late 1950s. And he lived in London, which made him much more interesting to Canadian producers than if he had stayed in Montreal.

Pierre Berton first appeared on CBC TV on September 9, 1952, three days after Canadian television began. Ten years later, his popularity on shows like *Close-Up* and *Front Page Challenge* got him his own late-night talk show on the new CTV network. He struggled on his own at first — kinder reviews called him "ill at ease" as a host — but the *Pierre Berton Show* found its legs in its third season in a reduced half-hour format devoted to a single guest, often taped outside Canada to get celebrities on the show. It also sold a lot of books, mostly his, but Marshall McLuhan, W. O. Mitchell, Farley Mowat, Irving Layton, and Leonard Cohen all appeared on the show over its eleven seasons. (Richler never did, which may have had something to do with his casting Berton as a woman in *The Incomparable Atuk*.)

Irving Layton made a name for himself outside the poetry community as a combative presence on CBC's *Fighting Words*, a CanCon copy of *What's My Line?* organized by Robert Weaver and hosted by the *Toronto Star*'s future drama critic, Nathan Cohen. On February 16, 1966, the CBC gave the National Film Board documentary *Ladies*

*and Gentlemen...Mr. Leonard Cohen* its first large audience, showing the forty-minute film on a Wednesday night after a Bob Hope
comedy special. In May, on *This Hour Has Seven Days*, Beryl Fox
asked Cohen how his mother felt about his poems, and on *Take 30*
Adrienne Clarkson asked him about getting high. That summer the
CBC announced that Cohen would co-host a new Montreal show
with a woman not yet chosen. In the fall he was named among
the on-air regulars for a live national current affairs show called
*Sunday,* billed as "the first experience in psychedelic television."
Cohen withdrew from the Montreal show two weeks before it was
set to air (he said it would have been "bad for my complexion"),
and *Sunday* was cancelled after its first season without his ever
appearing on it. But by then he had signed a recording contract
with Bob Dylan's label and no longer needed the CBC — or books,
for that matter.

The 1960s was not the CBC's best decade. Public radio lost listeners to private stations. Folk and rock music slaughtered the CBC's
drama and variety shows, programming made for a family sitting around the home radio rather than teens with transistor and
car radios. On television, the national network had to divide its
resources between two languages and lost much of its audience
to American programming. It also gave English Canadians few
reasons besides news, weather, and hockey not to switch the dial.

But because they didn't yet know what they were, public radio
and television gave a lot of time and attention to what they were
not. In Canada, the new media made the old media look better
than ever.

## Chapter 9

# Procedures for Underground

> Don't
> go mad in the face of their constant
> boredom before so much wonder
> —Victor Coleman, "Parking Lots for Greg Curnoe"

**BARRIE NICHOL'S FATHER** worked for the railroads that Purdy rode. Born in North Dakota, Glen Nichol found a job and a wife in Saskatoon and fathered four children. In 1937 the Canadian National Railway transferred him and his family to Regina. Two years later they sent him to Port Arthur, in northern Ontario. Two years after that, they promoted him to Burnaby, B.C., where he and Avis had their fifth and last child, Barrie Phillip Nichol, born the last day of September 1944. *Beep beep.*

When Barrie was three, the family moved to Winnipeg after another promotion. They bought a prefabricated home in a new subdivision tucked into a bend of the Red River called Wildwood Park, in section H. Little Barrie learned his alphabet by finding his way home. He attended Sunday School at the United Church because it was closest, and he could go by himself while his parents golfed. He liked the comics with people in funny white robes and heaven as a place in the clouds. A friend showed him a Dick Tracy comic strip. When Nichol died in 1988 after surgery to remove a spinal tumour, his Tracy collection filled a small room.

After five years in Winnipeg they were on the move again, back to Port Arthur. In the closest he got to an autobiography, Nichol said he fell into writing there, in what's now Thunder Bay — literally. In Grade 4 he fell into a ditch and caught a bad cold. Kept home for two weeks, he wrote a long story about a sailor from Mars. When he returned to school, his teacher read the story to the class, a bit a day for a week or two. She liked it, the kids liked it, and Barrie liked that they liked it. *Beep beep!*

In 1957 the family moved back to Winnipeg. Barrie was a good junior high student but "needs to try harder in language." He started a comic strip starring Bob de Cat and Dr. Nasty. In 1960 his father was promoted to Vancouver. The older children had by now left home, so the reduced family rented an apartment in Marpole. Barrie went to Winston Churchill High and to King Edward in Kitsilano for his senior year. At jazz clubs like the Black Spot and Java Jazz, he learned that it's not hip to shout hooray.

In the fall of 1962, Nichol enrolled in UBC's brand new faculty of education. He joined a student writing club and audited the English department's creative writing class, taught by Jacob Zilber. He met some of the student poets associated with *Tish* (launched the year before) but none took much notice of him. He was writing but not sharing anything, not yet. After passing his teacher-training program in the spring, he spent the summer with his brother in Toronto, then returned to Vancouver for his first teaching position, a Grade 4 class of "slow learners" in Port Coquitlam. He read a lot that year, including Sheila Watson's novel *The Double Hook*. The teaching wasn't going well. After compromising his beliefs by having a student strapped, he decided to quit and move to Toronto. On April 7, 1964, two weeks before he left, he wrote a poem in his journal that he signed simply "bp," the name by which he is known to literary history and the reason some called him Beep.

Nichol had experienced bouts of depression since adolescence. He moved to Toronto mostly to resume therapy with Lea Hindley-Smith, a self-trained psychoanalyst whom his brother had recommended the previous summer. Mrs. Smith, as she was known, supported her family by operating boarding houses and selling real estate, and, by the mid-fifties, as an unlicensed therapist. When Nichol arrived in Toronto, she had some sixty clients, half of whom lived in homes she owned in the Annex. Nichol moved into one, at 152 Howland Avenue, and in 1966 he began providing as well as receiving therapy. By decade's end he was vice-president of an incorporated commune that owned thirty-five houses in the Annex, four farms north of the city, and two vacation properties in Florida. Nichol belonged to Therafields until it fell apart in the mid-1980s. He met his wife and many of his closest friends there. A few years before he died, he told a grad student that Lea had saved his life.

The springboard of Nichol's literary career was his discovery of concrete poetry. He had seen and done some in Vancouver, but in January 1965 a friend mailed him British magazines on recent developments in concrete and phonetic poetry that "sort of blew my mind open." For over a year he swore off traditional poetry in favour of poems that played with letters and space. He and another friend started a newsletter that invited submissions from anyone interested in concrete poetry (they launched it at the Bohemian Embassy, on the night of a massive power failure that affected Ontario, Quebec, and nine north-eastern states). Around the end of 1965, Nichol rewrote some of his older poems in the light of his new work and submitted them to an anthology of new Canadian poets being put together by Ray Souster and Victor Coleman. "I had learned so much by doing visual poetry," he later said. "It was like I was *seeing*, like I had done eye-cleaning exercises."

The Centennial was a big year for him. In January a small British press published his first chapbook. He started a magazine, called *grOnk* after the sound made by the dinosaur in the popular comic

**BP (1967)**
**bpNichol**

★★★★

Nichol's first book isn't a book: it's a boxed set, what one puzzled reviewer called a "poetry kit." Inside, there's a book of poetry (*Journeying & the Returns*), a flexible record, a little flipbook called *Wild Things* (dedicated to the Troggs), and as many other "poem objects" as the Coach House irregulars and Nichol's friends could imagine, make, and pack inside — like a poem printed on a computer punch card, another with instructions for assembly and burning, and something called a "Mind Trap."

They made five hundred of them, each box painstakingly hand-assembled around the Coach House lunch table by many people long into many nights. It sold for $3.50. I asked Stan Bevington if they would ever do a reprint, and he laughed.

strip *B.C.* In February, Coach House Press released his first book, enclosed in a handmade box that also contained a record, a flip-book, and a dozen concrete poems. He and bill bissett appeared on CBC TV on July 2, interviewed by Phyllis Webb for a series on modern Canadian poetry. "This is the death of the poem," says Nichol, reading a poem. He is twenty-two years old. *Beep beep.*

**BEFORE THE 1960S,** you could count the literary magazines published in Canada at any one time on one hand. By the end of the sixties, counting them was a lot harder. Michael Ondaatje tried, but he gave up. One dies, he said, and more pop up to take its place.

Say the names: A *Cataract*, a *Delta*, a *Mountain*. *Evidence* of a *Canadian Forum* for *Canadian Literature*. An *Island* in a *Radiofree Rainforest*. A *Moment* in *Motion*, *examples* from the *Edge*, an *Open Letter* with a definite *Parti pris*. The *Impulse* for *Intercourse*. Say *Yes* to *Liberté — Maintenant, Now*. Subscribe to the *Tamarack Review*, but save some change for *20 Cents*. Take *Les herbes rouges* with *Salt*. *Imago* the *Ganglia* while *Up the Tube with One I (Open)*. Have a *Pop-See-Cul*. Run the *Alphabet*, from *The Ant's Forefoot* to the *White Pelican*. Call it *Talon*, call it *Teangadóir*, call it a *Prism* or a *Quarry*.

They came and went: the average lifespan was about two years, and many lasted no longer than their first issue. But from the mid-sixties to the mid-seventies, at least fifty French- and English-Canadian literary magazines were active at any one time, ten times as many as had ever existed before. There were also new student magazines, like the *Erindalian*, in which Harold Ladoo published drafts of his first novel, and *Tish*, the poetry newsletter printed by George Bowering and other students at UBC. Underground newspapers hit the streets, hungry for content and hip to poetry: *Logos* in Montreal, the *Yorkville Yawn* in Toronto, *Small Change* in Thunder Bay, *Loving Couch Press* in Winnipeg, the *Georgia Straight* in Vancouver.

There were more literary magazines and more magazines publishing literature because there were more people. Because more of those people had gone to university and read books. Because affluence let more of them imagine life as a writer, and because that same affluence gave them a reason to write. In the 1950s, postwar advertising and rising household income made *Reader's Digest*, *Star Weekly*, and *Weekend* the first magazines to reach a million Canadian readers. For the first time, alternative magazines had a reason to exist: successful commercial models and a booming consumer culture to define themselves against.

Machines helped. Low-cost printing technology developed for commercial purposes also served non-commercial purposes. The revolution was not televised; it was mimeographed. Milton Acorn and Al Purdy launched *Moment* in Al's living room on a mimeograph machine that Milt "liberated" from the Canadian Communist Party. Nichol used a Xerox machine at U of T's Sigmund Samuel Library. For small presses like Talonbooks and Coach House, an IBM Selectric (the so-called golf ball typewriter, with easily changeable typeface balls) together with a photo-offset printer meant major savings in time and money compared to setting type a line at a time. "Anyone can now become author and publisher," said McLuhan in his 1967 monster bestseller, *The Medium Is the Massage*.

Literary magazines are not commercial ventures. Many were free. Even if they did try to sell to bookstores or subscribers, their makers hoped at best to recover their costs. Most didn't pay contributors. The first issue of *Moment* said, "If you like it write and tell us so, maybe enclosing a buck or so. There's no charge and (curse it) no payment." With university and Canada Council support, *Prism* usually paid five dollars a poem. The *Tamarack Review* paid about eight dollars a page, less than what its editor, Robert Weaver, could pay for the

**PROCEDURES FOR UNDERGROUND (1970)**
Margaret Atwood

★★★

"Don't be alarmed by the title," Atwood wrote in an ex-boyfriend's copy. "It's neither a sewage manual nor a revolutionary handbook."

Written in Edmonton, Atwood's fourth book of poems is more of her by then trademark cottage Gothic, poems about ghosts and monsters hiding in the forest, emerging from the lake, living underground. They're frightening and frightened poems, poems entirely in keeping with Frye's notion that the signal achievement of Canadian poetry is the controlled evocation of terror — except the source of that fear is more fantastic than real, progressive insanities of a pioneer with an M.A. in English lit.

same work from his CBC office, but more than any other independent literary magazine of the period.

Most had no more than a few hundred readers. Mordecai Richler — then writing regularly for *Maclean's*, with a circulation over half a million — dismissed little magazines like Kingston's *Quarry* as "parochial." But in their defence, *Quarry* editor Michael Ondaatje responded that parochial "is precisely what most little magazines are proud of being. They are a private, local, regional art form." For their makers and their contributors (often the same people), little magazines let them share what they liked, not necessarily what anyone else might like. *Tish* had zero interest in printing poems that weren't *Tish* poems. Less experimental magazines like *Tamarack* and Allan Bevan's *Evidence* had no desire to compromise their editorial vision to attract readers. Their taste was all they had, so it was all that mattered.

Sent through the mail, little magazines connected physically dispersed but aesthetically united literary communities, the way *grOnk* linked Canadian with European and South American concrete poets and *Island* brought West Coast and American poetry to Toronto. Literary magazines may not have many readers, but they have a disproportionately high number of what for a writer are the best readers, their most important readers: friends and family, peers, more established writers, other editors and publishers. When Margaret Laurence published a short story in the first issue of *Prism* in September 1959, the magazine had only two hundred subscribers, but one of them was the novelist Ethel Wilson, Vancouver's premier writer, who wrote Laurence to say how much she liked it. "That meant more to me than I can ever express," said Laurence.

**OF ALL THE** little magazines that surfaced in Canada in the 1960s, none was more joyfully or persistently little than *blew ointment*. Its guiding force throughout its life as a magazine and a press was bill

**Harold Sonny Ladoo by Graeme Gibson ca. 1972**

Reproduced with the permission of Graeme Gibson.

**Hugh MacLennan in his Montreal apartment by Rosemary Gilliat Eaton, 1960**

Pierre Berton and Jack McClelland, Park Plaza Bookshop, Toronto, October 29, 1958. Photographed by Jean Gainfort Merrill for the launch of Berton's *Klondike: The Life and Death of the Last Great Gold Rush.*

Mordecai Richler in Classic's Little Books, Saint Catherine Street, Montreal, November 1957. Photographed by Horst Ehrict for Richler's debut in *Maclean's*, "How I Became an Unknown with My First Novel," February 1, 1958. "After an unspectacular career in seven countries, *The Acrobats* is tracked by author Richler to a bookseller's bargain counter."

**Mavis Gallant, Île Saint-Louis, Paris, 1960, photographer unknown**

Reproduced with the permission of Mary K. MacLeod for the Mavis Gallant estate.

**Northrop Frye by F. Roy Kemp ca. 1959, likely at Kemp's New York studio**

Frye Papers, Victoria University Library (Toronto), 1993 accession, box 7

**Marshall McLuhan by John Reeves, 1967**

Library and Archives Canada, 1980-194, PA-165118, e008295857.
Reproduced with the permission of John Reeves.

**John Metcalf in his Montreal apartment by Sam Tata, 1969**

Sam Tata Papers, Fisher Rare Book Library, MS COLL 00448, box 3.
Reproduced with the permission of Toni Tata.

HUGH HOOD, MONTREAL 1966          Sam Tata

**Hugh Hood by Sam Tata, 1966**

**Gwendolyn MacEwen in High Park, Toronto, by Sheldon Grimson, 1970**

**Milton Acorn in Toronto by Sheldon Grimson, 1970**

**Margaret Atwood on the ferry to the Toronto Islands by Sheldon Grimson, 1970**

Reproduced with the permission of Sheldon Grimson.

**Doug Jones by Sheldon Grimson, 1970**

Reproduced with the permission of Sheldon Grimson.

**Robert Weaver photographed by Horst Ehrict for "The Tiger of Canadian Culture Is a Pussycat,"** *Maclean's,* **April 1969. Possibly the only photograph of Weaver without his pipe.**

**Phyllis Webb by Kenneth McAllister, ca. 1962. This photo appeared on the dust-jacket of Webb's 1962 book of poems, *The Sea Is Also a Garden*.**

**Al Purdy by Sheldon Grimson, 1970. This and the other photographs in the book by Grimson were taken for Gary Geddes and Phyllis Bruce's 1970 anthology, *15 Canadian Poets*.**

bissett, the son of a prominent Halifax lawyer.* In the late 1950s, around the age of eighteen, bissett ran away and hitchhiked west with his first boyfriend. "We were trying to leave Western civilization," he says now. "We got as far as Vancouver." He found work at the Vancouver Public Library and at the university library while attending UBC. University wasn't for him, too many rules. He met Warren Tallman, but none of UBC's student writers. Instead, he became one of what they called the "downtown poets" — young writers who weren't in university, like Michael Coutts and Gerry Gilbert. He also became a serious drug user, including a brief heroin addiction and a longer relationship with LSD. He was busted for possession of marijuana in 1966 and again in 1968, the second charge earning him several weeks in prison and a $500 fine (the sentence would likely have been much higher, but the Crown dropped its appeal after bissett fell into a basement and received severe head injuries from which he wasn't expected to recover).

In 1962, bill and his partner Martina Clinton made a child and a magazine together. They named the child Ooljah April and the magazine *blew ointment*, bill's spelling of an ointment used to treat pubic lice. (bissett doesn't use capitals or punctuation and spells as he likes. He also likes "using th space uv th papr th page 2 avoid squares or rektanguls as th onlee shapes wun cud write in." He has been called a concrete poet but says "its all poetree 2 me.")

The magazine came out whenever they had enough to print and enough paper to print it, usually two or three times a year. A typical issue contained a hundred or so mimeographed pages of letter- or legal-size paper, stapled along one edge. The paper was often of different colours as well as different sizes; living on welfare, its makers scrounged what they could. In 1966 bissett bought an old Gestetner duplicator with the $300 the Canada Council gave him for attending one of their meetings. Its print quality wasn't great, but looking good wasn't the point. When a frustrated librarian wrote to complain about the magazine's

---

* Frederick Bissett, best known for representing black Nova Scotian Viola Desmond in her 1946 challenge of racial segregation in a New Glasgow movie theatre. They lost.

irregular numbering and illegible printing, bissett just printed the letter as more poetree.

Collating was done by hand, with as many hands as able: Lance Farrell, Judith Copithorne, Maxine Gadd, and others. Patrick Lane remembers the aftermath of one collating party circa 1966 in the warehouse where bill and Martina lived, off 4th Avenue in Kitsilano. bill lies naked on a mattress on the floor, rain falling on him through a large hole in the roof.

> He has pneumonia and his skin trembles with a fever of 104 degrees. For two days he has been lying here trying to find God. Four tabs of acid, fever, and the rain coming down, his bed sodden wet and cold.... The latest edition of *Blew Ointment* is finished, collated, stapled and ready to be mailed out. It lies in stacks against the wall. Everyone is in it, Avison, Newlove, Livesay, Birney, and every other poet from Canada and the United States.... We collated the pages of the magazine he had run off on his Gestetner, an ancient machine that had to be hand-cranked, hand-inked. It took days to print. He is not eating well. There's no money, hasn't been for a while. Martina and Ooljah have been staying somewhere else the past week.

*blew ointment* printed poems, drawings, collages, fiction, letters, rants — whatever it liked. Most contributors were from Vancouver, but it included writers and artists from elsewhere as it became better known. "Open it up and let everyone in," read an epigraph from Toronto poet Margaret Avison in the November 1965 issue, and it did. For that issue, as for most others, bissett did the cover art. Inside, Nichol contributed a lyric poem (later the prologue of his first book), some concrete poems, and a short comic called "Ooljah's Story." There's a tough poem by Pat Lowther about losing a baby and a sad poem by Patrick Lane about losing a brother. A couple from Seattle, George and Louise Crowley, argue for anarchy. Alan Neil remembers exposing himself to his sister. Fred Douglas remembers how high everybody got at the poetry reading last night.

Yvonne Bond writes disturbing poem-letters to some guy called darell: "Baby, you could twist / my head around backwards / and I wouldn't care / I'd go there."

Many issues contained objects tipped or bound into the magazine: a page torn from the phonebook, a glossy hairstyle photo from a beauty salon, a federal job posting for Expo guides. Rosemary Sullivan says she saw one with a small piece of wood bound into the spine, "presumably a gesture of gratitude to trees." ("Could be," says bill.) Some issues were focused loosely around a theme, like 1970's "Occupations Issew" — that is, the "occupation" of Canada by the U.S. — which included a poem from Atwood's *Power Politics* and excerpts from Nichol's *The True Eventual Story of Billy the Kid* and Ondaatje's *The Collected Works of Billy the Kid*, both of which later shared a Governor General's Award.

Subscriptions cost five dollars for six issues. In Vancouver, Duthie's sold it, and Don MacLeod's on West Pender and Dave Guy's Horizon Book Store in Kitsilano. You could buy it at bookstores in Montreal, Toronto (the Village Book Shop), and Cleveland (the Asphodel Bookshop, run by Jim Lowell, a friend of bissett's friend d.a. levy). Circulation peaked at seven hundred in the late sixties, a large number for a little magazine in a small market, then or now. Good luck finding a copy today.

It doesn't strike me as a magazine that rejected much, if anything, of what it received. As Atwood said at the time, "It can print poetry so awful you'd have to be high to appreciate it, and poems so good they create their own high." But little magazines like *blew ointment* were more interested in welcoming new words than in preserving the best

**THE COLLECTED WORKS OF BILLY THE KID: LEFT HANDED POEMS (1970)**
Michael Ondaatje

Ondaatje did with *Billy the Kid* what Sheila Watson did with *The Double Hook*: he reinvented the western. But he took the genre in a different direction, postmodern rather than modern, and brought back blood, bullets, and testosterone.

*The Collected Works of Billy the Kid* won a Governor General's Literary Award the same year as bpNichol's pamphlet *The True Eventual Story of Billy the Kid* (likely written as a joking response to his friend's book). Former prime minister John Diefenbaker expressed his displeasure with the award, calling Ondaatje's language "atrocious" and saying, "We have some great figures in our country every bit as colorful as that what's-his-name in the coonskin hat."

Billy doesn't wear a coonskin hat in either book; Diefenbaker appears to have confused him with Disney's Davy Crockett.

words. They were newsletters, really. "I didn't have to go gazing south of the border or across the sea for that hit of adrenaline that really new writing gives you," said Nichol. "It was happening right there in the first issue."

**THE *TAMARACK REVIEW*** began like this:

> If one's eyes could only ravish away the colour, the shape, the arrangement of this coast and its attendant ocean, and the ships, and place them securely in the mind forever in all their beauty and simplicity and evanescence... but no.

It's by Ethel Wilson, the Vancouver writer. Any similarities to *blew ointment* end there. She's not in Vancouver; she's holidaying in Portugal, describing the view from her balcony. A *blew ointment* writer couldn't afford that view and wouldn't describe it in those words if she could. "On a Portuguese Balcony" isn't "new writing"; it's a small masterpiece of established taste and style, recognizably beautiful words about a recognizably beautiful scene. It tells a story poignantly familiar to the reader it assumes, the affluent North American who knows just what it's like to love visiting Europe but look forward to coming home.

Cultured, cosmopolitan, Canadian: the *Tamarack Review* declared itself with the first piece in its first issue. For the next quarter-century, this was the country's most prestigious literary magazine.

It began because there was nothing like it. In 1956 the only literary magazine in English or French Canada was the *Fiddlehead*, then a magazine with few readers outside Fredericton and even fewer admirers. "Something had to be done," said Robert Weaver, "to give a certain kind of writer and a certain kind of reader a place to meet regularly in this country." And so, his day job notwithstanding, he did it. Partly so he wouldn't appear to be taking too much time off from the CBC, the masthead listed six editors: Macmillan editor Kildare Dobbs; Victoria College professor Millar MacLure;

William Toye and his boss, Ivon Owen, from Oxford University Press; poet Anne Wilkinson; and Weaver. In an effort at regional consultation that proved too difficult to sustain, *Tamarack* also had advisory editors outside Toronto, including Alan Crawley in Victoria and F. R. Scott in Montreal. Bill Toye designed, proofed, and produced the magazine and was the only editor besides Weaver to stay with it from the first to the final issue.

Weaver, Owen, and Toye put up $100 each to start the magazine. They raised another $1,700 by convincing friends to become founding subscribers at $25 each. Anne Wilkinson gave them money; Patricia Owen lent her dining room as boardroom and mailroom. The Canada Council began supporting them in 1958, with $3,000. Writers were paid from the start, but the editors and staff worked for free until the Ontario Council for the Arts helped hire John Robert Colombo as managing editor in 1965. Macmillan Canada advertised its books on the inside cover of every issue for eleven years. The Hudson's Bay Company bought the back cover for fifteen years, service ads featuring poems by Inuit and southern poets. Weaver and Toye shared delivery work; when Weaver travelled for the CBC, he left copies at bookstores around the country. The magazine's circulation never went over two thousand. On its tenth anniversary, Weaver said it could not have survived its first year without Anne Wilkinson, and the next nine without the Canada Council, Toronto publishers, and Hudson's Bay.

Circulation aside, *Tamarack* never thought of itself as a little magazine. The first issue promised a publication addressed not to "a little coterie of initiates but to the people at large." It avoided

**MEMOIRS OF MONTPARNASSE (1970)**
John Glassco

★★★

You'd have a hard time realizing that Glassco was bisexual from this account of his often sexual escapades. Without benefit of biography, you also wouldn't know that he allegedly wrote some of it in the late 1960s and made much of it up. He and his lover ("friend" in the book) Graeme Taylor arrived in Paris from Montreal in 1928, more to live the writer's life than to write. They insult Gertrude Stein at her own party, visit a brothel with Morley Callaghan, and drink brandy with Ernest Hemingway at La Coupole ("I found him almost as unattractive as his short stories," says Glassco). It's a fun book, if by the time it was published just one of many about Paris at that now legendary time. "*Nous voici encore une fois à Montparnasse*," said the *New Statesman* in its review.

manifestos, saying repeatedly that its only criterion was excellence. It published work by and often about Canadian writers but didn't like talking about "the Canadianness of Canadian literature." It reviewed more books from other countries than from Canada. Literary nationalism, it said, "is always and everywhere absurd."

Still, for its first two years the cover boasted a stylized forest of its namesake, a native Canadian tree known for being a pioneer and a survivor. The tamarack is the forest's avant-garde, the first tree to invade receding lakes. It can survive cold winters and flourishes in a wide range of soils. *Tamarack* didn't need a manifesto because it had one in its title.

The tamarack is also, not incidentally, a common tree in the Muskoka Lakes, where Ivon Owen got the idea for the title and where prosperous Torontonians were busily building summer cottages. The *Tamarack Review* was a new magazine for a new reader: middle-class English Canadians with time and money for leisure, including keeping up on culture. In the first issue, alongside the fiction and poetry, Massey commissioner Hilda Neatby tried to explain why so little had come from their report. CBC producer Vincent (Massey) Tovell said smart things about American movies. Poet Alan Brown measured the country's leading novelist in French, Gabrielle Roy, against its leading novelist in English, Hugh MacLennan (Roy won). Professors reviewed the letters of English historian Edward Gibbon and a sociological study of Toronto's Forest Hill neighbourhood. In their editorial, the editors declared their commitment to upholding civilization; in their design, they declared themselves modern.

They went looking for writers, often using Weaver's CBC contacts. Weaver tried repeatedly to get a piece from Leonard Cohen on his impressions of Greece. He convinced Montreal poet John Glassco to write a memoir about his hospitalization for tuberculosis, published under the pseudonym Silas N. Gooch. Mordecai Richler's *Cocksure* began as a short story in *Tamarack*, ten years before it won a Governor General's Award. The magazine printed three stories by Alice Munro before her first book. It published the first short stories by Timothy Findley, Hugh Hood, and Ray Smith. Many of its stories and poems became fixtures in CanLit classrooms, including Hood's "Getting to Williamstown," Al Purdy's "The Country North of Belleville," Clark Blaise's "A North American Education," and Austin Clarke's "Griff!" Less successfully, but because the Canada Council liked paying for them, they produced special issues on Canadian theatre and on literature from the West Indies. They printed French-Canadian writers in translation and articles on Québécois theatre and literature. Writers from tamarack-free Vancouver appeared, including professors George Woodcock and Warren Tallman and poets George Bowering and John Newlove. In 1967 Al Purdy curated a selection of West Coast poets that featured some of the *blew ointment* crew: bissett himself, Milton Acorn, Pat Lowther, Pat Lane, Salish poet Mary (Skyros) Bruce, and a half-dozen others.

FLYING A RED KITE (1962)
Hugh Hood

John Metcalf called *Flying a Red Kite* the first Canadian collection of stories with a command of modern technique. He's probably right, but maybe because they tried so hard to be modern stories about modern lives, they haven't aged well. Alice Munro's and Mavis Gallant's early stories are still full of colour; these feel black-and-white, like an old National Film Board documentary. They're at their best when they actually are documentary, like the autobiographical sketch "Recollections of the Works Department," about a summer job Hood had during college, "in the bad old, good old days before the creation of that warm featherbed for talent, the Canada Council."

"Apart from publishing your first novel," said Timothy Findley, "being published in *Tamarack* was the most exciting thing that could happen to you." The widely read American magazine *Esquire* bought a short story from Hugh Hood after the editor read his debut in *Tamarack*. Jack McClelland published Alistair MacLeod's *The Lost Salt Gift of Blood* after reading one of its stories in *Tamarack*. Unlike *blew ointment*, which seemed perfectly happy talking to itself, *Tamarack* assumed that influential people were listening — politicians with decisions to make, professors with syllabi to decide, publishers with lists to fill.

Around 1967, Milton Acorn submitted a poem called "The Tamarack Review" that began like this:

I pronounce a servantes against *The Tamarack Review*
Who's turned down my loveliest poems. But

Why should I condemn those people
Since they know and I know
That my beauty's a gun aimed at their ugly hearts?

They bought it. *Tamarack* had a massive backlog by this point, so it didn't appear in the magazine until 1971. In the title and throughout the poem, someone had changed *The Tamarack Review* to *The Canada Goose Review*.

**BEFORE TV TOOK** over the job, magazines like Montreal's *La revue populaire* and Toronto's *Star Weekly* sold hundreds of happy endings a year to hundreds of thousands of readers. Most of those magazines were American, around four of every five sold in Canada. Most of the authors were also American, and if they were by chance Canadian, or Tibetan, neither the editor nor the reader would have noticed or much cared. When the short story was popular, the story mattered more than the nationality or the name of the writer — just as people would soon know everything about their favourite TV show, except who wrote it.

By 1968 the only large-circulation magazine still regularly publishing fiction in either English or French Canada was the women's magazine *Chatelaine*. Its English editor, Doris Anderson, had pushed the magazine toward nationalist and often outspokenly feminist articles but preferred conventional romance fiction, much of it acquired from American agents and a New York–based fiction editor. As Anderson tells it, she didn't become interested in publishing Canadian writers until the launch of Alice Munro's first book, *Dance of the Happy Shades*. "I was invited to the press party and was incensed to read in the book's promotional material, 'None of these stories was published by *Chatelaine*.' The idea of a Canadian author, and a woman, boasting about not writing for *Chatelaine* deeply bothered me."* So she began to solicit and

---

* Munro had actually published three stories in *Chatelaine* in 1956–57 (when Anderson was an associate editor), including one from *Dance of the Happy Shades*.

publish exclusively Canadian stories. For her the results were less than successful. "Canadian writers, I found, tended to write moody, morose tales. I was guiltily aware that many of our readers, tired after a long day and looking for a little light escape, would not find it in *Chatelaine* some months."

*Maclean's* had stopped publishing fiction regularly by 1959 and paid declining attention to books, especially Canadian books. (By 1967, old furniture was getting more space in the magazine than new books, in a column called "Your Questions about Canadiana.") In the early sixties, Jack McClelland and Robert Weaver both thought the Canadian edition of *Time* carried more weight with book buyers, even though *Maclean's* had twice *Time's* circulation.

The most book-friendly consumer magazine in the decade's second half was Toronto's *Saturday Night.* It was also one of the smallest, with circulation of under 100,000. But it gave as much space to books as it did to movies or television, with new owner/editor Arnold Edinborough and other writers contributing substantial reviews of foreign and Canadian titles. Publishers obviously thought the revived monthly gave them the most bang for their limited buck, taking out seven pages for "Books for Christmas" in 1967 and twelve in 1968 (*Maclean's* and *Time* ads ran more to liquor, cars, and boats).

In 1965 Edinborough persuaded the tobacco company Benson & Hedges to sponsor an annual short story contest. Judges Yves Thériault and Robertson Davies awarded the $1,000 first prize to Austin Clarke for a story published in the December issue, "Four Stations in His Circle." Stories were submitted under pseudonyms, which made Mordecai Richler's suggestion (in his November 1968 column for the magazine) that Clarke had won because he was black especially unfair.* The policy probably discouraged more

---

* Clarke provoked Richler's column by giving an interview in which he said that if he were a white writer with his talent, he would have appeared by now on *Front Page Challenge.* Richler noted that he was at least as well-known a writer as Clarke, and he too had never appeared on the show. He called Clarke "a minor-league Leroi Jones" and suggested that his story had won *Saturday Night's* prize because he was being patronized by "Ol' Massa Edinborough."

established writers from submitting their work, and the next two prizes went to writers never heard of before or since. In 1968 the judges decided that none of the submissions were of sufficient merit, and the Belmont Award quietly disappeared.

The magazine did better by poetry, though it's doubtful if poetry did better by it. In Edinborough's first few years as publisher, traditional poems appeared in the magazine in the traditional way, as occasional filler for articles that had run short or ad space that had failed to sell. But in 1966 the magazine began to give much more prominence to poetry, starting with a two-page illustrated spread for Raymond Souster's "The Day Before Christmas" in December. The following spring, F. R. Scott got a full page and artwork for a poem about a dead poet, E. J. Pratt. George Jonas filled a page several times in the late sixties, including a poem about sex with an American woman that was printed over a photograph of one (at least according to the flag on her bed).

After the *Toronto Daily Star*'s book columnist Robert Fulford replaced Edinborough as editor in August 1968, *Saturday Night* became CanLit's journal of record. By the early seventies, reviews and articles on and by Canadian writers were appearing in every issue. In 1971 alone, the magazine published several columns by Richler, an essay on Canadian nationalism by Margaret Atwood, a cover story on Jack McClelland and Canadian publishing (Atwood appeared on the cover in November 1972, her first cover), a full-page excerpt from Dennis Lee's *Civil Elegies*, and six poems from Al Purdy's visit to Hiroshima. The following summer, Fulford and company (basically three other people) devoted an entire issue to "Fresh Flowering: The New

**DEATH GOES BETTER WITH COCA-COLA (1967)**
**Dave Godfrey**

★★

With the connivance of managing editor Kildare Dobbs, half the stories in Godfrey's first book first appeared in *Saturday Night* disguised as a sports column. The sport is mostly of the killing kind: shooting bears in Minnesota, pheasants in Iowa, ducks in Manitoba, antelope in Africa, and so on. Not far away is the killing in Vietnam. They're manly stories about manly men who have lost their way, again: hippie Hemingway.

At the time, Margaret Laurence called Godfrey the "Canadian writer most likely to produce first-rate work in the next decade." Robert Weaver said he was "easily the most talented of the short story writers who are still in their twenties." The brand new *Oxford Companion to Canadian History and Literature* said he was "probably the most gifted young short-story writer in English Canada." Time has proved them wrong.

Writing in English Canada." Donald Cameron explored the new freakiness of Canadian fiction. Dennis Lee waxed Heideggerian on Al Purdy. Valerie Miner Johnson contributed a superb profile of a now completely forgotten poet, Toronto's Ted Plantos. Anne Montagnes wrote about Sylvia Fraser's first novel, W. H. Rockett about Gwen MacEwen's new collection, and Doug Fetherling about the *Dictionary of Canadian Biography* and the Canadian section of *Playboy's Girls of the World*. Fulford himself discovered his inner nationalist at Factory Theatre Lab, without whose commitment to new Canadian plays "you might never have heard of David Freeman [profiled within], and I wouldn't have seen *Creeps*."

No less than *blew ointment* and the *Tamarack Review, Saturday Night* constantly struggled to find the money to keep going — it was just broke on a larger scale. In the same editorial in which he introduced the flowering of Canadian writing, Fulford said that rumours of *Saturday Night*'s demise had reached the point where the cbc had phoned to say a camera crew was on its way up to film their last day in business. Like so many last days for so many magazines, it wasn't; *Saturday Night* survived until 2005.

Publishing any kind of magazine in Canada has never been easy, least of all for a literary magazine. But people keep doing it, issue after issue, year after year. It's hard to call it anything else but love.

## Chapter 10

# New Wave Canada

often I
think of those headlong years with bafflement,
good friends and deaths ago,
when voice by voice we raged like a new noise in the orchestra
—Dennis Lee, *The Death of Harold Ladoo*

**HIS GRANDFATHERS WERE MINISTERS,** his parents teachers. Born the day before the war, Dennis Lee grew up in a town-becoming-a-suburb west of Toronto. Etobicoke had one high school and no library. Behind their house were fields as far as the eye could see. "Everything was new on our street," he says now. "A tree higher than yourself was unusual. There were lots of gaps between houses, because they were being built one by one. The geography was featureless: there was almost no sense of roots going back through the generations."

He earned admission to University of Toronto Schools, an independent boys' high school at Bloor and Spadina in downtown Toronto. They told him he had a future in math. On graduation he won the Prince of Wales Scholarship, fifty dollars awarded annually to the Ontario student with the highest average on any nine Grade 12 papers. He enrolled in Victoria College's English literature program with six other entering students, one boy and five girls, including seventeen-year-old Peggy Atwood. She thinks they met and danced together at a freshman mixer; he's sure they would have met before that, in their first classes. By second year they were both working on the college's literary magazine, *Acta Victoriana*. They wrote satirical sketches together under the pseudonym Shakesbeat Latweed.

Lee took third year off and wandered around Europe looking for his soul. He says he saw it briefly in a London railway station, but it got on a train and he couldn't catch it and that was that. He came home and married a Vic classmate, Donna Youngblut. A year later he graduated with the Governor General's Gold Medal in English.

After a year in England, the couple returned to Canada and had their first child. Lee started an M.A. at U of T and got a lecturing job at Vic. They lived at 29 Sussex Avenue, near his old high school. In 1965 Lee received his M.A. for a thesis called "Principles of Ekstatic Form." He and Donna had their second child the following year, another girl.

Lee and another young U of T lecturer launched their own publishing company with Lee's first book, a collection of poems begun in England called *Kingdom of Absence*. Av Isaacs gave him a photograph of a painting by Graham Coughtry for the cover. Lee dedicated the book to "Donna, who deserves a better."

That summer he quit his lecturing job to write and to work for his publishing company. He also landed one of two paid positions at the new Rochdale College, $10,000 a year provided by a federal program called the Company of Young Canadians. Lee provided intellectual *gravitas*, writing a long essay on the Rochdale experiment for *This Magazine Is about Schools* and telling *Star Weekly* they were building "a community of men and women who love wisdom." Maybe it was, for a moment. But within a month of the building's opening in September 1968, Lee realized that the questions he and others had brought to Rochdale were no longer part of the place, if they ever had been. He resigned in the spring, just ahead of the crashers and the bikers and the raids. By 1970 Rochdale was the best place in Canada to buy drugs.

Lee threw himself into his publishing company, by now called House of Anansi (originally Ananse, a spelling changed after its first book). Over the next few years he and others published some of the biggest books of the CanLit boom, including Graeme Gibson's *Five Legs*, Michael Ondaatje's *Billy the Kid*, Northrop Frye's *The Bush Garden*, and Margaret Atwood's *Survival*. He also revisited his own *Civil Elegies*, a long poem first published by Anansi in 1968. With editorial assistance from Atwood, he revised and expanded the main poem and added seventeen new ones. Anansi published *Civil Elegies and Other Poems* in April 1972, just as his relationships with his press and his wife were coming to a difficult end.

One year later, the Canada Council informed Lee that the book had won a Governor General's Literary Award. After all that had happened, it must have seemed small consolation.

**SMALL PRESSES LIKE** House of Anansi emerged at the same time as little magazines, and for much the same reasons. A prosperous consumer culture to define themselves against, including large foreign publishers and their Canadian branches. Cheaper and easier printing methods. Small but critical doses of public support. Mostly, so writers could publish themselves and their friends — what they liked, who they liked, and how they liked.

English Canada had few small presses before the mid-sixties. There was Aleph Press, which was Gwen MacEwen, a library copying machine, and a stapler. John Robert Colombo's Hawkshead Press printed Atwood's first chapbook, seven pages of poems for fifty cents. In Vancouver, artist Takao Tanabe's tiny Periwinkle Press produced a half-dozen pamphlets of new West Coast poetry. Fredericton's Fiddlehead Poetry Books published a steady stream of chapbooks,

**KINGDOM OF ABSENCE (1967)**
**Dennis Lee**

"For five years I wrote almost nothing but sonnet variations," Dennis Lee told an interviewer in 1972. "Isn't that absurd."

The result was his first book, a sonnet sequence called *Kingdom of Absence*. It has moments of whimsy, hints of the Dennis Lee to come in *Alligator Pie* and *Yesno*. But mostly it's an earnest book that wears its learning on its sleeve and loves darkness and elegies, because its author is at that time in life when there's little experience with real darkness and little need for real elegies. It's too hung up on its borrowed form to hear, much less say, what it wants to say. As Lee also said in 1972, he hadn't yet learned to speak the language of his own place in his own way, to "enact in words the presence of what we live among."

most of them paid for by owner/editor Fred Cogswell and his wife Pat. The cool kids wanted to be with Contact Press, founded in 1952 by Louis Dudek, Irving Layton, and Ray Souster. Contact was initially a vanity press, or what Dudek preferred to call a private press. It printed books mostly by its own editors, and authors paid for their own books. In 1959, Toronto banker Peter Miller replaced Layton and began paying for many of the books himself, shifting the press's centre from Montreal to Toronto and changing it into English Canada's first modern small press, the publisher of first books of poetry by Alden Nowlan, Al Purdy, Milton Acorn, Gwen MacEwen, George Bowering, John Newlove, and Margaret Atwood.

**LET US COMPARE MYTHOLOGIES (1956)**
**Leonard Cohen**

★★★

Most of Cohen is here, at the start. The religious longing. The eye that sees signs everywhere, the voice for which every ritual is a rite. The fascination, especially, with martyrs. "All the saints and prophets / are nailed to stakes and desert trees," he says here, and spent the rest of his life trying to join them.

There are of course also the poems about and for women. What's most impressive about both kinds of poems is their complete confidence in themselves (a confidence Cohen didn't share, which is what made him not Layton). They're over-the-top poems that have made up their mind to go big or go home, poems willing to be almost embarrassingly romantic. There's one, for heaven's sake, in which he's had a bottle made "to keep your tears in." He was made for a bigger stage.

Gaston Miron and five others established Éditions de l'Hexagone in 1953, the first significant French-Canadian small press and the first of any size devoted to Québécois poetry, "*la poésie du pays.*" Small presses flourished in Quebec in the early sixties, five years before their counterparts in English Canada: Éditions Hurtubise in 1960, Éditions du Jour in 1961, Éditions Parti pris in 1964. "We have found very compatible allies in the French-Canadian publishers," said English-Canadian small press founder and champion Dave Godfrey. "They loaned us much of our constitution, many of our principles, and a great deal of our inspiration. The model for us isn't Jack McClelland. It's Gaston Miron."

Some large publishers behaved at times like small literary presses, publishing poetry or fiction for prestige or to keep editors happy. Pierre Tisseyre agreed to run the Montreal office of New York-based Le Cercle du livre de France on the condition that he could publish Canadian writers. Toronto's Clarke, Irwin &

Company received most of its considerable income from textbooks, enough to tolerate editor Roy MacSkimming's buying the occasional collection of poetry or short stories (especially if it brought them a Governor General's Award, as Alden Nowlan's *Bread, Wine and Salt* did in 1967). Oxford University Press made enough money selling the Oxford name to the natives to let William Toye play with poetry as he liked, acquiring and designing handsome collections from Atwood, George Johnston, Miriam Waddington, Ray Souster, and Phyllis Gotlieb, among others.

Large presses also trained people who started small presses — like MacSkimming, who took what he learned from Clarke, Irwin (including what he disliked about it) and used it to help found New Press. In 1965 Bill Toye hired high-school dropout Victor Coleman as a part-time production assistant at Oxford. Coleman had worked as a copy boy at the *Toronto Daily Star*, and he knew the poetry scene from organizing readings at the Bohemian Embassy and from publishing his own little magazine, *Island*. He was also the father of two children, unemployed, and close to going on welfare. As he remembers it, he lost his job at the *Star* because copy boys couldn't be older than twenty. Toye "took me under his wing," teaching him the trade from production to sales.

The following year, Coleman left Oxford to work for a small publisher that had recently opened in downtown Toronto. They were calling it Coach House Press, and everyone called its owner Stan.

**STAN CAME FROM EDMONTON.** He came from Edmonton & arrived in Toronto on the bus. He was sitting there with an old ordinary Doukhobor hat on his head, a paper shopping bag between his feet, he never said a word on the bus. He wasnt much of a man for words. He was in love with books. He didnt read them. He loved them....

Pretty soon all the Toronto hippies were wearing black Doukhobor hats.

That's from *A Short Sad Book*, a novel in which Stan is a character trying to find the Pretty Good Canadian Novel. It's by George Bowering, so it's probably not entirely true. But it is a pretty good story.

Like Dennis Lee, Stan Bevington was the son of teachers. His interest piqued by classes at the Edmonton Art Gallery, he apprenticed in high school with a Hungarian artist who taught him everything from mixing pigments to gilding and silkscreening. On evenings when he wasn't with the artist, he worked for an architect who taught him drafting and darkroom techniques. By Grade 11 he could silkscreen on anything and make an enlarger from a tin can. His English teacher got him a job that summer at a country newspaper, where they let him run the backup linotype machine during his breaks. After high school he worked for a few months in a corrugated box factory, designing and painting sample cartons for beer and meat companies and getting the old guys on the shop floor to show him how to carve letters into rubber plates. He quit for a job as linotype operator for a weekly paper in Fairview, northwest of Edmonton. He wasn't fast enough yet, so he started early in the mornings, setting and proofing type before the boss showed up. He was nineteen years old.

In September 1962 he arrived in Toronto to begin two years at the University of Toronto's department of fine arts, as a prerequisite for the school of architecture. He didn't like writing essays and gave up in February. He tried the Ontario College of Art instead, hoping an art degree would get him into architecture without having to write too much.

The summer after his first year at OCA, Bevington launched his own printing business with handheld versions of the newly proposed Canadian flag — the so-called Pearson pennant — with blue sidebars and three red maple leaves in the middle. He hired women to sew the flags, silkscreened them in his basement, and paid hippies to sell them on the street in Yorkville. They sold hundreds a day through the summer of '64, enough to buy an antique printing press and help rent an old coach house on a back lane near Dundas and Bathurst, where Stan and a growing community of friends could live, work, and party. In November he dropped out of OCA to devote himself full-time to all three.

Coach House Press began when one of those friends, future art historian Dennis Reid, suggested they make a book. Wayne Clifford, an undergraduate English student at U of T, supplied poems. Two classmates lent money to buy paper. Another U of T friend, Janet Amos, let Reid photograph her naked for the illustrations. Professor Hugo McPherson provided a blurb. Bevington designed the book, handset the type, and silkscreened the photographs. Printed in March 1965 on his old foot-pedal printer in an edition of three hundred copies, *Man in a Window* set the prototype for a Coach House book: a unique collaboration between writer, artist, and printer for which the labour far exceeded the expected financial return.

Victor Coleman met Stan and Dennis at a party at the house of Earle Birney, U of T's new writer-in-residence. He helped them distribute *Man in a Window*, and when Wayne Clifford left for grad school in Iowa, he became their editor. In return, Stan trained him as a linotype operator and paid him for commercial work. With his taste and connections, Coleman grew Coach House from a vanity press for U of T students into a home for experimental writers, a publisher of outlandish books that were as well or better known in avant-garde arts communities in Buffalo, New York, Vancouver, and San Francisco than in Toronto. bpNichol came to Coach House about the same time as Coleman, bringing an additional set of international connections and an infectious enthusiasm for doing something new.

After publishing *Man in a Window* on their own, they asked the Canada Council for help. The problem was, the Council supported only university and French publishers; the only support available for English trade publishers was for translations of French books

ONE/EYE/LOVE (1967)
Victor Coleman

A very sixties book, from its unusual size (11 by 5¼ inches) and psychedelic illustrations to its declaration that "Any part of this book may be reproduced by anyone whose intention is not financial gain." The poems are mostly confessional first-person lyrics by a very earnest young man who says in his bio, "I stay high, most of the time."

My eyes are as naked as
the hashish ash in the pipe
& only crying gives them life

A half-century later and without benefit of drugs, the poems that stand up are the less overtly autobiographical ones, like "Song One," about New York, and especially "Speech & Invoice," a grisly inventory of scalps sent by the Six Nations to King George III in 1782.

into English or books about art or literary history. So in 1966, arts officer David Silcox disguised the first Council grant to help an independent press publish English-Canadian creative literature as an "arts bursary" for one Stan Bevington of Toronto, Ontario. The following year, the Council changed its policy and gave $3,500 to Coach House "for its activities in 1967" and $1,200 to Louis Dudek's Delta Canada to publish four books of poetry — the first grants openly awarded to assist original publication of English-Canadian non-academic books.

Coach House also received support in the early seventies from the Ontario Arts Council and the Opportunities for Youth program. Mostly it supported itself, the commercial work for Bevington Graphics underwriting books for the press. Stan did posters for the Toronto Public Library, flyers for Av Isaacs' gallery, stationery for Marty's bookstore, job printing for other publishers — whatever it took to keep his lost boys in paper and beer. They even sold some books, especially outside Toronto; people who lived in or were visiting the city were more likely to be given a Coach House book than to buy one. Writers were paid in books, their own and others'. Anyone who dropped in was encouraged to take as many as they liked — marketing, Coach House style.

In 1968, with Stan's lease about to expire, Dennis Lee invited Coach House Press to become Rochdale College's in-house printer. The new building wasn't ready, so they moved into a garage behind the site. Stan taught printing workshops for the college — arguably the best education Rochdale ever provided. He also printed Rochdale's popular diplomas, parody degrees in everything from a B.A. in Magical Apprenticeship for $25 to a Ph.D. in Poetic Justice for $100. He charged Rochdale five dollars to print each diploma: two dollars for labour and overhead, plus three dollars for a "special Dope fund or whatever."

According to rumour that became legend, all Coach House employees were given a tab of acid every morning. "It wasn't true," says Coach House author Matt Cohen. "Drugs were far too plentiful and available to require rationing or distribution, and besides, few people came to work in the morning." In Bevington's memory,

LSD arrived in Toronto in the summer of 1966. "We were early adopters," he admits. That summer they published Joe Rosenblatt's *The LSD Leacock*, illustrated poems with titles like "Waiter! There's an Alligator in My Coffee," "I Get High on Butterflies," and "The Egg Room":

> Hey baby! Step into my egg room
> you'll cool to dig the oval most;
> The walls have a shape of Brigitte Bardot
> And there's music flowing thru the love
>     tubes;
> you can hear Bob Dylan & the Hawks &
> Joan Baez.*

Coach House designed and sold LSD blotter paper (if you took acid in Toronto in the late sixties and it had a little green frog on it, the Canada Council helped get you high). Their 1968 pamphlet *Pink White and Clear* — three blank sheets stapled together that sold for $4.95 — allegedly included a drop of acid on the inside back cover. Most notoriously, they identified their books as "Printed in Canada by Mindless Acid Freaks," a phrase coined by bookseller John Douglas of the Fifth Kingdom Bookshop on Harbord Street. The first Coach House title to bear the colophon was Victor Coleman's first book, 1967's *One/Eye/Love*. Bowering says they had hidden it in very tiny print in books they printed for McClelland & Stewart the year before, but that might be just a very good story.

Coach House published over a hundred books in its first decade,

**BASEBALL: A POEM IN THE MAGIC NUMBER 9 (1967)**
George Bowering

★★★

"In the beginning was the word, and the word was / 'Play Ball.'" So says *Baseball*, a poem in nine innings about George Bowering's second great love. It's about growing up with baseball, playing it, following it, big-league and small-town games, about baseball as history, myth, and religion. Really, said George, it's about poetry, using his love for baseball as a disguise to talk about his love for poetry.

Coach House printed five hundred copies in a chapbook shaped like a baseball pennant, with green felt covers. When Bowering's friend and fellow *Tish* editor Frank Davey got his copy, he thought it was the first extraordinary book to come out of their circle, "the first that I'm sure will outlive us." It's still in print, so maybe he was right.

---

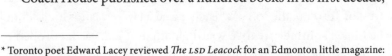

* Toronto poet Edward Lacey reviewed *The LSD Leacock* for an Edmonton little magazine: "Like all Coach House productions, it's lovingly designed, illustrated, and printed, but my advice to the prospective buyer is — try marijuana; it's cheaper."

plus countless magazines, brochures, broadsides, posters, post-cards, and anything else that could be made with paper and ink. As Coleman says, "Sure, we lit up after lunch. But look at the work. We got it done." Because of its unique design and manufacture, the best of that work can't be anthologized or reproduced. Except for a few titles — Daphne Marlatt's *Vancouver Poems*, Michael Ondaatje's *Rat Jelly*, Nichol's *The Martyrology* — early Coach House books are mostly museum objects now, not living books. But that's true of any publisher's backlist. Old Coach House books aren't just artifacts, they're art. When the Art Gallery of Ontario put on an exhibit in 2010 called *Canadian Art in the 1960s and 1970s through the Lens of Coach House Press*, the books were literally the centre of the show.

**THE DAINTY MONSTERS**
**(1967)**
Michael Ondaatje

★★★

Michael Ondaatje came to Canada in 1962 at nineteen without having written anything. Five years later he had a bachelor's degree, a wife and children, and a book of poetry, published with a gorgeous colour cover by Coach House Press after McClelland & Stewart turned it down.

*The Dainty Monsters* is a remarkably assured debut: skilful, confident poems with a surprising amount of wit for a writer who became much more earnest in the books that followed. I like the dragon tangled in the badminton net, and the houseplants that lust and fart while their owners sleep. The clearest sign of the darker Ondaatje to come is the suite of longer poems at the end, especially "Peter," about an artist figure who is literally tortured, hamstrung and has his tongue cut out. Next stop, Buddy Bolden.

**HOUSE OF ANANSI** was founded by Dave Godfrey and Dennis Lee, plus the patience of Ellen Godfrey. In the spring of 1967, Godfrey became angry about the lack of Canadian books in Canadian bookstores. He had been angry before (some say he was always angry), but this time his anger happened to coincide with a conversation in a pub with a poet who happened to have a manuscript of poems without a publisher. Six rounds of beer later, they had a publisher — themselves. It seemed like a good idea at the time.

Godfrey was born in Winnipeg and grew up west of Toronto, the son of a teacher and a lawyer. After high school he took a summer creative writing course at Harvard, enrolled in Trinity College at the University of Toronto, and worked in a lumber camp in Alberta. Trinity asked him to leave in his second year, according to him for protesting electroshock treatments for a class-mate diagnosed with depression (others said because he skipped too many classes). He finished his B.A. at the University of Iowa and then did an M.A. at Stanford, where he met his future wife, mystery novelist Ellen Swartz. In 1961 he returned to Iowa for an M.F.A. from their Writer's Workshop, and then stayed on to do a Ph.D. in American literature.

Like Margaret Atwood, Godfrey seems to have been made a Canadian nationalist by an American education. A successful short story writer while still in grad school, he liked to say he had refused to allow one of his stories to be included in the annual *Best American Stories* because the editors wouldn't change the title to *Best American and Canadian Stories*. (Apparently he changed his mind. His "Newfoundland Night," first published in the *Tamarack Review*, appeared in *The Best American Short Stories 1963*.) In the mid-sixties he taught English at an Anglican boys' school in Ghana, an experience that he said taught him to reject feelings of colonial inadequacy and look to his own culture for inspiration — to refuse, as Atwood said, to be a victim.

One year after returning to Toronto to teach at the college that had expelled him, he started a Canadian publishing company named for an African god, the Ashanti god of stories. It began in a basement, in a small room past the furnace in a house the Godfreys were renting from the university, at 671 Spadina Avenue, next door to the William Funeral Chapel. They had $5,000, half of it from the bank. After printing three hundred copies of Lee's first book in April, they applied to the Canada Council. With David Silcox's help they got a grant of $4,420 to publish four more titles in the fall: a reprint of *Kingdom of Absence*, a new edition of Atwood's *The Circle Game*, a book of poems by George Jonas, and a collection of Godfrey's short stories. By winter's end all four had sold more than five hundred copies, and *The Circle Game*'s run of a thousand had sold out. In their report to the Council, Godfrey and Lee concluded that "It is obviously possible to publish, promote, and sell reasonable quantities of books which will not outsell *Airport* but which will more likely remain readable and enjoyable in the years to come. All this requires is capital, boldness, innovation, time, and a seventy-five-hour work week."

A few months after they started, an eighteen-year-old draft resister named Douglas Fetherling arrived from Wheeling, West Virginia, and became their first full-time employee, paid $35 a week less $15 for a room, first in the attic and then in the basement with the inventory, dust floating from the ceiling whenever the bus stopped out front. Rochdale resident Ann Wall, from Virginia and unlike Fetherling from money, began volunteering along with her draft-age husband Byron in 1968. Godfrey ran the business, partly because Lee was busy with Rochdale and partly because Godfrey was better with money, more entrepreneur than editor. In a letter to Lee written sometime in the early fall of '68, he proposed selling debentures in an Anansi trust, what he called communal capitalism. "If Anansi survives five years, we pay off the debenture holders with shares, and fly to Spain with the $50,000 in the trust fund. Or buy machine guns for Biafra. Or have it as a free-of-debt trust fund to keep Anansi solvent."

Godfrey was writing from the south of France, where he and Ellen spent the academic year of 1968–69. He had won a $7,000 award from the Canada Council, and Trinity gave him the year off to write. In his absence, Dennis Lee became Anansi's main publisher and editor, maintaining regular correspondence with Godfrey. They agreed, for example, to fire Fetherling, whom Godfrey had hired and told Lee he could blame for firing: "Godfrey has turned Tory. Godfrey is a French wino. Or whatever. Farewell Doug."

Unexpectedly for a poet, Lee's most important contribution during his first year in charge was to push Anansi toward fiction. Small presses were about poetry, almost by definition. Some small presses published nonfiction on specialized subjects, like numerology or local history, but "fiction either got published by one of the big houses or it didn't get published at all." In the 1960s, many young Canadian writers followed European and American writers away from experimental poetry and into experimental fiction. In English Canada, such writers had no choice but to hope a commercial publisher would take a chance on them. That's why Lee and later Atwood had a sense of manuscripts emerging from attics and basements, of a dam bursting somewhere — because it did, when Lee opened the door.

Godfrey pointed the way to Anansi's fiction program with his own *Death Goes Better with Coca-Cola*, a book of genre-blurring stories about hunting, fishing, and being angry at America published in November 1967 that was later designated "AF1." In 1968, Nova Scotia writer Ray Smith sent Lee the manuscript of what became AF2, *Cape Breton Is the Thought-Control Center of Canada* — postmodern fictions about such things as Polish nationalism, liking turnips, and being angry at America. Next came Graeme Gibson's *Five Legs*, an experimental novel that four publishers had rejected before Lee edited it and sold two thousand copies in three months. That fall Anansi published five novels on the same day, under a new imprint dedicated to first novels. None did as well as *Five Legs*, but the point wasn't to publish bestsellers or even necessarily the best books. The point was to get new work out there quickly, to help young, adventurous writers like Marian Engel, Russell Marois, Peter Such, and Harold Sonny Ladoo "get into print, find an audience, and get on with their next book."

Godfrey supported Lee's move into fiction, but he pressed for more commercially viable nonfiction to support Anansi's literary publishing. The usual story is that Godfrey and Lee quarrelled and separated over this issue. The surviving correspondence, however, suggests more of a mutually agreeable divorce, in which Godfrey would publish commercial nonfiction "without compromising the Anansi name" by starting a new publishing company, appropriately called New Press.

**FIVE LEGS (1969)**
Graeme Gibson

★★★

*Five Legs* begins inside a hangover. It has two narrators, each with three chapters, on a bitterly cold winter day in southwestern Ontario, the funeral of a grad student killed by a hit-and-run driver. It jumps backwards, forwards, and sideways in the same paragraph. It blurs thoughts with dialogue. It's unorthodoxly punctuated and is fond of Yodaesque inversions like "Better, that feels." It moves from something like realism to something far from it.

*Saturday Night* called the book "the most sophisticated writing ever done in Canada." I'm not sure about that (partly because sophisticated means different things to different people), but it's certainly a challenging and important book, one of the more successful of the short shelf of books then catching up Canadian fiction of the 1960s to international fiction of the 1930s.

Not that there weren't fights. Ann Wall offered to buy Godfrey's shares in Anansi but he wouldn't sell to an American, so he sold them to Lee, who sold them to Wall. Shirley Gibson joined Anansi in 1969 to help promote her husband's novel and was soon clashing with Lee for control of the company. Her husband, meanwhile, would soon begin seeing Anansi poet Margaret Atwood — who herself joined the editorial board in 1971, a year before *her* husband, Jim Polk, began working for Anansi as a manuscript reader. As Polk later wrote (without naming names), "interpersonal relationships at the press were so involved by the summer of '72 that someone suggested we change the name to House of Atreus."

The early seventies were hard years for Anansi. Lee was exhausted, tired of working seventy-five-hour weeks for nothing. His own marriage was suffering. Sales were increasing but money was running out. He tried to sell the company to Macmillan; they offered a dollar. In February 1971 the editorial board decided they had to stop considering new manuscripts and reduce their publishing schedule for the upcoming year from twenty-seven to eight books. Two weeks later, water used to fight a warehouse fire destroyed half their inventory. In October, one of their new writers was killed by a train in an apparent suicide. Shirley Gibson replaced Lee as president in March 1972 and began issuing increasingly officious internal memos and requiring all editors to keep detailed timesheets. "She wanted to be the top banana," says Atwood. "She made life so difficult for Dennis that he just threw up his hands finally." In November he resigned from Anansi altogether.

**NO PAIN LIKE THIS BODY**
**(1972)**
**Harold Sonny Ladoo**

Nasty, brutish, and short, *No Pain Like This Body* takes place among South Asian indentured labourers in Trinidad. A boy drags his sister by the hair through a rice field in a growing storm. His mother goes mad and disappears into the darkness. The novel ends as it began, with another thunderstorm, another black sky twisting like a snake, the wind raging and the rain pounding the earth.

If there's any consolation, it's not in the book but is the book — the strength of will it took to write it and the faith it took to publish it. As Dionne Brand says in her introduction to a reprint of the novel in 2003, if you came from the place Ladoo did, you believed books could change your life. Not abstractly, as an English professor might believe it, but in the body, because you must.

Before he left, everyone — including Shirley Gibson — pulled together to help finish a book about Canadian literature, a kind of "CanLit for Dummies" they hoped might make enough to keep the doors open another year. Published in September 1972, *Survival* has since sold more than 150,000 copies. It's one of Anansi's bestselling books to date and the most influential book about Canadian literature ever published.

**IN THE MID-SIXTIES** Raymond Souster wanted to put together a Centennial anthology of new Canadian poets, including some too new for the taste of his fellow editors at Contact Press. He thought he'd call it *Poets 67*. He tried, unsuccessfully, to interest Ryerson Press, McClelland & Stewart, and the Centennial Commission in the project. He decided he'd publish it at his own expense, under the Contact name. Since the Centennial Commission wasn't interested, he changed the title to *New Wave Canada*.

Victor Coleman lived near Souster's home on Baby Point Road, and the two would often get together on weekends to throw around a ball in High Park (Souster would have been happy as a baseball player if he hadn't discovered he was a poet). Coleman actually was a new Canadian poet, twenty-three years Souster's junior, so he helped Souster plan and select the anthology and assembled it while working at Oxford University Press. He was going to print it too, but by then he'd begun working for Coach House, so they finished the job.

Launched on May 21, 1966, *New Wave Canada: The New Explosion in Canadian Poetry* was not the last book published by Contact Press, but it was its end. Louis Dudek hated it, and Peter Miller was so upset by his omission from the book that he quit. It was also the foundation of what became the Coach House list. Stan Bevington explains:

> If you look at the table of contents, it's a shopping list for the authors we published. Daphne Marlatt, bpNichol, Michael Ondaatje, David McFadden, one after another. That's

definitely the turning point for us, and they were Victor's choice. We published new work by most of the people that are in there, so it's kind of the cornerstone of the press.

*New Wave Canada* is not an attractive book. Magazine size, it looks more like a scrapbook than a book, laid out with a typewriter on cheap paper between thin cardboard covers. Surviving copies have faded badly. But the point wasn't to make a beautiful or lasting book; the point was to print news of the new. For that, its form fit its content. As McLuhan would have said, its medium was its message.

Much has been made of the differences between Coach House and Anansi. Coach House was the aesthete, Anansi the activist. Coach House was cosmopolitan, Anansi was nationalist. Coach House people used drugs and Anansi people drank. Anansi sold books and Coach House gave books away. Coach House was about making a community, while Anansi was about changing society. Coach House wanted to drop out; Anansi wanted in.

It's a pretty good story. Mostly, it's a true story. But it hides what they shared, with each other and with the many other small presses that followed. The main function and legacy of Canada's small presses of the sixties and early seventies was to publish new writers. Inevitably, most of those writers have been forgotten. But almost all the Canadian writers that we remember and read now were first published by small presses, especially after Anansi added fiction to the small-press repertoire. As Roy MacSkimming says in his history *The Perilous Trade*, without them, the literary landscape of Canada would be unrecognizable.

## Chapter 11

# The Boat Who Wouldn't Float

Yet this is the country of defeat
where Sisyphus rolls a big stone
year after year up the ancient hills
— Al Purdy, "The Country North of Belleville"

**AMONG HER PEERS,** Margaret Laurence was the most loved English-Canadian writer of the CanLit boom. Dennis Lee met her when she was writer-in-residence at the University of Toronto. "I knew some generous and warm people who were good writers," he says. "I'd never met such a concentration of those things in one person before." When the Writers' Union of Canada formed in 1973, Laurence agreed to serve as its chair until one could be elected. "It was unanimous," said Timothy Findley. "You couldn't possibly think of anybody else."

She was born in Neepawa, a Manitoba town big enough to have a hospital. Her father was a lawyer who would have liked to be a carpenter. Her mother would have liked to be a pianist. Both were from the good side of town, from old families in large old houses. They bought a little house on the wrong side of town.

Two days after Laurence's fourth birthday, her mother died of a kidney infection. Five years later, pneumonia took her father. She was raised by her mother's older sister Marg; to save money, they lived with Marg's father. Laurence began writing in the loft of her grandfather's garage, "leaving the little door open for light and

·filling scribblers with stories." At seventeen she had a short-lived romance with a twenty-seven-year-old British man from the nearby RAF training base. There were no boys in her grade that year; they were all away at war.

Laurence left Neepawa in 1944 to attend United College in Winnipeg, then affiliated with the University of Manitoba. She brought "two sweaters, two skirts, two blouses, one good dress, one pair of sensible shoes, and one pair of high heels." She did well in English, indifferently or poorly in all else. Canadian novels weren't taught in her classes, but she read some in the book department of the Hudson's Bay store. She met another English student who became her closest friend, Winnipegger Adele Wiseman. She also met a thirty-one-year-old Albertan named Jack Laurence, a former RCAF mechanic studying to become an engineer. They married within a year and lived in Winnipeg's North End while Jack finished his degree.

In 1949 they moved to London, England, the gateway to engineering jobs with His Majesty's Colonial Service. The following year Jack got a job supervising the construction of reservoirs in British Somaliland. They lived in the small mountain town of Sheikh, in a house with sandbags on the roof to keep the wind from blowing it away. Margaret liked Somalia but not colonialism, or becoming part of it. She helped translate a selection of Somali poems and tales into English, published by the Somaliland Protectorate as *A Tree for Poverty* — her first book.

She gave birth to her first child in London in the summer of 1952, a girl. In December, Jack took a new job building the port of Tema on the Gold Coast (now Ghana). They lived in Accra, the capital, then Tema. In June 1955, Margaret's former professor Malcolm Ross accepted for *Queen's Quarterly* what she called "my first real story," about a complicated friendship between the son of a British missionary and the son of his African nurse. Two months later she had an African-born son of her own.

The Laurences returned to Canada in 1957, partly for their children and partly because Margaret's stepmother was dying of cancer. They settled in Vancouver, in a small house on the west side near UBC. In 1960 McClelland & Stewart published her first novel, *This Side Jordan*. With Jack McClelland's help she got an agent in New York. A story in the *Tamarack Review* won the University of Western Ontario's President's Medal for best short story published in a magazine that year. Her novel won a $1,000 prize for first novels sponsored by the Canadian chapters of the Beta Sigma Phi sorority. And she wrote: book reviews for the *Vancouver Sun*, short stories for the *Saturday Evening Post*, a memoir of her time in Somaliland, and the first draft of what would become her best-known novel, all between 1960 and 1962.

Margaret and Jack separated in the fall of 1962. She loved Jack, but being the writer she wanted to be mattered more to her than being the wife he wanted. Jack took a job in Pakistan and Margaret took the kids and moved to London, "where I imagined, wrongly as it turned out, there would be a literary community that would receive me with open arms." One set of open arms she especially hoped to find belonged to the West Indian writer George Lamming, with whom she had an affair in Vancouver that summer. He lived in London, in the same Hampstead neighbourhood where Margaret found a flat. But she couldn't find him, and when she did (at a party at Mordecai and Florence Richler's apartment), he was with another woman. Winter was cold that year.

In the spring, Macmillan in London and McClelland & Stewart in Toronto published her Somaliland memoir and a collection of her short stories. Her agent got her a $5,000 advance from Knopf in New York to publish the memoir, the short-story collection, and the new novel, then called *Hagar*. She left London, renting a large old country house in the village of Penn

**THIS SIDE JORDAN (1960)**
**Margaret Laurence**

Set in Ghana a few months before its independence, Laurence's first novel is about the racially charged process of "Africanization," the hiring of African employees by British companies eager to stay in business after independence. Laurence said it was "the easiest novel I ever wrote because I knew absolutely nothing about writing a novel."

Reviews were mixed. All admired the writing but most found the ending "suspiciously sunny," as London's *New Statesman* put it. As several complained, the people in the novel are too rarely people, too often black or white. Still, it earned a Book Society Recommendation in England, a prize for first novels in Canada, and a half-hour adaptation for CBS TV in America. It was an important novel then, even if it's not now.

from her British publisher. She missed having a partner but she loved Elm Cottage. "It was home from the moment we moved in," she wrote in her memoir.

**THE STONE ANGEL (1964)**
**Margaret Laurence**

★★★★

*The Stone Angel* is a book about growing old and hating it — about raging against the dying of the light, as its epigraph says. "I'll have a word or two to say," says Hagar Shipley, "you can depend on that, before my mouth is stopped with dark." There are bits of Laurence in Hagar: growing up in Neepawa/Manawaka, the domineering grandfather turned into a domineering father, the sexual loneliness. But Hagar is mostly a creation of her imagination, the most realistic character she ever created because she isn't real, her only narrator that wasn't close to her own age. She's Laurence's most memorable character, the most likeable unlikeable character in CanLit.

In the summer of 1966, she came to Canada to promote her third novel, *A Jest of God*. Robert Weaver helped her get a Canada Council grant to pay her way over and McClelland & Stewart set up a five-city book tour. She sold the film rights to Paul Newman and Joanne Woodward for $30,000 and used some of it to buy Elm Cottage. The novel won a Governor General's Award, which she returned to receive in May 1967. She visited Expo with Adele Wiseman, by then a holder of her own GG. In the ladies' room at Government House, she met fellow winners Margaret Atwood and Claire Martin, each as nervous as the other. Afterwards she tried to have sex with Al Purdy, but they were both too drunk.

She didn't know it yet, but she had found the literary community she was looking for.

**TWO OF EVERY** three books sold in Canada in the 1960s and '70s came from outside the country. In some fields, such as pocketbooks and children's books, imports dominated the market almost completely. Of the five thousand new children's books available for sale in English Canada in 1969, thirty were published in Canada.

By the 1970s Canada was the world's largest importer of books, magazines, and newspapers, mostly from America. Canada, meanwhile, exported few books to the United States, partly because American publishers could legally pirate any Canadian book written in English that sold more than 1,500 copies in the States,* but mostly because distributors generally bought their books from American publishers.

By the early seventies, small Canadian publishers (fewer than twenty titles a year) had published 30 percent of the English-Canadian literary titles in print and got 8 percent of literary sales. Large Canadian publishers published a third of the titles and got half the sales. The rest were foreign-owned companies, though their share of the literary market shrank as Canadian literary publishing increased. In 1969 American subsidiaries made 60 percent of book sales in Canada but published just two new Canadian works of fiction.

As the publishers told it, Canadian companies struggled to compete against a flood of foreign capital and foreign books. The English-Canadian version of their story climaxes in the forced sale of venerable Ryerson Press to a New York company, and the French-Canadian version in "*l'affaire* Hachette," the takeover of Quebec's book wholesaling industry by a Parisian company. Readers and booksellers might tell a different story — for example, that Ryerson hadn't published much worth reading in decades, and that Quebec distributors were every bit as monopolistic as French distributors. Being Canadian didn't make capital any less capitalist.

The Governor General's Literary Awards also tell a different story, one in which foreign

**A BIRD IN THE HOUSE**
(1970)
Margaret Laurence

Linked autobiographical stories, *A Bird in the House* marked Laurence's first appearance on a bestseller list — though likely because there was no Canadian bestseller list until May 9, 1970, when it appeared at number two on the *Toronto Daily Star*'s very first list.

The stories are a step up from magazine melodrama, popular fiction lit up by a dose of symbolism and reflection on serious subjects. As Honor Tracy said in her review for the *New York Times*, "Were this collection to be judged by women's magazine standards, she would doubtless receive an A-plus." Like most of Laurence's fiction, it strikes me as an enjoyable and even important read in its day, but not good enough to survive its time. The respect other Canadian writers had for her has kept too much of Laurence's work around past its best-before date.

---

* After 1965, this licence to steal applied only to books by American authors. By then, however, seventy-five years of protectionism for American printers had entrenched permanent trade imbalances in the North American publishing industry.

publishers made significant contributions to Canadian literature. Of the ninety-five books awarded GGs between 1959 and 1974, twenty-eight were published by foreign publishers or Canadian branches of foreign publishers, including Hugh MacLennan's *The Watch That Ends the Night* (Scribner's), Réjean Ducharme's *L'Avalée des avalés* (Gallimard), Gwen MacEwen's *The Shadow-Maker* (Macmillan of Canada), and John Glassco's *Selected Poems* (Oxford University Press). The contribution of foreign-owned publishers was even greater in the *Toronto Star*'s new national bestseller list: about 40 percent of Canadian titles on the fiction list from 1970 to 1974. For Canadian publishers, every book sold in Canada by foreign publishers took money out of their pockets. For authors like Robertson Davies (Macmillan), Anne Hébert (Éditions du Seuil), and Alice Munro (McGraw-Hill Ryerson), it put money in theirs. Most readers don't much care who publishes the books they buy.

The publisher that made the most money for Canadian authors over this period was a Canadian company. Between 1959 and 1974, McClelland & Stewart won more Governor General's Awards, had more bestsellers, and paid more royalties to more writers than any other publisher in Canada. When Jack McClelland stepped down as president of M&S, his author Margaret Laurence wrote to honour him:

> Damn near singlehandedly, you transformed the Canadian publishing scene from one of mediocrity and dullness to one of enormous interest and vitality. Had it not been for M&S, I wonder if a whole lot of people such as myself, Mordecai, Al Purdy, Farley, Pierre, Peggy Atwood, and on and on and on would have found the wide audience of readers that we have. I doubt it.

**HIS STORY SHOULD** probably start with vodka, but let's start instead in a three-storey home in Toronto's Forest Hill, in a library made into a bedroom and school for an asthmatic child who read and read until the walls became the world all around. When he was ten, his doting mother and teetotalling father risked sending him to school, first to a public school on Avenue Road and then the University of Toronto Schools. Elsewhere in the city it was the soup kitchens and rubbing alcohol of the Depression, but at UTS it was Kipling, King, and Character.

Then north for the asthma to Aurora, to St. Andrew's College, where he captained the hockey team and the Literary Society, third-class marks in English be damned. He recorded his life ambition for the *College Review*: "to slay the fair sex." After graduation he started writing a few novels, realized he had nothing to say, and enrolled in engineering at the University of Toronto. In the fall of 1941, at nineteen, he joined the navy. The hockey captain became captain of Motor Torpedo Boat 747, hunting German E-boats in the English Channel. He lost his asthma, saw men die, and learned to drink, fuck, and curse. He said later that he never had a better time.

Back in Toronto after all that, he married a girl he had met on leave, his older sister's sorority sister Elizabeth Matchett. He finished his degree, abandoning engineering for a hasty B.A. from Trinity College. Before the war, his parents had strongly discouraged him from entering the family publishing business on the grounds that publishing could never make their only son truly wealthy. But in the flush postwar economy they recanted. If he wanted, the sailor had a job as well as a girl waiting for him. In November 1946, *Canadian Bookseller* announced an addition to the staff of the Toronto publishing firm McClelland & Stewart: John Gordon McClelland to his parents, Lieutenant Jake to the crew of MTB 747, and just Jack to a generation of Canadian writers.

To learn the business he worked in each department, starting in the warehouse and then moving on to accounting, publicity, and

**MIRROR ON THE FLOOR**
**(1967)**
**George Bowering**

★★

The plot of Bowering's first novel is simple: horny college student falls in love with beautiful woman with a mysterious past, nineteen-year-old Andrea Harrison. McLelland & Stewart tried to sell the novel by calling Andrea a "free living girl" (sixties code for promiscuous), but *Mirror on the Floor* is more a beat novel than a hippie novel, more Kerouac than Vonnegut — not postmodern excess but modern emptiness, its only moral that there is no moral, that "The world is a fucking awful place." The characters are rebels without causes, young men and women with time, angst, and lungs to burn. It's a young man's book by a writer pretending to be his heroes. He got better at fiction as he figured out how to be just George.

sales. In 1952 the firm moved to its new home at 25 Hollinger Road, just east of the Don Valley. Jack got a new office and a new title, general manager and executive vice-president. He and Elizabeth had their first child in 1948. Four children later, by which time Jack had become M&S's owner and president, they bought a large home at 141 Dunvegan Road in Forest Hill, a ten-minute walk from the house he grew up in. They also had a cottage in Muskoka, a Canadian-made mahogany speedboat, and a half-share with M&S author Farley Mowat in a leaky two-masted schooner out of Newfoundland. On land, Jack liked convertibles, preferably Mustangs. He worked wickedly long days, bringing files home every night and often working till four in the morning. To get through a day he had up to twenty cups of instant coffee, smoked two to three packs of cigarettes, and drank what his biographer could only describe as "a large amount of vodka."

Like other Canadian publishers, McClelland & Stewart survived by selling books for foreign publishers. Jack inherited his two most profitable writers from these agency relationships, as well as the writer he admired the most. Pierre Berton had pitched his first book to Robertson Davies' agent, who sold it to the New York publisher Alfred A. Knopf, then represented in Canada by M&S. Berton went to see McClelland, whom he'd never met, and Jack forever endeared himself to his new author by tearing the cover off the Knopf edition of Berton's book and promising something more "buyer-friendly."

Farley Mowat also went to M&S because it represented the American publisher of his first book, *People of the Deer*. Jack became close friends with both men. But by his own account the

**SELECTED POEMS (1972)**
· **Al Purdy**

★★★★★

Ignore the introduction: Purdy was more inclined to myth-breaking than myth-making. His John F. Kennedy is "only a man." His Cariboo horses are "only horses." His poems will not buy beer or flowers or a goddam thing. Sure, he said the trees were beautiful at Roblin Lake, but he also said, "I hate beautiful trees."

Purdy was a realist, but a hopeful realist, the happiest realist in Canadian literature. In 1973 he chastised another poet for writing angry rants à la Acorn and Layton. In a dark world, he said, a poem must include tenderness and pity. Wine and laughter also help.

If I had to pick one book of Canadian poetry to give to a friend from another country, it would probably be this one. *The Journals of Susanna Moodie* might scare them.

M&S writer with whom he fell "instantly in love" was the franco-phone novelist Gabrielle Roy. M&S was Canadian agent for the English translation of Roy's *Bonheur d'occasion*, published as *The Tin Flute* in New York in 1947. Jack met her that year on a sales trip with Elizabeth. They met in Saint Boniface, Manitoba, where Roy was visiting relatives to escape the publicity that came with sell-ing more than three-quarters of a million copies of her first novel. Jack was much taken with the older woman, with her charm, her "ethereal beauty," and especially her writing. He published twelve more of her books in translation, long after the world had stopped reading them. "As I have told you so many times," he wrote to her in 1974, "you are the greatest writer in the country."

From the point of view of literary history, Jack made the first important decision of his publishing career on August 8, 1958, when he told a forty-eight-year-old former schoolteacher from British Columbia that McClelland & Stewart would like to publish her book. Sheila Watson's experimental novel *The Double Hook* had been rejected by several prominent British literary publishers, including T. S. Eliot at Faber & Faber and C. Day Lewis at Chatto & Windus. M&S liked it enough to ask B.C. poet Earle Birney for his opinion. Birney admired the style but thought the story was cryptic and boring and advised rejection.

A few months later Jack received a letter from University of Alberta professor Fred Salter, calling Watson's novel "the most brilliant piece of fiction ever written in Canada." Salter offered to give Jack a foreword to the book and even suggested a publicity campaign: "I would get the book into the hands of avant-garde groups, and I would try to set up [some] sort of competition. The advertising copy should say: 'We don't know what it means. Can you understand it?'" Armed with Salter's letter, Jack tried to inter-est virtually every literary publisher in America in co-publishing the book. All of them passed. He took it anyway, telling Watson, "It's the sort of thing that makes a publisher feel it must be pub-lished." *The Double Hook* came out on May 16, 1959, and became the most influential Canadian novel ever published. "We all steal from Sheila," says Michael Ondaatje.

Jack wasn't entirely crazy. To offset the commercial risk of publishing a book like *The Double Hook*, he did something almost as radical as the book itself: he published it in paperback. M&S had begun publishing paperbacks the year before, in a series called the New Canadian Library. But the NCL was a reprint series; the newest title in its first batch was seventeen years old. Publishing original literary novels in anything other than hardcover was by then common in Europe and French Quebec, but still new in the States and not yet done in English Canada. Jack put house designer Frank Newfeld to work on the book (the cover is a much enlarged photo of a fishhook that Watson had bought in Paris, laid over an enlarged photo of the cross-section of a tibia bone), printed it in a larger "trade" size instead of the pocket size of pulp fiction, and priced it at $1.75. They sold all 2,500 copies of the first printing, plus 500 in a $3.95 cloth edition, mainly for libraries. Watson made $635 and Jack lost only $160. As Professor Salter promised, the book has been in print ever since.

**A RED CARPET FOR THE SUN (1959)**
Irving Layton

★★★

As promised (more like threatened) in his foreword, many of the poems in Layton's first collection with a commercial publisher attack commercial society. But also as promised, there are poems about pleasure, happiness, the "sudden glories" of ordinary life. He said "Good poems should rage like a fire," but he praised more than he burned. We just remember the attacks more, because he taught us to.

He loved the sound of words, especially his own. He never stopped being the teenager who once tossed a dictionary at a girl and said, "Ask me any word! I know them all!" It's what made him great but it's also why he couldn't stop himself, in his poems and his attacks on any who disliked them — because he believed what he said was true, every word of it, seduced by the power of his own voice.

In 1956 Ryerson Press reneged on an agreement to distribute Irving Layton's new book after deciding that calling churches "haemorrhoids upon the city's anus" was a bit much for the publishing arm of the United Church of Canada. Layton, being Layton, complained loudly and publicly that Canadian publishers were afraid to publish his poems. "You didn't try them all," wrote Jack. "Send us your manuscript and see what happens." Layton did, and Jack acquired the most popular English-Canadian poet of the early 1960s.

In 1959 he signed Margaret Laurence, Marie-Claire Blais, and Leonard Cohen. Richler jumped ship to M&S the following year, slipping out of his Canadian publisher's launch for *Duddy Kravitz* at the Park Plaza to cut a deal with Jack in the bar downstairs. Rudy Wiebe published his first novel with M&S in 1962. Peter Newman became an M&S author in 1963 after his publisher decided a biography of Prime Minister John Diefenbaker was premature. Jack didn't think so, and together he and Newman sold eighty thousand copies of *Renegade in Power* and established the political biography as a perennial Canadian genre. Purdy signed with M&S in 1963, Atwood in 1967.

They didn't always get along — with him or each other — but they all stayed with him. Jack always said he published authors, not books. "The author," he told his employees, "is king."

**HE SAID IT** so often the authors believed it. He said it so often *he* probably believed it. But while his letters certainly show a publisher dedicated to his writers, they also show him fully capable of telling them they're wrong or just to fuck off and quit bothering him (Earle Birney, frequently and apparently necessarily). He was exceptionally good at winning arguments, using praise when he could and force when he couldn't, all the while pretending ignorance. He could be charming or crude as best fit the correspondent. He was honest with himself and his writers, except for the forgivable lies of someone whose job is massaging egos into action. Writers were loyal to him because he was loyal to them. As Robert Fulford says, "Once he decided he was going to print Leonard Cohen, he was printing Leonard Cohen; that was it, to the end." (His loyalty had limits. Austin Clarke was so abusive to M&S staff that Jack suggested he look for another publisher. "What you need more than anything else," wrote Jack, "is a good swift kick in the ass.")

Legend had it that he never read the books he published, a story even some of his staff believed. It was nonsense. He read manuscripts constantly and carefully, usually at home. *Maclean's* got it right in 1963: being known as a publisher who didn't read manuscripts appealed to him, and he encouraged the rumour. "I haven't read it," Matt Cohen remembered Jack saying to him about *Johnny*

*Crackle Sings*, "but I hear it's great and that's all I need to know." He fed Atwood the same line about *The Edible Woman*, and like Matt she helped spread the story that Jack wanted told. He published lots of books he didn't personally like (pretty much all the poetry) but he didn't buy books blind. In 1959, when twenty-five-year-old Leonard Cohen showed up at his office with a manuscript, Jack bought it after reading just a few pages. He wasn't buying a book: he was buying the real product in the room, the young man in front of him. "We're going to publish this guy," he thought. "I don't give a shit whether the poetry's good."

In his retirement, Jack said his main innovation as a publisher was that he went looking for Canadian books. He watched the literary magazines and academic quarterlies for new voices. He maintained connections with librarians, professors, journalists — anyone who might suggest a writer or an idea for a book. To increase the firm's national representation, he made a very public tour of western Canada in search of manuscripts. "He Roams Afar to Find a Book," read a headline in the *Winnipeg Tribune*. Encouraged by Gabrielle Roy, he published French-Canadian writers in translation, including Roger Lemelin, Marie-Claire Blais, and Hubert Aquin. He launched national series like the New Canadian Library, the Canadian Centennial Library, and the Canadian Illustrated Library. When M&S began calling itself "the Canadian Publishers" in advertisements in the early fifties, it published about ten Canadian books a year. By 1963, when the phrase began appearing on its books, it was publishing more than fifty a year and on its way to a hundred. Competitors said there weren't that many publishable books in the country. "The Canadian Publishers" wasn't a boast anymore — it was a statement of fact.

**THE SPICE-BOX OF EARTH
(1961)
Leonard Cohen**

★★★★

He wanted a cheap paperback, not the usual slim hardcover. "I want an audience," he told his publisher. "I am not interested in the Academy." He got both: cloth and paper editions, with the cover cut out to introduce the face of McClelland & Stewart's newest poet.

A good part of the reason for Cohen's popularity was that he took poetry back to an earlier time, a time when love poems were love poems instead of ironic deconstructions of love poems. When he likened a lover's breasts to "the upturned bellies / of breathing fallen sparrows," he meant it — or his fans believed he meant it, which amounts to the same thing. No one understood better than Cohen the truth of the adage that the key to any performance is sincerity. If you can fake that, you can do anything.

Like Robert Weaver at the CBC, Jack created an audience at the same time that he was making a literature. He had to. Instead of the usual print runs of two thousand or so, he announced printings of ten thousand copies or more, creating a stir in the trade and the press. (He printed a *hundred thousand* copies of each title in the mail-order Centennial Library series, announced as "the most ambitious event in Canadian book publishing history.") Aided and abetted by staff such as Peter Taylor and Catherine Wilson, he staged some of the most memorable publicity stunts in the history of publishing anywhere. Guess which of these campaigns (all planned) was cancelled after sober second thought:

- caribou-skin gold pokes, some with real nuggets, sent to reviewers with Pierre Berton's *Klondike*
- packets of candied ginger and ground coffee included with review copies of Brian Moore's novel *The Luck of Ginger Coffey*
- miniature jockstraps with a book about sexism and racism in professional football
- with *The Snakes of Canada,* small boxes with a snake-sized hole and a label identifying the contents as "one of the hundreds of species described in the book"
- real estate signs on Toronto lawns declaring "Your Neighbour Is a Jew" to promote Rabbi Gunther Plaut's book of the same name
- a cocktail for *The Last Spike* called the Last Spike*

Jack did print advertising only to keep book review editors and authors happy. He preferred radio or television coverage, the free publicity of buzz. When Atwood objected to the publication date for *Lady Oracle* because she was due to have a baby that month, he suggested she could have the baby on television. "What if I die in childbirth?" she asked. "Great publicity," he said.

---

* The promotion for *Your Neighbour is a Jew* never happened. The rest all did.

It worked. Sales went up, from $1.5 million at the start of the sixties to nearly $5 million at the decade's end. Authors became well known, and a few well paid. For tens of thousands of Canadians who would never attend a poetry reading at the Bohemian Embassy, see a copy of *blew ointment* magazine, or get a free book from Coach House Press, CanLit was born.

Jack, meanwhile, nearly went broke. The number of copies sold increased, but so did the number of unsold copies, which reduced or erased the profits. In 1967 M&S achieved record sales with a record number of titles and lost money. Canada Council grants couldn't help a company the size of M&S, and Jack didn't believe in them anyway (he supported grants for writers but not publishers, because he thought they diluted a publisher's instincts). The company stayed afloat, barely, on Farley Mowat, Pierre Berton, and ever larger loans.

After M&S's financial problems became public in the early seventies, everyone had a theory to explain them. Too many Canadian books, not enough good books. Overexpansion. Too much money tied up in inventory. Distribution problems. A president with no head for business. Sloppy editing. The loss of textbook business. Competition from foreign publishers. Too much debt. Not enough debt.

"Jack cared a great deal more about his authors than about his books or his company," said Peter Newman. "He was the only businessman I have ever met in my life who figured his business was to better the human condition," said Farley Mowat. "He cared for books more than profit," said Pierre Berton.

They believed what they wanted to believe, what he wanted them to believe. But they were wrong. Jack didn't publish Canadian books for the sake of publishing Canadian books. He did it because he believed — impossibly, naively, and once in a while correctly — that Canadian books would sell.

**WRITING GOT HARDER** for Margaret Laurence. Two months after picking up her Governor General's Award for *A Jest of God*, she wrote to Jack, "It makes me laugh bitterly when I think that years ago I believed that one's second novel would be easier, and then that one's third would be easier, and so on. But no. They get more difficult all the time."

Life, too, got harder. Laurence had begun drinking heavily at the parties that were part of colonial life on the Gold Coast — not as much as many of the men, but more than their wives. After she and Jack finally divorced in 1969, she became a serious daily drinker. She was very lonely and, as she said, art is hard.

She was in Canada for the year, writer-in-residence at the University of Toronto. Given little to do, she printed her own posters advertising her presence to the university community and visited dozens of classes. In November she bought a three-season cottage on the Otonabee River, just south of Peterborough. She spent the next three summers there, writing what would become her last novel. Jack had a sign made for her: "No visitors allowed between Monday and Friday. An important work is going on." He signed it J. G. McClelland, "servant and publisher."

By January 1973 the draft was done. In the spring she found a surrogate for her marriage in the new Writers' Union of Canada, keeping herself busy and loved as the mother of the tribe. She sold Elm Cottage and came back to Canada for good in August, settling the following spring into an old house in Lakefield, Ontario, twenty miles upriver from her cottage.

**THE DIVINERS (1974)**
**Margaret Laurence**

Laurence put everything she could think of into her last novel — every memory, every narrative trick, every character, including many she had already written about. The resulting book is crowded and repetitive, sure, but Morag Gunn is still Laurence's most fully realized character after Hagar Shipley.

The real problem is the writing, much of which reads like lazy commercial fiction. It also hasn't aged as well as *The Stone Angel*, maybe because getting old never gets old. The very bits that helped it become a bestseller — what Phyllis Grosskurth in the *Globe* called Laurence's "extraordinary gift for describing sexual union" — seem most dated now, especially the cringe-inducing loss of Morag's virginity to her English professor and arguably the worst line in all of CanLit, another partner's invitation to "Ride my stallion, Morag."

*The Diviners* came out in May 1974. For the launch, M&S's new publicity manager, Patricia Bowles, won Jack's heart by suggesting a divining contest on the grounds of the Ontario Science Centre. A representative from the regional Conservation Authority agreed to supervise and people came from across the province. Laurence remembered CTV journalist Helen Hutchinson winning the contest; another account says three competitors found the target, a spot where two streams crossed under the bank behind the centre. Laurence hid in the bushes, drinking from a bottle hidden in M&S editor Anna Porter's purse.

By mid-July, *The Diviners* was number one on the *Star*'s national bestseller list. It won Laurence another Governor General's Award and sold over 200,000 copies in paperback alone. She tried several times, but she never wrote another novel. "I did my books when I was given them to do," she wrote in her journal shortly before her death.

> Seven of the fourteen turned out to be books of adult fiction. I wish many people could understand this. Well, they don't & won't. I guess I seem some kind of strange person because I have not published an adult novel for twelve years. And won't & can't. Lord, don't they know how anguished that has been for me? No. Why should they?

## Chapter 12

# The New Romans

I do not belong to any nation,
I hurl sharp poems at the world
—George Jonas, "Five More Lines"

**SOME SAY SHE** was born Mavis de Trafford Young, some say Mavis Leslie Young. Her father was probably Captain Albert Young, a British immigrant to Montreal. She usually told people he was an artist, a painter; he sold office furniture and dreamed of painting. Until recently we thought her mother was American, and few knew her name, partly because her daughter never spoke it. Turns out her mother was Benedictine Weissman, a Canadian of German heritage who said she was Romanian and went by "Bennie" and, for a time, "Jimmy," her name after she ran away from home and worked in Toronto as a man.

Bennie was arrested and sent back to her parents in Montreal, "properly garbed." Eight years later, in 1921, she was arrested again, this time in upstate New York, for cohabiting with a married man. She served three months in prison and was deported home, where she seems to have met and married Captain Young pretty much in the train station. Mavis was born the following summer.

At age four Mavis was sent to a French-language Catholic boarding school. "The only thing I remember," she told an interviewer, "is my mother putting me on a chair and saying, 'I'll be back in ten minutes.' She just didn't come back." Four years later, by which time the family was living part of the year across the river in Châteauguay, she found herself in an English school, learning her prayers and the alphabet all over again.

Her father died of kidney disease in 1932, or possibly by his own hand. Her mother promptly married a man with whom she had been having an affair, moved with him to New York, and packed off ten-year-old Mavis to a blurred succession of relatives, guardians, and boarding schools in Canada and the U.S. She finished high school in farming country, about thirty miles from Poughkeepsie, in the first year of the war.

That summer, at eighteen, she returned on her own to Montreal. She lived at first with her former nanny, then in her own apartment, downtown on Mackay Street. She worked for the Canadian National Railway and the National Film Board. Sometime before her twenty-first birthday she married a recent conscript, a jazz pianist named Johnny Gallant. Johnny went away to war, and with so many other men gone with him, Mavis Gallant landed a job in June 1944 as a feature reporter for a weekly Montreal newspaper called the *Standard*. She wrote about nurses in the Yukon, war brides arriving in Halifax, the high price of books, the Dionne quintuplets, the fashion for Freud, childless marriages. Her French opened a door on stories all over the province; her left-wing idealism drew her to articles about social workers and urban poverty. She had her own column for a while, a weekly review of radio shows that was cancelled after an advertiser complained she was making fun of jingles, and a film column that ended when a theatre chain pulled its ads in response to one of her reviews.

Meanwhile, she wrote for herself. Poetry left her around the time she left home, and she switched to prose: short stories, plays, attempts at novels. A colleague at the *Standard* showed two of her stories to her husband, one of the editors of a Montreal literary magazine called *Preview*. They were published in December 1944, her first literary publication. She kept writing, but aside from one story in the *Standard* that was also read on CBC Radio, she didn't show her work to anyone else or try to publish it. She didn't think she was ready, and she was afraid to find out.

The war ended and Johnny came home. The couple found themselves with little in common beyond an affection for American jazz and Russian literature; they divorced in 1948, when Mavis was twenty-five. Meanwhile, her reporting had attracted the attention of the RCMP, who visited the *Standard* to investigate her political activities. She decided that journalism was "a life I liked, but not the one I wanted." In the spring of 1950 she handed in her notice at the *Standard* and mailed a short story to the *New Yorker*. She planned to send them three stories; if they rejected all three, that would be that. They liked the first story and asked to see another. They bought the second one.

She went to New York to meet William Maxwell, the *New Yorker*'s fiction editor. Her first *New Yorker* cheque was waiting for her when she got home, for $600 (her pay at the *Standard* was then fifty dollars a month). She showed it around the office and bought herself a red alligator bag with gold trim from Birks for seventy-five dollars. She decided to give herself two years to find out if she could make a living from writing. Paris seemed the place to start — a clean break, "a place where I had no friends, no connections, no possibility of finding employment." A boyfriend in public relations at Air Canada got her a free plane ticket; her boss at the *Standard*, John McConnell, gave her $500 (perhaps for solving his problem as much as hers).* She left Canada with a typewriter, a year's pay, and a hell of a nice purse.

**THE OTHER PARIS (1956)**
**Mavis Gallant**

★★★

Janice Kulyk Keefer says in her book about Gallant that "she doesn't get better and better as she goes along — she was preternaturally good to begin with." I know what she means but I don't agree, and I doubt Gallant would have. She was better from the start than any of her Canadian contemporaries at the kind of writing she did, better than all but a few writers in the English language. But this is still a first collection by a young writer, and it shows, mostly in an irony that is at times just a touch too heavy, clever and powerful but not yet under control. Her lonely, scared characters too often become objects of laughter instead of sympathy. The trick, as she soon learned, was to make them both at the same time.

---

* Besides the RCMP, it seems that Mrs. McConnell was also happy that Mavis was leaving her husband's employ.

**THE MOMENT THAT** Canadians began imagining themselves as writers, they began to leave. They had few domestic models to encourage them otherwise, and they faced substantial obstacles to domestic authorship, among them a publishing industry intent on selling foreign books and a readership too preoccupied with economic progress to care about most kinds of writing — or about anything but "wheat, railroads and politics," as one writer fired back from exile in 1892. "I published a novel in Canada," said another in 1851. "I might as well have done so in Kamschatka." Aspiring writers grew up on British, French, and American books and magazines. At a professional level, their decision to publish in and move to cities like Paris, London, Boston, and New York wasn't about giving up one country for another. It was about moving from the margins to the centres of continental and transatlantic literary markets — markets that included Canada.

Like their predecessors, ambitious Canadian writers who began writing in the 1950s aimed their ambitions elsewhere. Pierre Berton and Farley Mowat sent their first manuscripts south, Berton to New York and Mowat to Boston. Margaret Laurence and Margaret Atwood both tried to interest American publishers in their first novels before sending them to Canadian publishers. "Because," said Mordecai Richler, "I didn't want to be taken for that pathetic provincial, the Canadian writer, I wouldn't allow my first novel to be compromised by the imprint of a Toronto publisher and went out of my way to have *The Acrobats* published in England." He was partly kidding — he published his first novel with a London press because that's who agreed to take it (with major revisions) — but only partly.

**GREEN WATER, GREEN SKY
(1959)
Mavis Gallant**

★★★★

Gallant's first novel tells the story of a mentally ill American woman in Europe of the 1950s, told at different times and from different perspectives. The green of the title isn't a pastoral green; it's the green of rot and disease. In one sense it's an old European story: *Death in Venice* with Aschenbach played by Americans. But Mann's rot was cultural while the rot for Gallant is in families, and the disease is psychological, not mythical. Her story is more American than European, more Freudian than Jungian.

Mostly it's a running portrait of a group of lonely, homeless people, told with intelligence, precision, and compassion. It's hardest to see the last in Gallant's writing, but that doesn't mean it's not there. She just doesn't like to point it out for you.

Berton went to Toronto as a stepping stone to New York. (*Maclean's* made him a nationalist and he stayed.) Norman Levine left Montreal for London in 1949 with the manuscript of his first novel and a promise from McClelland & Stewart to distribute it at home if he could find a publisher in England. Richler left the next year, arriving in Paris a month before Gallant. Over the years he gave many reasons for leaving, partly because TV shows and magazines kept paying him to tell the why-I-left-Canada story. He told an NFB filmmaker that "novelists are regarded as something of freaks in Canada." He told *Chatelaine* he left "to flee home and family," and that he stayed in London because it was cheap and he could work without a labour permit. His biographers have turned up additional reasons, like getting passed over as editor of his college newspaper, and because he found cheap prostitutes in Paris and a literary culture in London in which heavy drinking and clever abuse were normal.

The idea of becoming a writer in Canada didn't occur to Gallant any more than it did to Richler. "Canadian writing," she wrote in the *Standard*, "never hurt anyone's feelings." She chose Paris because it left her alone to live as she liked. When Canadian interviewers inevitably asked her why she had moved or stayed there, she often answered with a question: "Have you ever *been* to Paris?"

Arthur Hailey left for lower taxes and warmer winters. Margaret Laurence left for love, for her husband in 1949 and for a lover in 1962. Anne Hébert left because Quebec before the Quiet Revolution was a "*désert littéraire.*" To be a writer then, she told *Le Jour*, was "to be condemned to damnation" or, at best, "to display an immoderate taste

**ONE-WAY TICKET (1961)**
**Norman Levine**

Neither its Canadian distributor Jack McClelland nor Canadian readers much liked Levine's previous book, the travel book/ memoir *Canada Made Me*, but Jack nonetheless acquired Canadian rights to his first collection of short stories, *One-Way Ticket*. It's nine stories, the first and longest of which is about a Canadian writer living in St. Ives, Cornwall, where Levine and his family had themselves settled. In the last story, the narrator returns to Levine's hometown of Ottawa after an absence of some twenty years and learns the old lesson that you can't go home again. "I felt like a vagrant," he says at the end.

It's a better book than the few reviews I've found (almost all British) thought it was. They had read so much Hemingway and Fitzgerald by that point that it was all they could see in it.

for idleness." She left for Paris in 1954, found a French publisher for her first novel, and lived there for most of the rest of her life. Even after her Quebec City publisher declared her first novel the fastest-selling book in Quebec history, Marie-Claire Blais told CBC Radio that "I am not happy here and will have to leave to develop my talent. I want to go to Paris where the atmosphere is freer," she said. "One can write what one pleases there without any fear." After a year in Paris, she lived for most of the sixties in Massachusetts.

Irving Layton made his name through a fulsome introduction to one of his books by William Carlos Williams, then America's most important poet. American critic Edmund Wilson was instrumental in Blais's career, helping her win the fellowship that allowed her to leave Quebec and describing her as "in a class by herself" in his book *O Canada: An American's Notes on Canadian Culture*. Margaret Laurence's big break came with the announcement that Alfred A. Knopf of New York was publishing three of her books on the same day. "It certainly isn't common practice," said Knopf himself in a full-page ad in the *New York Times* on June 14, 1964. "I have no reason to believe that this has ever happened until now.... I don't think anything I could say about her singular gifts (or my pride in discovering her) could possibly be more impressive than this unusual gamble." The gamble didn't pay off in the States — unlike Atwood and Munro, Laurence never achieved an international reputation — but it made her the talk of the literary year in Canada.

The two Canadian writers who became celebrities in the 1960s were both made famous by America. Early in 1965, two California admen, Howard "Luck" Gossage and Dr. Gerald Feigen, read Marshall McLuhan's *Understanding Media*. The pair had a sideline in what they called "genius scouting," and they figured they'd found one. They flew to Toronto and, over dinner at the Royal York Hotel, convinced McLuhan to let them represent him. In May they introduced him to New York's media elite. In August they took him to San Francisco for a McLuhan festival in a converted firehouse. The *San Francisco Chronicle* called him "the hottest academic property around." Covering the festival for the *Herald Tribune*, Tom Wolfe wondered if McLuhan might be "the most important thinker since Newton, Darwin, Freud, Einstein, and Pavlov." A star was made, not born. *Understanding Media* sold 100,000 copies in an American paperback edition. A follow-up selection of McLuhan's deepest thoughts, *The Medium Is the Massage*, sold a million copies worldwide.

The spotlight was smaller for Leonard Cohen but stayed on longer. In 1967, American folksinger Judy Collins's version of "Suzanne" landed Cohen his first singing performances in the U.S., at several group concerts that included the Newport Folk Festival in July. In September he appeared on CBS's *Camera Three*, singing some songs, reading some poems, and peering poetically into store windows on Broadway. *Camera Three* was a highbrow Sunday morning show with a small budget, but it was national television, not a fading folk festival in Rhode Island. Cohen's appearance on it generated the greatest audience response in the show's fourteen-year history. Columbia Records released his first record, *Songs of Leonard Cohen*, on December 26. It failed to chart in Canada but reached eighty-three in the U.S. and thirteen in the U.K. That summer, McClelland & Stewart sold out its first printing of Cohen's new *Selected Poems*, five thousand copies. An American edition sold another 25,000 copies, and Bantam reprinted 1961's *The Spice-Box of Earth* in a virtually unprecedented pocketbook edition. "He is the best-selling poet in Canada," said a happy Jack McClelland. "In fact, he may be close to the best-selling poet in North America." The poetry had much to do with that, but it's not an accident that the bestselling poet in Canada was first a successful singer in America.

**THE MEDIUM IS THE MASSAGE (1967)**
**Marshall McLuhan and Quentin Fiore**

The best-selling Canadian book of the 1960s was turned down by seventeen publishers. Assembled by Jerome Agel and designer Quentin Fiore, *The Medium Is the Massage* was published in paperback before the hardcover edition from Random House, an unusual move. "We didn't have the time to wait a year to get Marshall's message into the hands of the people," said Agel. McLuhan contributed the title and approved the layout and text.

It's McLuhan for Dummies: an accessible, pocket-sized primer on his big ideas to date, with lots of illustrations, especially naked women and *New Yorker* cartoons. Agel called it "the first book designed for the TV age." The *New York Times* suggested that readers call McLuhan rather than debunk his theories by buying something as obsolete as a printed book, and provided his phone number at the University of Toronto.

**NO ONE WHO** participated in the CanLit boom — readers, civil servants, booksellers, critics, teachers, publishers, writers — lived or worked in a national vacuum. They took their affections and their influences where they found them.

Richler's model was Saul Bellow. Mavis Gallant's favourite writer was Proust. Rudy Wiebe learned from a play by Goethe that he could write about his own place. Michel Tremblay's early influences were Jean Ray, H. P. Lovecraft, and Edgar Allan Poe. Margaret Laurence found a licence to write in *As for Me and My House* and *The Mountain and the Valley*, but the contemporary writers she most admired were the Irishman Joyce Cary and the Australian Patrick White. Alice Munro told an interviewer in 1972 that "in terms of vision, the writers who have influenced me are probably the writers of the American South...Eudora Welty, Flannery O'Connor, Carson McCullers, Reynolds Price, James Agee. And Wright Morris. I'm sorry these are all Americans but that's the way it is."

It was the way it was because of the reach and quality of America's cultural exports, and because of the absence of home-made alternatives beyond a few scattered markers. "In most parts of Canada," said Richler in 1961, "only Mazo de la Roche and snow have been there before you." Atwood says she found the lack of literary ancestors liberating, like being handed a blank sheet of paper. Like everyone else, she learned how to fill the page from writers elsewhere — from Sylvia Plath, for example. Al Purdy learned how from D. H. Lawrence, Marie-Claire Blais from Baudelaire, Pat Lowther from Pablo Neruda. George Bowering calls William Carlos Williams his father, Charles Olson his hero, and Robert Duncan his mentor. Ginsberg's in there somewhere too.

The single most influential book of poetry of the CanLit boom was *The New American Poetry*, an anthology published in 1960 that defined half the country's anglophone poets and gave the other half something to complain about. Canada's first creative writing programs, at UBC and Concordia, were both modelled on the Writers' Workshop at the University of Iowa. The Readers' Club of Canada copied America's Book of the Month Club; McClelland & Stewart got the idea for its Centennial Library from Time-Life books. Jack's publishing role models were both Americans, Bennett Cerf at Random House and Alfred Knopf. He especially respected Knopf, from whom he got his interest in high-end literature and his conviction that good publishers publish authors, not books. "I learned more from Alfred than I ever learned from my father," he said.

Things were no different outside the mainstream. Alternative theatre in Toronto began by imitating alternative theatre in New York, at first by staging American experimental plays and then by applying American methods to Canadian plays. In the same program notes in which Ken Gass declared that the Factory Theatre Lab would present only original Canadian works, he said the best model for those works was American alternative theatre. Canada's most radical newspaper of the 1960s, Vancouver's *Georgia Straight*, was based on the *Los Angeles Free Press*. Marty Ahvenus's Village Book Store stocked American small presses beside the Canadians: books from City Lights, Oyez, White Rabbit, and Open Skull, little magazines like *December*, *Kayak*, and *ManRoot*. Coach House books belonged there, not in the Canadiana section at Coles.

Universities hired thousands of foreign professors. As the size and number of Canadian universities grew, the proportion of Canadian faculty plummeted, from 82 percent in 1951 to 53 percent in 1971 (Quebec was all that kept the figure above half). By 1971, three-quarters of new hires were foreign-born. Rates were higher still in the humanities and the arts, areas in which Canada was thought to have no history and therefore no experts. Future writers attending university in English Canada

**TEN GREEN BOTTLES (1967)**
**Audrey Callahan Thomas**

Thomas's first book, *Ten Green Bottles* contains stories born of her experiences working as an orderly at a psychiatric facility in upstate New York, studying for a year in Scotland, and living with her husband and two children in Ghana in the mid-sixties. You wouldn't know that from reading the stories — you can usually tell what country or at least what continent you're in, but unlike Mavis Gallant and Alice Munro, Thomas isn't much interested in specific places or times. She's a romantic, not a realist.

The stories range from conventional to experimental, from tales of a virginal college girl and a lonely housewife to an ellipsis-dotted collage about a woman giving birth to a dead child that was Thomas's first published story (in the *Atlantic Monthly*), the first story in the book and its best, a four-star story in a two-star book.

weren't just reading mostly British and American books, they were also taught mostly by British and American professors. Besides the institutional preference for foreign credentials, Europe and America provided a much larger academic labour pool, including many who were increasingly keen to leave their homeland. Nobody knows how many war resisters came to Canada during the Vietnam War, partly because the real number includes many partners and parents of draft dodgers and deserters. The usual guess is fifty thousand, most of them college educated. Many who stayed (more than half) ended up working in universities or elsewhere in the cultural sector. Margaret Atwood's husband and Anansi employee Jim Polk was a war resister; so were writers Doug Fetherling, Judith Merril, and William Gibson.*

The Canada Council replicated the structure of American foundations — the same executive positions, the same reliance on advice from research councils and voluntary associations. Like them, it administered its own fund and so wasn't dependent on the whims of Parliament, unlike the British Arts Council. The first speaker at the Council's first meeting was the president of the Rockefeller Foundation, there to welcome the new body and offer his advice, along with representatives from the Carnegie Corporation and the Ford Foundation. Historian Jeffrey Brison, from whose work these details come, argues that the notion of state support for the arts in Canada isn't "a rejection of the American model of private philanthropy but the adaptation of that model ... to a system of corporate patronage in which the nation-state was the major patron." At the other end of the cultural spectrum, the anxiety about American popular culture that prompted Minister Fulton's new obscenity

---

* Anansi's bestselling book in the 1960s was the *Manual for Draft-Age Immigrants to Canada*, a slim one-dollar paperback prepared by Toronto's Anti-Draft Programme, for which Coach House was the first printer and Anansi the agent. Published in six editions between 1968 and 1971, the manual sold more than sixty thousand copies, mostly on American college campuses.

Stan Bevington won't confirm Victor Coleman's statement that Coach House printed fake passports for war resisters. "I will admit," he says, "to having printed the letterheads for countless little companies' job offers. I will admit to having the technical skills to make a rubber stamp that looked like it was done by someone else."

law in 1959 mirrored American anxiety about popular culture—
like the comic-book burnings of the mid-fifties and the Senate
Subcommittee on Juvenile Delinquency, before
which Fulton eagerly appeared while still an
opposition MP.

America's star role in Canada's cultural
explosion was the vigour and clarity it gave
Canadian nationalism. By the Centennial,
almost half of Canadian manufacturing
industry was under foreign control, mostly
American. "No other Western nation," said
Pierre Berton, "had given up so much of its
economic control." But economics wasn't the
real worry: from a purely economic point of
view, nobody knew whether foreign investment
in Canada added up to a net gain or a loss for
the country, any more than we know now.
The worry was culture. In 1965 McClelland &
Stewart published a short book called *Lament
for a Nation* by George Grant, a philosopher at
McMaster University. Grant put the problem
succinctly. "Branch-plant economies," he said,
"have branch-plant cultures."

Grant had in mind things like Toronto's
O'Keefe Centre, opened in 1960 and home to
a steady parade of big-ticket foreign musicals,
ballets, and concerts (its first production was
a tryout for the Broadway musical *Camelot*,
bedtime listening in Kennedy's White House).
Off Front Street, however, the picture looked
increasingly different. Within a few years of
Grant's book, even a casual observer of English-
or French-Canadian literature would have to be
wondering if the opposite wasn't true: that branch-plant economies
create *national* cultures. *Littérature québécoise* emerged in opposition to English-Canadian power and French-Canadian literature;

**THE NEW ROMANS: CANDID
CANADIAN OPINIONS OF
THE U.S (1968)**
A. W. Purdy, ed.

A collection of fifty opinions of
America by Canadian writers
and academics, suggested and
introduced by Purdy. Mostly
they're angry, with Vietnam
heading the list of reasons
why. Ray Souster contributes a
"Death Chant for Mr. Johnson's
America." Ray Smith's short
story recommends sending
the President a Centennial gift:
"an American tourist's ear in
a matchbox." Québécois poet
André Major says, "The best I
can hope for is that Americans
will die of remorse before the
hatred of the world is unleashed
against them."

*The New Romans* was far
and away Purdy's most popular
book, selling thirty thousand
copies and splashing its
editor all over the news. It also
prompted a sequel of sorts, a
collection of Canadian opinions on Canada called *Notes
for a Native Land*, compiled by
a twenty-three-year-old undergraduate at Victoria College,
Andy Wainwright.

English-Canadian literature took off just as the rest of Canada began to look more American than English. "Some of us who read Grant's elegy," said his student Matt Cohen, "took it not as a statement of fact, but as a challenge."

House of Anansi would have never happened without Dave Godfrey's rage at American materialism and military power, or Dennis Lee's quieter but no less deeply felt disappointment with Canada for succumbing to it. Unlike Coach House, Anansi didn't have a defining literary or production style. What held the press together, said the poet who lived in the basement, was that "they were all, at some fundamental level, against more or less the same thing: Americanism, with its republican brutality and hatred of culture." For Fetherling and many other Americans and Canadians in the late sixties — after the assassination of Martin Luther King, the fights with police in Chicago, the massacre at My Lai — being against America was a full-blown philosophy, "a grid for responding to the world." And a reason for writing and publishing Canadian books.

In October 1970, the United Church of Canada sold English Canada's oldest publishing house to an American company. Ryerson author Milton Acorn was so angry he refused royalties from his new publisher. Gwen MacEwen said in a letter to the editor of the *Toronto Daily Star* that she wished she could take her books back. Al Purdy told the *Globe and Mail* he would risk a lawsuit rather than let an American company publish his new book. Graeme Gibson led a protest in front of the statue of Egerton Ryerson at the Ryerson Polytechnic Institute. Gibson climbed a ladder, draped an American flag over the statue's right arm, and led a chorus of "Yankee Doodle Dandy" for the television cameras. In response to the outcry, the provincial government appointed a royal commission that led (eventually) to federal block grants and protective legislation for Canadian publishers.

From the Massey Report to Ontario's Royal Commission on Book Publishing, America's enormously successful cultural industries gave Canadian cultural nationalism something to define itself against. At the same time, American counterculture gave

Canadians their most visible and exciting examples of political, social, and cultural rebellion. All Gibson would have had to do to make his protest against America fully American was to burn the flag he had brought. In Quebec, FLQ member Pierre Vallières took inspiration and the title for his book *Nègres blancs d'Amérique* from America's black liberation movement. "We got a political sense," says Daphne Marlatt, "through American culture, how they were getting politicized. The civil rights marches, the peace marches, the music. National identity became important to us because of a growing sense of how strong American culture was, just across the border, and how important it was for us to have our own sense of who we were, where we were."

MAVIS GALLANT ARRIVED in Paris in October 1950. She stayed in a hotel in Saint-Germain-des-Prés recommended by a musician she knew in Canada. Her room was all done up in red velvet and wasn't very clean. She explored the city she'd studied from a map pasted on the wall of her apartment in Montreal.

After a month she realized she was seeing too many expatriates — including young Mordecai Richler, who in her memory didn't like Paris, partly because he couldn't speak French, and was a "bit of a brat" (the two had been introduced in Montreal by a friend who heard they were both planning a move to Paris). She went to the Canadian embassy, which kept a list of French people with rooms to rent. "I wanted a good bourgeois family who had roots in France — in Paris — so I could study them," Gallant said at age eighty-six. "I sound as if I was collecting butterflies." She found a young family with two little boys who lived on a respectable street on the Right Bank, rue de Monceau. Her Left Bank friends were horrified. Her room was large and the radiator small. "If I am working," she wrote to a friend, "my hands get numb and I have to soak them in warm water. I can now understand why the French never sleep alone. They aren't any sexier than any other race, but it's the only way of keeping warm." She wrote a story called "The Other Paris," about a young American woman who fails to find the Paris of her imagination.

She spent much of the next ten years roaming around Europe from city to city, hotels and *pensions* and apartments — "collecting butterflies" — writing notes in her journals that became the precisely observed places and people of her fiction, often stories about other wanderers. In the spring of 1951 she used another cheque from the *New Yorker* to rent a flat on the French Riviera, in Menton. She lived in Austria, in Italy and Sicily, a winter in Strasbourg, two years in Spain. The agent she'd found in New York was selling her stories without telling her and keeping the cheques, leaving her doubting herself as a writer. She was so poor in Madrid in the spring of 1952 that she pawned her typewriter for fifteen hundred pesetas, her clock for a breakfast, her watch, her grandmother's ring, her clothes, and her books. "I hang on the edge of hunger," she wrote in her journal. "We are all as pale as this paper. I can't wear my blouses because they are dirty and I haven't soap for them and for me and it has to be me."

**THE PEGNITZ JUNCTION (1973)**
**Mavis Gallant**

★★★★

Gallant's fifth book focuses on stories about postwar Germans: a fashion model, a concentration camp survivor, a former member of the Hitler Youth, a teacher, a travel agent, and a well-to-do family and their servant. She described it as "a book about where fascism came from.... Not the historical causes of fascism — just its small possibilities in people."

As reviewers complained, the novella's experiments in narrative perspective are more distracting than effective. The best stories in the collection are "The Old Friends," in which a Jewish survivor dines with a German police commissioner, and "An Autobiography," a devastating dramatic monologue by a teacher at a private girls' school in Switzerland. They're the only two from this collection that Gallant didn't include in her *Selected Stories*, so either I'm wrong or she was.

> Chambrun [her agent] says he has sold only one story in twenty months.... I am revolted at the idea of exposing any more of the things I write. I have always despised the people who write "for themselves" — who keep things in a trunk as if they would fade or disintegrate in the light and air. Now I begin to understand it. Each story means as much to me as the one before. I think of each one as honest. If they are *bad*, that is something else.

I wish there were someone who could say "yes" or "no," "keep on writing" or else "give it up." As long as there is no one

but myself I shall of course keep on, but can I be trusted?
And how could I trust an editor? Is he free to trust himself?

In June she learned from the *New Yorker* about her agent's fraud.
She got her confidence back, and some of her money.

She also found an editor she could trust: William Maxwell, her
editor at the *New Yorker* until his retirement in 1975. "I owe him
everything," she wrote in the introduction to her *Selected Stories*.
When she published her first collection in 1956, nine of its twelve
stories had already appeared in the *New Yorker*. By the mid-sixties
she had published more than forty stories in the magazine and
they had signed a first-reading agreement, guaranteeing it the first
look at anything she wrote. The *New Yorker* ultimately printed 116
stories by Gallant, less than only John O'Hara and John Updike.
An unpublished *New Yorker* cartoon (probably made for her as a
private joke) shows two bored socialites over the caption "Mavis
Gallant in the *New Yorker* every so often is all the Canadian culture
I can stand."

From 1960 until she died, Gallant lived in a rented apartment
at 14 rue Jean Ferrandi, on the Left Bank between Montparnasse
and Saint-Germain-des-Prés. CBC TV's Fletcher Markle visited her
there in 1964 for a two-part documentary about her on *Telescope*.
The cameras show a woman in her early forties in a small, bright,
modern apartment with paintings on the walls and flowers on
the table. She spoke French and was almost entirely unknown by
Parisians as a writer in English. "Most of my European friends," she
told an interviewer in 1977, "have never heard of the *New Yorker*."

Gallant's generation grew up believing that real careers and
real lives happened elsewhere. One of the biggest changes for the
next generation — both a cause and a consequence of the CanLit
boom — was that ambitious Canadians began staying home. They
stayed partly because moving somewhere else had got harder: more
rules, more paperwork, more lawyers. But they also stayed because
Canada looked better than it had to any generation before them —
more exciting, more possible. For every young Canadian who wandered around Europe in the fifties, a hundred hitchhiked across

Canada in the late sixties and early seventies. Many also went to Europe or California or somewhere off the usual map for a while, but they came back: Hubert Aquin from France, Leonard Cohen from Greece, Graeme Gibson from England, Margaret Atwood and Alistair MacLeod from the United States, and even, eventually, Mordecai Richler and Margaret Laurence. Richler said he had always intended to return. Maybe so, but surely it didn't hurt that by the time they came back, he and Laurence were both better known at home than anywhere else. There wasn't a Canadian literature when they left; there was when they came back, and they were two of its stars.

## Chapter 13

# Cocksure

**The 15-year-old girls
I wanted when I was 15
I have them now...
I advise you all
to become rich and famous.**
**—Leonard Cohen, "The 15-Year-Old Girls"**

IRVING LAYTON HAD the largest ego of any Canadian poet yet born. The beat poets, his American contemporaries, howled. Layton *roared.* "You are not aware of the vast reservoirs of self-confidence that I possess," he told an interviewer when he was seventy. "The truth of the matter is that if I hadn't had that arrogance, I could never have survived the kind of shit that has been hurled at me. I never had the slightest doubt at any time after I had written 'The Swimmer' that I was a great poet."

He was born Israel Pincu Lazarovitch, the last of eight children of a Jewish bookkeeper in a tiny village in northern Romania. His mother called him Issie or Flamplatz, Yiddish for "exploding flame." He began calling himself Irving in his late teens and added Layton at age twenty-four, he said because it rhymed with Satan.

His family had immigrated to Montreal in 1913, when he was still a baby, leaving behind laws that kept Jews out of schools and good jobs and would have forced his oldest brother into the Romanian army. They rented a four-room flat in an alley off St. Elizabeth Street above St. Catherine, the heart of a French ghetto becoming a Jewish ghetto. French and Italian boys taunted and stoned *les maudits juifs*, most joyfully at Easter. Issie and his brothers learned how to fight and run across rooftops to avoid the gangs. His father hid in his room, finding in religion the understanding that evaded him in this new land. His mother supported the family by selling groceries from their home. She was a hard woman, a master of vicious, carefully cadenced Yiddish curses that Layton said twisted his soul and helped his poetry.

He claimed to be his elementary school's "best scrapper." His father forced him to attend Hebrew school after classes, which made him into an atheist scrapper. At thirteen, with his father dead, his mother moved to a rickety shack ten blocks north, at 4158 City Hall Avenue (now a small park). Layton went to Baron Byng High, Mordecai Richler's school twenty years later. He had to repeat his first year, dropped out for a while in Grade 10, and was expelled a month before graduation for refusing to apologize to a teacher he disobeyed. But he had another teacher, Amos Saunders, who thundered poetry aloud in class and turned Layton into a reader who spent every cent he could find on adventure novels and British poetry from Diamond's used bookstore. By fourteen he was writing his own poems. "He'll grow out of it," said his mother.

By sixteen he was keen on communism. He joined the Young People's Socialist League and hung out at Horn's Cafeteria, drinking five-cent cups of coffee and arguing politics with socialists, communists, and anarchists. The Wall Street crash of 1929 left him and millions of others with little to do but lots to talk about.

His mother had remarried that spring and he moved out on his own, renting a room on brothel-lined De Bullion Street. He paid the rent by teaching English to Jewish immigrants in his room and at the Jewish People's Library. Because the Quebec government wanted to develop farming, tuition at McGill's agricultural college was free for the first two years and fifty dollars a year for the last two, a quarter what the main campus charged. He enrolled in September 1933 and did his best to ignore cows and classes equally.

Instead he joined the boxing, wrestling, and debating clubs, started a political discussion club, and wrote fractious left-wing commentaries in the student paper. In the classroom he earned two F's in his first year and five in his second year and failed third year altogether. After a year he tried again, this time managing a 71 percent average. He graduated in May 1939, so far as I know the only Canadian poet with a B.Sc. in agriculture.

He was by then a married man. The first of Layton's five wives was Faye Lynch, a short, overweight junk-dealer's secretary from Yarmouth, Nova Scotia. Faye's parents invited them to Nova Scotia, where Layton sold Fuller brushes door-to-door in Dartmouth. His in-laws offered to set them up with a stationery store; he agreed and then bolted, leaving Faye in Halifax and hitchhiking back to Montreal. She followed him, so he joined the army.

On leave four months into his training, Layton met Betty Sutherland, a painter and the sister of a McGill poet who had just launched a little mimeographed poetry magazine called *First Statement*. He read his poems to her, rhyming verses of romantic sentiment and praise for the proletariat. She thought they were awful. He began seeing Betty every leave, and his poems got better. Jealous, Faye told the army her husband was a Communist. The army didn't much care, since it had already decided he was incompetent and gave him an honourable discharge in June 1943.

**THE SWINGING FLESH**
**(1961)**
**Irving Layton**

Layton's second book for M&S combines short stories and poems because he felt they complemented each other. They don't. It was a serious mistake to publish the short stories at all, but both would have done better left on their own.

The autobiographical stories have nothing to recommend them as fiction: they're just sketches with a vaguely literary ending tacked on, like someone leaving or a door closing, something to signal the end and squeeze profundity from it. A friend, the critic Desmond Pacey, called them "stiff." Layton said, "They're the best thing since Joyce's *Dubliners* and they have much more to say."

He moved in with Betty, in an apartment above a thrift store on University Street. She worked in restaurants and painted; he worked where he could and wrote. He published poems in her brother's magazine and helped him edit it, together with a young poet he had met at a lecture at McGill, Louis Dudek. In 1944 he wrote "The Swimmer," one of his best-known poems, in under five minutes on a napkin in a restaurant on St. Catherine. "It was like hearing the voice of God," he said. God didn't offer to pay for it, so he began printing slim chapbooks at his own expense, starting with *Here and Now* in 1945.

**BALLS FOR A ONE-ARMED JUGGLER (1963)**
Irving Layton

The short opening poem, "There Were No Signs," suggests a welcome development for Layton, a book that would temper his contempt for us mortals with understanding, maybe even sympathy. This is not that book. His declared subject — the organized evil of the twentieth century — and his concern about it are legitimate, but the poems are overwhelmed by their self-righteousness. In one he hears the scream of an insect, a scream "I alone heard." That's Layton's problem: he thought he was the only one to see the truth, the only one who wasn't a hypocrite, the first to have had sex, the first to think and feel, the first poet. In casting himself as superhuman, he made it all but impossible to write human poems. Occasionally one slipped out. But as the *Globe and Mail* said in its review, most of his work is a "nasty bore."

Betty and he had a son the following year and Faye finally gave him the divorce he wanted. He married Betty, and her father helped them buy a little farmhouse in Côte-Saint-Luc. Layton taught history and poetry at an orthodox Jewish high school and completed an M.A. in economics, with ambitions of becoming a professor. Poets beyond Montreal began to notice his poems. In 1953 the American poet Robert Creeley wrote to ask if he could publish some. Al Purdy wrote a fan letter from Vancouver. His sixth chapbook brought praise from William Carlos Williams and a postcard from Ezra Pound. "Cheers," it said.

His relationship with Betty deteriorated into what they optimistically agreed to call an open marriage. In the summer of 1955, now forty-three, he met a twenty-one-year-old Australian woman named Aviva Cantor. "I have left you for another," he wrote to Betty in a poem, "who wears black panties and is as crazy as the birds." He wouldn't ask Betty for a divorce and never married Aviva, his partner for over twenty years. He did agree to buy her a wedding ring, but when he took her to the store, he changed his mind and bought a bracelet for Betty instead. Leonard Cohen was with them that day; he bought Aviva a ring, put it on her finger, and said, "Now you're married."

The chapbooks kept coming, many of them from a private press that Layton, Dudek, and Ray Souster had spun off from Souster's magazine of the same name, *Contact*. In November 1956, a small

American press associated with Black Mountain College in North Carolina published his first real book, a selection of his poems to date called *The Improved Binoculars*. William Carlos Williams provided an introduction in which he said Layton was capable of anything. "There will, if I'm not mistaken, be a battle: Layton against the rest of the world. With his vigor and abilities who shall not say that Canada will not have produced one of the west's most famous poets?"*

When Layton learned that the *Globe and Mail* was planning a story about Ryerson's refusal to distribute the book in Canada, he was ecstatic. "This may be it," he wrote to his publisher, "the long-expected break we've been hoping for, the long gravy slide into fame and fortune. The *Globe and Mail* story will be carried all over the country, I being the first Canadian poet to be so treated. I expect it will become national news, a cause célèbre." The *Globe* story turned out to be noncommittal, its headline — "Poet Attacks Publisher's Attitude" — not what he wanted. The *cause célèbre* never happened, but Williams's introduction and the poems themselves pushed the book into a second printing and won Layton a $4,000 award from the Canada Foundation. Most important, he received a letter from Jack McClelland inviting him to submit his next book to McClelland & Stewart.

**IRVING LAYTON MADE** Canadian poetry almost hip. Unlike many of the American beat poets, he wasn't himself much of a bohemian. He liked his house kept tidy, his tea on time, and his bank account comfortably balanced — exactly the man he scorned in his poetry. He didn't use drugs, drank very little, and hated hippies. He supported Kennedy against Castro, America against Vietnam, and Trudeau's invocation of the War Measures Act. Even his much celebrated virility was just poetry. "He was inhibited sexually," says

---

* In 1964 an anonymous reviewer noticed a framed letter from William Carlos Williams hanging in Raymond Souster's living room. It said, "I read Irving Layton, but try as I may it doesn't come off. Maybe the age is at fault. But somehow when I read you, I am moved. Have confidence in yourself. You've got it."

Aviva, the woman who was with him longest. "He was unable to penetrate me for a long time."

But in print or for an audience, Layton was a hot-blooded Jewish satyr, "The Lusty Laureate from the Slums." He was the poet who finally made Canadian poetry "respectably unrespectable," said Jack McClelland. "For his ice-breaking role, everyone writing in Canada today should be profoundly grateful," said Edward Lacey. "Irving Layton gave us fire," said Kenneth Hertz, one of many young poets who circled around him in Montreal. "Without his influence," said Gwen MacEwen, "Canadian poetry would have been nowhere." "Irving Layton converted a whole generation to poetry," said Leonard Cohen.

**THE CAPTAIN POETRY POEMS (1971)**
bpNichol

A combination of Nichol's childhood and adult affections, *The Captain Poetry Poems* collect twenty pages of drawings and poems about their eponymous superhero, a flying poet with a rooster's head. See Captain Poetry eat a meal and take a bath. Hear him sing. Watch him write a sonnet when his girlfriend tells him he can't. Thrill to his contest for the affections of Blossom Tight, the girl with "the biggest cans in town."

Nichol later said that the Captain Poetry poems were ironic, intended to satirize the "macho male bullshit tradition in canadian poetry." I'm sure they were, but I think he was also saying goodbye to the poet he had dreamed of becoming before he learned what poetry was. "I loved you so," says bp to CP. "But now it seems / in all my dreams / you just look funny."

In September 1959, Irving and Aviva returned to Montreal from a summer in Europe courtesy of the Canada Council. Jack McClelland had arranged a party for his new author, a joint launch at the palatial Windsor Hotel with romance novelist Katherine Roy, billed as "Beauty and the Beast." Layton was becoming known for his barbs on CBC's *Fighting Words*, and the attention, together with Roy's socialite friends, filled the room. "Everyone in T.V. or Radio, in the Newspaper or Bookselling game was present when I made my great entry," he wrote to a friend the next morning. "And what an entry it was! I was flanked by Aviva on one side, and by Leonard Cohen on the other, and I needed both of these to run interference for me as the mob bore down." His book, *A Red Carpet for the Sun*, was M&S's second experiment with original paperbacks, after *The Double Hook*. It sold five thousand copies in three months — English Canada's bestselling book of poetry since Robert Service's *Songs of a Sourdough* in 1907.

In February, *Star Weekly* — circulation just under a million — published a lengthy profile by June Callwood, a pivotal article that completed Layton's transformation from private-press poet to public figure. "As a boy he was in a fist fight every day," read the deck. "Now he shocks readers with his sexy rhapsodics." One photo showed him lifting weights at the YMCA, "looking more like a caged animal," said the caption, than a "wistful poet." "We had a hunch Layton can be sold successfully," Jack told Callwood. "His poems don't suffer from the problem of most modern poetry, which has developed so that poets are communicating only to other poets and the average person can't comprehend the symbolism."

In March Layton gave a reading at the Montreal Museum of Fine Arts from which more than a hundred people had to be turned away for lack of even standing room. The orthodox high school he'd been teaching at for fourteen years fired him a month later, just after he picked up his GG for *Red Carpet*, because of complaints from parents about "anti-Jewish ideas" in his books and his classroom. That stung, but over the next two years he had fifteen offers to read or teach at universities to console him.

One of the most talked about cultural events of the early 1960s was the first Canadian Conference of the Arts, held over three days in May 1961 at Toronto's new O'Keefe Centre. On the first night, five poets — Layton, Earle Birney, Gilles Hénault, Jay Macpherson, and Leonard Cohen (who also read for the absent Anne Hébert) — read for two hours to an overflow crowd of about two hundred. "Take away the socialites, hangers-on, 'culturettes' and merely curious," said the *Globe*, "and it might still safely be claimed that the remaining crowd of earnest listeners was one of the largest live audiences ever faced by Canadian poets." As expected, Layton stole the show, prefacing his reading by calling the speakers at the opening plenary session that afternoon pompous "rightniks" and the greatest threat to art. "I don't want to hear poetry discussed in terms of scholarship, education, or responsibility," he said, "but in terms of love and madness and ecstasy." He illustrated his point by reading a new poem, "Why I Don't Make Love to the First Lady." "Of course I could have her!" he began. But "I'll wait until / the international situation has cleared. / After that it's every poet for himself."*

When Layton read at Le Hibou coffee shop in Ottawa in January 1962, the lineup ran two blocks down the street. He gave a second reading two hours after the first to accommodate the overflow. "This sort of thing would have been inconceivable ten years ago," he said. "Writing poetry then was something to be enjoyed privately and not talked about, like masturbation." In April 1963, Jack McClelland said his best poets were outselling his average novelists. Canadian poetry, ventured a *Globe and Mail* headline, had entered its "Golden Age."

And the man with the golden voice was just getting started.

**LEONARD COHEN GREW** up twenty years later a few miles from the Lazarovitches' ghetto, in a sun-filled Westmount home with a maid, a nanny, and a gardener.** His father was a Montreal-born clothing manufacturer, his mother a rabbi's daughter from Russia. He went to Roslyn Elementary and Westmount High, a Protestant school with about a third Jewish students, and Hebrew school two afternoons a week, as well as the synagogue on Saturdays with the family (one older sister) and for Sunday school.

In his early teens Cohen became interested in hypnosis and tested his new skill on the maid by instructing her (successfully) to remove her clothes. He wandered downtown late at night, by himself and then in a friend's Cadillac. When he was fifteen, he picked up a copy of the Spanish poet Federico García Lorca's selected poems outside a used bookstore, read "Gacela of the Morning Market," and became a poet. He said Lorca's voice hooked him, but the poem's eroticism likely didn't hurt.

He became a musician the same year. In the park behind his home he saw a young Spanish man playing a guitar flamenco style, surrounded by a group of admiring girls. Leonard liked the style,

---

* He had already mailed the poem to President and Mrs. Kennedy, with a copy of *A Red Carpet for the Sun*.

** It's for sale as I write, for $1.6 million.

and he liked the girls. He bought a Spanish guitar from a pawn-shop and convinced the Spaniard to teach him. After three lessons the Spaniard killed himself, presumably for reasons unrelated to Leonard.

In September 1951, just turned seventeen, he showed up at McGill University. People remember him with a notebook or a guitar, playing by himself on the lawn or for friends at parties. He had Louis Dudek for modern literature and Hugh MacLennan for the modern novel. Mostly he avoided classes, spending his time drinking, writing, girl-watching. He had to take supplementary exams to graduate, with a 56 percent average and a B.A.

He showed some of the poems he was writing to MacLennan. "Perhaps a time is coming which will be more favourable to your kind of talent than the present or the last twenty years," his professor wrote to him. "Eliot should soon be embalmed. . . . I do have a feeling that a brighter day, a singing day, must come if there is to be any future at all, and then a poet will want to make his work resemble music instead of an equation enclosed in a cryptogram."

Cohen invited Irving Layton to read at his fraternity house and became a regular at the Laytons' farmhouse in Côte-Saint-Luc. In March 1954 his first published poems appeared alongside Layton's and Dudek's in a Montreal little magazine. The following summer, Layton took Cohen with him to the Canadian Writers' Conference in Kingston and invited him onstage to read and play a little guitar. In May 1956 Contact Press published Cohen's first book, *Let Us Compare Mythologies*. It sold about four hundred copies, half of them on campus. Margaret Avison liked it the most of seven new poetry books she reviewed for the first issue of the *Tamarack Review*. "The discovery of a new poet of stature is so exciting that it is hard to repress superlatives. . . . Poetry is Leonard Cohen's natural language."

That fall he went to New York to become a writer, with graduate school at Columbia as a cover for his family. Publishers rejected the novel he sent them and he hated grad students — "Nothing smells more like a slaughterhouse than a graduate seminar," he wrote in his next novel — so he came home. He sold some poems to Robert

Weaver's *Anthology* and read at Dunn's Birdland with a jazz group, like the poets he'd seen in New York. On Layton's suggestion, he went to Toronto and pitched Jack McClelland a book of poems. Jack bought it on the spot, with a $400 advance.

In December Cohen used a $2,000 grant from the Canada Council to go to London and write another novel. He lived in a boarding house in Hampstead (a few blocks from Richler, though they didn't meet till several years later), wrote every day, and finished the draft of *The Favourite Game* in March. London in spring was too cold and rainy, even with his new blue raincoat, so he went to Jerusalem, Athens, and finally Hydra, a little Greek island in the Aegean with a small expatriate community of writers and artists. He rented a house, and when his grandmother left him $1,500, he bought his own, three storeys of whitewashed stone two hundred years old, with no plumbing or electricity. And he met Marianne Jensen, a beautiful young Norwegian woman with a six-month-old son and a soon-to-be-ex-husband.

For the next five years Leonard, Marianne, and her son moved between Hydra and Montreal. McClelland & Stewart published his second book of poems, *The Spice-Box of Earth*, and a New York press brought out *The Favourite Game* after readers' reports left Jack with little choice but to reject it. *Saturday Night* and the *Toronto Daily Star* called Cohen the best young poet in Canada. On CBC Radio Phyllis Webb said, "It is hard to imagine Leonard Cohen opening his mouth to speak and uttering anything but poetry." Reviews for *The Favourite Game* were more bad than good, but there were many more of them, and some of the bad reviews helped sales by complaining about the sex and dirty words. It earned about US$2,700 in its first year, including $750 for an excerpt in *Playboy*-style *Cavalier* magazine (*Playboy* itself said no, along with *Esquire*, the *New Yorker*, and *McCall's*).

In October 1964, McClelland & Stewart organized a tour of six Ontario and Quebec universities for Cohen, Layton, Earle Birney, and Phyllis Gotlieb. The Ontario government helped pay for it and an NFB camera crew followed the tour. "Everywhere, the readings have been packed," reported the *Toronto Daily Star* when the tour came to Hart House at the University of Toronto. "I'm wondering whether this is supposed to be Canada's answer to the Beatles," said Layton on the *Pierre Berton Show*. Layton got the most media attention, but he thought Cohen outshone him and said so, calling him "the most exciting member of the peripatetic quartet" and "the most talented, the most promising young writer in this country." The NFB obviously agreed: the film that was supposed to be a documentary about the tour became a biography of Leonard Cohen, *Ladies and Gentlemen...Mr. Leonard Cohen.*

**THE FAVOURITE GAME**
(1963)
**Leonard Cohen**

Like many first novels, *The Favourite Game* is mostly about its author. It's a *Bildungsroman*, almost, about a young Jewish boy growing up, going to college, and falling in love. Lawrence Breavman is a poet, a man who wants to believe in magic but doesn't and so decides to enchant everyone else but himself. "I want to touch people," he says, "to leave my brand, make them beautiful. I want to be the hypnotist who takes no chances of falling asleep himself. I want to kiss with one eye open."

It's a juvenile, self-centred novel. And like everything else Cohen wrote, it's also honestly and at times beautifully written. As Vancouver *Province* columnist Lorne Parton said in one of the kinder reviews, "I'm not sure that Leonard Cohen has something to say, but whatever it is, he says it well."

By December Cohen was back on Hydra and back at work on his new novel. He wrote up to twenty hours a day, with help from hash, acid, and especially speed. Ray Charles's *The Genius Sings the Blues* played until it warped in the sun. He ate little and often nothing at all for days. After he finished he went on a ten-day fast and dropped to 116 pounds with a fever of 104 degrees. He needed intravenous protein injections and had to spend weeks in bed, looked after by Marianne.

*Beautiful Losers* was published in March 1966 in Toronto and New York. The poet who said he didn't want to write for academics had written a novel only academics could like. Almost the only good reviews were from scholars, who knew a book that needed an article to explain it when they saw it. The kindest of the mainstream reviewers was likely Robert Fulford, who called it both the "most interesting" and the "most revolting" book ever written in Canada. The only completely positive review I've seen was bill bissett's in *Alphabet*, and I'd guess he was at least as high when he wrote it as Cohen was when he wrote the book.

Despite aggressive promotion by M&S (including hints before publication that it was likely to be censored), *Beautiful Losers* sold only a thousand copies in Canada, plus another two thousand worldwide. Cohen wanted to write for a real audience, not just for other poets and academics. In the summer of 1966 he decided he wasn't going to get one with poetry or fiction. He packed his guitar and left Montreal for New York. He would follow popular poetry where it had gone, into music, and become a songwriter.

**FLOWERS FOR HITLER
(1964)**
Leonard Cohen

Cohen's third book of poetry is a much more obviously modern book than its predecessor, no longer drawn to Bible stories and fairy tales. Instead of a falcon, the first poem references a mushroom cloud. There are poems about the Canadian parliament, Quebec separatists, and, of course, Hitler. In another sign of the times, many of the poems are about and/or affected by drugs, often wandering off into stoner surrealism. The clearest sign of Cohen's new territory, though, is the tone. Where *Spice-Box* was romantic, *Flowers for Hitler* is more often angry, sarcastic, cynical, or just plain disappointed. Never mind the Holocaust, "I would like to remind / the management / that the drinks are watered / and the hat-check girl / has syphilis."

**WHEN IT STARTED** up in 1959, *Canadian Literature* set out to review every book of poetry published in Canada. That year it found twenty-four books and reviewed them all. In 1971 the journal predicted that between 250 and 300 books of poetry would be published in Canada during the year, and announced that it was abandoning even the pretence of reviewing them all.

Literary titles increased threefold over the 1960s; poetry titles, tenfold. Between 1960 and 1973, almost six hundred poets published more than 1,100 books of poetry, not counting anthologies. "Canadians," said Margaret Atwood, "had become the highest per capita consumers of poetry in the world." Pierre Berton sold more books, but Irving Layton, Leonard Cohen, and, in Quebec, Gilles Vigneault were the rock stars of CanLit.

There were many reasons for this. The example of Irving Layton, the doors he opened. The sexy rebelliousness of the American beat poets. Later, the sexy rebelliousness (and the audiences) of American popular music, especially after Dylan crossed the barrier between poetry and song. More leisure meant more time to read and write for leisure's sake. The same was true for fiction, but you could publish poetry yourself; all it took was a library with a copying machine and the ability to fold a piece of paper in half. Most of the new little magazines published mostly (and often only) poetry. At the same time, mainstream media remained open to poetry for content and a lingering desire for its cultural credentials. When Robert Kennedy was assassinated, *Star Weekly* called Al Purdy and asked him for a poem. The *Globe and Mail* reviewed as much poetry as the *Tamarack Review*. The Hudson's Bay Company used poems in its ads. The CBC let poets read on television...Poets. Reading poems. On *television*. In 1967 they let Margaret Atwood read on TV with tape holding her glasses together. Everybody, it seemed, was writing poetry, and everybody wanted a piece of it.

**LOVE IN A BURNING BUILDING (1970)**
**Al Purdy**

Faced with titles like "After the Miscarriage" and "Ballad of the Despairing Wife," you can understand Jack McClelland's reaction that this wasn't the collection of love poems he was expecting. Most aren't love poems but poems about love, its ups and downs, what Purdy calls "the whole comic disease." "Love is a broken oath by day," he says, "but sealed at night again." Judging by this book, he and Eurithe did a lot of both.

The poems are at times adolescent, selfish, even stupid: but so is love. As a collection, its main problem was that readers had seen well over half the poems before. Purdy revised some of the older poems for this collection, but as Atwood said in a smart review for *Canadian Literature*, "It's like eating leftovers — they've been warmed up but you know you've had them before."

They turned to poetry to replace the world as advertised with the world as imagined. Poetry was a way out with a way in, an easy and inexpensive challenge to bourgeois respectability within the safety of bourgeois respectability. In Layton's "Paging Mr. Superman," the poet walks into a hotel lobby of the affluent society, asks the desk clerk to page Mr. Superman, and then stands back and watches the flash of hope in people's eyes that he might actually appear, that something heroic might wake them from their comfortable, boring lives. "What offends us / is the sanities," said Atwood in *The Circle Game*. "The houses in pedantic rows, the planted / sanitary trees." "This is a time of starvation," Leonard Cohen told a reporter the summer he became a songwriter. "We're just hungry for something human."

For Layton, Cohen, and many of the rest of the boys, the hunger often took the form of a dick-swinging masculinity that easily became sexism, especially for Layton. "The poetry of the future will be written by the guy with the biggest fist," he wrote to a friend in 1956. He called one book *The Swinging Flesh*, another *Balls for a One-Armed Juggler*, in part because it pleased him to imagine a woman in a bookstore asking for Layton's balls. "I placed my hand upon her thigh," he wrote in a poem.

**THE STUDHORSE MAN (1970)**
**Robert Kroetsch**

★★★

"Horny books abound," began the *New York Times* review of *The Studhorse Man*, "but few of them are about horses." A comic mash-up of the western tall tale and the *Odyssey*, Kroetsch's Governor General's Literary Award-winning novel has more cocks in it (and more words for cocks) than any Canadian novel I know. Its hero, a studhorse man who gets more work than his stallion, calls his "Old Blue." The narrator likes to fold his notes for the book into little hats and wear them on his penis in the bathtub.

It's a good book, more controlled than Cohen's equally dick-driven *Beautiful Losers*, less misogynist than Layton's dick-driven poems, as or more fun than Bowering's equally postmodern send-up of Canadian history, *Burning Water*. It's very Canadian, and very funny — two words that don't often appear together, at least at Rideau Hall.

> By the way
> she moved
> away
> I could see
> her devotion
> to literature
> was not
> perfect.

If you think he's being ironic, read his memoirs, letters, and biographies. Layton's sexuality was mostly a self-constructed myth, but it was a myth he believed.

Layton, Purdy, Cohen, and many others all began writing poems for the oldest reason for poetry, the oldest reason for anything. But it wasn't all they wrote poetry for or about. Mostly, they wrote poetry because they believed in it. When McClelland & Stewart launched Purdy's anthology of new Canadian poets, *Storm Warning*, at Toronto's St. Lawrence Hall in March 1971, twelve hundred people showed up at the four-hundred-seat facility. For a while, poets weren't the only ones who believed in poetry.

The backlash against poetry's popularity began immediately, led from the academy by Layton's old friend Louis Dudek. In his review of *A Red Carpet for the Sun*, Dudek said Layton had graduated from "Canada's most neglected poet to the most over-rated poet anywhere." Writing in the *Montreal Star*, he attacked M&S's 1964 tour as a prostitution of poetry, "popular buffoonery — and since Canadians don't know poetry anyhow, it passes for poetry." In 1969 he lamented "the degeneration of poetry to a teeny-bopper fad," an age of "Advertisements for Myself" led by fame-hungry poets, supported by Jack McClelland's thirst for sales and the media's thirst for celebrities, and fed by hippies looking for art that would endorse their immoral lives without making them think too hard. About the only good he could see was that "A collapse of this South Sea Bubble is no doubt inevitable and eventually the run for poetry will lose its interest."

Envy made him harsh, but he was right. In the 1970s academics and poets drove poetry back into the cloister, aided by the advent of specialized literary theory and the rising number of poets with academic positions. By the mid-sixties Layton had begun his long fade from the top of English-Canadian poetry, replaced by Purdy and then eclipsed by Cohen. In 1969 the prof-hater became a prof, picking up a tenured position (and wife number four) at York University. Cohen's career took off in 1967 but was from then on driven by music. He turned down a Governor General's Award for his *Selected Poems* in 1969, saying the poems themselves wouldn't permit it. He has since published just four books of original poetry in almost fifty years.*

Poetry continued to do just fine, song even better. But the age of poets was over.

**THE LAUGHING ROOSTER**
**(1964)**
**Irving Layton**

Layton was going to call his new book *Poems in Poor Taste* but decided it was more fun to watch reviewers realize that on their own. If nothing else, *The Laughing Rooster* is trademark Layton, still writing long-winded prefaces, still firing away at professors and social workers, still publishing dirty minded misogynist poems, including one in which his darling's heaving breasts are all that stop him from hitting her.

Reading this, you can understand why the *Tish* poets thought Layton and his humanist lyric line had exhausted themselves. Even Layton seems a little bored, tired enough of "affirming life" to consider stepping in front of a car. Maybe that's why in this book he goes back so often to rhyme: because rhyme means not having to think so hard about what comes next. Lust leads to dust, and so on, to the end.

---

* And now there won't be any more. Rest in peace, Leonard.

## Chapter 14

# George, Vancouver

**Through the feckless years we have come to the time
when to look on this quilt of lamps is a troubling delight**
**—Earle Birney, "Vancouver Lights"**

**IRVING LAYTON SAYS** he was born circumcised. Apparently, rabbis came from as far away as Russia to see the first Jew since Moses born without a foreskin. George Bowering says *he* was born sideways. I have a hard time imagining either event, but that's what they say. You could look it up.

There were mostly doctors and nurses in the room for the two days it took to bring George Harry Bowering into the world. (His father Ewart visited when he could get away from his bridge game.) For Layton's mother, her son's penis was a messianic sign. Bowering's mother, nineteen-year-old Pearl Brinson from Three Hills, Alberta, may have taken the difficult birth of her first child as some kind of sign, but she wasn't sure of what. In her son's baby book, under "Remarks," she put a question mark.

Bowering was born and raised in south central British Columbia. He went to school mostly in Oliver, then more orchards than vineyards, where his father was a chemistry teacher at the new high school. He barely passed his father's class and was briefly expelled several times in Grades 10 to 12. He wasn't a bad student, just a bit rebellious and a class clown. They let him come back to write his final exams, and he passed.

He read westerns, science fiction, sports novels. "Literature," he says, "got me when my guard was lowered by books." He wrote songs, skits, poems, and stories, sang in the choir, acted, did stand-up. Mostly he played, followed, and wrote about baseball, reporting baseball news for the weekly *Oliver Chronicle* and the daily *Penticton Herald* while still in high school. He wanted, more than anything, to be a sportswriter.

After high school his girlfriend went to college in Victoria, so he did too. Then she dumped him and he dumped college and went and hid in the trees of northern B.C., working for a government survey company. On July 10, 1954, at age eighteen, he enlisted in the Royal Canadian Air Force. They put him to work at the Macdonald weapons training base in Manitoba as an aerial photographer, taking pictures of training targets for fighter pilots. He wrote for the base newspaper and published his first poem in a national magazine, twenty-six stanzas of rhyming verse called "The ABCs of the NHL" for Montreal's *Hockey Pictorial*.

Three years later he enrolled at UBC in Vancouver. Most days he hung out in the cafeteria below the theatre with Red Lane, an RCAF buddy from Macdonald, and Lionel Kearns, a new buddy from the Kootenays. Nights, he ranged downtown, looking for material for a novel he wrote and never published. He found William Carlos Williams in the library, and Kearns introduced him to Kerouac. In second year he published a parody of Ginsberg's *Howl* in the *Ubyssey* ("I have seen the best minds of this campus...") and a poem in the second issue of *Prism* about seaweed and death.

He graduated in the spring of 1960 with a B.A. in creative writing and history, then did a victory lap to prepare for a master's degree in English. During his M.A. studies he wrote a sports column for the *Oliver Chronicle* and an arts column for the *Ubyssey*, helped edit a poetry magazine, reviewed books for *Canadian Literature*, and sent poems to every little literary magazine he could find, including *blue grass* in Dobbs Ferry, New York; *Amethyst* in Wolfville, Nova Scotia; *Teangadóir* in Toronto; *Delta* in Montreal; *Mountain* in Hamilton; *Sun* in San Francisco; *South and West* in Fort Smith, Arizona; *Hawk & Whippoorwill* in Sauk City, Wisconsin; and *Wild*

*Dog* in Pocatello, Idaho. "Say he was a real sucker for his name in print," he explained in a note to future biographers.

And he got married. Angela Luoma was a third-year UBC student, half Finnish and half Anglo-Scottish. She was beautiful with green eyes and blond hair. They married in December 1962 at Vancouver City Hall and lived in an old apartment building on steep Yew Street. The following spring they heard his love poem to her, "Rime of Our Time," on CBC Radio.

One month later he submitted his M.A. thesis and got a book of poems accepted by Contact Press in Toronto. The University of Alberta in Calgary offered him a full-time teaching job at $5,200 a year and they moved in the fall to a furnished basement apartment, where he worked as superintendent to reduce the rent. It was cold and the wind never stopped, and the closest thing he could find in the city to an art gallery was a framing shop on 17 Avenue SW. When he wasn't teaching, they ran to Mexico.

In the fall of 1966 Bowering started a Ph.D. at the University of Western Ontario. Angela worked in a psychology lab, transplanting pigeon brains while George took his courses. They became close friends with Greg and Sheila Curnoe, then at the centre of the exploding London art scene that included the sculptor twins David and Royden Rabinowitch, clay artist Margot Ariss, poet/playwright James Reaney, guitar/jet designer Murray Favro, and the painters Jack Chambers, Ron Martin, and Tony Urquhart. Bowering sat in once with Curnoe's Nihilist Spasm Band, a jazz collective with homemade instruments that aimed somewhere just south of total noise. ("After ten beers," said the bar

**ROCKY MOUNTAIN FOOT:
A LYRIC, A MEMOIR (1969)**
**George Bowering**

The poet most associated with Vancouver won his first Governor General's Award for a book about Calgary. *Rocky Mountain Foot* collects poems from the two years he spent teaching at the University of Alberta in the mid-1960s, "a poet in cow country." It's *Tish* technique applied elsewhere: pay attention to the local, map it, name it. Cadillacs and churches, Natives in bellbottoms, dinosaur bones in Drumheller, the mountains, the prairies, the snow, the dust, and the wind, always the wind. The *Tish* rebellion against the lyric ego shows up in interruptions by other poets, found letters, local histories. But it's the traditional lyrics that make the book, poems like "The Plain," "The Name," and "Calgary." Unusually for poetry, it's also a good *book*, a collection held together by its setting, like Purdy's *North of Summer*.

manager, "they sound like Guy Lombardo.") He made the mistake of keeping time, so they took away his drumsticks.

The Centennial was a big year for Bowering, the year the "fuckin' Easterners" (as he still calls them) took notice. In April McClelland & Stewart published his first novel. Two weeks later he appeared on CBC TV talking about poetry of the sixties with Earle Birney, Victor Coleman, and bpNichol. In July he wrote his first book review for the *Globe and Mail*, and the *Globe*'s books editor William French interviewed him in August on CBC Radio. His poems appeared in the Oxford anthology *Modern Canadian Verse* and *The Penguin Book of Canadian Verse*.

Sir George Williams University offered Bowering its first writer-in-residence position. He quit his Ph.D. and he and Angela moved to Montreal, renting one of the few flats left available by Expo, a long, narrow series of rooms on Grosvenor Avenue, just off Sherbrooke in Westmount. He met loads of poets, locals and visitors brought to Montreal by Roy Kiyooka and others for the SGW Reading Series: Alden Nowlan, John Newlove, bpNichol, Robin Blaser, bill bissett, Al Purdy, Daphne Marlatt, Allen Ginsberg, and many others, friends old and new. Margaret Atwood was teaching at SGW that year; she remembers meeting the Bowerings at a party, Angela in a mini-dress and white go-go boots and George wearing a Donald Duck tie and quacking like a duck.

When the writer-in-residence gig ended, Bowering stayed on as an assistant professor of English. In April 1970 he won the Governor General's Literary Award for poetry for his sixth and seventh books, M&S's *Rocky Mountain Foot* and Anansi's *The Gangs of Kosmos*. "I'd given myself until 1971 to make it," he told the *Toronto Daily Star*. "It was just a little game I played with myself—just like at the beginning of the baseball season I write down who's going to finish in first place." He accepted the award at Rideau Hall, wearing a ruffled shirt under a bright green velvet suit with pearl buttons. The Governor General couldn't take his eyes off him.

IN A FICTIONALIZED memoir written many years later, the Bowerings and some of their friends remembered the arrival of the New American poets in Vancouver in the summer of 1961 as an explosion of light, a "Gigantic White Flash" that lit the sky above North Vancouver. The light, they said, burnt hicroglyphs into the wall of a brewery near the Burrard Street Bridge, addling the already addled minds of three young poets staggering home from drinking and dodging poet-hating loggers in the basement of the Hotel Georgia. A man appeared to them and said the flash was a sign. *You must find your calling,* the man said. *You must make harmonies for the new world unlike those of, say, Robertson Davies.*

> What did you do to us that summer? What did we let our-
> selves in for? It was an enchantment. The lovely enchantment
> of words. Did you save or damn us? You American poets,
> bent on your own salvation, damnation...
>
> The hangover lasted for decades. Did we ever recover?
> No, thank God. Yes, thank God. That was the real writing
> on the wall. They marked us as their own. We had to write
> our way out of that rapture we'd been caught up in, not to
> be overcome by it.

It all started in 1959, when Warren Tallman began teaching a third-year course in contemporary poetry at UBC. Tallman was from Tumwater, Washington, at the southern end of Puget Sound. While doing graduate studies at the University of Washington, he had met and married Ellen King, a grad student from San Francisco who knew poets associated with the San Francisco Renaissance — Robin Blaser, Jack Spicer, Robert Duncan. Warren fell in love with Ellen and, through her, with the poets she loved. They both got teaching jobs at UBC and moved to Vancouver in 1956.

In the fall of 1960, Tallman began teaching *The New American Poetry,* the anthology that had come out that spring, and intro- duced a generation to a new kind of poetry — for some a new world, "like that moment in *The Wizard of Oz,*" remembers poet Michael Boughn, "where the world suddenly switches from black and white to colour." The Tallmans invited the leading *New American* poets to give readings and informal talks at their home in Kerrisdale. Robert Duncan read in the basement to an audience on rented chairs. The giant Charles Olson slept upstairs. Robert Creeley spoke around the kitchen table late into the night. Allen Ginsberg and his beard talked in the living room. Students listened, talked back, read their own poems, emptied the fridge, borrowed the car, slept on the floor.

They didn't do it on their own — Tallman himself attributed the explosion of young writers at UBC in the early sixties to the openness of Earle Birney's teaching, the attention of George Woodcock's *Canadian Literature*, and the support of the Canada Council — but the Tallmans were fundamental to what happened next. "Ellen and Warren Tallman gave us everything," says Bowering in his memoirs. "Their house seemed to me to be the nerve centre of anything that was going to happen in verse all our lives."

Which brings us to 1961. That February, the Tallmans arranged for Robert Duncan to read at the first UBC Festival of Contemporary Arts. He read at noon. Some of the student poets in the audience asked him to read again that night. As he read to this smaller group, he talked to them. The students, says Tallman, let Duncan in. This wasn't your usual poetry reading. This was something closer to a conversion.

In the audience that night were George Bowering, Lionel Kearns, Frank Davey, Fred Wah, David Dawson, and Jamie Reid. At Tallman's suggestion, those six and others formed a poetry study group that met weekly through the summer of 1961. They contributed five dollars each to offer Duncan $100 to come back to Vancouver and talk to them about modern poetry. Duncan came up by bus, gave three lectures, and stayed for nearly a month.

It seems to have been Fred Wah who proposed a magazine. Wah suggested it to his friend Lionel Kearns, Kearns suggested talking to his friend George Bowering, Bowering suggested talking to his friend Frank Davey, Davey said let's ask Tallman, and Tallman suggested forming the study group first. At the group's last meeting, on a Sunday afternoon at the Tallmans' house in August 1961, they agreed to start a monthly poetry magazine. Duncan was there, a houseguest of the Tallmans on his last day in the city. He encouraged the idea and gave them the magazine's name, a polite anagram for *shit*.

The first issue appeared in September, mimeographed on legal-size paper. The masthead listed Frank Davey as editor, with Reid, Bowering, Wah, and Dawson as contributing editors. Kearns declined to be an editor but contributed all the same. Tallman helped out with money and beer. UBC unknowingly provided paper, printing, and stamps. They didn't want to wait for subscribers, so they just mailed it to university libraries and anyone else they thought might be interested. They offered to continue providing it free to anyone who wrote to the editor once every three issues. Al Purdy took them at their word; his letter published in the fourth issue said he liked bits of it and hoped they kept it up.

Established literary magazines were too slow in those heady days: by the time your poems came out in them, you'd moved on. At *Tish* you wrote your poems one week, showed them to the other editors the following week, argued about them the next, and then printed, addressed, and mailed them. Like *blew ointment*, it was more newsletter than magazine, what Davey called "a record of on-going literary activity, a record that preserved every roughness, insight, and stupidity." The whole point was to keep things moving, to circulate the proof and results of a *movement* — a *Tish* movement, as the running joke went.

It was a boys' club, with boys' jokes and mostly boys' poems. Tallman describes Vancouver Islander Gladys Hindmarch as a seventh, unnamed editor, but Davey says no women volunteered

**D-DAY AND AFTER (1962)**
**Frank Davey**

Davey's and *Tish* magazine's first book, a slim chapbook that sold for sixty-five cents. They're mostly poems about getting over a girl, first-year student Daphne Buckle (now Marlatt). She's the "D" in the title poem and the "Buckle" in the epigraph, from Hopkins's "The Windhover."

Wandering margins aside, they're traditional lyrics on traditional subjects. Their main fault is the assumption that something becomes important simply by putting it in a poem. Maybe all lyric poets have to assume that what happens to them matters more than what happens to you or me, or else they wouldn't be lyric poets. But the *Tish* practice of stripping away adjectives and other ornaments risks overexposing the arrogance. "I lose a pen this morning / the third / in two weeks / and my last / and now / I must go out and buy another."

as editors or helped out with production other than his soon-to-be wife, education student Helen Simmons. Hindmarch, who lived with the Tallmans for several years, didn't herself publish in *Tish*. Daphne Marlatt remembers her as "a kind of muse figure for the boys." (Not just the boys, apparently. Tallman said that when she walked outdoors, "the leaves on nearby trees would flutter into a welcoming dance.")

**VANCOUVER POEMS (1972)**
Daphne Marlatt

A little homesick, Marlatt wrote most of her *Vancouver Poems* while in Wisconsin with her husband for a year, before she left him and came home. Like the title says, they're poems about Vancouver: its places, people, and past. Gulls and the sea, the rain, Chinese grocers, the Sylvia Hotel, Lions Gate Bridge, a bakery on Robson, beer parlours on Pender, junk shops on Main. The poems have a cluttered, crowded feel to them, like those junk shops, like an archive. Her fourth book, it's her turning point, the book in which she worked out her differences from the boys in the band. It's still the *Tish* project of heeding the local, but on a larger and longer scale, letting a whole city, as she said in her journal, "speak *thru* the poems."

So was Marlatt, especially for Frank Davey. Then Daphne Buckle, she had immigrated to Vancouver from Malaysia with her family. She arrived at UBC in 1960 at the age of eighteen for what ended up as a double major in English literature and creative writing. Her first-year English teacher pushed her into joining a writing group of upper-year students, where she met Bowering, Davey, and Jamie Reid. Davey fell for her hard, spending more time writing poems to her than working on his courses. Like Hindmarch, Marlatt participated informally in *Tish* editorial conversations, and in her case published poems in it herself. But she knew it wasn't her sandbox. "I always felt perilously on the edge," she later told Bowering about her four years at UBC. "I never felt that I was part of even the *Tish* group."

Meanwhile, the Americans kept coming. Lawrence Ferlinghetti and Robert Creeley read at UBC's second Festival of Contemporary Arts in 1962; with the Tallmans' help, Creeley came back in the fall to teach creative writing for a year. Michael McClure ("Pat McLear" in Kerouac's novel *Big Sur*) came in 1964 and Jack Spicer in 1965. In May, Robin Blaser, Stan Persky, and Spicer read at the New Design Gallery on West Pender; Spicer stayed on and gave three lectures at the Tallmans'. Brand-new Simon Fraser University in Burnaby tried to hire Spicer, but after alcohol killed him in San Francisco, they offered Blaser the job. Blaser brought with him his partner Stan Persky, later co-founder of the *Georgia Straight Writing Supplement*, and became what his student Sharon Thesen remembers as an "enormous force as a poet-professor," the cen-tre of a circle from which came *Iron* magazine and writers such as Thesen, Brian Fawcett, and Michael Boughn.

The most important Canadian literary con-ference of the 1960s was neither a conference nor especially Canadian. Organized by the Tallmans and Robert Creeley, the Vancouver Poetry Conference was a three-week creative writing course combined with a non-credit course of evening poetry readings, held at UBC from July 24 to August 16, 1963. "Poetry in the morning, poetry in the afternoon, and poetry in the evening," remembered Tallman, and then parties and more poetry at the Tallmans' and at Jamie Reid's pad in Coal Harbour. They would have kept going all night if Ellen Tallman hadn't handed out sleeping pills. Creeley, Olson, and Ginsberg led the workshops. Robert Duncan came back for it. Denise Levertov and Margaret Avison (the only Canadian faculty member) came for a week; they were a bit outside the action, Avison partly because her father's death during the conference took her away early. Phyllis Webb, then teaching at UBC, interviewed the faculty for CBC Radio.*

Forty-one students took the course: eight-een Americans and twenty-three Canadians,

**NAKED POEMS (1965)**
**Phyllis Webb**

★★

A product of Webb's encounter with New American poets at the Vancouver Poetry Conference, *Naked Poems* was a radical departure from her previous books. Gone are the metaphysic-al conceits and philosophical musings, replaced by stripped-down snapshots of blouses on the floor, flies on the ceiling, sunlight through curtains. Much of the credit for the book goes to designer Takao Tanabe, who spread its fewer than 250 short lines over forty-six pages. Charitably, the space gives the poems room to breathe. Less charitably, it lends weight to what needs it, what couldn't be a book without it. This is the book that made Webb's reputa-tion, but today it seems a much lesser accomplishment than the poems that came before and after. John Robert Colombo got it about right in his review in the *Globe*: "A private achieve-ment, striking but not strong, a gift-book for lovers."

---

* The interviews were vetoed by Robert Weaver and never aired. Filmmaker Robert McTavish found Webb's working tape of *Five Poets* uncatalogued at Library and Archives Canada and used it to help make his 2013 documentary film about the Vancouver Poetry Conference, *The Line Has Shattered*.

including Hindmarch, Marlatt, and all the *Tish* editors but Davey. Many more audited or attended the readings. Bowering had finished his M.A. by then but somehow managed to register anyway, meeting Olson for the first time and hearing Ginsberg recite Shelley's "Adonais" on the grass, an experience that changed his direction as a poet. "I was electrified," he says. "I felt an honest-to-God *aura* around the person of Allen."

Some of it was that, the fame and charisma of the Americans. Ginsberg was by then a celebrity, notorious enough to attract undercover police to one of the after-parties at the Tallmans'. Charles Olson was a towering force, six feet eight of bristling intelligence and fierce devotion. For Duncan — for all of them — poetry wasn't a career but a calling. But what they had to say also made sense to many young Canadian writers, not just those in Vancouver. The poet, they said, isn't Layton's commanding ego, what Olson called the private self crying at any public wall. Instead of imposing yourself on your perceptions, let your perceptions shape your self. Don't impose form on content; let the content decide the form. Don't force traditions from other places and times onto your place and time; listen to your place, your environment, and let it show you what stories to tell and how to tell them.

It's not hard to understand how such an aesthetic, such a philosophy, would appeal to a generation of writers with only foreign traditions to go on, especially the part of that generation cut off by big mountains from the few places on Canada's existing literary map. The American imperative to write as you like about where you live gave British Columbia's writers a licence to create their own traditions — a rapture, as Bowering said, and a way past it.

FOUR OF THE five founding editors of *Tish* left the magazine in the summer of 1963, leaving Dave Dawson as the new managing editor. Frank and Helen Davey left for a job at Royal Roads Military College in Victoria, where he started a new magazine. Fred Wah and Pauline Butling went to the University of New Mexico, where he started a magazine. George and Angela Bowering went to Calgary, where he started a magazine. Jamie and Carol Reid stayed in Vancouver and eventually gave up poetry to work for the Communist Party of Canada. When they let him go twenty years later, he started a magazine.

Daphne Buckle became one of *Tish's* new editors during her last year at UBC. She married psychologist Alan Marlatt and they moved to Indiana, where she did an M.A. in comparative literature and wrote her first book. Gladys Hindmarch also became a *Tish* editor, then went to work at Vancouver City College. She married Clifford Andstein at the Tallmans' house in 1967. Warren Tallman gave the toast to the bride and Robin Blaser read a poem he had written for the couple.

*Tish* kept going until 1969. Its first two years are generally regarded as its best, after which its energy spread out with the editors and the Vancouver poetry scene moved downtown. Often left out of this story is how much of the scene was already downtown, clustered around so-called downtown poets like bill bissett, Gerry Gilbert, Judith Copithorne, Curt Lang, and John Newlove. To Jamie Reid in 1959, then still in high school, bissett especially was a highly visible presence in the city, "the embodiment of the truly hip, a real Ginsberg, a real Kerouac, right here in Vancouver." Copithorne and bissett both tried UBC but dropped out. "I never melted with the university scene," says bissett. Tallman tried to bring them in, inviting Gilbert and others to gatherings at his house in the early sixties. When bissett was charged with possession in 1968, Tallman put up his house for the bail money.

Most movement went the other way, from UBC to downtown. For starters, UBC didn't sell beer. The *Tish* crew drank at the Georgia

**STEVESTON (1974)**
Daphne Marlatt

★★★

Marlatt's fifth book grew out of an oral history project at UBC. She wrote the poems and sociologist Robert Minden provided the photographs. It's a powerful book, better than *Vancouver Poems*, I think because the smaller setting lets the book contain more of the subject within its canvas. But it has the same dedication to the local and the physical — to "perceive it as it stands," in the words of the epigraph. The title of the first poem asks the reader to "Imagine: a town" that's gone, a way of life lost during the Japanese internment and disappearing again beneath encroaching development. In a sense, *Steveston* is a version of Dennis Lee's *Civil Elegies*, except it's lamenting the loss of a real rather than a possible community. And America is not the enemy, never even mentioned. Canada did this to itself, twice.

and the Cecil Hotel, on the north side of the Granville Bridge, the closest bar to campus. Many of the downtown poets and artists favoured the beer parlour at the Hotel Alcazar, on the northeast corner of Dunsmuir and Homer, also the regular for nearby bookseller Don MacLeod and friends.

In the late fifties and early sixties, Vancouver's bohemia was on downtown Robson Street, among the shops and restaurants of German and other East European immigrants. Judith Copithorne met Saskatchewan friends Roy Kiyooka and John Newlove there, at the Little Heidelberg Coffee House or the public library at Robson and Burrard, where Newlove scrounged cigarette butts. Just up the street, Duthie's paperback manager, Binky Marks, bought ten copies of the first issue of *Tish* for twenty-five cents each and gave them away. George Bowering had his first taste of Al Purdy's wild grape wine at Doug and Hannah Kaye's bookstore across Robson from the library, a Christmas gift mailed to the Kayes marked as "books" (he said it reminded him of when they used to take tar off the streets and chew it, but worse).

Over the water, in a dark concrete basement near Broadway and Main, the Cellar jazz club hosted poetry readings perhaps as early as 1956. Hipsters brought bottles of whisky in brown paper bags and bought overpriced ginger ale and ice from the house. Jamie Reid remembers seeing bissett perform there in full fey mode, reading poems in a breathless falsetto while angry drunk men in their thirties and forties yelled "fruit" and "fairy" at him.

bissett and UBC student Brian Belfont ran their own reading series at the Black Spot, on Dunbar Street between West 27th and 28th. Also a jazz club, the Black Spot drew mostly students from nearby UBC and Lord Byng High School. bpNichol went there in his last year of high school. Frank Davey took Daphne Buckle there on a hopeful date in January 1961. bissett lived upstairs with his best friend, poet Lance Farrell. He read there many times, and at other clubs like the Flat Five on 4th Avenue and the Inquisition Coffee House downtown.

Artist/poet Roy Kiyooka began a poetry reading series in 1963 at the Vancouver School of Art (now Emily Carr University) in which several *Tish* and most of the downtown poets appeared. That same year, Milton Acorn started a poetry series at Vanguard Books on Granville Street, a stumble from the Cecil. Acorn built bookshelves for the store and fixed up a space in the back room where bissett, Maxine Gadd, Pat and Roy Lowther, Red Lane, Dorothy Livesay, and many others read.

In the mid-sixties, bohemia grew its hair and crossed the Granville Bridge, re-forming along 4th Avenue amid UBC's student ghetto. Students and artists lived in old apartment buildings and warehouses near Kitsilano Beach and English Bay. bill bissett, Martina, and baby Ooljah moved to Kitsilano around this time and lived in a variety of places, most famously a large warehouse space on the corner of Yew and York that produced *blew ointment* and epic parties. John and Susan Newlove lived upstairs; Gladys Hindmarch lived for a while in an apartment in the same building.

A few blocks inland, the Psychedelic Shop at 2057 West 4th Avenue provided incense, beads, and "many other Trips." The Phase 4 Coffee House across the street stayed open until three a.m. In the old Russian Community Hall at number 2114, the Afterthought staged rock concerts and a psychedelic dance and light show until one a.m. Dave Guy's Horizon Book Store, near the corner of 4th and Arbutus, stocked *blew ointment* and books from Coach House Press in Toronto, along with used books and records, amid "an air of intellectualism." At Kitsilano's western edge, left-minded UBC students opened a non-profit coffee house in an empty mattress factory at 10th and Alma. They left the old sign up, and the place became known as the Advance Mattress. Milton Acorn hosted another

**LETTERS FROM THE SAVAGE MIND (1966)**
Patrick Lane

Lane's first book, printed by Very Stone House, a small press he started in Kitsilano with bill bissett, Seymour Mayne, and Jim Brown. People generally called it the "very stoned house."

There are many stones in the poems too: stones in the ground and on beaches, stones thrown at birds and dogs, stones on graves. Some of the poems wave the *Tish* colours with their wandering margins, but they're mostly traditional lyrics, perceptions of moments: a kid on a tricycle, cougar tracks outside his door, an otter rolling in the sand. There's a fair bit of drugs, alcohol, and death, as there was in Lane's life. "I think it was poetry that saved me from killing myself or killing others," he says in his superb 2004 memoir, *There Is a Season*. (It's more about gardening than writing poems. There are, however, many stones in it.)

reading series there, and bissett performed his first chant poem there in 1966 or '67, at a benefit for Vietnamese communist leader Ho Chi Minh.

On February 1, 1967, Leonard Cohen came from New York to appear at UBC's seventh Festival of the Contemporary Arts. He was scheduled to read at the 400-seat Frederic Wood Theatre, but the crowd that showed up was too large and the reading was hastily relocated to a large lecture hall. Cohen surprised the audience by coming onstage carrying a guitar. Some of those present had heard Judy Collins's recording of "Suzanne," and some knew Cohen had written it. But nobody in that lecture hall thought of Leonard Cohen as a singer, not yet. He read a few poems, picked up the guitar, sang "Suzanne," and ended his career as a poet.

Legend says that the idea for a counterculture Vancouver street paper first came up at a party after Cohen's UBC performance. Whether that's true or not, Cohen's guitar and the *Georgia Straight* came from the same place, the same desire to bring news from the underground to a larger audience. The *Straight*'s editor, UBC math student Dan McLeod, was himself a poet and a *Tish* editor who left *Tish* to help found the *Straight*. Poets Milton Acorn, Stan Persky, Robin Blaser, and Gladys Hindmarch supplied much of its journalism; a year's subscription came with a free copy of Robert Creeley's *Pieces*. When *Tish* ended in 1969, it was "unofficially replaced" by the *Georgia Straight Writing Supplement*, a twenty-page poetry and fiction insert included every three months in what was by then a weekly newspaper with a readership around 25,000. "Instead of a couple of hundred people getting to see what's being written," read an editorial in the second supplement, "it goes directly to a large audience in the city."

The *Georgia Straight* is still publishing today but the writing supplement folded in a year, and its contributors and poetry returned to the small magazines and presses from which they had come. They too are still alive: the *Georgia Straight Writing Supplement* became Vancouver Community Press, which became New Star Books, which in 2015 published George Bowering's thirty-sixth book of poetry.

**IN OCTOBER 1970,** the Front de libération du Québec went from blowing up mailboxes to killing people. Soldiers patrolled the streets of Montreal. "When the permanent nitrous fog moved below the twentieth floor windows of the Place Ville Marie," the Bowerings decided it was time to go home. With the help of a Canada Council grant, they returned to Vancouver in the summer of 1971 and moved into a old house in Kitsilano known as the York Street Commune. There were seven of them in the house, including Gladys Hindmarch and Stan Persky. In October Angela had a baby, and then there were eight. The Bowerings bought a little house on Balaclava Street. George got a teaching job at Simon Fraser and they bought a bigger house on West 37th Avenue, where they lived for the next twenty-five years. It's just two doors east of where *Tish* began, the home of Ellen and Warren Tallman.

Daphne Marlatt also came home. In 1968 Alan got a job at UBC and they moved into a house in Dunbar, near the campus. They had a son, Kit. But Alan didn't like Vancouver and they moved back to the States in the fall of 1969 for a job at the University of Wisconsin. A year later, Marlatt left her husband and returned to Vancouver with her son, this time to stay. She published her *Vancouver Poems* in 1972 and *Steveston* in 1974 — a book of poems and photographs about a salmon-canning town that was once home to some two thousand Japanese Canadians interned during the war. As she says in a documentary about the Vancouver Poetry Conference, for her the most important lesson of that time was to pay attention to where you are.

**GEORGE, VANCOUVER:
A DISCOVERY POEM (1971)**
George Bowering

★★★

When Bowering moved to Ontario to start a Ph.D., he couldn't find any poems because he couldn't find his place. Then, in the University of Western Ontario's library, he found a journal kept by the ship's botanist aboard George Vancouver's HMS *Discovery*, and he found his place and a story to tell: a long poem about Captain Vancouver and other West Coast explorers. Like Ondaatje's later *Coming Through Slaughter*, it's as much about the author as the character, history as confessional.

It's at times too clever for its own good, but I like the poem more each time I read it. I certainly like it more than anything I've read by Olson. The big difference between Bowering and the New American poets that inspired him is that he cares if readers understand and enjoy what he has to say.

## Chapter 15

# Next Episode

I'm a Cuban a nigger a white nigger from Quebec fleur-de-lys-
decked Canada-Council-sponsored I'm anger in the taverns
anger in two hundred years of vomit
     —Paul Chamberland, "The Signpainter Screams"

**MICHEL TREMBLAY DIDN'T** just revolutionize French-Canadian theatre, said *Le Devoir*'s Michel Bélair. "He gave it a right to exist." Born in Montreal in the first week of the summer of 1942, Tremblay was the youngest of five children. His family lived on rue Fabre in the then working-class neighbourhood of Plateau Mont-Royal. "We were three families in the same house: thirteen in seven rooms," he told *La Presse*. "That's the only place I've ever known, the place I love, the place where I'm from."

In the early fifties, Tremblay's family moved up and out to an apartment of their own on nearby rue Cartier. The move wasn't easy for him. He missed his old friends, didn't like his new school, and slowly realized, alone and with difficulty, that he was what the boys at school called a *tapette*, a fag.

He read a lot, a passion he shared with his mother and grandmother. The cinema and the theatre were forbidden, so he went to both as often as he could. At thirteen he won a provincial scholarship to a Catholic college, but he found it snobbish and quit after a few months. He went back to high school and read his way through the *collège classique* curriculum on his own.

In 1959, at seventeen, he saw on television Marcel Carné's *Les visiteurs du soir*, a French wartime film about the devil preventing a marriage. Like many Parisians, Tremblay saw the movie as an allegory about France's refusal to yield under German occupation. "The next day," he said, "I started to write." He wrote short stories, a novel, and his first play, *Le train*, about two men and a murder set in a train compartment. After high school he followed his father into the printing trade, enrolling at the Institute for Graphic Arts on rue Saint-Hubert. He worked as a delivery boy for Ty-Coq Barbecue and, after finishing his printing program, as a linotypist for the Judicial Printer of Montreal.

If his mother hadn't died prematurely, Tremblay says, he would have kept his writing to himself. Her encouragement and tastes were so important to him that he hid his writing for fear it would disappoint her. In 1964, a few months after her death, he submitted *Le train* to a Radio-Canada contest for young writers and won first prize.

He kept writing, including a new and very different kind of play he was calling *Les belles-soeurs*, the sisters-in-law. In 1966 he left his $167-a-week printing job to work for $60 a week in the costume department at Radio-Canada. Éditions du jour published his first book in its Novelists of the Day series: *Tales for Late Night Drinkers*, a collection of short fantasies written when he was a teenager trying to escape from real life. In December, Tremblay's friend and some-time lover André Brassard directed *Cinq* at Le Patriote-en-Haut, a 170-seat theatre above a coffee house on rue Sainte-Catherine (a play about the daily life of working-class Montrealers, *Cinq* was later expanded into *En pièces détachées*, "in separate parts"). The following year, the Canada Council gave him a travel grant to go to Mexico. He stayed in Acapulco for two months, writing a fantasy novel for Éditions du jour and *The Duchess of Langeais*, a one-hander about an aging transvestite.

On March 4, 1968, soon after Tremblay returned from Mexico, *Les belles-soeurs* had its first public reading. Tremblay had begun writing the play in 1965, but after it was rejected by Quebec's Dramatic Arts Festival he put it away. One evening during Expo 67, at a restaurant across from La Fontaine Park, Brassard and another friend, costume designer Louise Jobin, convinced him that giving up on the play meant giving up on himself as a writer.

*Les belles-soeurs* is about a Montreal woman who wins a million trading stamps. She invites fourteen women, relatives and neighbours, to her home to help her glue the stamps into booklets that she can redeem for consumer goods to fill the house of her dreams. Her helpers steal the stamps for themselves while complaining about their shitty lives. Comedy, then tragedy, ensues.

Tremblay grew up in a house filled with women. "My first vision of the world," he told *L'actualité* in 1992, "was of those women who forgot I was there, and who said things they would never have said if they had known I was listening." *Les belles-soeurs* shows that he was listening, and carefully — not just to what those women said, but how they said it. The play is written in *joual*, the French of working-class Montreal. Brought to attention in an October 1959 *Le Devoir* editorial, the term gained currency with teacher Jean-Paul Desbiens's complaint in his 1960 bestseller *Les insolences du Frère Untel* that "our pupils speak *joual*, write *joual*, and do not wish to speak or write anything else."

For young writers looking to establish a distinctive Québécois literature, *joual* was not a problem but a solution. "I am proud to write badly," declared poet Paul Chamberland. The first *joual* novel appeared in 1964, a year before Tremblay began writing *Les belles-soeurs*. Jacques Renaud's *Le cassé*\* is about a man from Montreal's east end who thinks his girlfriend is sleeping with a drug dealer. It's written, said Renaud, in the language he learned from his people, full of words adapted from English and slurred in speech. So, for example, in *Le cassé* the standard French phrase *à cette heure* becomes *astheure*, because that's closer to how it sounds when people say it.

*Les belles-soeurs* premiered on August 28, 1968, at the Théâtre du Rideau Vert in Tremblay's home neighbourhood of the Plateau.

---

\* Translated from "Quebekish" by Gérald Robitaille in 1969 as *Flat Broke and Beat*, and by David Homel in 1984 as *Broke City*.

The oldest professional French-language theatre in Canada, the Rideau Vert staged the same kind of plays as its English-Canadian counterparts, classical plays by foreign and, typically, dead writers like Molière and Shakespeare. But for the slower summer season, they had advertised a Canadian play that was suddenly cancelled. *Les belles-soeurs* was called in to fill the hole. On opening night the response was decidedly undecided. The laughter was forced, uncertain; people shifted uncomfortably in their seats. Some left before the end. When the curtain came down, "cries of all kinds blended together, applause was irregular, mouths stayed open." Outside on rue Saint-Denis after the show, the questions began: Was Tremblay making fun of the working class? of the French language? of Quebec? Was it a tragedy or a parody?

In *La Presse* the next day, Martial Dassylva said the Rideau Vert had done Tremblay a disservice by accepting his play. "It's the first time in my life I've heard, in one night, so many curses, swear words, and trashy language." Tremblay, he said, had a choice: to devote his talents to "true dramatic writing" or to "take pleasure in applied vulgarity and continue to follow paths that lead nowhere." Speaking for the other side of what became one of the most heated cultural debates in Quebec history, Jean Basile in *Le Devoir* called the play a masterpiece, "one of the first real critical gazes that a Québécois playwright has cast on Quebec society."

Martial Dassylva spoke for many at the moment; Jean Basile, it turned out, for posterity. *Les belles-soeurs* marked the dividing line between French-Canadian and Québécois theatre, between a borrowed and a native art. "*Joual*," said André Major, "permits a drama to be one" — to be both legitimately dramatic and legitimately realistic.

**MAURICE DUPLESSIS HATED** writers almost as much as he hated scientists, communists, labour unions, the Liberals, Jehovah's Witnesses, and anyone who ever said no to him. In September 1959 the Boss died in office, ending eighteen years as premier of Quebec and the period in Quebec known as the Great Darkness. The Liberals

came to power the following summer, inaugurating the Quiet Revolution. Literature's fortunes, along with a great deal else, changed.

Cultural nationalism in Canada began in
French-speaking Quebec, with writers united
by a common discontent, readers hungry for
stories about their own place, and publishers
supported by the provincial and federal governments. "Young people," wrote Pierre Vallières,
"were seized with a desire to read and to know,
and the book trade enjoyed an unprecedented
expansion." Literature became important
to French Canadians because words — their
words — were all they had. Journalist Malcolm
Reid explained it in his insider account of the
writers associated with the socialist magazine
*Parti pris*: when Anglo Montreal said poets
can't run a country, the *partipristes* responded,
"Indeed, history has so far given power, cash,
stocks, bonds to you, words to us. We shall use
our words to plan how to take them from you."
Says the hero of Hubert Aquin's second novel,
"We must name everything, write everything
down, before we blow everything up."

Ottawa was happy to help out. Half the
Canada Council's first arts fellowships went
to Quebeckers, and until 1967 the Council
directed most of its limited support for trade
publishing to French-Canadian firms. Quebec
didn't join the Centennial celebrations, but it
did accept Centennial funding — more than
any other province, though it also contributed
more of its own. The CBC sustained dozens of
French-Canadian writers; the National Film
Board (based in Montreal since 1956) employed as many or more,
including Anne Hébert, Jacques Godbout, and Hubert Aquin.
Jean Roberts, theatre officer for the Canada Council from 1967

**WHITE NIGGERS OF
AMERICA (NÈGRES BLANCS
D'AMÈRIQUE) (1968)**
**Pierre Vallières**

★★★

Written in a New York jail after a
month-long hunger strike, *White
Niggers of America* is a very
good book if you can get past the
first fifty pages. It opens with a
Marxist history of Quebec: a
long catalogue of crimes and
criminals that includes British
and American imperialism, the
French Canadian petite bour-
geoisie, priests, Confederation,
Henri Bourassa, Lester Pearson,
the "traitor" Trudeau, and René
Lévesque. After that it's a mix
of memoir and argument, an
account of Vallières's life from
growing up in east-end Montreal
and the suburban slum of Ville
Jacques-Cartier to his embrace
of revolutionary socialism and
his conviction for manslaughter
in 1968. He's thoughtful, honest,
intelligent, and angry — much
more with capitalism than with
English Canadians. Despite
how the story played out in
the English press at the time,
Vallières was a communist first,
a separatist second.

to 1971, remembers Quebec having eight of the seventeen theatres the Council was then supporting and getting the lion's share of the funding, "because it was so active" and because "the Council tried very hard to respond to that kind of healthy activity in those days."

The motives for this extra effort were complicated. Federal institutions clearly and no doubt sincerely wanted to promote French writing inside and especially outside Quebec, for Quebec's sake and to support the federal projects of bilingualism and biculturalism. They also hoped, of course, that some of those writers would themselves endorse the federal projects. The Centennial Commission, for example, paid for Montreal broadcaster Solange Chaput-Rolland to cross Canada looking for the answer to her question *Mon pays, Québec ou le Canada?* because she was a known federalist and because they were betting on (and sort of got) a federalist book. But from the separatist point of view, English Canada's support for French-Canadian arts was a way to keep the more entertaining bits of French culture around while the culture itself withered and died.*

Quebec helped pay for those entertainments. In 1961 the provincial government established its Ministry of Cultural Affairs, which supported events like the Salon du livre de Québec. In 1963 the Ministry launched a program called Aid to Creativity and Research Service specifically to encourage artists, including writers. By 1971 the program had awarded 430 grants totalling $1.2 million to authors, playwrights, musicians, and filmmakers. The province became the literary-prize capital of Canada, adding eight prizes to its existing seven in the 1960s and twenty-two more in the 1970s. Undecorated French-Canadian writers became hard to find.

But most of the money came from Ottawa, which made for some difficult decisions as Quebec nationalism heated up over the decade. Gaston Miron accepted one of the first Canada Council

---

* "The domination of one human group by another," wrote Hubert Aquin in 1964, "places an exaggerated importance on those powers of the inferior group which are harmless: sex, artistic proclivities, natural talent for music or creation, and so on." Think Inuit sculpture, or African-American hip hop.

grants, but when Expo organizers asked if they could inscribe a few lines of his poetry on the walls of the Quebec pavilion, he said no. Michel Tremblay also accepted Canada Council grants but refused until 1976 to allow his plays to be performed in English in Quebec. Hubert Aquin worked for the National Film Board but turned down a Governor General's Award. Separatist poet Gérald Godin continued to work for the CBC, partly, he said, because the network's French-Canadian employees couldn't be disciplined without stirring up a major protest, which left him freer than English-Canadian producers to say and air what he liked. Most separatist writers accepted some form of federal support, but on their own terms — like the French Quebeckers who went to Expo 67 in droves but saw it as Quebec's triumph, not Canada's.

**KAMOURASKA (1970)**
Anne Hébert

Anne Hébert's best-known novel is based on historic events in Quebec in the winter of 1839. It is ... cold. A young wife and her lover conspire to murder her husband. They send her maid to poison him. The husband ... survives. The lover does the deed himself. With a pistol. There is ... blood. On his black horse. On the white snow.

The novel's literary sources also hail from the previous century, stories closer to *Madame Bovary* than anything from Hébert's time. Today, *Kamouraska* doesn't have much to recommend it besides being a good argument for divorce. Something may have got lost (or added) in translation, but both the story and its style reach for pathos and land too often in bathos for the translator to take all the blame.

Except during the Second World War, when Quebec publishers briefly flourished in the European publishing vacuum, most books sold in French Canada before 1960 came from wholesalers for foreign publishers, especially French publishers. In the early sixties, independent French-Canadian publishers re-emerged to publish new ideas and new writers for an increasing and increasingly politicized readership. Claude Hurtubise founded Éditions Hurtubise HMH and launched a popular nonfiction series called Collection constantes, which included books by Jean Le Moyne, Pierre Vadeboncoeur, Pierre Elliott Trudeau, and other liberal intellectuals associated with the anti-Duplessis magazine *Cité libre*. Jacques Hébert's Éditions du jour introduced young Quebec writers in one-dollar paperbacks, selling ten thousand copies of Jean-Louis Gagnon's short-story collection *La mort d'un nègre* and six thousand copies of Marie-Claire Blais's novel *Le jour est noir*. The separatist magazine *Parti pris* appeared in October 1963 and created its own imprint four months later, publishing plays, essays, and fiction, including the *joual* novel *Le cassé*. All received Canada Council funding, as did older French-Canadian literary presses like Le cercle du livre de France and Gaston Miron's Éditions de l'Hexagone, focused like its famous editor on poetry and also the publisher of *Liberté*, the premier literary magazine of the Quiet Revolution. Whatever federal arts funding meant for Quebec, it was a major boon for Quebec literature.*

**ST. LAWRENCE BLUES (UN JOUALONAIS SA JOUALONIE) (1973)**
Marie-Claire Blais

A novel narrated by an orphan and ex-con nicknamed Ti-Pit, "little nothing." Much of it is dialogue: conversations in the streets and taverns of Montreal with other drifters, criminals, drug addicts, poets, and prostitutes — the people you'd meet today in a Heather O'Neill novel. It's Blais's only novel written in *joual*, which Ralph Manheim's translation renders as a kind of hillbilly American English. But it's a satire rather than an endorsement of the "Joualonese," Blais's shot at the pretensions that Québécois literature had acquired in her absence, along with many other targets. The general strike at the end — on Christmas eve, during a snowstorm — was a good idea, but the mixture of sordid naturalism and smug satire doesn't fit the picaresque plot. No doubt fun to read at the time, it's more of a chore now. Read O'Neill instead, or Michel Rabagliati.

**HUBERT AQUIN DID** not write in *joual*. "Some authors think that just because they spice up a familiar sentence with a few curses they have given a literary existence to their birthplace," he wrote in 1962. He continued to reject *joual* after its rise, arguing that it pitted Quebec against the French language rather than its English-Canadian masters, and that a "defective" language made for defective thinking.

He was born October 24, 1929, the day Wall Street began to crash, the second of three sons in a middle-class French family living on rue Saint-André, near La Fontaine Park. He went to a Catholic boys' school at Roy and Drolet, then the Holy Cross day college on Sherbrooke and the Jesuit Collège Sainte-Marie on rue Bleury.

From 1948 to 1951 he studied philosophy at the Université de Montréal, specializing in the

* Le cercle du livre de France received the most Council support, an average of about $4,400 a year in the sixties. The separatist press Parti pris received about $400 a year, but it published far fewer books and didn't do translations, a favourite of the Council.

German phenomenologist Edmund Husserl and the French existentialist Jean-Paul Sartre. He worked for the U de M student paper *Le Quartier latin*, publishing essays and fiction under a variety of pseudonyms. After earning his *licence* (B.A.), he went to Paris on a provincial scholarship to study at the Institute of Political Studies, a public university housed in pre-revolutionary mansions on the Left Bank. Like many future separatists, he became sympathetic to Algeria's growing struggle for independence. He wrote a short novel, "The Redeemers," and started a Ph.D. in aesthetics that he didn't finish.

Aquin returned to Montreal in the summer of 1954 and went to work for Radio-Canada, writing and directing radio plays, adaptations, and educational programming. He married a CBC script assistant and had two sons. They lived on a quiet residential street in Outremont, a few blocks north of the Université de Montréal, where Aquin began a master's degree in history. In 1959 he directed an NFB documentary written by Roland Barthes called *Le sport et les hommes* that explored the meaning of sports like auto racing, a passion of Aquin's (he founded a company the following year that tried unsuccessfully to bring Grand Prix racing to Montreal). He produced and occasionally directed a dozen more NFB films, including an affecting documentary about the first day of school in a working-class Montreal neighbourhood, *In Saint-Henri on September 5.*

Radio and television didn't pay all the bills, so from 1960 to 1964 he worked as a St. James Street stockbroker's assistant. He joined the Rassemblement pour l'indépendance nationale, a new organization dedicated to promoting Quebec's independence. He also began writing regularly for *Liberté*, founded in 1959 by poet Jean-Guy Pilon and other writers. In May 1962, *Liberté* published a long essay by Aquin responding to a controversial article by Pierre Elliott Trudeau in *Cité Libre* the previous month. Trudeau had argued against French-Canadian nationalism because of nationalism's history of war and racism; Aquin countered that nationalism was neither good nor evil but whatever people made of it. Without its own nationalism to assert itself against the English-Canadian majority, French Canada was depressed and dying. "The Cultural Fatigue of French Canada" quickly became Aquin's best-known essay and a pivotal document in Quebec history, the lever that lifted a conversation into action.

The following year Aquin founded a terrorist cell. In January 1964 he helped steal weapons from a military barracks and published an emotional essay in *Parti pris* in which he renounced his profession as a writer. "In this flaming bordello of a country in pieces, writing is like saying one's prayers while sitting on a nitroglycerine bomb.... In rejecting domination I refuse literature, the daily bread of the dominated." Six months later, on June 18, he wrote to *Montréal-Matin* and other newspapers announcing that he was leaving public politics for clandestine activism. "I declare total war on all the enemies of Quebec independence. My harmonious relationship with a society that cheats is definitively ruptured. For a while, I will be far away. Then I will return among you. Let's prepare ourselves. The revolution will take place. *Vive le Québéc!*"

On a Sunday morning, July 5, Aquin was arrested while sitting alone in a car parked behind Saint Joseph's Oratory of Mount Royal, the largest church in Canada. He had a loaded revolver in his belt. When the police asked him his profession, he said he was a revolutionary. They charged him with car theft and possession of a semiautomatic pistol. On the advice of his lawyer, he pleaded temporary insanity, and on July 15 was remanded to a psychiatric hospital, the Institut Albert-Prévost in Cartierville, to await trial.

He asked for paper. They gave him fifty pages a month and let him write in the common room, where guards could watch him. "I learned to write small," he said. He wrote up to eighteen hours a day, the words spilling from his pen. In "Occupation: Writer," the essay in which he had said the year before that he was abandoning writing, he left himself an out: the only way to write in an incoherent country, he said, was to write incoherently. So he let what he was writing ramble where it wanted, giving himself up because he couldn't give up.

By September it was finished. Aquin was released on bail after the judge heard the psychiatric report; in December he was tried and acquitted because of insufficient evidence. Two months later, on February 10, his book was accepted by Pierre Tisseyre for Le cercle du livre de France. With $1,000 help from the Canada Council, Tisseyre published Aquin's book in October 1965.

It ended up being a spy novel, sort of — the story of an unnamed FLQ terrorist assigned to kill a counter-revolutionary in Switzerland, told by an unnamed political prisoner in a Montreal psychiatric clinic who is trying to write a spy novel about an unnamed FLQ terrorist assigned to kill a counter-revolutionary in Switzerland. He called it *Prochain épisode* — next episode — because it doesn't end, and couldn't end until the revolution. The French-Canadian press adored it, using phrases like "truly inspired" and "a literary bomb." "There is no need to look further," said *Le Devoir*'s literary critic, Jean Éthier-Blais. "We have found him, our great writer. The Lord be praised."

*Prochain épisode* outsold all other French-Canadian books in the year of its publication. By the end of 1966 it had sold over ten thousand copies. In 1970 — the closest Aquin's novel has yet come to getting the ending it wanted — it was still selling four thousand copies a year.

**MOST WRITERS OF** Quebec's Quiet Revolution went unnoticed in France. Marie-Claire Blais may have felt freer to write in Paris than at home, but the French were also freer to ignore her, and her first novel sold poorly when it was published in Paris. When Anne Hébert's *Les chambres de bois* came out from Paris's Éditions du Seuil in 1958, over 90 percent of its sales were in Quebec. Hubert Aquin's publisher sold the French rights

**NEXT EPISODE
(PROCHAIN ÉPISODE)
(1965)**
Hubert Aquin

Aquin's first book is a prison memoir, a love letter to Quebec, a political allegory, and a postmodern spy novel. Its hero is Aquin's double outside the walls of the psychiatric institute in which he wrote it, his "proxy." Despite what the French edition said about the book being "a true action novel," nothing that happens in it is real — nothing but its author's hand moving across the paper, writing "to stave off sorrow and to feel it."

The admittedly improvised book loses its way in its spy story, becoming too interested in what was only ever a metaphor. Genre novels are harder than artists think. In its place and time — which is how Aquin insisted it be read — *Prochain épisode* was both an important and a great novel. Today it's a good memoir that gives too many pages to a poor spy novel.

for *Prochain épisode* to the Paris house Robert Laffont, but the novel was panned in France as derivative and didn't have anything like its success at home.

**THE SWALLOWER
SWALLOWED
(L'AVALÉE DES AVALÉS)
(1966)**
**Réjean Ducharme**

★★★★

"I can't wait to be one of the wicked," says nine-year-old Bernice Einberg near the beginning of her story. It doesn't take her long. She poisons her mother's cat about fifty pages in, then beats its replacement to death. After she's exiled to New York, she wills her only friend to be killed by a car. "Murder by telepathy," she calls it.

Bernice is, of course, mad. But there's a method to her madness, and a resonance with readers of her time and place that helped make her story a bestseller. Like many French Canadians of her generation, she wants to remake the world as she sees it, reason be damned — to avoid being swallowed by her world by swallowing it herself. *The Swallower Swallowed* is occasionally wearying and could have shed some pages. But it's a passionate book that has a lot of fun with its darkness.

There were exceptions, books whose success in France helped them find readers at home. In 1966 the prestigious French house Éditions Gallimard published the first novel by an unknown twenty-four-year-old taxi driver from Saint-Félix-de-Valois, north of Montreal. Réjean Ducharme's *L'avalée des avalés* (published in English as *The Swallower Swallowed*) sold more than ten thousand copies in France in two months and was nominated for the Prix Goncourt, France's highest literary award. Back home, the novel sold thousands of copies in a pirated edition and won a Governor General's Literary Award.* That same year, Blais's *A Season in the Life of Emmanuel* became the first Canadian book to win France's Prix Médicis, awarded to a work of fiction in French by a writer whose "fame does not yet match their talent." Quebec sales of Hébert's *Les chambres de bois* got her noticed in France, where she sold more than half of her subsequent books. Jacques Godbout, like Hébert published by Éditions du Seuil, also sold well in France.

The first firm to publish books from the Quiet Revolution in English was Montreal's Harvest House, founded in 1962 by Maynard

---

* Ducharme remained unknown, giving just a few interviews and refusing to appear on television or pick up his GG in person. "My novel is public, not me," he told *Le magazine Maclean*. Rumours circulated that photos of him were of a dead student and that *L'avalée des avalés* was written by someone else. Candidates included Hubert Aquin, literary critic Naïm Kattan, actress Luce Guilbeault, and the French novelist Raymond Queneau. Ducharme himself suggested that his books had been written by the Swiss-born poet Blaise Cendrars, then five years dead.

Gertler and his wife Ann. Harvest House translated about a dozen French-Canadian books in the sixties, starting with Pierre Laporte's critical biography *The True Face of Duplessis* and including Jean-Paul Desbiens's *The Impertinences of Brother Anonymous*. Glen Shortliffe translated Gérard Bessette's novel *Le libraire* as *Not for Every Eye* for Macmillan in 1962. *Maclean's* published a two-page excerpt from Penny Williams's translation of Aquin's *Prochain épisode* for McClelland & Stewart on June 4, 1966, the last fiction ever to appear in *Maclean's*. M&S also published Marie-Claire Blais's novels in translation and English versions of René Lévesque's argument for sovereignty association (*Option Québec*) and Pierre Vallières's pro-separatist memoir *Nègres blancs d'Amérique*.

The House of Anansi took a special interest in introducing French-Canadian writers to English-Canadian readers. One of the five titles in its 1969 Spiderline series of new novels was Pierre Gravel's *À perte de temps*, published in French with generous notes for English readers trying to remember their high-school French. By far Anansi's most successful translation was Roch Carrier's first novel, *La guerre, yes sir!*, translated by Sheila Fischman. Fischman was part of a bilingual literary community that flourished in the sixties and seventies in Quebec's Eastern Townships around the lakeside village of North Hatley. The group included permanent and summer residents of the area, writers and professors like Ralph Gustafson, Hugh MacLennan, F. R. Scott, Roland Giguère, Gérald Godin, and Fischman's husband, D. G. Jones.

Carrier often spent summers in North Hatley, and he gave Fischman a copy of *La guerre*. She loved it, asked if she could translate it, and found a publisher. Published in April 1970, Anansi's

**THE TELEPHONE POLE**
**(1969)**
Russell Marois

A bilingual French Canadian from Sherbrooke, Quebec, Russell Marois was twenty-four years old when he published his first and only book. *The Telephone Pole* is a darkly humorous and very disturbing short novel about young, bored Montrealers. Its characters look out the windows of their apartments ... nothing. They look in their wallets ... nothing. They try to have sex or masturbate ... nothing. So they watch the clock and smoke (the novel rivals George Bowering's first novel for most cigarettes smoked in a Canadian novel). Maybe they'll go out and get drunk at the Swiss Hut, maybe not. All that's certain is that "in an hour it will be six-thirty and in two hours it will be seven-thirty." Eventually they do something to end the monotony, to do and feel *something*. What they do is the disturbing part.

*La Guerre, Yes Sir!* made it to the bottom of the *Toronto Daily Star*'s top-ten bestseller list in June. The *Globe and Mail* printed a full-page review by Jack Ludwig, who said Carrier "puts us *anglais* novelists to shame." George Woodcock described it in the *Star* as the "curtain scene to the rural novel that dominated the French-Canadian literary scene for 100 years." Carrier published nine more books with Anansi and became English Canada's best-known French writer. Fischman used the $250 she earned for her first translation to buy herself a blue suede coat. She became Canada's most prolific translator, with around 150 book-length translations from French to English.

**LA GUERRE, YES SIR! (1968)**
Roch Carrier

★★★

*La guerre, yes sir!* is a funny book, assuming you like your humour a little coarse. The main character is a dead man, blown up by a landmine while taking a shit behind a hedge in France and now lying in his coffin while English-Canadian soldiers and French-Canadian villagers drink and brawl around him.

It's easy to read a national allegory into the plot: French Quebec is Corriveau's coffin, draped with an English flag, fought over by the English and the French, and destined for the cold ground. But you don't need the allegory to pick up the sadness beneath the comedy. As one woman thinks of the corpse at the centre of it all, "He had been born a French Canadian so he couldn't have been very happy."

By 1972 some forty Quebec novels existed in English translations. Literary Canada had one solitude, not two: Quebec, where only six English-Canadian novels had so far been translated into French. Three were by Hugh MacLennan, starting with a Paris-published translation of *Two Solitudes* in 1963. Éditions HMH published French translations of Northrop Frye's *The Modern Century* and *The Educated Imagination* and Marshall McLuhan's *The Gutenberg Galaxy* and *Understanding Media*. *Liberté* published an occasional English-Canadian short story in translation, while Éditions du Jour and Ryerson Press collaborated on a bilingual poetry anthology. And that's about it.

French Quebec translated fewer books than English Canada partly because there were more francophones who could read in English than anglophones who could read in French. (One of the most thoughtful and sympathetic reviews of Leonard Cohen's first novel came from *La Presse*.) But it was mostly because young, politicized literary French Canadians had no interest in what they called *canadian* literature (deliberately spelled in English), or even in *canadienne-française* literature. *Parti pris* magazine declared that there was not and never had been any such thing as French-Canadian literature, only Canadian literature and *littérature québécoise*, a term it introduced in 1965. Separatist André Major condemned Éditions du Jour and Ryerson's anthology as part of federalism's "enterprise of mystification" — the myth of bicultural equality. "Fighting poets (and I am one)," he said, "denounce this trap." Mind you, he still appeared in it.

**THE CONTROVERSY OVER** *Les belles-soeurs* made Michel Tremblay a celebrity in Quebec. He and director André Brassard played up to their fame, accepting any and all invitations for public appearances and showing up wearing boas and extravagant sunglasses. In November 1972, Toronto's Tarragon Theatre staged the first English-language production of a Tremblay play, *Forever Yours, Marie-Lou*. The same translators — Bill Glassco and John Van Burek — brought *Les Belles-Soeurs* to the St. Lawrence Centre in April 1973, then *Hosanna* to Tarragon in May 1974. All three were commercial and critical successes, especially *Hosanna*, about the relationship between a Montreal drag queen and a gay biker. Its Tarragon debut was what theatre historian Denis Johnston calls "one of the most celebrated Canadian productions of its decade," winning rave reviews and three weeks on Broadway.

Tremblay has written many more plays and even more fiction, including a series of six novels set in the Plateau neighbourhood where he grew up. *Les Belles-Soeurs* has been performed in several countries in many languages, including Scots (*The Guid-Sisters*) and Yiddish (*Di Shveigerins*). Cree playwright Tomson Highway rewrote it in English and later in Cree as *The Rez Sisters*, swapping trading stamps for bingo. One language it has never been performed in is standard French, at Tremblay's insistence. When the play went to France in its original *joual* in 1973, Quebec's minister of cultural affairs refused to help out with a grant because she thought the language was degrading. She needn't have worried; Parisians thought it was cute.

In May 1966, Hubert Aquin left his wife and family for a sociology professor with whom he'd been having an affair for several years, Andrée Yanacopoulo. They flew to Switzerland together and tried to stay in Lyon, but his application for a residency permit was rejected. Back in Montreal, Aquin wrote and starred in a TV spy movie called *Faux Bond* and served as a consulting filmmaker for the Quebec pavilion at Expo 67. He taught French studies for two years at his old college, Sainte-Marie, then aesthetics and literature for a year at its successor, the new Université du Québec à Montréal (UQAM).

Aquin won the Governor General's Award for fiction for his second novel, *Trou de mémoire* (translated as *Blackout*). He refused it, telling the Governor General that his decision was "in keeping with a political commitment that I have made publicly." (This was the same year that Leonard Cohen turned down a GG for his *Selected Poems*. Mordecai Richler, who won one GG that year for two books, said he'd be happy to accept their prize money.)

Two more novels and a major literary prize, Quebec's Prix Athanase-David, followed. But Aquin was struggling, unemployed and relying on Andrée for support, and suffering from either epilepsy or advanced alcoholism, maybe both. He tried to kill himself in March 1971 by overdosing on epilepsy pills in a room at the Queen Elizabeth Hotel but woke up in the hospital. In 1975 *La Presse* hired him to direct a new literary press, then fired him eighteen months later after a public quarrel with his boss, novelist and *La Presse* CEO Roger Lemelin. Two weeks later he landed another job as the editor of a new weekly version of the separatist newspaper *Le Jour*, but the paper folded a few days after he started work.

**BLACKOUT
(TROU DE MÉMOIRE)
(1968)**
Hubert Aquin

*Blackout* is the confession of a murderer edited by his publisher. Like Aquin's first novel, it's also an allegory of Quebec separatism. The confusing plot and Pierre's hyperactive writing style are meant to fulfill Aquin's pledge to write illogically while his country remains illogical, to mimic the French-Canadian's experience of colonization. More disturbing, the repeated drugging and raping of English-Canadian women in the novel is an extended metaphor for Quebec's political impotence and its solution. "Revolution is a crime," says Pierre. Fair enough, but why must the revolution be figured as the rape of women, their death a "stand-in for victory"?

Then, on November 15, the separatist party that Aquin had been one of the first to argue for won the Quebec election. He spent the next two weeks sitting by the phone, waiting for a call from René Lévesque that never came. He told Andrée he would probably kill himself soon. In February Aquin used the money he'd won in a law suit against *La Presse* to pay back what he'd borrowed from Andrée and to give himself what he described to her as "a last chance to choose life" — a three-week trip to Rome, Sicily, Lyon, and Geneva. He didn't tell her he was bringing along another woman, a University of Toronto French lecturer he'd been seeing for a year. He broke off the affair in Rome and returned to Montreal on his own.

Two weeks later he shot himself in the head in a laneway behind a convent school in Notre-Dame-de-Grâce. "My act is positive," he said in a letter to Andrée, "the act of someone who is alive. My life has reached its end. I have lived intensely and now it's over."

## Chapter 16

# In Hardy Country

I am there now
because I am away
—Tom Dawe, "Vortex"

**THE ATLANTIC PROVINCES'** most renowned writer was born on the prairies.

It was his parents' fault. Well, it was the Depression's fault. In the 1930s, Alexander and Christena MacLeod left their home in Cape Breton and went west for work. They landed in North Battleford in western Saskatchewan, then a town of about five thousand people. They had their first child here, a son they named John Alexander Joseph MacLeod. They called him Alistair, Gaelic for Alexander.

Alistair MacLeod's ancestors came to Cape Breton from the Scottish Hebrides in 1791, leaving one small island for another. His parents grew up speaking Gaelic, learning and using English only outside the home, as the language of work — words like *rock* and *shovel*, picked up in the coal mines where his father and other relatives worked, on the island and away. He could understand his parents' language but he never learned to speak it. "You're just like the dog," his grandfather would tell him. "You can understand me, but you can't talk back."

When he was three or four his family moved to Mercoal, a company mining town in western Alberta. They had another child, a girl named Marylin. After the war ended they went home to Cape

Breton, to where they had come from, the west-coast community of Dunvegan. Alistair was ten. He liked the blue of the sea and the green of the hills. He also liked reading — westerns, mostly, Zane Grey and the like — and he liked his new school, all the one room of it. For Grade 12 he bused down the coast a bit to Inverness, where he won the English prize for best essay.

After high school MacLeod hitchhiked to Elliot Lake in northern Ontario to work in the uranium mines. He moved to Edmonton for a year, living with an aunt and delivering milk for Northern Alberta Dairy Products. "It was a good job," he said. "They were going to make me route foreman. When I turned it down, the manager said to me, 'You're making a big mistake, MacLeod.'"* Instead he got a teaching certificate from the Nova Scotia Normal College in Truro and taught for a year in a one-room school on Port Hood Island, off Cape Breton (current population two). As it had for his father, teaching meant security, something to fall back on when the fish ran out or the mines closed. But he found he liked it.

In 1957, now twenty-one, he began a combined B.A. and B.Ed. at St. Francis Xavier University in Antigonish, followed by an M.A. at the University of New Brunswick. He worked his way through university fishing, logging, and mining, whatever and wherever the work was. In 1963 he began a Ph.D. in English at the University of Notre Dame, a Catholic university outside South Bend, Indiana. He wrote his dissertation on Thomas Hardy's *A Group of Noble Dames*, historical stories told by members of an antiquarian club. Four decades later, Hardy's Jude Fawley, a stonemason who dreams of becoming a scholar, was still his favourite fictional character. "He tries to do the very best he can," said MacLeod.

He was thinking of writing, of becoming a writer. He chose Notre Dame partly because he hoped to study with Frank O'Malley, who was known for his equal devotion to faith and to English literature. Instead he took a creative writing course with the Catholic novelist Richard Sullivan. Two things, he said, got him writing in earnest.

---

* MacLeod told CBC's Shelagh Rogers the same thing about leaving a logging job on Vancouver Island. He never let the truth get in the way of a story.

At some point I decided that instead of just analyzing Joyce's "The Dead" or Faulkner's "A Rose for Emily," maybe I should try and write a few stories of my own. The other thing related to being so far from home. I found myself becoming more and more thoughtful about where I'd grown up. I'm not saying that it was simply "absence makes the heart grow fonder," but I do think it's true that sometimes when you're removed from your home, you start to think about it differently, which certainly happened to me. So I decided to write my own stories and set them in my native landscape.

He wrote his first story for Sullivan's class. A teacher at a Midwestern university sits alone drinking coffee in an all-night diner, remembering fishing as a boy off Cape Breton and his father's death at sea, "the cuttings from an old movie made in the black and white of long ago." He called it "The Boat." The *Massachusetts Review* published the story in the spring of 1968. The contributors' page identified its author as a native of New Brunswick's Inverness County, getting the county right but not the province.

MacLeod was by then himself teaching at a Midwestern university, nineteenth-century British literature at Indiana and Purdue Universities' new joint campus in Fort Wayne. In 1968 the head of the English department at the University of Windsor needed someone to teach English Romantic literature. He saw MacLeod's name on a list of Canada Council recipients teaching in the States and invited him up for an interview. Despite his expertise in a later period, the university liked what it saw and offered him a job. MacLeod went home to pack and began work in the fall of 1969. In his first

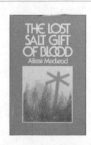

**THE LOST SALT GIFT OF BLOOD (1976)**
Alistair MacLeod

★★★★★

MacLeod's first book, seven stories written in the late sixties and early seventies. They're set mostly in Cape Breton, about young men leaving because they must and returning because they must, in body or in memory. "There is nothing for one to do here," says the mother of one. "There never was anything for one to do here."

There's more heart in one of MacLeod's sentences than in whole stories, whole novels, by other writers. He's not clever or ironic, though he can be funny. He sincerely loves these people and this place. But that doesn't stop him from seeing the bad and the dark, people twisted by place and blood. Hugh MacLennan thought *The Lost Salt Gift of Blood* was the finest book ever published in Canada. He might be right still.

month of teaching, "The Boat" was reprinted in *The Best American Short Stories 1969*. The *North American Review* called it perhaps the most effective story in the collection and quoted the entire opening paragraph. The University of Windsor had set out to hire a British scholar and got a Canadian writer.

**ALDEN NOWLAN WAS** born at home in the village of Stanley, in Hants County, Nova Scotia. His father was twenty-four at the time, his mother fourteen. She read poetry to her children — Alden and a sister born two years later. His father made up stories for them when he wasn't working at the sawmill beside their house. His grandmother, who lived with them, told ghost stories, sang Irish folksongs, and lectured from the Old Testament. She made her own medicines and was known in the village as an eccentric (some said a witch).

By the time he was four his parents' marriage was falling apart. His father was drinking more and his much younger wife was going out more. One night after she came home from a dance, they fought and he kicked her out. She took the children and went to live with her mother in nearby Mosherville. While she wandered, her mother looked after the children.

In September 1939, at the age of six, Nowlan started school in a one-room schoolhouse next door to his father's house. He was shy and kept to himself. "He never wanted to play outside," his sister recalls. "He'd always have his nose in a book." The following spring his grandmother died and he and his sister ended up back with their father. His mother lived with a boyfriend for a couple of years, then moved to Dartmouth to live with another man. She eventually became a nurse and left Nova Scotia in the early sixties. If anyone asked, Nowlan would say his mother had died when he was young.

They were very poor. His father's house had no plumbing, no electricity, no telephone. They had a radio that worked when they could afford batteries. "I am one of the few North American writers," Nowlan told a student in 1967, "who knows anything about the world outside the affluent society." His favourite name for Stanley (one of several) was "Desolation Creek."

He had to repeat Grade 3, mostly because he rarely attended, and left for good after failing Grade 4. He was by this time writing for himself: rhyming poems, romances about knights, detective stories. He wrote, as he read, in secret. "My father would as soon have seen me wear lipstick," he said. He saw a movie about Jack London growing up poor, writing books, and becoming rich and famous, and that looked good to him.

He spent his first year out of school reading, including scores of pamphlets that he discovered he could get free from religious and political groups by answering ads in the *Family Herald*. He built a fort in the woods where he could read alone, sometimes aloud, sometimes in the dark by firelight. People started talking about his being crazy. He had his first publication, a letter in a Cape Breton labour magazine called *Steelworker and Miner*.

By the following summer Nowlan had become increasingly withdrawn and listless. He was taken to the hospital in Windsor, possibly after an intervention by Children's Aid, and transferred to the Halifax Children's Hospital and then the Nova Scotia Hospital for the mentally ill in Dartmouth. He spent nearly two years here, a time he never spoke about except in poems and fiction. He told people that he had learned about the institution from an uncle who worked there, or that he himself had worked there in his teens — likely true in part, as his treatment would probably have included occupational therapy, including vocational and social skills.

He came home early in 1948, almost sixteen. He helped his father cut trees and when summer came got a job as night watchman at the sawmill. He spent his shift reading magazines and avoided the other men as much as he could, going to work after they had left and leaving before they started. Saturday nights he got a ride into Windsor to see a movie and visit the library. The librarian liked him. "I'd come home with a knapsack crammed with books: Whitman, Rupert Brooke, Jack London, H. G. Wells, Shaw, even Darwin and, God help us, Herbert Spencer."

He found a list of magazines that published poetry, bought a typewriter from the Eaton's catalogue, and began working his way through the list. At eighteen he had his first poem published, a vaguely Celtic lyric about a castle in the mist, under the name Max Philip Ireland in an Oregon magazine. Later that year he had his first Canadian poetry publication, "A Letter to Tomorrow" by "Del Acadie," in the communist weekly *Canadian Tribune*. He began reviewing books for the *Windsor Tribune*, starting with a book about the Bible.

The sawmill fired him for poor work and suspected communist sympathies. He hitchhiked to Halifax and tried to enlist for the war in Korea but was rejected because of poor eyesight. In February 1952 he took a two-week farming course sponsored by the Department of Agriculture. He applied immediately afterwards for a reporter position with a small-town New Brunswick newspaper, padding his résumé with a high school education and a year's experience. They offered him the job, and he arrived with a suitcase full of books.

His new employer was the Hartland *Observer*, a Conservative weekly in a Conservative town on the Saint John River in western New Brunswick. He covered mostly local news, things like county fairs, council meetings, the occasional accident or crime. Still painfully shy, especially around women, he made friends at the paper and in the community organizations they encouraged him to join: the Young Conservatives, the Knights of Pythias, the Masons, the Fish and Game Association. He spent most of his free time alone, reading late into the night in the room he rented in a boarding house.

He sent his poems to American little magazines, because they were what there was. He also began writing to other poets. The most important of these was Fred Cogswell, a professor of English at the University of New Brunswick in Fredericton and then editor of the only poetry magazine in the country. Cogswell sent him magazines and books, introduced him to the work of Canadian poets like Louis Dudek and Raymond Souster, and published his poems in the *Fiddlehead*. In November 1958 he printed Nowlan's first collection of poems, a sixteen-page chapbook called *The Rose and the Puritan*.

By then his poems had begun appearing in Canadian literary magazines, partly because by then there were Canadian literary magazines. *Anthology* aired seven poems. He had poems in the newborn *Prism* and the toddler *Tamarack*. In Montreal, Milton Acorn took some for *Moment* and Michael Gnarowski for *Yes*. For his twenty-seventh birthday Nowlan got a contract from Toronto's Ryerson Press for another chapbook. A month later, on February 20, 1960, he gave his first reading in Toronto, at the Isaacs Gallery for Ray Souster's Contact Poetry Readings series.

The Canada Council gave him a $2,300 Arts Scholarship in June 1961. He left the *Observer* and spent most of the next twelve months writing a novel about his childhood that Ryerson and then M&S rejected. He felt so bad about it he considered sending his Council grant back. But the money was gone, so he swallowed the rejections and returned to his old job. "I work at the *Observer*, drink vodka, and brood," he wrote to Cogswell.

In 1963 he published his first book-length collection of poems, found a new job, and got married. Contact Press published the book, *The Things Which Are*. The *Telegraph-Journal* in Saint John provided the job. And Claudine Orser, a linotype operator at the *Observer*, said yes to the marriage. She was a year older than him, with a son from a previous marriage. Nowlan loved them both.

They moved to Saint John the day after the wedding, living for the first year in a second-floor tenement on Britain Street in the city's south end. In 1964 the *Telegraph* promoted Nowlan to provincial editor and they moved to a larger apartment in the north end. That year saw his poems in the New Canadian Library's *Poetry of Mid-Century*, edited by U of T's Milton Wilson. Nowlan read at the Montreal Museum of Fine Arts in November 1963 and at UBC in the spring. (Milton Acorn crashed the lunch for Nowlan at UBC's faculty club. He told Nowlan he could write but needed to learn how to read for an audience.)

In March 1966, Nowlan finally gave in to his wife's urging and saw a doctor about a lump on his neck. He ended up in hospital for six weeks, undergoing three complex surgeries to remove a malignant tumour from his thyroid gland. The operations were successful but left him with a raspy voice and a propensity to obesity. "I thought I was going to die," he said. "The thing I was worried about after worrying about what would become of my wife and son was how much I wanted to write — how much time I'd wasted when I could have been writing." That summer he wrote a series of adaptations of Mi'kmaq legends for the *Atlantic Advocate* and put together his next book of poems. Fred Cogswell led a group of friends who got him a special grant from the Canada Council for $5,500. The following spring he won a Guggenheim Fellowship, enough money to let him write full-time for the rest of the year.

After McClelland & Stewart rejected his new book, Nowlan sent the manuscript to Clarke, Irwin in Toronto at the urging of the company's new editor, Roy MacSkimming. They accepted the book in April 1967 and published it that fall under the title *Bread, Wine and Salt*. Nowlan said the title represented the holiness of ordinary life.

*Bread, Wine and Salt* won the 1967 Governor General's Literary Award for poetry, shared with Eli Mandel's *An Idiot Joy*. Claudine and their son went with him to Ottawa to accept the award. "It always seems sort of funny to me," he wrote to a cousin just before leaving, "when anyone gives me money for simply writing down what I feel. When I did the same thing back in Stanley everybody thought I was a half-wit."

**BREAD, WINE AND SALT**
**(1967)**
**Alden Nowlan**

★★★

Nowlan's first book of poetry in five years was designed and illustrated for his new publisher by Mary Cserepy, a Hungarian-born Toronto artist, with Impressionist drawings of rock-like people, all spiky around the edges. The drawings have a kind of rough beauty, not unlike the poems.

Most of the poems are about family, friends, and neighbours in and around Hartland, New Brunswick. Some are about Nowlan himself and a few about the world, Vietnam and Ottawa. His voice inclines to tenderness, verging on sentimental. "Gentle words are whispered," he says in one poem, "and harsh words shouted." He was more of a whisperer than a shouter, which is maybe why Layton and Purdy have drowned him out.

**IN THE SPRING** of 1976, *Saturday Night* published a long illustrated article under the title "The Newfoundland Renaissance." "Destruction of the outports," declared the deck, "has unexpectedly spawned Newfcult, the miraculous and exciting revival of art and theatre on Canada's poor, bald rock."

Newfoundland's version of Canada's cultural boom came a

little later than elsewhere in the country, but it came for mostly the same reasons: new government support, new universities, and new resources, a society both excited and worried about profound economic change. On its own time, the island also had its own reasons, first among them the forced resettlement of Newfoundlanders from the outports to larger "growth centres" — a heart-torn dislocation that gave art a subject, a feeling, often an anger. Art feeds more on loss than grants.

Joey Smallwood didn't care much for art himself, but he was willing to pay for it. One of his first acts as premier of the new province of Newfoundland was to make Memorial University College in St. John's a degree-granting institution, a "power-house," as he saw it, for the "dissemination and encouragement of a distinctly Newfoundland culture." Two years later, in 1951, his minister of education established an Arts and Letters Competition for all residents of Newfoundland and Labrador. Faculty and librarians at Memorial began assembling a provincial archive and a dictionary of Newfoundland English. In 1961 Memorial opened a new campus, a new art gallery, and an extension service to take the university to rural communities and encourage local artists, musicians, and writers.

Their new country helped. The Canada Council supported the archives and the dictionary, helped Memorial develop an artist-in-residence program in the outports, and funded a travelling agitprop theatre company called the Mummers Troupe. Centennial funding established the Newfoundland and Labrador Folk Arts Council for arts from home and the St. John's Arts and Culture Centre for arts from away. The St. John's CBC TV affiliate launched *All Around the Circle*, a variety show devoted to Newfoundland folk music

**HOUSE OF HATE (1970)**
Percy Janes

*House of Hate* is a novelized study of the damage wrought on children by an abusive father, a perpetually angry man who takes out his disappointment and rage on his wife and children. "Fear was the governing principle of our entire family existence," says Juju Stone. Ultimately Juju puts the blame on environment more than family, on the crushing poverty, isolation, and ignorance of rural Newfoundland and the damage it caused his father and so his father's children. He sees his baby brother as "the last in that long line of Newfoundlanders who stood rooted in time, storing up through the centuries, dumbly waiting for their Van Gogh to come and set down the pity and the terror of their lives." Janes isn't quite that Van Gogh, but besides a few poems by Tom Dawe, I've read nothing from the period that comes closer.

that aired nationally from 1969 to 1975. In 1967 the National Film Board paid Alberta-born director Colin Low to make a group of films on and about the isolated community of Fogo Island, part of an NFB program that used communally pro-

**THE BOAT WHO WOULDN'T FLOAT (1969)**
**Farley Mowat**

★★★

In the spring of 1960, Farley Mowat and his publisher, Jack McClelland, bought a fishing schooner laid up on Newfoundland's Avalon Peninsula. The idea was they'd sail it together to Bermuda, the Azores, Rio de Janeiro — wherever the wind took them.

They never got out of Placentia Bay. The wind couldn't take them far, since the masts and sails were rotten. The boat had an engine, but it started unpredictably in either forward or reverse, when it started. To say it leaked like a sieve would be a grievous insult to sieves. The compass missed north by a good forty degrees. (St. John's writer Harold Horwood found the boat for them. Harold was published by Doubleday.)

I can't see why anyone ever thought Mowat was writing non-fiction: his stories are too good to be true.

duced media to spark social progress. The three books that came out of Farley Mowat's eight years in Newfoundland — *This Rock Within the Sea* (1968), *The Boat Who Wouldn't Float* (1969), and *A Whale for the Killing* (1972) — struck some islanders as condescending but turned a national light on the place and its people. "He began the literary movement [in Newfoundland], however badly," wrote St. John's publisher Clyde Rose in 1973. "He taught us we were worth writing about."

Resettlement mattered more. From the mid-fifties to the mid-seventies, the provincial and later the federal government paid families living in the outports to move to larger centres, a massive experiment in demographic engineering designed to adjust the province to a life after fishing. By 1975 nearly thirty thousand people had been moved and more than 250 communities abandoned. Resettlement brought isolated writers and artists to the towns and cities and in contact with other artists. It sent young people to schools and universities, creating a class for the creation and consumption of art. And it gave Newfoundlanders a subject for art: the life they were leaving behind, literally or in their collective imagination. "People were forced to recognize what they were losing," said playwright Michael Cook.

Then, oil. The discovery of offshore oil in the 1970s fuelled hopes of economic recovery and launched a long argument over ownership of the oil, constitutionally under federal jurisdiction because not on provincial land. A new provincial government, the Progressive Conservatives led by Frank Moores, fought for control, declaring that Newfoundlanders wanted to be "masters in our own house." As in Quebec, an economic grievance fostered cultural pride and the rise of Newfoundland nationalism.

By the time St. John's–born journalist Sandra Gwyn had published her *Saturday Night* article in 1976, what she called the Newfcult phenomenon was in full swing. Her article begins in Philadelphia, on tour with the "commedia dell'outport" troupe CODCO for the American bicentennial.* She comes back to Newfoundland for a performance in Badger by the Mummers Troupe, a play about the loggers' strike that Joey Smallwood broke, in the town where he broke it. She visits artist-in-residence Gerry Squires in Ferryland, who shows her a work in progress called *No Longer May Seagulls Cry in Their Ears* and tells her, "We're starting to get our identity back." She mentions actor Gordon Pinsent, novelist Harold Horwood, columnist Ray Guy, painters Christopher and Mary Pratt, printmakers Heidi Oberheide and David Blackwood, lithographer Frank Lapointe, folk-rockers Figgy Duff, Memorial University's Extension Service, art curator Edythe Goodridge, playwrights David French, Michael Cook, and Grace Butt, and many others. "Suddenly, all over this rock," she says, "painters and actors and poets are popping up in sweet and splendid profusion."

**DEATH ON THE ICE (1972)**
Cassie Brown

In March 1914, a series of mistakes left 132 men on shifting ice off the north coast of Newfoundland for two nights during a blizzard. Seventy-eight of them died. "All the details of this story are true," says journalist Cassie Brown in her novelized account of the disaster, reconstructed from evidence given in the inquiries that followed. She also had the evidence of the bodies themselves, photographed on their return to St. John's, stacked three deep on the deck, still frozen in the positions in which they had died.

A bestseller at the time and for years afterwards required reading in Newfoundland high schools, *Death on the Ice* is still a powerful story, starkly told. It's not an indictment of sealing but of the sealing industry, in which men endured inhuman labour conditions for thirty dollars a year. This is not Farley Mowat's Newfoundland.

---

* CODCO grew out of the Newfoundland Travelling Theatre Company. It debuted with the revue *Crime and Punishment/Cod on a Stick* at Toronto's Theatre Passe Muraille in October 1973.

**TOM DAWE WAS** born and now lives again near Long Pond on Conception Bay, about twenty-five kilometres from St. John's. In 1963 he began teaching high school in Lewisporte, on Newfoundland's north coast. "I always liked poetry," he says. "I started writing poetry when I was teaching school. The books started to change: you started to see less of Bliss Carman and the boys, and more of the mildly contemporary poets. I was teaching history and English, and I thought, I could write as well as this."

E. J. Pratt showed him that poetry could be about Newfoundlanders. But the poets who moved him first, he says, were people like Alden Nowlan, writers who expressed great feeling in plain language. "He still stirs me." Margaret Laurence was also an important influence.

> When she talks about the small place, she says people might think nothing happens here, in little Manawaka. The train just goes through, and if you're not looking, you'll miss it. But she says, in one of her essays, that everything happens here. That made me feel better about writing about some of the small places. Everything happens here. It all happens, wherever a few people are living.

Like Nowlan, he sent most of his early poems away, to little magazines in Britain, in the States, and on the mainland. Aside from the antique *Newfoundland Quarterly,* there was nowhere else.

In 1968 Memorial established a junior division to help first-year students from small communities adjust to the university and to city life. To staff it they hired many teachers straight out of Newfoundland high schools. "I'm teaching out at Lewisporte in 1969," says Dawe, "and here's an offer which says, you're probably interested in doing an M.A. So come on in and do the M.A. and teach for us, be a lecturer, and we'll give you free courses. My M.A. didn't cost me one cent. That new structure got us in there, us young writers, because that's how we got our jobs, coming in from teaching high school in the outports."

In 1971 he sent a poem to a magazine in Montreal called *Intercourse.*

The editor who responded happened to be a Newfoundlander: Al Pittman, part of an Atlantic expatriate community in Montreal that included Clyde Rose and singer Pat Byrne and the magazine's founders, New Brunswick writers Raymond Fraser and LeRoy Johnson. Pittman was from Corner Brook, and like Dawe a teacher and a poet. He wrote to Dawe that his were the first poems that *Intercourse* had seen from Newfoundland and that he'd love to publish them but couldn't, because the magazine was folding.

Two years later, Pittman, Rose, and Byrne found themselves back in Newfoundland, all teaching at Memorial. Driven by the need for books from home to teach, they united with Dawe and English professor Richard Buehler and in 1973 established Newfoundland's first commercial publishing house. Breakwater Books' first publication was an anthology of Newfoundland literature called *Baffles of Wind and Tide*, edited by Rose, which sold over twenty thousand copies. A collection of Ray Guy's columns for the St. John's *Evening Telegram — You May Know Them as Sea Urchins, Ma'am —* sold five thousand copies in just two weeks. They published plays by Michael Cook and Tom Cahill and their own poems, Dawe's first solo book and Pittman's third. A book of poetry for "children and young fish" by Pittman won an award from the Canadian Association of Children's Librarians. A second collection of Guy's columns, illustrated by Gerry Squires, won the Leacock Award for Humour. In three years Breakwater had produced a dozen commercial successes and won two national prizes, all without national distribution.

To promote their list and its interest in Newfoundland's heritage, all five publishers, along with fiddler Rufus Guinchard, were

**HEMLOCK COVE AND AFTER (1975)**
Tom Dawe

There are some fond memories of rural life in Dawe's first book, but more strikingly the poems capture the hostility of small communities to strangers, to anyone not like them. An Inuk man is beaten by locals; a new teacher in an isolated outport is scorned for making children read "poets with queer ideas"; a boy is shunned by other boys because he prefers reading books to killing frogs. Like Purdy's poems, Dawe's are myth breaking, not myth-making.

The best introduction to Dawe's poetry is 1993's *In Hardy Country*, a selection from his first three books. His style is deceptively accessible — simple words about deep feelings. They're poems that aren't afraid of pathos, poems that don't hide from sentiment in modern cynicism or postmodern play. But their sentiment is tough-minded, their nostalgia never candy-coated: hardy poems for a hardy country.

"available for dances and convivial evenings" to give readings, perform jigs and reels, and sing folksongs. "Let Jack McClelland top that," said the *Globe and Mail*.

**AFTER PICKING UP** his Governor General's Award, Alden Nowlan became writer-in-residence at the University of New Brunswick. The Canada Council paid his stipend of $5,500 a year and the university provided a small house at the edge of campus. He wasn't expected to teach any classes, just write and meet with students and faculty. Partly to keep up his health benefits, he stayed on the *Telegraph* payroll with a weekly column.

That summer of 1968, Clarke, Irwin published a collection of his short fiction called *Miracle at Indian River*. Mostly autobiographical stories about poor people in rural Nova Scotia and New Brunswick, the book was savaged by Dave Godfrey in *Canadian Forum*. Nowlan had given a poor review to Godfrey's own first collection of stories in the *Forum* earlier that year, and Godfrey shot back behind a pseudonym: "I thought your stories were real neat, Ald, just real neat.... You really got poverty right, Ald. Sometimes I get a little embarrassed reading [Hugh] Garner. It's almost as though he had been poor himself once. But you have that certain distance." Nowlan responded in a furious letter to the editor, saying that until he received his first paycheque at age fifteen he had lived on boiled potatoes flavoured with vinegar. "Don't get funny when you talk to me about poverty, you presumptuous anonymous jerk."

He hung on to the writer-in-residence position until 1972, and the *Telegraph* column for fifteen years. In return for some speechwriting, New Brunswick premier Richard Hatfield agreed to replace the Council's funding and eventually to provide an annual stipend. For the rest of his life, Nowlan was a kind of adjunct at UNB and the unofficial poet laureate of New Brunswick. In the late sixties and early seventies, his and Claudine's university home on Windsor Street — dubbed Windsor Castle — was Fredericton's literary centre, home and tavern for young faculty and student poets like Louis Cormier, Ray Fraser, and Fraser's friend Al Pittman. "A typical

scene in those years would have been three students mimeograph-
ing a little magazine on my dining-room table," said Nowlan. "Or
a student knocking on my door at 4 a.m. to tell me that he'd had a
poem accepted by the CBC."

He kept publishing his own poems in magazines and books.
In 1973, Clarke, Irwin published a novel he called a fictional mem-
oir. He did a ten-stop tour of western Canada for the League of
Canadian Poets with New Brunswick poet Elizabeth Brewster. The
CBC and the NFB made documentaries about him. He co-wrote
several plays with Theatre New Brunswick artistic director Walter
Learning, most successfully an adaptation of *Frankenstein*. In 1979 a
collection of his *Telegraph* columns won an award from the Writers'
Federation of Nova Scotia.

In 1983, now fifty, Nowlan's drinking and his weight problem
caught up with him. After a cardiac arrest, he fell into a coma. Two
weeks later Claudia had the hospital disconnect his respirator. She
buried him in Fredericton's Forest Hill Cemetery, right behind
Bliss Carman. "If there's anything I'd like to be remembered for
in years to come," Nowlan had told a reporter in 1977, "it would be
that I had given confidence to writers to write about places where
they actually lived."

**ALISTAIR MACLEOD MARRIED** Anita MacLellan, who grew up in
Cape Breton in a house near his. "My wife and I are from the same
community," he told the *Globe*. "We've known each other since
pre-birth." They had six sons — one of whom died in infancy — and
a daughter together. Family mattered more to him than writing,
more than anything, which is one reason he wrote just one novel
and seventeen short stories in his fifty years as a writer.

While he was still in the States, before he moved to Windsor for
his new job, he had sent a story off to the *Tamarack Review* called
"In the Fall," about a man remembering his mother forcing his
father to sell their horse because the horse is old and they're poor.
Given its backlog, *Tamarack* took more than five years to publish
it, in October 1973. Soon after the issue came out, Jack McClelland

read the story. He wrote to MacLeod the next day at the University of Windsor, calling it "probably the best piece of Canadian writing, either short or long, that I have seen for a considerable period of time." He said he had called Bob Weaver, and Bob had said MacLeod had more stories. MacLeod sent Jack three more to look at, and by the following spring he had a contract for his first book. M&S published *The Lost Salt Gift of Blood* in January 1976. For MacLeod, the blood in the title meant family, and salt the sea and bitterness. All the stories, he said, were about loss.

He stayed with the University of Windsor until his retirement, teaching and editing the *Windsor Review*. He and Anita bought the house back home in Dunvegan that his great-grandfather built, the house in which his grandfather and his father were born. Their growing family spent most summers there. Neighbours built him a small writing shack near the house, on a grassy cliff above the ocean.

Ten years after his first collection, MacLeod published a second, and thirteen years after that a novel, *No Great Mischief*. The novel was the first by a Canadian to win the International IMPAC Dublin Literary Award, then the world's richest literary prize, equivalent to $172,000 Canadian. In 2009 more than seven hundred authors, editors, and critics elected *No Great Mischief* the greatest Atlantic-Canadian book of all time, just ahead of *Anne of Green Gables*.

Alistair MacLeod died in 2014 and is buried with his ancestors in Cape Breton. The *New York Times* titled its obituary "A Novelist in No Hurry."

## Chapter 17

# Lives of Girls and Women

**In the shadows, far from the smoking men,**
    **the women wove**
        **—Marie-Claire Blais, "The Sleepers"**

**ALICE MUNRO GREW** up on a small farm at the end of a road just outside the town of Wingham, in Huron County, southwestern Ontario. Today she lives a half-hour's drive away. Her stories have travelled far in the years between, but that bit of the world has always been the centre of her life and work.

Her father, Robert Laidlaw, was born on a farm cleared by his grandfather. In an unpublished fragment of memoir, Munro described her father as a Huron County farm boy who preferred the woods and trapping to fields and farming. In 1925 he became a fur farmer, raising mink and foxes. Two years later he married Annie Chamney, a schoolteacher from eastern Ontario. They bought a five-acre farm on the Maitland River with a brick house and a barn. They could see the town hall and church towers of Wingham to the east when the leaves were off the trees.

Alice Ann Laidlaw came along in the summer of 1931, later joined by a brother and sister. Until the fur trade dried up in the war years they had a hired girl to help out around the house. They had a car, even if it didn't always run, and annual holidays on the beach at Goderich. Alice walked to school, first to Lower Wingham and then across the river into Wingham proper for Grades 4 to 13.

She says the first book she ever read was Charles Dickens's *A Child's History of England*, a book they had at home. Later she devoured Lucy Maud Montgomery's *Emily of New Moon* and a collection of Tennyson's poems she found in an abandoned farmhouse. "Reading in our family was a private activity," she wrote in a 1962 essay. "There was nothing particularly commendable about it.... But once the addiction was established, nobody thought of interfering with it." Both her parents were readers, her mother a little ostentatiously for her surroundings. "My mother," says Del Jordan in a draft of Munro's autobiographical novel *Lives of Girls and Women*, "thinks you can solve anything by writing a letter to the principal."

Munro began caring about school in Grade 8, under a new teacher who cared whether his students enjoyed what they were learning. She finished Grade 9 with the second highest average in Wingham High School, 80.7 percent. On graduation she was Wingham's highest-scoring student and class valedictorian. She won $550 worth of scholarships to the University of Western Ontario for having the highest average in six subjects, including the highest score of any applicant in English. Her family was cash-poor, so a government bursary provided another $400 a year. She enrolled in journalism but switched to honours English for second year. To make ends meet, she worked in libraries and the cafeteria and sold her blood. When summer came, she waitressed at a hotel in the Muskoka Lakes.

She had been serious about writing since she was fourteen. In high school she made up, wrote, and abandoned stories, including an imitation of *Wuthering Heights*, and submitted poems to *Chatelaine*, all unpublished. Near the end of her first year at university, the undergraduate literary magazine published a story by her about a small-town female teacher infatuated with a male student. The contributor's note described her as "overly modest about her talents, but hopes to write the Great Canadian Novel some day."

Early in 1951, halfway through her second year, her stories reached the desk of CBC producer Robert Weaver. In May he bought one for $50. "The Strangers" was scheduled for broadcast on

*Canadian Short Stories* on June 1. Alice Munro's first professional story was bumped for coverage of the release that day of the Massey Report, the national inquiry into the absence of Canadian writers. Her story aired in October, on the first episode of the show's fall season.

By then she had left university and was about to be married. She loved university — "those are the only two years of my life without housework," she told her biographer. And she did exceptionally well at it, earning a prize at the end of second year for the highest marks in English. But the scholarships were only for two years and there was no more money. She could go back to Wingham or she could get married. On December 29, 1951, she married Jim Munro, an accountant's son from Oakville whom she had met in the library.

The newlyweds took the train to Vancouver, where Jim had a job at Eaton's downtown store and half the main floor of a pink stucco house facing Kitsilano Beach. Alice worked at the Kitsilano branch of the Vancouver Public Library, looked after the house, had children — three, including a second daughter born without functioning kidneys who died that day — and read a lot, "most of the writers of the twentieth century that you're supposed to have read." With help from Jim's father they bought a bungalow in North Vancouver and then a larger house on Lawson Avenue in West Vancouver, on the hill above Marine Drive.

**DANCE OF THE HAPPY SHADES (1968)**
Alice Munro

Munro, not Richler, is our great satirist. We just don't think of her as one, because, unlike Richler, she's subtle enough to lull you into thinking her caricatures are real. But like him she's got a mean streak, a fondness for poking at the way people, especially those with little education, look, speak, and think.

Like all social satire, the book feels a bit dated now that its society is gone. Today, Munro's first book is most important as an early run at *Lives of Girls and Women*, without the novel's sympathetic distance because without the escape Del Jordan achieves. It's still a very good collection, especially the auto-biographical story "The Peace of Utrecht." Munro knows how to end stories better than any short-story writer I know.

Weaver bought a half-dozen more stories from Munro in the fifties and encouraged her to send them elsewhere as well. She landed her first commercial publication, "A Basket of Strawberries," in the November 1953 issue of *Mayfair*, a high-society Toronto monthly. Others followed in *Canadian Forum*, *Queen's Quarterly*, *Chatelaine*,

*Tamarack Review,* and the *Montrealer.* She also tried the *New Yorker,* unsuccessfully.

With references from Weaver and two English professors, she applied for a Canada Council grant to pay for some babysitting. Her application was unsuccessful. Also encouraged by Weaver — and, by 1961, Jack McClelland — she made many attempts at a novel. None satisfied her, and she fell into a lengthy depression in the late fifties during which she wrote little and published nothing. She rented an office above a drugstore on Marine Drive and tried again to write a novel. All that came of it was a short story about a woman renting an office in which to write.

**LIVES OF GIRLS AND WOMEN (1971)**
**Alice Munro**

★★★★★

The writer who couldn't write novels wrote one of the best novels anywhere, in any time. *Lives of Girls and Women* is about an ambitious young woman in a place and time faintly suspicious of ambition, a small town in southwestern Ontario much like the one in which Munro grew up. She had to trick herself into writing it, adding stories about the same girl until she had what she and her publisher agreed to call a novel. Until the epilogue came to her, she said, it was "just the story of a young girl."

It's still that, but it's also the story of how that young girl became Canada's best writer ever. The trick, as Del Jordan realizes, is to see that there is nothing ordinary about ordinary lives. That, and a lot of hard work.

By the summer of 1963 Jim was tired of working at Eaton's. With his retail and her library experience, they decided on a bookstore. They rented a storefront in downtown Victoria and a house a half-hour's walk away at 105 Cook Street, next to Beacon Hill Park. For Munro, those first years in Victoria were the happiest of her marriage. Jim worked at the store all day, coming home for supper. She worked there afternoons and evenings. "We were very poor," she says, "but our aims were completely wound up with surviving in this place."

In August 1966, with Alice pregnant again, they got a bargain price on a large house at 1648 Rockland Avenue, a twelve-room Tudor-style home with five bedrooms, five fireplaces, and two sets of staircases. Jim and their oldest daughter, Sheila, by now a teenager, wanted the house. Alice hated it from the start — it was too large to heat and look after, too grand. She told her first biographer that her marriage never recovered from the move.

Weaver had by then interested several publishers in Munro. McClelland & Stewart and a New York publisher (Appleton-Century-Crofts) both wanted a novel first, though Jack told her that if a novel was too far off, he would consider a story collection. John Robert Colombo at Ryerson Press offered to publish a collection, but Munro resisted. Colombo's successor, Earle Toppings, met Munro for lunch in Vancouver in 1962 or '63 and got a sense that a book wasn't a priority for her. During her first three years in Victoria, she completed only two stories, both published in the *Montrealer*.

Then, in March 1967, Munro and Toppings agreed on a book. As Jim Munro tells it, her change of heart came from reading books in their store. "Hell," she said, "I can write better books than these." Ryerson published *Dance of the Happy Shades* the following fall: fifteen stories, three of them new. Ryerson author Hugh Garner provided a preface, Weaver a blurb. She dedicated the book to her father.

*Dance of the Happy Shades* won the 1968 Governor General's Literary Award for fiction. Munro attended the ceremony with her husband, her father and his new wife (her mother had died in 1959 after a long fight with Parkinson's disease), her sister, and Jim's parents. Her father was exceptionally proud — "astounded," said Munro many years later — especially when Pierre Trudeau showed up unannounced, the first prime minister to attend the ceremony in its thirty-three years. Until that night, she added, her family had thought of her writing as "something I would get over." For her the award meant that now she could tell people she was writing, that writing was what she did.

**THE YEAR ALICE** Munro's mother turned twenty, 1918, women became eligible to vote in Canadian federal elections. When Annie was a twenty-three-year-old schoolteacher, Canadians elected their first female member of Parliament. One year into her marriage, she saw women on Canada's Olympic team for the first time. During the Second World War she read about women suddenly working in all sorts of jobs, from factory floors to newsrooms.

After the war — after the men came home and needed their jobs back, when men and women wanted homes where they could for-get the loneliness of war and the new threat of the Bomb — becoming a woman mostly meant becoming a wife and a mother. By the mid-1950s, 60 percent of American women were dropping out of college, either to get married or because they saw no point in continuing. By the end of the decade, the average marriage age of women in America had dropped to twenty. In their magazines, women became or hoped to become happy housewives, content in a reduced world of "bedroom and kitchen, sex, babies, and home."

So said American journalist Betty Friedan in her 1963 bestseller, *The Feminine Mystique*. Encouraging representations of working women in postwar commercial magazines were not as rare as Freidan suggested. But the house-wife/mother was the ideal, even if she now also had to work outside the home to help with the mounting bills. *Life* had a working woman on its cover for Christmas 1956, but it showed her looking happily into the eyes of a child.

The situation was very similar in Canada, partly because its most popular women's maga-zine, *Chatelaine*, was modelled on American magazines and bought much of its fiction from American agents. Alice Munro got married at twenty, the American average. Phyllis Brett Young's *The Torontonians* amounts to a fic-tional version of *The Feminine Mystique*: social history disguised as a novel about a housewife who has everything — children, husband, house — and wonders, like Friedan's housewives, if that's all there is. At the other end of the spectrum, Maria Campbell's *Halfbreed* shows a woman and a

**HALFBREED (1973)**
**Maria Campbell**

Strange but true: Maria Camp-bell's autobiography became a bestseller the same year that Cher's "Half-Breed" was a num-ber one pop hit in the United States and Canada.

Of mostly Scottish, French, and Cree descent, Campbell recounts her life from occa-sionally happy poverty north of Prince Albert, Saskatchewan, through prostitution, addiction, and suicide attempts in Van-couver, Calgary, and Edmonton in the fifties and sixties. At twelve she became mother and father to seven brothers and sisters after her mother died in childbirth and her father disappeared into drink.

Jack McClelland's request to connect the manuscript to larger issues of poverty and discrimination in a "biography with a purpose" resulted in the book's weakest passages, hasty histories of things like the Riel rebellions and Native activism that get in the way of Camp-bell's story. It's still a good book, and still important.

mother left out of the affluent society (and Friedan's book), a life of poverty, racism, and abuse in rural Saskatchewan and the slums of Vancouver.

For a decade defined by change, not much changed in the lives of girls and women in the 1960s besides longer hair and shorter skirts. As the decade was beginning, the CBC cancelled an interview with French philosopher Simone de Beauvoir because she approved of divorce. Three years later, CTV pulled Pierre Berton's interview with Helen Gurley Brown about her book *Sex and the Single Girl*, partly because of the shitstorm generated by Berton's recent *Maclean's* column defending premarital sex, including for his own daughters. At the end of the most iconic English-Canadian film of the 1960s, Don Owen's *Nobody Waved Good-bye*, the rebel-without-a-cause hero leaves his pregnant girlfriend at the side of the road — the fate of an increasing number of teenage girls over the decade. The pill gave women more control but gave men no side effects, no consequences, and increased expectations. "In the fifties," as one veteran of the so-called sexual revolution put it, "the message was 'Nice girls don't screw.' In the sixties it was 'Nice girls don't say no.'"

WRITING IN THE sixties, says Margaret Atwood, was no different from life in the sixties: "pretty much a guy thing, in Canada as elsewhere."

> The people involved in starting the publishing houses and the magazines are mostly guys who opted out of being the guy in the grey flannel suit. They didn't give much of a piss about whatever Betty Friedan had to say because it didn't concern them. They're much more interested in the fact that the pill has made sex freely available.

Layton's poems line up at the left margin and Bowering's don't, but they both contain a lot of tits and asses. Atwood says Layton interrupted one of her readings by shouting from the audience that her poems were putting him to sleep, and that "women are only good for screwing, men are good for screwing *plus!*" She based David, the loud-mouthed sexist husband in *Surfacing*, on Bowering. *Tish*, Coach House, and *Parti pris* were all male domains that published almost entirely male writers.* "They looked at girls as potential muses or hangers-on," says Daphne Marlatt. "Quebec is a woman just conquered," said a young Québécois commentator on CBC Radio — an image used over and over again in French-Canadian literature. For all their much proclaimed and much exaggerated differences, western and eastern poets, French and English, were united by simple, common, ordinary sexism.

At the height of poetry's new popularity, several prominent Canadian women poets stopped writing or publishing. Jay Macpherson and P. K. Page published only one book of new poetry each in the 1960s. Phyllis Webb published nothing for fifteen years after 1965's *Naked Poems*. They quit for their own reasons (Page, for example, because she was studying Portuguese and learning to paint), but it's hard to avoid thinking that they went silent partly because the men were so loud. If it were true, as Layton said — and his popularity suggested — that the poetry of the future would be written by the guy with the biggest "fist," then there was no future for a woman poet.

Mavis Gallant told an interviewer in 1978 that if she had stayed in Canada she would have become a frustrated housewife. Alice Munro's oldest daughter says that her mother couldn't write for a year after she visited a creative writing class at the University of Victoria in the mid-sixties, where a male student dismissed the story she had brought them as "something a typical housewife would write." Margaret Laurence wrote in her memoirs that when she began writing at university,

> Writing by women, in those and the following years, was generally regarded by critics and reviewers in this country with at

---

* bill bissett's *blew ointment* was a rare exception, publishing many now-forgotten women writers. "To me," says bissett, "the canon is not male-centred. I don't accept that. I know it exists, but that's not what I'm interested in."

best an amused tolerance, at worst a dismissive shrug. It still makes me angry how thoroughly I had been brainwashed by society, despite having been greatly encouraged by two of my male professors at college, whom I bless to this day. But when I first submitted poems to the University of Manitoba student paper, *The Manitoban*, I sent them in under the name of Steve Lancaster....I cringe with shame to recall it now. Later, I dared to use my own name, but it was J. M. Wemyss, I think, not Jean Margaret. In one of my early stories, published in the United College magazine, *Vox*, I actually used a first-person narrative, but the narrator was a man. How long, how regrettably long, it took me to find my true voice as a woman writer.

**SURFACING (1972)**
**Margaret Atwood**

★★★★

*On Golden Pond* meets *The Shining*. A young, recently divorced woman returns to her family cabin after her father disappears. As Atwood said, the ghosts are all in her narrator's head, the disease coming up from the south, the Canadians she thinks are Americans.

Today the novel seems more marred than aided by its use of the United States as a socioeconomic bogeyman. Even if the narrator is seeing things, the book still uses Americans in the same way Joseph Conrad used Africans in *Heart of Darkness*, as the inhuman Other against which to define what's human. "This above all," it famously ends, "to refuse to be a victim." That's still important to hear. Me, I like the story more than the lesson: the perfectly paced revelation of madness, the uncanny wilderness, the clarity of the writing.

Reviews improved over the sixties, partly because of several supportive and prolific male reviewers (notably Robert Fulford and Robert Weaver), partly because more reviews were being written by women. In 1971 Margaret Atwood asked the students in her Canadian Women Writers course at York University to survey magazines and newspapers for evidence of sexual bias in Canadian reviewing; they didn't find as much as they expected. Still, they found many examples, all by men against women, such as commenting on the attractiveness of an author's photo or praising a woman for writing like a man. When they asked Canadian authors if they felt reviews of their work had been slanted because of their gender, four of the nine women who responded said yes.

Because of her representations of men and women, because of her success, because she's never been good at silence, Atwood took the brunt of Canadian literary sexism in the 1960s and '70s. In the spring of 1974, *Canadian Forum* printed a juvenile parody about a pretty little girl named Margaret who lives at the bottom of a lake guarded by male leprechauns. Little Margaret urges everyone in the lake to "stop being victims" and eats so many of the leprechauns that she gets bigger and bigger and grows tentacles, becoming "the octopus of Lake Canada." She grows so powerful that she rises from the lake, shouting, "I'm surfacing."*

That fall, the *Globe and Mail* published a review of Atwood's sixth book of poetry (*You Are Happy*) that her biographer Rosemary Sullivan says epitomized the pervasive image of Atwood in those years as a man-eating monster. Written by the poet Alan Pearson, the review describes Atwood as both a fey Brontean figure and a "snaky-haired Medusa," a frightening beauty of Canadian letters. "The male psyche knows to beware," says Pearson, "lest this sinewy female unleashes all the thermotropic weaponry of her rhetoric."

"Both the 'male' writers of my generation," said Atwood in a letter to Margaret Laurence (I think she means Layton and Purdy), "had trouble with me at first, didn't know whether to shake my hand or grab my ass." But "they're ok now," she added.

**MARIE-CLAIRE BLAIS CREATED** her own monsters. "I write about monsters because they are alone and unloved," she told a CBC reporter in 1960. "They are incapable of love. That is the tragedy of life."

She grew up alone for the first six years of her life, the oldest of five children, including a sister of whom she was very fond who was sent away to a mental institution. Her father had a good job as an electrician at Quebec City's Laval Dairy, but with seven mouths to feed, money was tight. At fifteen she quit school and got a typing job to help out.

---

* The *Forum* took some of the sting out of the anonymous attack by printing an article in the same issue by journalist George Galt that called *Surfacing* "likely the best piece of fiction produced by Atwood's generation in North America or anywhere." But as Atwood said in a letter to Dennis Lee (who along with Jay Macpherson wrote to the *Forum* condemning the parody), what bothered her about "The Lady of the Lake" wasn't so much the personal attack as the "rampant sexism."

She wrote her first novel that year, about a boy sold to the circus by his father. She had been writing since she was six. "I really thought something was wrong with me," she said, "because I kept feeling I had to put things down on paper. I lived in a dream world and invented imaginary characters." By the time she was nineteen she had written four novels, a dozen plays, and some two hundred poems.

Her family teased her about the hours she spent writing but regarded it as a harmless hobby. Then her mother read one of her stories she had found in a drawer. Horrified by what she read, she threw it into the fire. Blais was furious. "You burned my babies!" she screamed when she came home that night. "You burned my children!" She was still angry when she told the story to the CBC several years later, speaking about her family with what struck the reporter as "actual hate." She began taking her manuscripts with her to work, a habit that got her fired by employers who thought she was working for others on their time. She found other jobs and kept writing.

In 1958 she began taking evening classes in literature and philosophy at Laval University. Her teacher and mentor Jeanne Lapointe remembered her running around with but somewhat outside a wild bunch of students who hung out at the Porte des Arts Café and hitchhiked to Montreal for the beatnik cafés on Stanley Street. "She just followed them around," she said, "taking it all in."

In the early fall of 1959, Blais wrote to Father Georges-Henri Lévesque, former dean of Laval's faculty of social sciences and vice-president of the Canada Council. "I have written many novels, plays and poems but have been unable to get them published," she said. "You are my last hope." Lévesque asked for a sample of her work; she mailed him a stack of manuscripts a foot high. "All," said Lévesque, "were stories of tormented, tangled, and utterly unpublishable relationships between human monsters." But he agreed to meet her. After he got over his shock at her youth, he told Blais she needed to be more selective, more disciplined. She said she had a story in mind about a smart, ugly girl and her stupid, beautiful brother. "Like a beautiful beast," said the priest. "That's it!" said Blais. "That will be the title."

Fifteen days later it was done. Lévesque took the manuscript to Paul Michaud at the Institut littéraire du Québec, who decided to publish it immediately. *La Belle Bête* was published near the end of October 1959, a few weeks after its author's twentieth birthday. As promised, it's the story of an ugly girl who shoves her beautiful brother's face into boiling water. At the end she burns her hated mother's house to the ground, an ending that has been championed as clearing the way for a new Quebec society, a new Quebec literature, and a new women's literature. (I'd guess Blais's mother interpreted it differently.)

*La Belle Bête* sold five thousand copies in six weeks and made Blais a celebrity in Quebec. "We salute the monsters," said French CBC Radio. "The most beautiful, the most marvellous beginning," said *Le Devoir*. The Catholic young people's magazine *Lecture* helped sales by labelling it "dangerous." *Saturday Night* published a four-page profile of Blais called "Lightning on the Literary Landscape" in March, by which time her book was in its third printing. A French edition came out in Paris in the spring; McClelland & Stewart, Jonathan Cape in London, and Little, Brown in Boston published an English translation in the fall. The Canadian Press named Blais woman of the year in literature and the arts. She had by then already published her second novel, about a young boy who enjoys killing small animals and doesn't know why.

**MAD SHADOWS
(LA BELLE BÊTE) (1959)
Marie-Claire Blais**

Mad Shadows is a tragedy, about the fall of a noble house, but *tragedy* doesn't do justice to its cruelty. Set on a country estate in a never-named Quebec, the novel feels and reads more like the nineteenth than the twentieth century, like vintage Baudelaire: decadence and disease, madness and evil, "the consuming passion of the damned." With few contemporary models, the early writers of Quebec's Quiet Revolution may have spent too much time reading older French writers.

The Gallic affection for the beauty of darkness is usually a bit much for my taste. But what saves Mad Shadows is the tightness and brevity of its construction. It sends you to hell but it doesn't leave you there long — just long enough to enjoy the trip and be glad it's over.

She moved to Montreal in 1960. Father Lévesque pulled some strings at the Council and got her a scholarship to study in Paris for the following year. She shared a room with other students at the Hôtel Aiglon in Montparnasse and hitchhiked around Europe with a girlfriend. While she was there, the French

Academy awarded the Prix de la langue française to *La Belle Bête*, which helped make up for the book's meagre sales in France.

A year and another Quebec bestseller after her return from Paris, in May 1963, Blais's landlady came to her room in a Montreal boarding house with news that would change her life. She had won a fellowship from the Guggenheim Foundation, and the man who had helped her win it, American literary critic Edmund Wilson, was expecting her with his wife Elena for a drink at the Ritz-Carlton. Together the Wilsons and Blais decided at this first meeting that she would spend her Guggenheim year in Cambridge, Massachusetts, close to libraries and to the Wilsons' home on Cape Cod.

Blais arrived in Cambridge in June, bringing with her only what she considered essential: table, chair, radio, typewriter. She rented a basement apartment in a drug-ridden black neighbourhood, losing two bicycles to thieves in a month. That summer of race riots in cities across America, she read James Baldwin, Richard Wright, and Ralph Ellison, becoming deeply sympathetic to black oppression and activism. She was also learning to speak English, writing several novels, and publishing a weekly journal in *Le Devoir*.

In October she made her first visit to the Wilsons, staying in a guest cottage behind their house in Wellfleet. By the summer she had found a place of her own nearby, a small house lent to her by the journalist Barbara Deming and her partner, painter Mary Meigs. The beach was a bike ride away. Blais met many others in Cape Cod's affluent arts community, both residents and visitors like Mary McCarthy (Wilson's ex-wife), John Cage, and Bessie Breuer. "I'll feel less alone," she wrote in her notebook, "with all these writers close

**DAVID STERNE (1967)**
**Marie-Claire Blais**

Eighteen-year-old David Sterne is an orphan, a former seminary student, and a rapist. For this and perhaps other crimes he's been found guilty by judges who speak in dark verse and may be figures of his imagination. Blais said the title character was inspired by two American friends, a Harvard student destroyed by drugs and a young black writer twisted by racism. "My friends live again in the hero of this novel, a character whose youth was shattered." She modelled the novel's fragmented form on the music of John Cage after seeing him perform in Maine, where part of it was written.

It's a book born of great sympathy that fails to engender that sympathy in the reader. I admire the attempt, but the result is too artful, too pretentious. John Cage can do that to you.

by, these artists for whom writing, music, painting, is the sacred goal of their lives."

Blais lived for the next six years in Wellfleet, some of it in Maine, where Cape Codders fled tourists in the summer. She would return to Quebec and France to launch a book or pick up a prize, including the Prix Médicis in 1966 for her fourth and best-known novel, *A Season in the Life of Emmanuel*. In May 1969 she won the first of her four Governor General's Awards for *The Manuscripts of Pauline Archange*, the same year that Alice Munro won for her first book. Blais invited a fan to accompany her to Ottawa: Gwendolyn MacEwen, who had written to her around 1964 in schoolgirl French to thank her for inspiring her when she began writing.

When Pierre Trudeau showed up at the ceremony, it wasn't Alice Munro's father he had come to meet, or Leonard Cohen or Mordecai Richler or Hubert Aquin. It was Marie-Claire Blais, the young woman who started a storm.

**A SEASON IN THE LIFE OF EMMANUEL (1965)**
**Marie-Claire Blais**

★★★★

*A Season in the Life of Emmanuel* is actually a season in the life of Emmanuel's large, poor French Catholic family. Emmanuel is their sixteenth baby, born the winter morning on which the book begins. We don't hear much from him besides his thinking he's cold or hungry.

It's much more comic than her earlier novels, more Beckett than Baudelaire. The humour is at times folksy but more often grotesque, *La guerre, yes sir!* with more anger (and more masturbating). "People thought it was realist," said Blais many years later, "that it was a portrait of my friends, of my country, and it was not. It was a kind of Gothic tale of what it is to be deprived, but with humor." The lady doth protest too much, but it's not a political allegory. It's just a story, one of Canada's best.

**IF CANADIAN LITERATURE** in the 1960s was "pretty much a guy thing," why does the Can-Lit boom now seem so dominated by women writers? By Anne Hébert and Marie-Claire Blais in Quebec; by Margaret Atwood and Alice Munro in English Canada; by the long shadows cast by *The Double Hook* on writers, by *The Stone Angel* on classrooms, by *Survival* on criticism? Why does Canada have so many great women writers?

It's a common misconception that progressive artistic communities are also socially progressive. In Canada, as elsewhere, the most avant-garde literary circles were often the worst behaved. Sexism was more common among writers (especially poets) than among professional reviewers and commercial publishers. Even if only because few women held positions of cultural power at the time, many of the establishment's literary men were vital to the early careers of women writers — men such as Malcolm Ross for Margaret Laurence, Georges-Henri Lévesque for Blais, and Robert Weaver for Munro. Laurence may have struggled to find her voice, but she told Graeme Gibson around 1970 that she hadn't experienced many difficulties as a woman author. Atwood said much the same in the same interview series, that she had experienced sexism from reviewers and other writers but seldom from publishers. "Publishers are in business to make money," she said. "If your books do well they don't care whether you are male, female, or an elephant."

Commercial publishers like McClelland & Stewart were not as gender-blind as Atwood said. They bought books by women partly because women were becoming their largest audience, especially for fiction. In the fifties and sixties, half the educated adult population with money to buy books had little to fulfill them outside the home. "There was something horribly wrong," thinks the housewife hero of *The Torontonians*, "with a system that insisted first on compulsory education, and then lured you into a full-time occupation that any reasonably intelligent illiterate could have handled without a qualm."

Many women were no doubt happy being wives and mothers, or too busy to do anything else. But many were not. After and between babies, some golfed, some drank, some had affairs, many turned to therapy and tranquilizers. And some turned to art, a cheaper form of therapy: painting, pottery classes, music, reading. In Betty Friedan's 1957 survey

**A JEST OF GOD (1966)**
**Margaret Laurence**

As several reviewers noted, the plot of Laurence's third novel sounds like a soap opera: the milkman's son seduces the undertaker's daughter. He's dark, handsome, mysteriously tragic; she's a thirty-four-year-old virgin who still lives with her mother. "Put it in, darling," Nick tells her their first time. "A brief searing hurt, and then his sex is in mine and I can feel him piercing warmly, unhurtfully."

If you can set that novel aside, there's another novel here, a better, braver book: a self-portrait of a lonely, scared woman and the social inhibitions that helped make her that way. One reason why the sex and the talk about it feel so false in the novel is that they come from a time that had almost no models of either that *weren't* fictional. This was one of the first that tried not to be.

of women graduates of Smith College, nine in ten of her classmates had become housewives, women who claimed to read from fifteen to a staggering three hundred books a year. "More often than not — far more often than not," said Hugh MacLennan at the University of Saskatchewan in 1959, "the profession of the serious reader today, when the reader applies for a passport, is classified as housewife."

When Atwood sent Laurence a copy of the 1970 feminist anthology *Sisterhood Is Powerful*, Laurence wrote back that although she strongly agreed with the women's liberation movement, she wasn't a "joiner." Atwood herself didn't hear about feminism until about the same time. When *The Edible Woman* was published in 1969, she was living in Edmonton, "where, believe me, there was not a feminist in sight. They didn't even know what the word meant; neither, basically, did I. I never even thought about it." In a reluctantly written article about being a woman writer, she said, "It seems to me that the proper path for a woman writer is not an all-out manning (or womaning) of the barricades, however much she may agree with the aims of the movement. The proper path is to become better as a writer." Like Laurence — and like Blais, Gallant, and Munro — she wrote as a writer first, a woman second, and a feminist third, if at all.

But books become what their readers want. By the early seventies, feminism was another reason for women to buy books by women, turning novels like *The Edible Woman* and *Mad Shadows* into feminist icons and creating women's studies programs and women's bookstores. The Vancouver Women's Bookstore, the first in the country, opened on Richards Street in July 1973, selling books by and for women with an emphasis on Canadian writers. The Toronto Women's Bookstore began that same year as a rack in a corner of a women's centre on Dupont Street. Feminism did not create the writers of the CanLit boom, at least not feminism by name.* But both feminism and the conditions that awoke it did give women writers a large and interested audience. "Whether you

---

* "I was a feminist all my life before the word ever came into being," said Gwen MacEwen. "It never occurred to me that I couldn't do anything I wanted to."

were in the movement or not," says Atwood now, "you were going to be read by those women."

Apart from Robert Weaver's support at the CBC, it's hard to see why Canada produced disproportionately more great women writers than countries with similar social circumstances. Perhaps, as Atwood suggests, the consumer capitalism that fed postwar sexism was less powerful in Canada than in America, a smaller effect because a smaller economy. With fewer ads to tell them what they were supposed to be, maybe Canadian women were a little freer to be what they wanted. Perhaps it was just chance — a few writers who happened to be born the same gender at the same time in the same place. All we can be sure of is that despite the importance of male mentors to many of them, Canadian women writers wouldn't have succeeded without the women who were their largest audience. It wasn't just affluence that created the CanLit boom; it was also one of affluence's most powerful and lasting by-products: women with the time and the need for books.

**IN 1970 MARIE-CLAIRE** Blais moved to France with Mary Meigs. They had become lovers while Meigs was still in her relationship with Barbara Deming, though you'd have a hard time realizing that from Blais's side of the story. She has kept her private life mostly private, including her sexual orientation; her memoirs, *American Notebooks* and a talk she gave in 2010 for the Writers' Trust, are more about other writers than herself. She didn't write about lesbian experiences until 1976, for a play by a Quebec feminist collective. "She does not like labels," said Meigs. "She does not see herself as a lesbian writer. She is a writer. That's her only cause."

They lived in a small village in Brittany, eight miles from the coast. "There are fifty people and one telephone," Blais told the *Globe and Mail* in the fall of 1974 — "ideal conditions for writing." It was lonely, she said, but Paris was only four and a half hours away. And she was coming home in the spring. "I want to be on the Quebec scene now, to be with Quebeckers, close to them... We're so passionate about our feelings, so bound to each other in

Quebec." She moved to a writers' colony in the Eastern Townships. In the 1980s she began dividing her time between Quebec and the Florida island of Key West, where Michel Tremblay also has a home.

**THE MANUSCRIPTS OF PAULINE ARCHANGE (1968)**
Marie-Claire Blais

★★★★

Pauline Archange has finally written the story she wanted to write: her own story, remembering when she was a young girl living among the working poor in a rat-infested alley in an unnamed Quebec city. Her best friend, the only person she loved, is killed. She's sent to live in the country with relatives, savages who whip her blind. She's raped by the priest who visits her sick mother. And she writes.

Like *Lives of Girls and Women* (with which it won a GG), the *Manuscrits de Pauline Archange* is an autobiographical novel about growing up that's also a novel about the making of a writer. "Born into the very story I wanted to write," says Pauline at the end, "I aspired only to find a way out of it." She and her maker did both.

Alice Munro used the $2,500 from her Governor General's Award to rent a cottage on Gabriola Island and write. By December 1970 she had finished the draft of her next book. *Lives of Girls and Women* was published in the fall of 1971 in Toronto and a year later in New York (out of loyalty to her editor, Audrey Coffin, she stayed with Ryerson despite their sale to McGraw-Hill). Her marriage, meanwhile, was ending. She spent the summer of 1972 in Toronto with her daughter Andrea. With the help of a $7,500 Canada Council grant (the only one she has ever received), she rented her own apartment when they returned to Victoria in the fall for school. She still did the cooking and cleaning at the Rockland house and worked on stories for her third book, *Something I've Been Meaning to Tell You.*

The following summer she took her daughters with her to Nelson, B.C., to teach a three-week writing course at a private Catholic university. She and Jim separated in September. As she was packing, she got a call from the chair of English at York University, offering her an emergency teaching job because of unexpectedly high enrolment in a creative writing class. She rented an apartment for herself and her sixteen-year-old daughter Jenny in less expensive London and commuted to Toronto once a week by train. She thought her teaching was a fraud, and she hated York. She quit in January, citing health reasons.

Munro spent much of the summer of 1974 in Montreal, staying at Hugh and Noreen Hood's house and ending a relationship

**bpNichol, early 1970s, photographer unknown**

Provided by Rick/Simon. Reproduced with the permission of the bpNichol estate.

bill bissett at his home/studio in Kitsilano, Vancouver, early 1960s,
by Duncan Horner

Reproduced with the permission of bill bissett.

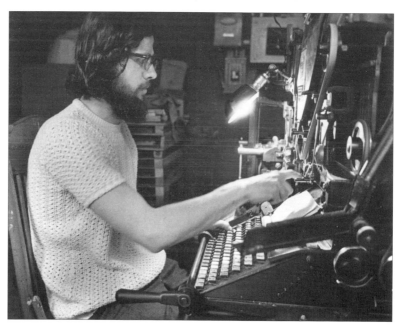

Victor Coleman at Coach House Press, Toronto, 1970, by Sheldon Grimson

Reproduced with the permission of Sheldon Grimson.

**Michael Ondaatje, Toronto, 1970, by Sheldon Grimson**

Reproduced with the permission of Sheldon Grimson.

**Dennis Lee at Rochdale College, December 1968, photographer unknown**

York University Libraries, Clara Thomas Archives and Special Collections,
Toronto *Telegram* fonds, ASC35606. Reproduced with the permission of York University.

**Dave Godfrey and (Douglas) George Fetherling at 671 Spadina Avenue, Toronto, the entrance to Anansi's space in the cellar, May 1968, photographer unknown**

Provided by and reproduced with the permission of George Fetherling.

Margaret Laurence at her cottage on the Otonabee River, Ontario, summer 1970. Photographed for Donnalu Wigmore, "Margaret Laurence: The Woman Behind the Writing," *Chatelaine*, February 1971. Photographer unknown.

**Irving Layton, York University, Toronto, 1970, by Sheldon Grimson**

Reproduced with the permission of Sheldon Grimson.

**Leonard Cohen, Hydra, Greece, 1963, by M. Fish**

**George Bowering, University of Toronto, 1970, by Sheldon Grimson**

Reproduced with the permission of Sheldon Grimson.

**John Newlove, 1970, by Sheldon Grimson**

Reproduced with the permission of Sheldon Grimson.

**Daphne Marlatt, ca. 1974, by Roy Kiyooka,
probably on a camping trip to Bowen Island**

Reproduced with the permission of Daphne Marlatt.

**Michel Tremblay at Salon de la Femme, Place Bonaventure, Montréal, May 1971, by Réal Filion**

Reproduced with the permission of Réal Filion.

Hubert Aquin as agent Hubert Desaulniers in *Faux Bond* (CBC, 1967).
Photograph by André Le Coz, March 19, 1966.

Alistair MacLeod outside the barn of his family home in Dunvegan, Cape Breton, 1962. The occasion for this rare photograph of MacLeod in these years may have been his departure to begin his PhD at Notre Dame.

**Alden Nowlan by Horst Ehricht, 1973**

**Alice Munro at home in West Vancouver, ca. 1961, by Jim Munro**

Provided by and reproduced with the permission of Sheila Munro.

**Marie-Claire Blais as she appeared in "Lightning on the Literary Landscape,"**
*Saturday Night*, March 19, 1960

with John Metcalf that had begun when they met in June 1973 at the first planning meeting of what would become the Writers' Union of Canada. For the academic year 1974–75, she took over from Margaret Laurence as writer-in-residence at the University of Western Ontario. Over martinis at the faculty club she reunited with Gerald Fremlin, a Western classmate and old flame. "*This* time it's real," she wrote to her friend Audrey Thomas in March. "He's 50, free, a good man if I ever saw one, tough and gentle like in the old tire ads, and this is the big thing — grown-up." In August she left London to live with Fremlin and his mother in their house in Clinton, thirty-six kilometres south of Wingham.

Like Margaret Atwood, Mordecai Richler, Margaret Laurence, and Marie-Claire Blais, Alice Munro had come home. A remarkable chapter in the history of Canadian literature was over. Another, of course, was beginning.

## Chapter 18

# Civil Elegies

**What do you expect after this?**
**Applause? Your name on stone?**
— Margaret Atwood, "Small Tactics"

**"NO PAIN LIKE THIS BODY** is selling like shit," wrote Harold Ladoo to Dennis Lee in November 1972. "The time is coming when I will perhaps say fuck writing and fuck literature, and return to the land of my birth."

Instead he wrote more. Training himself to get by on just a few hours of sleep, he locked himself in his bedroom for days at a time until he had a draft. Then he'd call Lee or Peter Such, announce he'd finished a book, and start another. He talked about writing twenty-five novels, thirty, fifty — a vast saga of West Indian life from Trinidad in the early twentieth century to Toronto in the 1970s.

By the spring of 1973 Anansi had accepted a second novel from him. He won a second Canada Council grant, for $4,000. In June he graduated from Erindale. Writer-in-residence Dave Godfrey held a little party for him.

That summer Ladoo learned that his mother in Trinidad was destitute, begging on the street. Peter Such drove him to the airport and he flew home. A week later, Ladoo's wife called Such to tell him Harold was dead. He had been found in a ditch beside a country road near Couva, with severe head injuries and most of his teeth knocked out, nearly dead. Trinidad police suspected foul play, possibly a family feud. Ladoo died in the hospital, leaving behind his wife, three children, two finished novels, and drafts of about ten more. He was twenty-eight years old.

"Harold Ladoo always said he would die young," wrote Robert Fulford in his *Star* column. *Saturday Night* published a eulogy by Peter Such, "The Short Life and Sudden Death of Harold Ladoo." Dennis Lee wrote a long elegy that tied Ladoo's death with the end of his own years at Anansi and the end of the sixties, with much work and what felt like little to show for it. "Your dying," he said, "diminished the thing on earth we longed to be." Timothy Findley was deeply moved by the poem. "It has become a part of my totem," he wrote to Lee, "like the stones in Virginia Woolf's pocket."

They mythologized themselves and each other, these people who created a Canadian literature. Writers lived larger lives then, so there was more mythic material. Creating a profession, they were not yet themselves professional; they took chances, made mistakes, wrote risky books and lived risky lives. Mostly, I think, they saw themselves as heroes because they saw nothing behind them. "Rampant with making," says Lee in *The Death of Harold Ladoo*, "we recognized no origin but us."

They had no stories, so they made themselves into story. "The artist is strong," wrote Ladoo to Lee. "He can fight until he becomes a myth." "I enjoy creating myths about myself," said Milton Acorn. "When I create my poems a demon possesses me," said Layton. "I am Lilith," said Gwen MacEwen. "I'm your man," said Leonard Cohen.

The country helped, as hungry for cultural heroes as its writers. We repeated their stories and invented others. Margaret Laurence, mother of the tribe. Irving Layton, lusty laureate of the slums. Girl genius Marie-Claire Blais. Milton Acorn, the people's poet. Dark goddess Gwen MacEwen. Margaret Atwood, man-eating Medusa. Jack McClelland, the hard-drinking pirate. Marshall McLuhan, oracle of the electric age. Backwoods Al Purdy. The unknown, unread Mavis Gallant. The damned Hubert Aquin, *écrivain maudit*.

It didn't matter if the stories weren't true — that Purdy had a larger library than any of them, that McLuhan preferred books to television, that Layton was more bourgeois than bohemian. Milton Acorn probably wasn't descended from Bavarian devil-worshippers, but like the Mi'kmaq in his blood and the plate in his head, it was a story that others liked telling as much as he did. At that moment, Canada needed storied writers even more than the stories they wrote. The stories didn't have to be true, they just had to be good.

**AT LEAST SO FAR,** audiences have not rewarded any Canadian visual artist of the 1960s with the fame of an Emily Carr or a Tom Thomson. The most well-known Canadian paintings today from the sixties are by Alex Colville, who had begun painting two decades earlier and whose realistic style was outside the main currents of sixties art. The best-known Canadian artists to emerge in the sixties are likely Michael Snow and Norval Morrisseau, neither of them household names. In Canada, as elsewhere, the sixties were a time when artists tried out a rapidly changing succession of international styles: video art, performance art, pop art and op art, art made from quilts and nails, from anything and everything. Perhaps conceptual art had a harder time imprinting itself on the Canadian imagination than paintings of lakes and trees; perhaps Canadian artists simply didn't stand out on the international stages.

Something similar happened in the Canadian theatre that emerged at the end of the sixties. Most of its energy came from experimental collective productions that were exciting to develop (and sometimes to watch) but have not survived their initial enthusiasm. Almost twenty years after Nathan Cohen noted that by 1967 Canada had not produced a full-time playwright in either language, literary critic Bill Keith thought the number of Canadian plays that "may reasonably be expected to form part of a permanent repertory is still disappointingly low." Quebec might point to Michel Tremblay, and a critic more sympathetic to the politics and methods of sixties theatre might argue that the problem lies with the author-oriented, script-loving theatrical canon. But even so, few Canadian plays from

the period are regularly staged today. In 2015, Hannah Moscovitch —
"Canada's hottest young playwright," says the *Globe and Mail* and
others — told an interviewer that "None of the Canadian playwrights
I admire are dead. Or even old. There is no such thing as an A-list
Canadian playwright, no recognizable names."

Pop music had bigger stars, but of all Canadian arts in the 1960s,
literature not only experienced the biggest boom in Canada during
the 1960s, more of it has survived the time than any other art. There
is a remarkable correlation between the writers in Frank Davey's
1974 survey of Canadian writers of the 1960s and those who still
appear in anthologies and even bestseller lists of the past twenty
years. Not all writers today might admire Margaret Atwood, but
they all know who she is.

For many associated with the little magazines and small presses
that emerged in the sixties, the legacy of the period isn't individual writers or books but the communities they created. For Victor
Coleman, who left Coach House in 1974 in a dispute with Stan
Bevington about the press's commercialization, that community
has moved to places like Jay MillAr's BookThug press. For publicist
Sarah Sheard, who joined Coach House after Coleman's departure,
it survived there, in "the acute and enduring pleasure our company
gave one another."

> It was this that warmed all of us, participation in a conversa-
> tion that was to span decades, not only among ourselves but
> among other writers and artists, printing and computer tech-
> ies, photographers, publishers, typographers.... This salon —
> of Stan's, really, although he wouldn't like me singling him
> out — may possibly turn out to have been of greater singular-
> ity than the work of any of its individual artists.

The legacy of *Tish* isn't its theories or its poems, it's the process:
collective editing, self-publishing, free magazines, and free readings by poets for poets. These are practices still followed today
by experimental Canadian poets, many of whom name *Tish,* bill
bissett's *blew ointment,* or bpNichol's *Ganglia* as models.

For others, especially those with a more national audience and perspective, the main legacy of the CanLit boom is the literary infrastructure it left behind. As Atwood says,

> Many of the conditions taken for granted today — that there is a Canadian "canon," that a Canadian writer can be widely known, respected, and solvent, that you can get a grant or a film contract or teach creative writing or win big prizes, that there are such things as book-promotion tours and literary festivals, that it is possible to live in Canada and function as a professional writer with a national, indeed an international "career" — these conditions scarcely existed in the writing world of the 50s and 60s.

"What has happened," said Robert Fulford in *Books in Canada* in 1976,

> is that serious literature in English Canada has built, for the first time, a structure to contain its activities. The structure remains unsound. Of course. From time to time bits of it fall off. There is no way of being sure, when you wake up in the morning, that the House of Anansi or the *Malahat Review* or CBC *Anthology* or the University of Toronto writers-in-residence program will still be there. But the structure exists and it seems to me that its outlines at least are permanent.

Bits have fallen off. The house that Jack built is no more, sold to an American publisher in 2011 and now an imprint of a German media corporation. *Anthology* retired with Robert Weaver in 1985. The *Tamarack Review* and *Saturday Night* are gone, though the *Malahat Review* is still publishing, as is *Canadian Literature*. The University of Toronto and many more universities, colleges, and public libraries have writers-in-residence still. The Canada Council still helps writers, still helps the performing arts more. The House of Anansi and Coach House Books are both still here, both still loyal to their founding spirits. Coach House is in the same building it was in the sixties, in an alley now called bpNichol Lane, which is just east of Matt Cohen Park and a short walk from statues of Northrop Frye and Al Purdy. As Fulford said, the structure created in the 1960s remains more or less in place.

Writers have also fallen. Some, like Harold Ladoo, did not themselves survive their time. Michael Coutts, bill bissett's best friend and the first blewointment press author, died of a heroin overdose at twenty-one. Anansi author Russell Marois was found dead on the train tracks near Port Hope in 1971, two years after publishing his only novel. Pat Lowther was killed by her husband two weeks after Oxford University Press accepted her second book. Novelist Juan Butler was committed to a psychiatric ward in 1975 and later hung himself in a Toronto halfway house.

Many others, especially women, left the literary world, or it left them. For every artist we remember there are hundreds we don't, like the poet Luella Booth, who wrote to Lee at Anansi in 1969 begging for any help he could give her.

> I am short of time, exhausted from overwork and personal trouble, namely my husband's desertion, eviction and breakdown of my marriage of 23 years. Economically my circumstances are dreadful — and I've two young sons who have suffered and who concern me because I love them. We have had some extremely brutal things done to us, almost unbelievable. So I have the collected works to publish. . . . Don't snow me — I've had to use old newspapers for lack of money for toilet paper, my gums are rotting from lack of enough or proper food to eat — I have not had a holiday for 7½ years. . . .

No less than in any other time, success did not come to everyone. As Lee says in *The Death of Harold Ladoo*, "the breakdown quotient was high" — of minds and marriages, careers and lives.

Others had more successful careers but have since lost their place. Once highly regarded, Hugh Hood, Dave Godfrey, and Audrey Thomas are mostly unread today. Marian Engel has been reduced to *Bear*, Rudy Wiebe to *The Temptations of Big Bear*. I'd guess Margaret Laurence and George Bowering aren't far behind, likely to be remembered for only a book or two once the generation that loved them has gone.

But many survive still in classrooms and bookstores, here and elsewhere.* Since the office was created in 2001, two founding members of *Tish* — Bowering and Fred Wah — have been poet laureates of Canada. Alice Munro won the Nobel Prize in 2013. Marie-Claire Blais won Quebec's version of the Nobel in 2005, the Prix Gilles-Corbeil, and has been repeatedly nominated by PEN Quebec for the Nobel itself. Hubert Aquin's *Next Episode* won CBC's national battle of the books, Canada Reads, in 2003. Atwood's fifteenth novel is number six on the *Globe*'s Canadian fiction bestseller list as I write, and a documentary about Al Purdy is at Toronto's Hot Docs Cinema.

Perhaps literary taste is slow to change; perhaps we're still reading the boomers' books. But I think we mostly still know Canadian writers of the 1960s because they were and still are important to Canada, in the same way we still know Shakespeare because of his importance to Britain. It wasn't literary quality that once made Sir Walter Scott unavoidable, or Jane Austen now. Writers don't make classics; readers do, and they pick the books they need as much as the books they like.

From where I sit, the lasting importance of the writers who emerged in Canada in the 1960s is the literature they created. "Those years were crucial," wrote Matt Cohen in his posthumously published 2000 memoir,

> not because all the best books were written then (they weren't), but because the universe of Canadian literature mutated into a new existence at that time, and has retained approximately the same definition even as it evolved over three decades into something much richer and more

---

* In the spring of 2015, Book Culture — a literature-friendly bookstore in New York's upper west side at Columbus and West 81st — had on its shelves one Gallant, a half-dozen Atwoods, and a foot or so of Munros.

unpredictable than its narrow base might have suggested.... Within a few years a visible explosion had begun, a burst of energy that transformed CanLit from a curiosity sometimes talked about at Commonwealth conferences into a prominent world literature.

**WHAT TO CALL IT?** Many call it what Cohen does, an explosion. "The New Explosion in Canadian Poetry," announced the subtitle of Ray Souster and Victor Coleman's 1966 anthology. In his conclusion ten years later to the second edition of the *Literary History of Canada*, Northrop Frye talked about the "colossal verbal explosion that has taken place in Canada since 1960" — likely the main source for the shorthand term that I and others have since used, the CanLit boom.*

Historian Donald Creighton called the final chapter of his 1959 bestseller *The Story of Canada* "The First Elizabethan Age" — a reference both to Canada's first Elizabeth, Elizabeth II, and to the artistic renaissance that took place in England under her namesake, and that Creighton saw coming again in Canada in things like the Canada Council and the Stratford Festival. Long-time *Toronto Star* books columnist Philip Marchand calls the sixties and seventies "the heroic age of Canadian literature." Politician Roy Romanow calls it a "golden age." Pierre Berton called it a "literary renaissance."

*Renaissance* is not the right word for what happened in Canadian literature in the 1960s and '70s. It did share one feature with the European Renaissance and others like it around the world: the rise of a vernacular literature. W. O. Mitchell's prairie lingo, Quebec's *joual*, Newfoundland's embrace of its own words, Mordecai Richler's and Ray Souster's urban slang, the colloquial poems of Al Purdy and Alden Nowlan — all echo the giant step

---

* The first use of the phrase "CanLit boom" that I've found is in a 1986 article about Robert Weaver for the CBC's *Radio Guide* magazine. In his book about Expo 67, journalist John Lownsbrough says the energies of the time produced a "boomlet" of Canadian literature, which is kind of sweet.

that Dante took into his own language six centuries before. But except in Newfoundland's return to folklore and a few isolated conversations elsewhere in English Canada (Atwood with Susanna Moodie, Bowering with George Vancouver), it wasn't a rebirth of classic artists and stories — at least not Canadian classic artists and stories, because there weren't any, not as the writers saw it. Quebec didn't revisit its rural classics *Maria Chapdelaine* and *Thirty Acres*; it burned them down. In quality as well as quantity, the CanLit boom deserves its title. But it wasn't a renaissance. It was what novelist Katherine Govier calls a *naissance*, "the cultural *naissance* of Canadian literary identity." A birth, not a rebirth.

For George Grant, the triumph of modern liberalism — its emphasis above all else on freedom, especially the freedom to get and spend — brought the end of Canada as a nation. If the purpose of life is consumption, then borders are anachronisms, here and everywhere. "Perhaps we should rejoice in the disappearance of Canada," begins the last chapter of his *Lament for a Nation*.

> We leave the narrow provincialism and our backwoods culture; we enter the excitement of the United States where all the great things are being done. Who would compare the science, the art, the politics, the entertainment of our petty world to the overflowing achievements of New York, Washington, Chicago, and San Francisco? Think of William Faulkner and then think of Morley Callaghan.

He was being ironic, of course. If by the end of *Lament for a Nation* you think Grant might actually rejoice in the end of Canada, start over. But the comparisons he invokes were fair enough in 1965, especially for older readers. The question is, were they fair a decade later? Maybe Morley Callaghan really was the best example Grant could dredge up in the early 1960s. But wouldn't we now think of different names, names that might stand up better against Faulkner? Munro. Atwood. Blais. Gallant. MacLeod. Depending on your education and taste, you might still put Faulkner on top, but at least now the comparison isn't a joke. The Canadian literary boom of the 1960s contradicts Grant's claim that branch-plant economies have branch-plant cultures. Canadian culture didn't disappear in the 1960s. It arrived.

Why did Canadian culture in the 1960s become more nationalist, more *Canadian*, than ever before or since? Why was this the time that finally instituted the spirit of the nearly forgotten Massey Report, the time that created the literary infrastructure we have today — and the time that produced so many laments like Grant's? "If Canada no longer exists," asked the poet Edward Lacey in 1969, "why so much chatter about it?"

Because death is a great subject. Because in both English and French Canada, nationalism was a panacea for continentalism, a smokescreen and a comfort, while below the surface, as Grant said, integration continued.

The CanLit boom was mostly a product of economic circumstances, of increasing affluence and education. But it was also fuelled by the most productive force in art: loss. As Noah Richler says about the Québécois version in his book *This Is My Country*, it is "much more inspiring for a person to pine after something he imagines he does not have, than to possess whatever it is that he imagined he needed." The sense among many Canadians that their identity was disappearing, either into the larger identity of English Canada or the still larger American identity, didn't just produce a string of elegies for a Canada that once was or might have been. It also fuelled an entire literature of loss — poem after poem and novel after novel about lost people and lost places.

They weren't all elegies. But it's the elegies that best caught and have since held our imagination, the books they wrote and the books we wrote about them and their time. Books about doomed cowboys and doomed Indians, lost children and lost explorers, martyred saints and suicidal revolutionaries, all those beautiful losers. Poems and stories about vanished communities, villages and small towns lost in the past: Tom Dawe's abandoned outports and Al Purdy's abandoned farms, Daphne Marlatt's bulldozed Steveston, Laurence's Manawaka, Munro's Jubilee, Davies' Deptford. Pierre Berton's book about 1967, *The Last Good Year*. Sam Solecki's book about Purdy, *The*

*Last Canadian Poet.* Stephen Cole's book about the NHL's 1966–67 season, *The Last Hurrah.* The only story by Hugh Hood that we still read is the anthology standard "Getting to Williamstown," about a dying Montreal businessman dreaming of a small town in the sun. For Hood, the story was about life after death. Maybe so, but it became part of the canon because of what it said to its readers about life on earth: about wanting a life that's more than a new Chrysler or a new television, a life in the green, golden past.

Things weren't all bad, of course. Being better off than ever before made up for a lot, and American movies were pretty darn good. Absolute despair, as Grant said, produces suicides, not books. In his case, his belief in God precluded total despair: he couldn't be certain that Canada's disappearance wasn't part of God's plan. Canadian writers of the 1960s had other things besides God to temper their despair, things like grants, readers, awards, even fame. A few did kill themselves. But many turned stories of failure into successful books.

All literature, all art, is more about things lost than things gained. But there is something deeply elegiac about this time, both in what it produced and the way we remember it. The CanLit boom was an epitaph for a Canada that no longer existed, because the moment of Canadian literature's arrival was also the moment when such a thing as a "Canadian" literature no longer seemed necessary.

**BARRING SOME CATACLYSMIC** event that starts history over, it can't happen again. The demographic and economic circumstances that produced the CanLit boom now appear to have been unique to their time. As economist Thomas Piketty showed in his 2013 best-seller, *Capital in the Twenty-First Century* — today's version of *The Affluent Society* — economic growth in Europe and North America has slowed since 1980 to below the return on capital, which is why wealth is concentrating in the hands of those who already have it. In Canada, as elsewhere, the only class that's significantly better off today is the very wealthy, a class too small to drive a consumer boom in anything other than luxury goods.

It was a boom, too, because the numbers were so small to begin with. We have seen and will again see better books, but we will never again see a larger increase in such a short period of time. "It was like opening a floodgate," says Atwood. "A surge poured through. You wouldn't find that now because the floodgates aren't closed, there's no buildup — you don't get a sudden explosion."

Just as international free trade agreements like NAFTA have made the main economic and cultural debate of the 1960s in Canada — foreign ownership of domestic industry — not just irrelevant but actionable, the very idea of a national literature is now an artifact of history. Atwood is still writing elegies, but now they're for the species. The last all-Canadian bookstore in the country, Montreal's Double Hook, closed in 2005. Saskatchewan and British Columbia require students to read a Canadian novel or two, but Canadian literature is once again optional in Ontario high schools. At eleven of Canada's largest twenty universities, English and French, you can complete a major in literature without any of it being Canadian. (At all twenty you can earn a B.A. without ever reading a Canadian poem or novel.) When an American company bought Ryerson Press in 1970, there were public protests, threats of boycotts from writers, and a royal commission. When an American company bought the infinitely more important McClelland & Stewart in 2011, the few complaints felt quaint, never mind useless. "Literary nationalism is something your grandparents did," says Toronto novelist Stephen Marche, "like macramé." The younger Québécois writers with whom Noah Richler spoke for *This Is My Country* cared even less about a distinctly Québécois literature than they did about a distinct Quebec; they just wanted to "get on with their art."

Canadian literature is more alive and more exciting than ever. Regardless of who owns it, M&S still publishes books by Canadians, as do other and now larger foreign-owned publishers and imprints. New publishers like Gaspereau Press in Kentville, Nova Scotia, Drawn & Quarterly in Montreal, and Biblioasis in Windsor, Ontario, are producing better (and better-looking) books than the country has ever seen. New prizes like the Griffin and the Giller have made Canadian poetry and Canadian fiction glamorous for an evening. The CBC is again doing more than anyone to foster a national audience for Canadian books, especially in the annual gathering around the literary campfire known as Canada Reads and (until 2015) as *Le combat des livres.*

The country is producing many more writers and many more books than ever before, books by and about many more different kinds of Canadians than ever before. It also has more readers — they're just spread out now, among so many more books and so many more ways to read, that it's hard to see them all. And last but not least, the average quality of the literature published in Canada is higher today than in the sixties, partly because of increased awareness of increased competition, partly because of the creative writing programs that are now a booming industry at universities and colleges. Quite simply, there has never been a better time to be a Canadian reader.

As Northrop Frye said as early as 1967, Canada moved faster and farther than most countries toward the emerging post-national world. Much the same happened with its literature, which became a post-national literature almost in the moment of its arrival as a national literature. The first recorded use of the term "Can. Lit." is the title Earle Birney gave one of his poems in 1962 — a poem about its absence (what America did in poetry, says Birney, Canada did in railways). The next use is in a 1969 *Globe and Mail* column by William French, reporting four new series of books about Canadian authors. "All of a sudden," says French, "we've got CanLit coming out of our ears."

Just ten years later, in an article for *Saturday Night*, Matt Cohen declared CanLit dead, displaced by the desire of agents and publishers for commercial international fiction.

Canadian writers have always been influenced by writers from elsewhere, and Canadian publishers have always tried to sell their products internationally to compensate for the limited domestic market. What's really changed is that the whole context for Canadian writing — its production, reception, and definition — is no longer national. The Canadiana section at the bookstore is no more.

For literary nationalists this is cause for concern, the abandonment of Canadian stories for international settings and international sales. For literary cosmopolitans it's cause for celebration: the end of a homogeneous, state-sponsored literature and the coming of age of Canadian writing on the international stage. For Frye, and for me, it's just part of the inevitable maturing of a capitalist society, a society that is now politically national, economically international, and culturally regional. Our writers may not be writing stories about Canada any more (if they ever did), but they are writing stories about Montreal and the Saguenay, Edmonton and Calgary, the Okanagan and the Annapolis Valley, Vancouver, Toronto, Winnipeg, Kitimaat Village and Nogojiwanong, Saint John and St. John's, as well as stories set elsewhere on the globe.

If more of those stories are now being read and recognized around the world, so much the better for their writers and publishers. What matters more is that we now have the stories themselves, both those from the sixties and those that came after. We have something we did not have before the CanLit boom — a literary canon, a shifting but now recognizable body of writing for critics to describe, students to read, the public to celebrate, and writers to steal from or define themselves against. Like the literatures of other large countries today, it's not a national literature, not in the sense of a national project, or something that is definitively and uniquely Canadian. "Canadian literature" is now just the sum of its parts, a useful abstraction. But that abstraction did not exist until the CanLit boom of the 1960s, and that's the legacy of that remarkable time.

CanLit ended when it arrived because that was its job — to arrive. "We opened the box," says Graeme Gibson. "Out came the writers."

# Acknowledgements

No publisher could afford to pay what it really costs to produce a book like this: memoir is cheap, but history is expensive. *Arrival* could not have been written without the long-standing support of the University of Toronto and the students and citizens who keep it alive. You gave me your confidence, you gave me ideas, you gave me time, and you gave me money. I am especially grateful to three past and current chairs of the Department of English: Brian Corman, who hired me; Alan Bewell, who promoted me; and Paul Stevens, who hasn't yet fired me.

Many people gave their own time for interviews for this book. I have acknowledged specific debts in the notes that follow; let me add what should be obvious, that an acknowledgement doesn't imply agreement or endorsement, and offer here special thanks to Margaret Atwood, Stan Bevington, bill bissett, George Bowering, Russell Brown, Victor Coleman, Tom Dawe, Nicky Drumbolis, Robert Fulford, Graeme Gibson, David Helwig, George Jonas, Bill Keith, Richard Landon, Dennis Lee, Daphne Marlatt, Dave Mason, John Metcalf, David Silcox, and Andy Wainwright.

Brandy Ryan was the book's first research assistant and spent many hours investigating things like Pierre Berton's mistake about Canada's affluence, Dorothy Cameron's obscenity conviction, and a "Meet the Authors" dinner at Toronto's Royal York Hotel in 1959 that unfortunately didn't make it into the book. Esther de Bruijn, Nick Morwood, Miriam Novick, and Laurel Ryan transcribed interviews recorded under less-than-studio conditions, like Dennis Lee at a table in Pauper's Pub beside the cash register. Sean Allingham worked on the book for several years, initially in U of T's Work Study Program; he tracked down dozens of loose ends, and assembled invaluable databases on the publishers of best-selling and Governor General's Award–winning books. The fact that you were all paid for your labour does I hope settle my debt to you, but does not at all diminish my gratitude.

Because little has been written about Québécois writers in English and my French is inadequate, the chapters on French-Canadian literature and much else in the book could not have been written without the research and translations of Dr. Myra Bloom. Even with help from her and others, I have surely got things wrong about Quebec and its writers. But the usual solution to this long-standing problem in Canadian literary history is silence on both sides. For better or worse, I have decided in this book (and consequently, in my classrooms) that reading in translation and making mistakes is better than ignoring each other. The literary cultures of English and French Canada are not as different, or as separate, as we like to think.

Norah Franklin and Scott Herder spent more than three hundred hours subjecting the manuscript to a *New Yorker*–style fact check that saved me from countless embarrassments, like calling Quebec's sixteenth premier "Marcel Duplessis" and claiming that the Issacs Gallery opened across the street from a library that didn't yet exist. Michael Boughn read the chapter on Vancouver and has gently tried to tutor me in the wonders of the avant-garde. If I fail to grasp them still, it's not his fault. Janet Paterson provided invaluable corrections for the chapter on Michel Tremblay and Hubert Aquin, and Lisa Moore for the chapter on Newfoundland. My thanks to Sara Peters, Sheila Fischman, Donald Winkler, and especially Robert Fulford, for taking the time to read and respond to the manuscript in whole or part.

My first and most important reader is my partner and wife of twenty-seven years, Bernadette (Baran) Mount. She read every chapter before anyone else, and she more than anyone else paid the price for the time it took, the nights and weekends lost to stupid words. I won't say she never complained about it, because we both know that isn't true. But I am routinely floored by her love and support, and deeply grateful. I got very lucky thirty-two years ago at a house party in Trail, B.C., and luckier still that the luck and the love is with us yet.

For expert archival knowledge and gracious help, special thanks to Jennifer Toews at the Fisher Rare Book Library; Agatha Barc at Victoria University; Karen Smith at Dalhousie's Killam Library; Nick Drumbolis at Letters Bookshop in Thunder Bay; Florian Daveau at Bibliothèque et Archives nationales du Québec; Suzanne Dubeau, Anna St. Onge, and Jula Holland at York University Libraries; and Jean Matheson, Megan Butcher, and Samantha Shields at Library and Archives Canada. For photographs, thanks especially to George Fetherling, Réal Filion, Graeme Gibson, Shelly Grimson, Robert Kory, Alexander MacLeod, Sheila Munro, Norman Nehmetallah, Eleanor Nichol, Andy Phillips, Toni Tata, and Phyllis Thomas.

Boris Castel at *Queen's Quarterly* and John Macfarlane at the *Walrus* published early versions of portions of this book. Sarah MacLachlan at Anansi bought it before it was a book. Thanks to my first editor at Anansi and closest friend, Jared Bland; I wish we could have done this book together, but it wasn't to be. My next editor, Janice Zawerbny, believed in the book and pushed it forward even if she too never got to see its end. The editor who did the actual work on the manuscript was Peter Norman, as careful and smart a reader as any book could hope for. Gillian Watts copy-edited it, and Cheryl Lemmens proofed it. The people at Anansi who saw *Arrival* through its last stages included Maria Golikova, Cindy Ma, Douglas Richmond, Alysia Shewchuk, Alex Trnka, and Janie Yoon. Thanks to all of you and to everyone else at Anansi, past, present, and future. I'm glad it's your name on this next chapter in the story.

# Notes

## Chapter 1: Surfacing

3    *"staring straight ahead"*: Such, "The Short Life of Harold Ladoo," *Saturday Night*, May 1974.

4    *called him Plato*: Dionne Brand, introduction, *No Pain Like This Body* (Anansi, 2013).

5    *"could not stop"*: Ladoo to Dennis Lee, Nov. 20, 1971, Lee Papers, Thomas Fisher Rare Book Library, University of Toronto, MS COLL 271, box 6.

    *"canon of images"*: Jo Nordley Beglo, "Picturing Canada," *History of the Book in Canada: Volume III, 1918–1980*, ed. Carole Gerson and Jacques Michon (UTP, 2007), 73.

6    *"fallen far behind"*: *Royal Commission on National Development in the Arts, Letters and Sciences* (King's Printer, 1951), 222.

7    *first daily book column*: "Robert Fulford on Books" began Aug. 31, 1959, with a review of Vladimir Nabokov's *The Real Life of Sebastian Knight*. It ran for eight years, two periods of four years each. Fulford interview, July 4, 2012.

    *Le Devoir*: Malcolm Reid, *The Shouting Signpainters: A Literary and Political Account of Quebec Revolutionary Nationalism* (M&S, 1972), 18.

    *Purdy's first public reading*: poster for Contact Readings, reproduced in Donnalu Wigmore, ed., *Isaacs Seen* (Hart House, 2005), 44.

    *Readers' Club*: Peter Martin, "Canadians Buy Books," *Quill & Quire*, March/April 1964.

    *Atwood's first professional publication*: "Fruition," *Canadian Forum*, Sep. 1959.

7     *Writers' Union*: Christopher Moore, "The Writers' Union of Canada," Feb. 2007, www.writersunion.ca.

*Best Canadian Stories*: Metcalf, *An Aesthetic Underground* (Thomas Allen, 2003), 121–22; cf. David Helwig, *The Names of Things* (Porcupine's Quill, 2006), 141.

8     *"Elizabethan period"*: Sutherland, "Canada's Elizabethan Age?" TLS, Oct. 26, 1973; *"fifteen years ago"*: Atwood, "Poetry in the Buffer Zone," ibid.

*freaks and geeks:* Delores Broten, *The Lumber Jack Report: English Canadian Literary Trade Book Publishers' Sales, 1963–1972* (CANLIT, 1975). The CANLIT fonds are in Special Collections, University of Calgary Library, MsC 221.

9     *American titles also increased*: Broten, *Lumber Jack Report*, 15.

*"mass distribution"*: Robert Escarpit, *Trends in Worldwide Book Development, 1970–1978* (UNESCO, 1982), 3–4.

*eight times the global rate*: based on figures in Escarpit, 3, 10–11, and Broten, 14.

*number of bookstores*: *History of the Book in Canada: Vol. III*, 393.

*"must be a million"*: Ondaatje, "Little Magazines/Small Presses, 1969," *artscanada*, Aug. 1969.

9–10     *value of goods*: Statistics Canada, *Annual Census of Manufacturers: Printing, Publishing, and Allied Industries, 1970* (Minister of Industry, Trade and Commerce, 1972), 19.

10     *"suddenly an outlet"*: Atwood interview, Dec. 15, 2010.

*"up from a basement"*: Lee interview, June 26, 2012.

*claimed to write*: *Occupational Trends in Canada, 1931 to 1961* (Department of Labour, 1963); *Occupational Trends, 1961–1986* (Minister of Supply and Services, 1988), 57; and "National Occupational Classification for Statistics Canada," 1996, 2001, and 2006. The chart below summarizes the data from these sources. Occupation figures are extrapolated from a 20 percent sample and include both creative and technical writers, editors, and journalists. Journalists have been counted separately since at least the 1996 census but not from 1931 to (I think) 1986, so the only way to make historical comparisons is to leave them in.

| Census Year | Writers, Editors, and Journalists | Increase over Past 10 Years | Per Capita |
|---|---|---|---|
| 1931 | 3,344 | | 1 per 3,100 |
| 1941 | 4,147 | 24% | 1 per 2,770 |
| 1951 | 7,217 | 74% | 1 per 1,940 |
| 1961 | 13,024 | 80% | 1 per 1,400 |
| 1971 (# 3352) | 14,780 | 13% | 1 per 1,490 |
| 1981 (# 3352) | 28,755 | 95% | 1 per 860 |
| 1986 (# 3352) | 33,855 | | 1 per 770 |
| 1996 (F021–23) | 39,010 | 15% | 1 per 760 |
| 2001 (F021–23) | 46,960 | | 1 per 660 |
| 2006 (F021–23) | 54,555 | 40% | 1 per 600 |

11    *coming Native renaissance*: see Stephanie McKenzie, *Before the Country: Native Renaissance, Canadian Mythology* (UTP, 2007).

*"golden age"*: Noah Richler, *This Is My Country, What's Yours?* (M&S, 2006), 385.

*novel serialized in Chatelaine*: Phyllis Brett Young's *The Torontonians*, condensed in *Chatelaine*, Oct.–Dec. 1960. Quoted from McGill-Queen's UP 2007 edition, 174.

*Painters Eleven*: Iris Nowell, *Painters Eleven: The Wild Ones of Canadian Art* (Douglas & McIntyre, 2010).

12    *"generally ignored"*: Dennis Reid, *A Concise History of Canadian Painting*, 2nd ed. (OUP, 1988), 256.

*model's naked body*: Iris Nowell, "Tom Hodgson," *CNQ* 72 (2007).

*Isaacs' new gallery*: Wigmore, *Isaacs Seen*.

*"like TV sets"*: Lotta Dempsey, *Globe and Mail*, Feb. 16, 1956.

*first exhibit devoted to indigenous art*: Ruth B. Phillips, "Morrisseau's 'Entrance,'" *Norval Morrisseau: Shaman Artist*, ed. Greg A. Hill (National Gallery of Canada, 2006).

*"command post"*: Sandra Gwyn, "The Newfoundland Renaissance," *Saturday Night*, April 1976.

*"swingingest city"*: Barry Lord, "Swinging London (Ontario)," *Star Weekly*, Jan. 13, 1968.

*"wall painters"*: Stan Bevington interview, Aug. 25, 2010; Victor Coleman interview, July 13, 2010.

12    *performance art*: David Wisdom and Stephen Osborne, "Glenn Lewis," *Geist* 88 (2013).

13    *full-time playwright*: Nathan Cohen, "A Copy Theatre," *Century, 1867–1967: The Canadian Saga*, ed. John D. Harbron (Toronto Daily Star, 1967), 66.

*Smaller theatre companies*: Denis W. Johnston, *Up the Mainstream: The Rise of Toronto's Alternative Theatres, 1968–1975* (UTP, 1991).

*Fortune and Men's Eyes*: Kate Taylor, "Playwright Wrote Landmark Drama," *Globe and Mail*, June 26, 2001.

*just 3 percent*: editorial, ACTRA 4.3 (Fall 1967).

13–14    *pop music*: Jack Batten, "Can. Pop," *Chatelaine*, Sep. 1969.

14–15    *American imports*: Statistics Canada, *Canada Year Book, 1951*, 919; *Canada Year Book, 1961*, 971.

15    *"unprecedented rise"*: Michael Fellman, "Sleeping with the Elephant," *Parallel Destinies*, ed. John M. Findlay and Ken S. Coates (MQUP, 2002), 287.

*"just writers"*: Atwood quoted in Rosemary Sullivan, *The Red Shoes: Margaret Atwood Starting Out* (HarperFlamingo, 1998), 200.

*collective effort*: James Polk, "Anansi at Fifteen," *Canadian Forum*, June/July 1982.

16    *sold 50,000 copies*: Sullivan, *Red Shoes*, 266.

## Chapter 2: Beautiful Losers

17–19    *MacLennan*: Elspeth Cameron, *Hugh MacLennan: A Writer's Life* (UTP, 1981).

19    *Scribner's window*: MacLennan, "New York, New York," *Scotchman's Return* (Macmillan, 1960).

20    *Fridays off*: Sid Ross and Ed Kiester, "Do You Really Want a Four-Day Week?" *Parade*, Sep. 1957.

21    *taxi drivers in Edmonton, Cadillacs in Toronto*: Peter C. Newman, *Renegade in Power* (M&S, 1963), 202.

*charge account at Dupuis Frères*: Mavis Gallant, "The Chosen Husband," *Varieties of Exile* (NYRB, 2003), 188. Yes, I know this is fiction. She's a better historian than most historians.

*home ownership increased*: from 30 percent in 1948 to 60 percent in 1961, according to Mary Louise Adams in *Love, Hate, and Fear in Canada's Cold War*, ed. Richard Cavell (UTP, 2004), 137.

*"a rich country"*: Fulford interview, July 4, 2012.

*Doug Wright*: for a loving introduction, see *The Collected Doug Wright*, ed. Seth and Brad Mackay (Drawn & Quarterly, 2009).

22    *"massive development projects"*: Newman, *Renegade in Power*, 204. Bryan Palmer's *Canada's 1960s* (UTP, 2009) paints much the same picture (34–35).

23    *"second most affluent"*: Berton, *1967* (Doubleday, 1997), 15. OECD rankings from *The World Economy* (OECD, 2006), clarified in correspondence with the report's author, economist Angus Maddison. Professor Maddison thought Berton might have been misled by a newspaper article.

    *Century, 1867–1967: The Canadian Saga*: my copy is from the *North Bay Nugget*, Feb. 13, 1967.

24    *"terrifyingly affluent"*: "Expo 67," *Hunting Tigers under Glass* (M&S, 1968), 32.

25    *Abstracts at Home*: "Tom Hodgson of Painters Eleven Dies," CBC *Arts*, March 6, 2006.

    *"culture is our business"*: quoted by Claude Bissell in "The University and the Intellectual," *Queen's Quarterly* 68.1 (1961).

    *"Our task"*: *Royal Commission on National Development in the Arts, Letters and Sciences* (King's Printer, 1951), 5.

26    *"expansion in leisure-time"*: quoted in Kenneth F. Watson et al., *Leisure Reading Habits* (Infoscan, 1980), 5.

    *bartering printing work*: Bevington interview, Aug. 25, 2010.

    *"writers didn't have money"*: Marlatt interview, July 17, 2012.

    *"larger aspirations"*: Davey, *When Tish Happens* (ECW, 2011), 58.

    *Tamarack subscribers*: Elaine Kalman Naves, *Robert Weaver* (Véhicule, 2007), 56.

29    *Ohmann's account*: "The Shaping of a Canon," *Critical Inquiry* 10.1 (1983). The phrase "happy problems" comes from a remarkable essay by Herbert Gold in *Mademoiselle*, Feb. 1958.

30    *revolting*: Jack McClelland to Cohen, June 15, 1965, *Imagining Canadian Literature: The Selected Letters of Jack McClelland*, ed. Sam Solecki (Key Porter, 1998), 102.

    *"wash my mind"*: Gladys Taylor, "The Beautiful Losers at the Altar to an Arty Baal," Toronto *Telegram*, clipping [1966?], Cohen Papers, Fisher Library, MS COLL 122, box 9, folder 11.

## Chapter 3: Fifth Business

33–35    *Richler*: Charles Foran, *Mordecai: The Life and Times* (Knopf, 2010); Michael Posner, *The Last Honest Man* (M&S, 2004); Reinhold Kramer, *Mordecai Richler* (MQUP, 2008).

34    *Joyce Weiner*: see also John Ayre, "Richlerian Tales," *Books in Canada*, Sep. 2002.

34*     *"caricature of Jewish life"*: quoted in M. J. Vassanji, *Mordecai Richler* (Penguin, 2009), as excerpted in *Maclean's*, March 12, 2009.

35      *reference from MacLennan*: MacLennan to Marian Engel, May 16, 1981, *Dear Marian, Dear Hugh*, ed. Christl Verduyn (U of Ottawa P, 1995), 117.

        *Council agreed*: Canada Council, *Second Annual Report, to March 31, 1959*, 77.

        *"No other Canadian commission"*: Claude Bissell, *The Imperial Canadian* (UTP, 1986), 233.

        *"vibrant literary culture"*: Robert Lecker, *Dr. Delicious* (Véhicule, 2006), 261.

        *British production company*: for *Room at the Top* (1959), winner of an Oscar for best adapted screenplay (Foran, *Mordecai*, 224).

        *"Next year I will give a grant"*: quoted in Posner, *Last Honest Man*, 109.

36      *"totally unrealistic"*: quoted in Christine Wiesenthal, *The Half-Lives of Pat Lowther* (UTP, 2005), 311.

        *"American technology"*: quoted in George Grant, *Lament for a Nation* (Carleton UP, 1997), 11.

        *wealthy American families*: Jeffrey D. Brison, *Rockefeller, Carnegie, and Canada: American Philanthropy and the Arts and Letters in Canada* (MQUP, 2005).

37–40   *Massey Report*: Paul Litt, *The Muses, the Masses, and the Massey Commission* (UTP, 1992).

37      *"complete cross section"*: *Royal Commission on National Development in the Arts, Letters and Sciences* (King's Printer, 1951), 9.

38      *"a bit shy"*: quoted in Litt, *Muses*, 41; *"bit of a savage"*: ibid., 30; *milk a cow*: ibid., 65.

39      *"trouble with the intelligentsia"*: ibid., 176.

        *"American books"*: Vancouver Branch of the Canadian Authors' Association, Brief to the Royal Commission, 1949.

        *"le danger d'américanisation"*: Association canadienne des éducateurs de la langue française, Mémoire soumis à la commission royale, Jan. 1950.

        *avoiding the word "culture"*: see Hilda Neatby, "The Massey Report: A Retrospect," *Tamarack Review* 1 (1956).

39*     *"organized resistance"*: James Doyle, *Progressive Heritage: The Evolution of a Politically Radical Literary Tradition in Canada* (WLUP, 2002), 190.

40      *Neatby noted privately*: Litt, *Muses*, 230.

41    *two wealthy men*: financier Izaak Walton Killam and steel baron James
      Dunn. See "Sir James Dunn" (obituary), *Saint Croix Courier*, Jan. 5,
      1956.

      *"foster and promote"*: Canada Council Act, quoted in Canada Council,
      *Second Annual Report*, 11.

42    *"recognition on 75th birthday"*: Canada Council, *First Annual Report,
      to March 31, 1958,* 59.

      *$11.4 million*: *Second Annual Report*, 49, 52.

      *inaugural arts fellowships*: ibid., 76–77.

      *"hand on to our children"*: "The Canada Council and the Writer,"
      *Canadian Author & Bookman* 39.3 (1964).

43    *Canada Foundation*: "Canada Foundation," *Montreal Gazette*, June 14,
      1945.

      *"whatever we wanted to do"*: Silcox interview, Oct. 1, 2013.

      *tenable only abroad*: Canada Council, *First Annual Report*, 49–50.

      *$461,000*: Canada Council, *11th Annual Report, 1967–1968*, 21.

      *Ontario Council for the Arts:* Ontario Royal Commission on Publishing,
      *Canadian Publishers and Canadian Publishing* (Queen's Printer, 1973),
      254. Paul Litt's claim that the Ontario Arts Council spent "not a penny"
      on literature in 1967 appears to be wrong, in fact if not in spirit (*History
      of the Book in Canada: Vol. III*, 525n47).

44    *Council helped Purdy*: Canada Council to Purdy, March 17, 1965, Papers
      of A. W. Purdy, University of Saskatchewan, MSS 4, box 21, folder IX, D;
      *Gibson*: Gibson interview, Oct. 26, 2010; *Lee*: *Civil Elegies* (Anansi, 1972),
      copyright page; *Laurence*: James King, *The Life of Margaret Laurence*
      (Knopf, 1997), 226; *Cohen*: Ira B. Nadel, *Various Positions: A Life of
      Leonard Cohen* (Random House, 1996), 66, 87; *Munro*: Robert Thacker,
      *Alice Munro: Writing Her Lives* (M&S, 2005), 145–46; *Atwood*: interview,
      Dec. 15, 2010.

      *two thousand copies*: Victor J. Ramraj, "Mordecai Richler" (1987),
      University of Calgary Special Collections; *half a million readers*:
      according to figures collected by the Ontario Royal Commission
      on Publishing, *Maclean's* circulation in 1962 was 522,409 (*Canadian
      Publishers*, 281).

45    *"chapter with a recipe"*: quoted in Foran, *Mordecai*, 378.

      *"jew-ville"*: Richler to Brian Moore, Feb. 16, 1959, quoted in Posner,
      *Last Honest Man*, 129.

46    *"campus vaudeville circuit"*: Richler, "Endure, Endure," *Maclean's*,
      March 1971.

## Chapter 4: The National Dream

47–50    *Berton*: A. B. McKillop, *Pierre Berton* (M&S, 2008); Berton, *My Times* (Doubleday, 1995).

47       *"The following six books"*: quoted in McKillop, *Pierre Berton*, 105.

50       *Diefenbaker's tastes*: Peter C. Newman, *Renegade in Power* (M&S, 1963), 10, 174; *Fulton*: ibid., 111.

         *cover story*: ibid., 237.

         *royal commission on magazines*: Ken Kelly, "New Commission," *Ottawa Citizen*, Oct. 20, 1960.

50–51    *Eli MacLaren: Dominion and Agency: Copyright and the Structuring of the Canadian Book Trade* (UTP, 2011), 12.

51       *Canada Council and GGs*: Marie-Pier Luneau and Ruth Panofsky, "Celebrating Authors," *History of the Book in Canada: Vol. III* (UTP, 2007) 118.

         *Obscenity law*: Shannon Bell, Brenda Cossman, and Lise Gotell, *Bad Attitude/s on Trial: Pornography, Feminism, and the Butler Decision* (UTP, 1997); L. W. Sumner, *The Hateful and the Obscene* (UTP, 2004).

         *crime comics ban*: "'Obscenity' Hearing Put Over to Fall," *Manitoba Ensign*, July 5, 1952. See also Fulton's testimony to the United States Senate Subcommittee on Juvenile Delinquency, archived at http://www.thecomicbooks.com/fulton.html.

         *"any publication"*: *Criminal Code of Canada*, pt. 5, 163, para. 8.

         *puritan on a crusade*: "Citizens Beware," *Quill & Quire*, Dec. 1959/Jan. 1960.

52       *"genuine literary merit"*: "Government Defines Obscenity," *Quill & Quire*, Aug./Sep. 1959.

         *"objectionable material"*: quoted in Bell, Cossman, and Gotell, *Bad Attitude/s*, 15.

         *paid a few fines*: the first of which, so far as I know, was Toronto magazine and bookseller/distributor Gordon McAuslane, charged in 1966 and sentenced to six months in prison, plus a $500 fine for his company, Bookazine Enterprises, for possession of obscene literature, including the paperbacks *Executive Lesbian*, *Bedroom a-Go-Go*, and *Flesh Worshipers* ("Book Firm Official Jailed," *Globe and Mail*, May 19, 1966; "Loses Appeal," ibid., May 2, 1967).

         *"orgy of filth"*: John Fisher to Jack McClelland, Aug. 22, and McClelland to Fisher, Aug. 26, 1966, *Selected Letters of Jack McClelland*, ed. Sam Solecki (Key Porter, 1998), 110–13.

52      *refused to sell Beautiful Losers*: McClelland to Cohen, May 9, 1966, ibid., 105; *escaped obscenity charges*: McClelland worried about censorship of *Beautiful Losers* "but didn't hear a word" (quoted in Posner, *The Last Honest Man*, 153).

52–53   *Lady Chatterley's Lover*: "Bestsellers in Canada," *Quill & Quire*, Oct./Nov. 1959; "Chatterley Obscene," *Globe and Mail*, April 8, 1961; "Chatterley's Lover Cleared," ibid., March 16, 1962.

53      *Dorothy Cameron*: "Art Dealer Charged," *Globe and Mail*, May 27, 1965; *Berton spoke*: *My Times*, 282; *"lesbian activity"*: Patrick Watson, *This Hour Has Seven Days*, CBC TV, Feb. 6, 1966; *lost her appeals*: Farrell Crook, "No Right to Appeal," *Globe and Mail*, June 7, 1967.

53*     *testimony by art experts*: Robert Fulford, *Best Seat in the House* (Collins, 1988), 106–9.

53–54   *"Mike's artistic interest"*: John English, *The Worldly Years: The Life of Lester Pearson*, vol. 2, *1949–1972* (Knopf, 1992), 73; *"lowly board"*: ibid., 389.

54      *influenced by Galbraith*: ibid., 238 (cf. 218–19).

        *not a government idea*: Pierre Berton, *1967* (Doubleday, 1967), 20.

        *"moving panorama"*: *Expo 67: Guide officiel/Official Guide* (Maclean-Hunter, 1967), 308.

55ff.    *Expo*: John Lownsbrough, *The Best Place to Be: Expo 67 and Its Time* (Penguin, 2012).

55      *neither was enthusiastic*: Newman, *Renegade in Power*, 93 (Diefenbaker); Berton, *1967*, 261 (Pearson).

        *"awfully good fun"*: "Expo 67," *Hunting Tigers under Glass* (M&S, 1968), 32.

        *some $25 million*: Peter H. Aykroyd, *The Anniversary Compulsion: Canada's Centennial Celebrations* (Dundurn, 1992), Appendix J; *Council worried*: Canada Council, *11th Annual Report, 1967–1968*, 14.

        *centennial song*: Bobby Gimby's "Ca-na-da" (Quality Records, 1967).

56      *"commissioned by a commission"*: Gerald McNeil, "Centennial Play," *Montreal Gazette*, Jan. 6, 1967. Written by Halifax surgeon Arthur Murphy, Montreal playwright Yves Thériault, Ontario writer Robertson Davies, prairie novelist W. O. Mitchell, and Vancouver humorist Eric Nicol, *The Centennial Play* closed three days after it opened.

        *Toronto for a month*: Zena Cherry, "Pageant of Canada," *Globe and Mail*, Oct. 16, 1967. The incident led to creation of the Canadian Artists' Representation/Le front des artistes canadiens.

        *bought Canadian books*: Aykroyd, *Anniversary Compulsion*, 132–33.

        *"mountain of non-books"*: Richler, "Expo 67," 28.

56     *"Canadian subjects"*: "Competitions: Short Stories, Essays and Poetry,"
       brochure, Dennis Lee Papers, Thomas Fisher Rare Book Library, MS
       COLL 271, box 21, folder 17.

       *Atwood won the poetry prize*: Rosemary Sullivan, *The Red Shoes:
       Margaret Atwood Starting Out* (HarperFlamingo, 1998), 213; *essay prize*:
       "She Wins First Prize," *Toronto Daily Star*, July 29, 1967.

       *Cohen read his poems*: "Leonard Cohen in Expo," *Montreal Gazette*,
       July 13, 1967.

       *Richler at* CAA *conference*: Charles Foran, *Mordecai: The Life and Times*
       (Knopf, 2010), 338.

57     *"Story of Man"*: *Expo 67 Official Guide*, 57; *Frye*: Lownsbrough, *Best
       Place to Be*, 129.

       *"latest screwdriver"*: Robillard quoted in *Ottawa Journal*, Dec. 30, 1967,
       45.

       *beyond scarcity*: Fulford, *Remember Expo* (M&S, 1968), 8.

       *"history buffs"*: Berton, *1967*, 48.

58     *"greatest international exposition"*: quoted ibid., 274.

       *"Nationalism has its limits"*: *The Names of Things* (Porcupine's Quill,
       2006), 129.

58–60  *Trudeau*: John English, *Just Watch Me: The Life of Pierre Elliott Trudeau*,
       vol. 2, *1968–2000* (Vintage Canada, 2010); Nino Ricci, *Pierre Elliott
       Trudeau* (Penguin, 2009).

58     *Trudeau and McLuhan*: see also Philip Marchand, *Marshall McLuhan:
       The Medium and the Messenger* (Random House, 1989), 222–24.

       *Trudeau and Richler*: see also Foran, *Mordecai*, 665–66.

59     *two new programs*: John Burns, "Student Job Program," *Globe and
       Mail*, March 17, 1971; Associated Press, "Canadian Project Helps on
       Local Level," *Spokane Daily Chronicle*, May 1, 1975.

       *Tamahnous Theatre*: John Gray, "Pierre Elliott Trudeau," *Globe and
       Mail*, Oct. 2, 2000.

       *Toronto Free Theatre*: Denis W. Johnston, *Up the Mainstream: The Rise
       of Toronto's Alternative Theatres* (UTP, 1991), 171.

       *James Reaney*: Linda Gaborian, "Best English-Canadian Play Yet,"
       *Montreal Gazette*, Dec. 7, 1974.

59*    *Gardner complained*: William Kilbourn et al, "The Canada Council
       and the Theatre," *Theatre Research in Canada* 3.2 (1982).

59–60  OFY *aid for Coach House*: interviews with Stan Bevington, Aug. 25,
       2010, and Victor Coleman, July 13, 2010.

60     *demanded a royal commission*: Berton, *My Times*, 367.

60      *"my countrymen"*: "June Callwood's Canada," *Maclean's*, Jan. 1972.

        *Gibson*: interview, Oct. 26, 2010.

        *Wieland*: English, *Just Watch Me*, 99.

## Chapter 5: The Diviners

61–63    *McLuhan*: Philip Marchand, *Marshall McLuhan: The Medium and the Messenger* (Random House, 1989); *Frye*: John Ayre, *Northrop Frye: A Biography* (Random House, 1989).

62      *Frye versus McLuhan*: B. W. Powe, *Marshall McLuhan and Northrop Frye: Apocalypse and Alchemy* (UTP, 2014), 136, 92. Portions of this section have been adapted from my review of Powe's book in the *Literary Review of Canada*, July/Aug. 2014.

        *"de rigueur"*: Atwood, "The Great Communicator," *Globe and Mail*, Jan. 24, 1991.

63      *ninety-seven magazines*: Berton, *1967* (Doubleday, 1997), 206.

        *"oracle of the electric age"*: McLuhan, *Understanding Media* (Signet-NAL, ©1964), front cover.

        *"future of work"*: ibid., 300–301.

64      *new universities*: "List of Universities in Canada," Wikipedia, counting U du Q as one and adding Regina, which became a university in 1974.

        *increased enrolments, "full scale…shift"*: Stuart Henderson, *Making the Scene: Yorkville and Hip Toronto in the 1960s* (UTP, 2011), 16.

65      *"Shakespeare and after"*: Rosemary Sullivan, *The Red Shoes: Margaret Atwood Starting Out* (HarperFlamingo, 1998), 61; *"English and dead"*: Atwood, "Nationalism, Limbo, and the Canadian Club," *Saturday Night*, Jan. 1971.

65*     *Britnell's offered*: Frank Moritsugu, "Books & People," *Toronto Daily Star*, Feb. 5, 1963.

66      *"little yid"*: Richler, *The Apprenticeship of Duddy Kravitz* (M&S/NCL, 1989), 280.

66–69    *Jim Foley*: Al Purdy, "The Salvation of Canadian Literature," *Weekend Magazine*, June 15, 1974; Paul William Roberts, "A Passionate Believer," *Toronto Star*, July 1, 1989.

66      *almost evangelical*: Lee interview, June 26, 2012.

67      *"only country"*: quoted in Purdy, "Salvation."

67–68    *Canada Day*: William French, "Canada Day," *Globe and Mail*, Jan. 13, 1973, and "Canada Day Writ Large," ibid., May 12, 1975; Foley, "Canada Day," *Canadian Literature* 64 (1975).

68      *Brown remembers*: interview, July 3, 2012.

        *Gibson recalls*: interview, Oct. 26, 2010.

68      *Atwood wrote*: "Travels Back," *Maclean's*, Jan. 1973.

68*     *Montreal Story Tellers*: J. R. Struthers, *The Montreal Story Tellers* (Véhicule, 1985).

69      *Canadian studies*: Ian Underhill, *Starting the Ark in the Dark: Teaching Canadian Literature in High School* (University of Western Ontario, 1977), 3; *literature*: Don Gutteridge, *Stubborn Pilgrimage: Resistance and Transformation in Ontario Teaching, 1960–1993* (Our Schools/Our Selves, 1994), 233n27.

        *Berton said*: quoted in "Literary Stars Make His Day," *Winnipeg Free Press*, Jan. 25, 1973.

        *debated in Parliament*: "After Canada Day, Quebec Day?" *Globe and Mail*, Feb. 25, 1976.

        *CanLit in universities*: Paul Martin, *Sanctioned Ignorance: The Politics of Knowledge Production and the Teaching of the Literatures of Canada* (U of Alberta, 2013).

        *courses devoted to Canadian literature*: Janet B. Friskney, *New Canadian Library* (UTP, 2007), 44, 67.

70      *"suddenly in demand"*: Clara Thomas, "Irving Layton," *Books in Canada*, March 2006.

        *university bookstores*: *The Book Publishing and Manufacturing Industry in Canada* (Department of Industry, Trade and Commerce, 1970), 2; Fernande Roy, *Histoire de la librairie au Québec* (Leméac, 2000), 191.

        *bookseller David Mason*: Mason, *The Pope's Bookbinder* (Biblioasis, 2013), 167–68.

70–71   *bought manuscripts*: Robert Fulford, "A Hot Market for Manuscripts," *Toronto Daily Star*, clipping [March 1966?], Cohen Papers, Fisher Library, MS COLL 122, box 9, folder 11.

70      *McGill wasn't interested, Newlove's teeth*: Richard Landon interview, May 5, 2008.

71      *MacLennan's papers*: "Archives Sold," *Montreal Gazette*, July 14, 1973; *Richler's papers*: Charles Foran, *Mordecai: The Life and Times* (Knopf, 2010), 439.

        *Atwood's first novel*: Atwood, introduction, *The Edible Woman* (Virago, 1980).

        *"excelling in the classroom"*: John T. Saywell, *Someone to Teach Them: York and the Great University Explosion, 1960–1973* (UTP, 2008), 86.

72      *ninety appointments*: Nancy Earle, "The Canada Council for the Arts Writer-in-Residence Program," *History of the Book in Canada: Vol. III*, 115.

        *started with Avison*: Donald Hair, "Canadian Literature and Culture at Western," *Canadian Poetry* 65 (2009).

72–73 *"Purdy's crocuses"*: versions of this story can be found in John Metcalf, *Kicking Against the Pricks* (ECW, 1982), 133; Susan Musgrave, "Remembering Al," in *Al Purdy*, ed. Linda Rogers (Guernica, 2002); and Riffs & Ripples (blog), Marvin Orbach to Chris Faiers, July 12, 2012. Orbach's version has the cans.

73 *Richler at George Williams and Carleton*: Foran, *Mordecai*, 362, 416–17, 425.

 *"I played darts"*: Metcalf, *Kicking Against the Pricks*, 124, 120.

74 *a home in the academy*: George Whalley, ed., *Writing in Canada: Proceedings of the Canadian Writers' Conference, 28–31 July 1955* (Macmillan, 1956); *celebrated its arrival*: Clara Thomas, "Seeing Niagara and After," *Lakehead University Review* 6.2 (1973).

 *poets paid*: George Bowering interview, July 17, 2012; cf. Bowering, *A Magpie Life* (Key Porter, 2001), 154–55.

 *Salter convinced*: Rudy Wiebe in *A Writer's Life: The Margaret Laurence Lectures* (M&S, 2011), 294.

 *UBC committee*: George Woodcock, "Getting Away with Survival," *The Sixties: Writers and Writing of the Decade* (UBC, 1969).

 *Birney insisted*: George McWhirter, "Creative Writing at UBC," *Making Waves: Reading B.C. and Pacific Northwest Literature*, ed. Trevor Carolan (Anvil, 2010), 163.

 *Blaser taught*: George Bowering to Michael Boughn, email ca. 2012, my copy.

74–75 *"intended by fate"*: David Solway, "Dudek Made Poetry Irresistible," *Quill & Quire*, May 2001.

75 *Blaise proposed*: Blaise, "The Muse-C of Metcalf," *CNQ* 88 (2013).

## Chapter 6: The Double Hook

77–79 *MacEwen*: Rosemary Sullivan, *Shadow Maker: The Life of Gwendolyn MacEwen* (HarperCollins, 1995).

77 *$400 plus $71.23*: contract for *Julian the Magician*, Nov. 7, 1962; Theodore Wilente to MacEwen, Aug. 22, 1963, and Aug. 11, 1965, MacEwen Papers, Fisher Library, MS COLL 00121, box 28.

78 *didn't much care for the poems*: e.g. Victor Coleman, interview, July 13, 2010.

 *Acorn*: Chris Gudgeon, *Out of This World: The Natural History of Milton Acorn* (Arsenal Pulp, 1996).

 *"important book"*: Bowering, "A Complex Music," *Canadian Literature* 21 (1964).

 *Telegram profile*: Cynthia Kelly, "A Poetic Life," *Telegram*, Jan. 11, 1964.

78    *outgrown the Embassy*: Linda Munk, "Four Women Poets," *Globe and Mail*, Jan. 28, 1965.

*paid no advance*: contract, Jan. 13, 1965, MacEwen Papers, box 28.

*agents gave up*: Harold Ober Associates to MacEwen, March 15, 1971, and David Higham Associates to MacEwen, April 17, 1973, ibid.

79    *"jammed to overflowing"*: Helen Worthington, "Recital Draws Full House," *Toronto Star*, April 28, 1972.

80    *didn't stop publishers*: e.g. Macmillan's advertisement in the Sep./Oct. 1963 *Quill & Quire*, which invited readers to "Choose your bestsellers from the Macmillan fall list," including MacEwan's [*sic*] *Julian the Magician* — a book not yet available and printed in an edition of five hundred copies.

*"creative wasteland"*: Metcalf, *An Aesthetic Underground: A Literary Memoir* (Thomas Allen, 2003), 64.

*less than Grade 9*: Audrey M. Thomas, *Adult Illiteracy in Canada* (Canadian Commission for UNESCO, 1983), 66, table 11; 61, 63. The figures for Quebec and Montreal are from the 1976 census, presumably an improvement there, as for the country.

80–81    *consulting firm*: Ernst & Ernst Management Consulting Services, *The Book Publishing and Manufacturing Industry in Canada* (Department of Industry, Trade and Commerce, 1970).

81    *study at York*: Delores Broten, *The Lumber Jack Report: English Canadian Literary Trade Book Publishers' Sales, 1963–72* (CANLIT, 1975).

*largest distillery*: Samuel Bronfman's Distillery Corporation, with 1969 revenue of $1.4 billion ("Top 30 Canadian Companies," *Annual Review of the Canadian Equity Market and Economy*, Toronto Stock Exchange, 1969).

*first survey of Canadian readers*: for the Ontario Royal Commission on Publishing, reported in *Canadian Publishers and Canadian Publishing* (Queen's Printer, 1973), 162–67.

81–82    *government's first survey*: "Survey of Selected Leisure Activities: Reading Habits," Feb. 1978, reported in Kenneth F. Watson et al., *Leisure Reading Habits* (Infoscan, 1980).

82    *"twenty-five book shops"*: *Royal Commission on National Development in the Arts, Letters and Sciences* (King's Printer, 1951), 229.

*1,260 businesses*: *History of the Book in Canada: Vol. III*, 393. The number of college and trade bookstores is an estimate, based on 1971 membership of 112 trade bookstores in the English-speaking Canadian Booksellers Association (Ontario Royal Commission on Publishing, *Canadian Publishers*, 136), plus the same number per capita for Quebec.

82    *"pitifully underdeveloped"*: Royal Commission on Publishing, *Canadian Publishers*, 138–39.

83    *Mel Hurtig's store*: Roy MacSkimming, *The Perilous Trade* (M&S, 2007), 230.

    *Duthie's*: Alan Twigg, "Bill Duthie," *Quill & Quire*, June 1984.

    *Classic Books*: William French, "Porcelain Pigless Bookstores," *Globe and Mail*, Feb. 4, 1967.

    *"Victoria's largest assortment"*: quoted in Robert Thacker, *Alice Munro: Writing Her Lives* (M&S, 2005), 179.

    *"right behind Berton"*: William French, "In Alice Land," *Globe and Mail*, June 19, 1973.

84    *guide to Toronto's bookstores*: *Anything But Son of Rochdale* 1.1 (Sep. 1967), Lee Papers, Fisher Library, MS COLL 271, box 15, folder 17.

    *Third World Books*: Kevin Plummer, "Third World Books," Torontoist, Feb. 7, 2015.

84–86    *Ahvenus*: undated memoir, Ahvenus Papers, Thomas Fisher Rare Book Library, MS COLL 574, box 15, folder 3; Don McLeod, "Notes on Martin Ahvenus," CNQ 69 (2006); Richard Landon interview, May 5, 2008; David Mason interview, June 18, 2012.

85    *$125 a month*: Declaration of Business, Ahvenus Papers, box 1, folder 1.

    *"living in Toronto"*: Purdy to Ahvenus [ca. late sixties], Ahvenus Papers, box 10, folder 12.

    *dark poem on the wall*: Gudgeon, *Out of This World*, 114.

    *"every Thursday"*: Mason interview. See also Douglas Fetherling, *Travels by Night* (Lester, 1994), 231–32.

86    *Atwood's first book*: invoices, Ahvenus Papers, box 1, folders 6–8.

    *850 titles*: Berton, unlocated *Daily Star* column of April 30, 1962, quoted in Jamie Bradburn, "Past Pieces of Toronto: The Book Cellar," OpenFile, June 24, 2012.

    *Book Cellar regulars*: Robert Fulford, "The Book Cellar's Storied Past," *Globe and Mail*, Jan. 14, 1998.

    *"out-of-the-way books"*: "Bookstores," *Anything But Son of Rochdale* 1.1.

    *Forms of Loss*: sales record, April 30, 1965, Lee Papers, box 6, folder 35; "The Forms of Loss: Balance," n.d., ibid., folder 32; "A Very Special Poet," *Toronto Daily Star*, April 28, 1965.

87    *W. H. Smith and Cocksure*: Urjo Kareda, "Banned in Britain," *Toronto Daily Star*, June 1, 1968.

87    *"carcan"*: Philippe Roy, *Le Livre français au Québec, 1939–1972* (Publibook, 2008), 156, trans. Myra Bloom.

87–88   *Longhouse Book Shop*: William French, "The Longhouse," *Globe and Mail*, May 9, 1972, and "The Flag Sells," ibid., March 19, 1974; Brian Brett, "We Worked Hard," ibid., Nov. 27, 1999.

88    *Books Canada*: "Bookstores Boomed in 1972," *Ottawa Citizen*, April 7, 1973.

      *A Pair of Trindles*: Paul McCormick, "What's a Pair of Trindles?" *Canadian Bookseller*, April 1984.

      *Oxford Canadiana*: Mark Pittam interview, Oct. 22, 2014.

88–89   *Double Hook*: Sheila Fischman, "Quebec Social Notes," *Globe and Mail*, Jan. 11, 1975; "Novelist Puts Her Bookshop First," *Montreal Gazette*, Feb. 5, 1976; Linda Leith, "A Heroine of Canadian Literature," *Globe and Mail*, March 11, 2014.

90    *"wrote for ourselves"*: Atwood interview, Dec. 15, 2010.

91    *"register our protest"*: Lee Papers, box 6, folder 41. See also Gudgeon, *Out of This World*, 135–43.

      *party for Acorn*: see also Kaspars Dzeguze, "Prize for Poet," *Globe and Mail*, May 18, 1970; Purdy to Earle Birney, May 18, 1970, *Yours, Al: The Collected Letters of Al Purdy*, ed. Sam Solecki (Harbour, 2004), 159.

## Chapter 7: The Torontonians

93–96   *Atwood*: Rosemary Sullivan, *The Red Shoes: Margaret Atwood Starting Out* (HarperFlamingo, 1998).

93    *Forum accepted*: Milton Wilson to Atwood, March 28, 1959, Atwood Papers, Thomas Fisher Rare Book Library, MS COLL 335, box 119, folder 7:8.

      *"young Toronto poets"*: "Coming Attractions," Atwood Papers, MS COLL 200, box 1, folder 7.

94    *three publishers*: "Up in the Air So Blue" was rejected by M&S (Atwood Papers, MS COLL 200, box 1, folder 47), Ryerson (folder 70), and Clarke, Irwin (folder 25). Atwood adds Macmillan to the list, but I can't find any record of this.

      *"way ahead of its time"*: Atwood interview, April 7, 2010.

      *Contact Press accepted*: Raymond Souster to Atwood, postmarked Aug. 25, 1965, Atwood Papers, MS COLL 200, box 1, folder 74; *suggested title*: Peter Miller to Atwood, Sep. 29, 1965, ibid., folder 50B; *290 copies*: Miller to Atwood, March 23, 1967, ibid.

      *only newspaper*: *Toronto Daily Star*, Dec. 10, 1966, 33; *sold the manuscript*: to Laurie Hill Limited for an unknown amount (Atwood to Laurie Lerew, Jan. 11, 1967, MS COLL 200, box 92, folder 2).

95    *Edible Woman reviews*: *Time*, Sep. 26, 1969, 16; George Woodcock,
      "Are We All Emotional Cannibals?" *Toronto Daily Star*, Sep. 13, 1969;
      Eileen Johnson, "Poet Does Well by Novel," *Vancouver Sun*, Oct. 31,
      1969; Dorothy Bishop, "Novel of the Week," *Ottawa Journal*, Jan. 17,
      1970; MariJo Amer, *Peterborough Examiner*, Dec. 11, 1969.

96    *"ugly vitality"*: Dudek, "The Montreal Poets," *Culture* (1957), reprinted
      in *Language Acts: Anglo-Québec Poetry*, ed. Jason Camlot and Todd
      Swift (Véhicule, 2007), 38, 41.

      *centred on Toronto*: Dudek and Michael Gnarowski, *The Making of
      Modern Poetry in Canada* (Ryerson, 1967), 114.

97    *Toronto liquor laws*: Edward Lacey, "Poetry Chronicle III," *Edge* 8 (1968),
      reprinted in *Canadian Poetry* 58 (2006), 97. Lacey's account may be a
      tad exaggerated.

      *Berton counted five*: *My Times* (Doubleday, 1995), 8.

      *couldn't find a bar*: Mason interview, June 18, 2012.

      *"misery reigned"*: Kildare Dobbs, *Running the Rapids* (Dundurn, 2005),
      129.

      *"cemetery with lights"*: e.g. in Jim Coleman's column, *Ottawa Citizen*,
      Aug. 1, 1962.

      *floor-length tablecloths*: Phyllis Brett Young, *The Torontonians* (MQUP,
      2007), 150–51, 207–8, 243. See also Doug Taylor, "The Infamous Casino
      on Queen St.," Historic Toronto, Nov. 6, 2013.

98    *"swinging Toronto"*: *Globe and Mail*, April 29, 1967, 27. For a glimpse,
      see Don Owen's documentary *Toronto Jazz* (National Film Board, 1963).

      *House of Hambourg*: Herbert Whittaker, "Grimy Expose," *Globe and
      Mail*, Nov. 30, 1960, and "Revue Offers Mixture of Exotic Dances,"
      ibid., Feb. 21, 1961.

      *Isaacs' first gallery*: Donnalu Wigmore, ed., *Isaacs Seen* (Hart House,
      2005), 8. The gallery's official opening was on Feb. 1, 1956 (ibid., 37).

      *Council's first grant*: Cameron Anstee, "The Canada Council for the
      Arts and the Funding of Poetry Readings," *Amodern* 4 (2014).

      *"attendance varied"*: quoted in Wigmore, *Isaacs Seen*, 44.

99    *"Finnish rugs"*: *Toronto Daily Star*, Nov. 4, 1964, quoted in Stuart
      Henderson, *Making the Scene: Yorkville and Hip Toronto in the 1960s*
      (UTP, 2011), 111.

99–103 *Bohemian Embassy*: Don Cullen, *The Bohemian Embassy* (Wolsak &
      Wynn, 2007).

100   *"lost causes"*: quoted in Sullivan, *Red Shoes*, 103.

100     *café boheme*: photograph, Nov. 5, 1965, Toronto *Telegram* fonds, York
        University, #ASC05472. Rosemary Sullivan incorrectly says the walls
        were black, likely misled by Atwood, whose memory plays the same
        trick on her in her fictionalization of MacEwen reading at the Embassy
        in the short story "Isis in Darkness," in *Wilderness Tips* (M&S, 1991).

        *students smashed glasses*: Matthew K. Thomas, "Voice of a Nation,"
        *Varsity*, Feb. 26, 2004.

        *"a sweet guy"*: Coleman interview, July 13, 2010.

        *Libby Jones*: Antony Ferry, "Stripper Lectures Poets," *Toronto Daily
        Star*, Nov. 18, 1960, and Lux advertisement below.

        *tried a happening*: "Canada's First Happening," *Close-Up*, CBC TV, Feb.
        17, 1963; *didn't happen*: John Porter, "Toronto Artists' Film Activity
        1949–1969," *CineZine*, 1983–84.

101     *Nathan Cohen*: *Toronto Daily Star*, Dec. 3, 1963, 16.

102     *"didn't have a budget"*: Coleman interview. Cullen never mentions
        Coleman in *The Bohemian Embassy*. His book and Christopher Ban's
        2010 documentary *Behind the Bohemian Embassy* both leave the
        impression that Colombo was the first Embassy's only literary host.

        *"beatnik housewife"*: Donald Grant, "Poet Babies Grown Up," *Telegram*,
        Jan. 17, 1962.   .

        *Acorn passed out*: Atwood interview, Dec. 15, 2010.

        *filed an objection*: *Cullen v. Triple Canon*, 2011 TMOB 231, Nov. 30, 2011.

103     *Love-In*: "4500 at Queen's Park," *Globe and Mail*, May 23, 1967.

        *"crossing boundaries"*: Wainwright interview, June 5, 2008.

104     *Park Plaza*: Fulford, *Best Seat in the House* (Collins, 1988), 144; *wolf
        howl*: Graeme Gibson interview, Oct. 26, 2010.

        *Pilot Tavern*: Wigmore, *Isaacs Seen*, 75.

        *Rochdale*: Dennis Lee, "Judy Merril," *Body Music* (Anansi, 1998);
        Rochdale Calendar 1967–68, Lee Papers, Fisher Library, MS COLL
        271, box 14, folder 21; Rochdale College catalogue, Sep. 1968, ibid., folder
        30.

        *municipal tax grants*: Minutes, Rochdale College Governing Council,
        Sep. 13, 1966, Lee Papers, folder 5; Coordinators Report, May 29, 1967,
        ibid., folder 16.

        *Rochdale inhabitants*: Drumbolis interview, Sep. 16, 2014; Coleman
        interview.

        *"published nothing"*: Matt Cohen, *Typing* (Vintage Canada, 2001), 85.

104*    *Garrard's Tom Paine*: Denis W. Johnston, *Up the Mainstream: The Rise
        of Toronto's Alternative Theatres* (UTP, 1991), 37–38.

105     *the Pit*: Iris Nowell, "Tom Hodgson," *CNQ* 72 (2007).

105     *Church Streeters*: Fetherling, *Travels by Night*, 205, 230–31.

        *Lane remembers*: "Lives of the Poets," *Geist* 17 (1995).

        *Stanley Street*: Abraham Tarasofsky, "Layton as I Knew Him," CNQ 72 (2007), 60.

        *partipriste hangouts*: Malcolm Reid, *The Shouting Signpainters* (M&S, 1972), 40–41.

        *London scene*: Barry Lord, "Swinging London (Ontario)," *Star Weekly*, Jan. 13, 1968.

106     *decided on her own*: Sullivan, *Red Shoes*, 67.

107     *"part of a community"*: quoted in Roy MacSkimming, "Perilous Trade Conversations Four," CNQ 72 (2007).

        *Cohen and Clarke versus Richler*: Foran, *Mordecai: The Life and Times* (Knopf, 2010), 315, 366.

        *Cohen left Anansi*: Typing, 102, and letter to Dennis Lee [ca. 1969], Lee Papers, box 3, Cohen folder.

108     *"a moral in this"*: Ontario Royal Commission on Publishing, *Canadian Publishers and Canadian Publishing* (Queen's Printer, 1973), 49. See also Kildare Dobbs, "Writers Make Fools of Themselves," *Toronto Daily Star*, Dec. 10, 1971, and Michael Smith, "Book Probe Hears Writers," *Globe and Mail*, Dec. 10, 1971.

        *"each other's company"*: Munro, "Wood," *Too Much Happiness* (M&S, 2009).

## Chapter 8: Understanding Media

109–112  *Purdy*: Purdy, *Reaching for the Beaufort Sea* (Harbour, 1993); *Yours, Al: The Collected Letters of Al Purdy*, ed. Sam Solecki (Harbour, 2004).

109     *"big man"*: Helwig, *The Names of Things* (Porcupine's Quill, 2006), 145.

110     *"euphoric period"*: Purdy, *Beaufort Sea*, 213.

        *Purdy and Acorn*: Purdy, introduction to Acorn's *I've Tasted My Blood* (Ryerson, 1969).

111     *first Canada Council grant*: Lillian Breen for the Council to Purdy, June 1, 1960, Purdy Papers, University of Saskatchewan, box 21, folder IX, D.

        *Tsimshian territory*: "Al Purdy's Canada," *Maclean's*, May 1971.

112     *Mitchell*: Barbara and Ormond Mitchell, *The Life of W. O. Mitchell: The Years of Fame, 1948–1998* (M&S, 2005); cf. Catherine McLay, "The W. O. Mitchell Papers," www.ucalgary.ca.

113     *"My name is Al"*: "No Other Country," *Tuesday Night*, CBC Radio, Nov. 21, 1967, Purdy Digital Archive, University of Saskatchewan, tape 27.

        *earned about $4,000*: based on contracts in the Purdy Papers, box 21, IX, A.

113      *radio dramas*: Concordia University Centre for Broadcasting and Journalism Studies, bibliography of CBC radio drama scripts, vol. 2, 1962–86.

114      *Tremblay's last full-time job*: Gilbert David and Pierre Lavoie, eds., *Le monde de Michel Tremblay* (Cahiers de théâtre Jeu, 1993), 9.

         *"I went to the* CBC*"*: Jonas interview, Sep. 10, 2013.

115      *"natural madness"*: "Phyllis Webb's Canada," *Maclean's*, Oct. 1971.

         *Ideas*: Pauline Butling, "Phyllis Webb as Public Intellectual," *Wider Boundaries of Daring*, ed. Di Brandt and Barbara Godard (WLUP, 2009).

115–116  *Modern Canadian Poetry*: produced by John Kennedy and aired from April 30 to July 23, 1967; from brochure in MacEwen Papers, Fisher Library, MS COLL 00121, box 32.

116–122  *Weaver*: Elaine Kalman Naves, *Robert Weaver: Godfather of Canadian Literature* (Véhicule, 2007). Quotations not otherwise cited are from "Bob Weaver Has Lots of Friends," *Performing Arts Magazine* (Fall 1973).

117      *November 9*: Naves says *Anthology* first aired on Oct. 19, but the *Globe and Mail*'s radio guide for that day doesn't mention *Anthology* and lists another show, *Latin American Music*, in its eleven p.m. time slot. *Anthology* first appears in the *Globe*'s radio guide for November 9.

         *five poems*: CBC to Leonard Cohen, Oct. 23, 1957, Cohen Papers, Fisher Library, MS COLL 122, box 10B, folder 10.

         *bought work from Munro*: Robert Thacker, *Alice Munro: Writing Her Lives* (M&S, 2005), 565–66; *from Atwood*: Robert McCormack to Atwood, June 19, 1961, Atwood Papers, Fisher Library, MS COLL 200, box 1, folder 24; *from Bowering*: Roy Miki, *A Record of Writing* (Talonbooks, 1990), E3.

         *"fatuous nonsense"*: Weaver to Phyllis Webb, Jan. 27, 1964, quoted in Butling, "Phyllis Webb," 248.

118      *"not sexist"*: quoted in Naves, *Robert Weaver*, 102; *"special affection"*: ibid., 146.

         *"tweed jacket"*: Cohen, *Typing* (Vintage Canada, 2001), 110.

         *"clean his pipe"*: Fetherling, *Travels by Night* (Lester, 1994), 170–71.

119      *"lunches with Bob"*: Purdy, *Beaufort Sea*, 284.

         *Metcalf remembers*: interview, May 18, 2012.

         *"greatest gossips"*: quoted in Naves, *Robert Weaver*, 96.

         *budget of $48,000*: William French, "Listeners All Have First Names," *Globe and Mail*, Oct. 5, 1968.

120      *"Kraft Dinners"*: quoted in Rosemary Sullivan, *Shadow Maker: The Life of Gwendolyn MacEwen* (HarperCollins, 1995), 179.

120 *"big"*: Atwood interview, Dec. 15, 2010.

*"reminded me"*: Munro, foreword, *The Anthology Anthology* (Macmillan, 1984).

120–121 *"pretty sparse"*: quoted in Naves, *Robert Weaver*, 100.

121–122 *"call into existence"*: ibid., 123–24.

122 *Educated Imagination*: John Ayre, *Northrop Frye* (Random House, 1989), 286.

*"More fatherly"*: quoted in French, "Listeners All Have First Names."

*Canadian content*: ACTRA 4.3 (fall 1967).

123 *Factory Theatre Lab*: Denis W. Johnston, *Up the Mainstream: The Rise of Toronto's Alternative Theatres* (UTP, 1991), 96–97.

*dramas on CBC*: Fulford, "Radio and TV," *Century, 1867–1967: The Canadian Saga*, ed. John D. Harbron (Toronto Daily Star, 1967), 53.

123–124 *Hailey*: Sheila Hailey, *I Married a Bestseller* (Bantam, 1979); Kevin Plummer, "Hailey's Comet," Torontoist, Aug. 13, 2011.

124 *Festival*: Blaine Allan, "CBC Television Series, 1952–1982," Queen's University Film and Media, www.queensu.ca.

*"artsy-craftiest nonsense"*: Shields, "Enter Bilingualism," *Toronto Daily Star*, Feb. 21, 1967. Blais is quoted in the same piece.

125 *"really pretty bad"*: Miller, *Turn Up the Contrast: CBC Television Drama since 1952* (UBC, 1987), 231.

*three million viewers*: A. B. McKillop, *Pierre Berton* (M&S, 2008), 536.

*Jest of God adaptation*: James King, *The Life of Margaret Laurence* (Knopf, 1997), 236. The Newman film was called *Rachel, Rachel*.

*movie editions of Duddy*: Charles Foran, *Mordecai: The Life and Times* (Knopf, 2010), 438.

126 *"bowling alleys"*: "Mordecai Richler," *Close-Up*, CBC TV, Nov. 5, 1961, CBC Digital Archives.

*Berton on CBC*: McKillop, *Pierre Berton*, 278.

*"ill at ease"*: Berton, *My Times* (Doubleday, 1995), 234.

*Layton on CBC*: Elspeth Cameron, *Irving Layton: A Portrait* (Stoddart, 1985), 381.

127 *Cohen on CBC*: Robert Fulford, "Leonard Cohen, the TV Star," *Toronto Daily Star*, clipping [July 1966], Cohen Papers, Fisher Library, MS COLL 122, box 9, folder 11.

*"psychedelic television"*: Roy Shields, "Daryl Duke," *Toronto Daily Star*, Oct. 20, 1966.

127     *"bad for my complexion"*: "Cohen's Body Told Him," *Toronto Daily Star*, Sep. 2, 1966.

CBC *in 1960s*: Barry Kiefl, "On Treacherous Ground," LRC, June 2014.

## Chapter 9: Procedures for Underground

129–132     *Nichol*: Frank Davey, *aka bpNichol: A Preliminary Biography* (ECW, 2012).

130     *closest he got to an autobiography*: *Selected Organs* (Black Moss, 1988).

*"needs to try harder"*: quoted in Davey, *aka bpNichol*, 33.

131     *Therafields*: Grant Goodbrand, *Therafields: The Rise and Fall of Lea Hindley-Smith's Psychoanalytic Commune* (ECW, 2010).

*"blew my mind open"*: Ken Norris, "Interview with bp Nichol, Feb. 18, 1978," *Essays on Canadian Writing* 12 (1978).

*"eye-cleaning exercises"*: ibid.

132     *Ondaatje tried*: Ondaatje, "Little Magazines / Small Presses 1969," *artscanada*, Aug. 1969.

133     *"liberated"*: Chris Gudgeon, *Out of This World: The Natural History of Milton Acorn* (Arsenal Pulp, 1996), 82.

*"author and publisher"*: *The Medium Is the Massage* (Bantam, 1967), 123.

*"enclose a buck"*: quoted in Gudgeon, *Out of This World*, 82.

*Prism paid*: e.g. Jacob Zilber to Al Purdy, April 7, 1966, Purdy Papers, University of Saskatchewan, box 21, folder IX, E; Zilber to George Jonas, Feb. 14, 1968, Jonas Papers, Fisher Library, uncatalogued correspondence, folder P.

*Tamarack paid*: e.g. J. R. Colombo to George Jonas, Sep. 15, 1970, ibid., folder A–C.

134     *"parochial"*: Ondaatje, "Little Magazines."

*"meant more to me"*: Laurence, "Ten Years' Sentences," *The Sixties: Writers and Writing of the Decade*, ed. George Woodcock (UBC, 1969).

135     *"as far as Vancouver"*: bissett interview, Jan. 27, 2015. Biographical details not from this interview or otherwise cited are from bissett's entry in www.abcbookworld.com.

*"space uv th papr"*: bissett, acceptance speech for Woodcock Award, 2007, archived at www.abcbookworld.com.

*"its all poetree"*: bissett to Dennis Lee ca. 1971, Lee Papers, Fisher Library, MS COLL 271, box 2, bissett folder.

135–136     *frustrated librarian*: letter in Ken Norris, *The Little Magazine in Canada* (ECW, 1984), 145.

136     *"He has pneumonia"*: Lane, "Lives of the Poets," *Geist* 17 (1995).

137     *"gratitude to trees"*: Sullivan, *The Red Shoes: Margaret Atwood Starting Out* (HarperFlamingo, 1998), 150.

        *peaked at seven hundred*: bissett to Dennis Lee ca. 1971, Lee Papers, box 2, bissett folder.

        *"you'd have to be high"*: Atwood, "Some Old, Some *New*," *Alphabet* 17 (1969).

138     *"hit of adrenaline"*: quoted in Sullivan, *Red Shoes*, 150.

138–142   *Tamarack Review*: Elaine Kalman Naves, *Robert Weaver* (Véhicule, 2007); Roy MacSkimming, *The Perilous Trade* (M&S, 2007).

138     *"Something had to be done"*: editorial, *Tamarack* 41 (1966).

139     *Ontario Council for the Arts*: Canada Council, *Eighth Annual Report, 1964–65*, 13.

        *"people at large"*: editorial, *Tamarack* 1 (1956).

140     *"Canadianness"*: "A Point of View," *Tamarack* 10 (1959).

        *piece from Cohen*: Cohen Papers, Fisher Library, MS COLL 122, box 10A, folder 39.

141     *Council liked paying for them*: Canada Council, *Third Annual Report, to March 31, 1960*, 85, and *Sixth Annual Report, 1962–63*, 101.

        *"most exciting thing"*: quoted in Naves, *Robert Weaver*, 58.

        *Esquire bought*: "A Point of View," *Tamarack* 16 (1960).

141–142   *Acorn poem*: Gudgeon, *Out of This World*, 216; *Tamarack* 57 (1971).

142 143  *"deeply bothered me"*: Doris Anderson, *Rebel Daughter* (Key Porter, 1996), 168–69.

143     *Time carried more weight*: Weaver, "Notes on a Royal Commission," *Tamarack* 18 (1961); McClelland to Norman Levine, Jan. 9, 1959, *Selected Letters of Jack McClelland*, ed. Sam Solecki (Key Porter, 1998), 34.

143–144  *Belmont Award*: "The Inside Story," *Saturday Night*, Dec. 1965 and Dec. 1968.

143*    *"minor-league LeRoi Jones"*: Richler, *Saturday Night*, Nov. 1968. Clarke's interview appeared in Dan Proudfoot, "What Makes Austin Clarke Canada's Angriest Black Man?" *Canadian Magazine*, July 5, 1968.

144     *American woman*: Jonas, "Encounter," *Saturday Night*, Aug. 1968.

145     *Factory Theatre Lab*: Fulford, "Reporting Back," *Saturday Night*, July 1972.

## Chapter 10: New Wave Canada

147     *"Everything was new"*: Lee interview, June 26, 2012.

147     *Prince of Wales scholarship*: J. C. Evans (U of T Registrar) to Lee, Sep. 3, 1957, Lee Papers, Fisher Library, box 21, folder 4.

        *She thinks they met*: Atwood, "Dennis Revisited," *Tasks of Passion*, ed. Karen Mulhallen, Donna Bennett, and Russell Brown (Descant, 1982).

148     *$10,000 a year*: "Rochdale: People and Money," Lee Papers, box 14, folder 26.

        *long essay*: "Getting to Rochdale," *This Magazine Is About Schools* 2.5 (1968).

        *"a community"*: quoted in Alan Walker, "Rochdale," *Star Weekly*, Jan. 13, 1968.

        *within a month*: Lee, "Judy Merril," *Body Music* (Anansi, 1998), 114.

        *resigned in the spring*: Lee, letter to members, May 31 [1969], Lee Papers, box 14, folder 34.

149     *Council informed Lee*: Claude Gauthier to Lee, April 12, 1973, Lee Papers, box 64, folder 7.

        *Aleph Press*: Rosemary Sullivan, *Shadow Maker: The Life of Gwendolyn MacEwen* (HarperCollins, 1995), 115.

        *Hawkshead Press*: Sullivan, *The Red Shoes: Margaret Atwood Starting Out* (HarperFlamingo, 1998), 110.

        *Periwinkle Press*: Marya Fiamengo, "Private Presses in Vancouver," *Canadian Literature* 22 (1964).

149–50  *Fiddlehead*: Michael VanTassell, "Fiddlehead Poetry Books," 2012, New Brunswick Literary Encyclopedia, w3.stu.ca.

150     *Contact Press*: Peter Miller, "Contact Press," *CNQ* 51 (1997).

        *"compatible allies"*: Godfrey, "The Canadian Publishers," *Canadian Literature* 57 (1973); *"isn't Jack McClelland"*: quoted in Roy MacSkimming, *The Perilous Trade* (M&S, 2007), 187.

151     *"under his wing"*: Coleman interview, July 13, 2010.

        *"came from Edmonton"*: Bowering, *A Short Sad Book* (Talonbooks, 1977), 139–40, 144.

151–152 *Bevington*: Sarah Hipworth, "Stan Bevington: The Making of a Master Printer," Historical Perspectives on Canadian Publishing, Jan. 2009, http://hpcanpub.mcmaster.ca; Bevington interview, Aug. 25, 2010.

152     *Canadian flags*: Dennis Reid, "Old Coach House Days," *Open Letter* 9.8 (1997).

153     *Coleman as editor*: Coleman, "Coach House: An Emotional Memoir," ibid.

153–154 *Council only supported*: Canada Council, *First Annual Report, to March 31, 1958*, 26.

154      *"arts bursary"*: Silcox interview, Oct. 1, 2013.

*"activities in 1967"*: Canada Council, *10th Annual Report, 1966–67*, 76.

*stationery for Marty's bookstore*: invoice, Jan. 29, 1968, Ahvenus Papers, Fisher Library, MS COLL 574, box 1, folder 8.

*"Dope fund"*: quoted in David Sharpe, *Rochdale* (Anansi, 1987), 171.

*"It wasn't true"*: Cohen, *Typing* (Vintage Canada, 2001), 144–45.

155      *"early adopters"*: Bevington interview.

*Pink White and Clear*: Stephen Cain, "Imprinting Identities" (Ph.D. diss., York University, 2002), 82.

*Mindless Acid Freaks*: Bevington interview.

*"tiny print"*: Bowering interview, July 17, 2012.

155*    *"try marijuana"*: Lacey, "Poetry Chronicle II," *Edge* 7 (1967–68), reprinted in *Canadian Poetry* 58 (2006).

156      *"Sure, we lit up"*: Coleman interview.

*Godfrey became angry*: "Small Presses: An Interview," *Canadian Forum*, Aug. 1967.

*six rounds later*: Anansi Books in Print, January 1969, Lee Papers, box 17, folder 53. For Godfrey's version of the founding, see also Roy MacSkimming, "Perilous Trade Conversations Five," CNQ 73 (2008). For Lee's, see his interview in *Canadian Fiction Magazine* 6 (1972).

156–157  *Godfrey*: James Adams, "Writer Created Three Publishing Houses," *Globe and Mail*, July 4, 2015.

157      *made a nationalist*: Eleven Canadian Novelists Interviewed by Graeme Gibson (Anansi, 1973), 176–77.

*he liked to say*; e.g. to MacSkimming, see *Perilous Trade*, 175.

*had $5,000*: Brief to the Ontario Royal Commission on Publishing, March 31, 1971, Lee Papers, box 20, folder 3.

*Lee's first book*: Lee to Atwood et al., April 10, 1967, Lee Papers, box 6, folder 32.

*grant of $4,420*: Canada Council, *11th Annual Report, 1967–1968*, 45.

157–158  *"obviously possible"*: Report to the Canada Council, April 15, 1968, Lee Papers, box 17, folder 6.

158      *first full-time employee*: Fetherling, *Travels by Night* (Lester, 1994), 105–7, 117.

*"communal capitalism"*: Godfrey in MacSkimming, "Perilous Trade Conversations Five."

*"machine guns"*: Godfrey to Lee, n.d., Lee Papers, Fisher Library, box 17, folder 4.

158 *$7,000 award*: Canada Council, *11th Annual Report*, 43.

 *"Farewell Doug"*: Godfrey to Lee, n.d., Lee Papers, box 17, folder 4.

 *"didn't get published"*: Lee interview.

159 *Smith sent Lee*: John Metcalf, "CNQ Interviews: 4, Ray Smith," *CNQ* 81 (2011).

 *Five Legs*: Gibson in MacSkimming, "Perilous Trade Conversations Four," *CNQ* 72 (2007).

 *"get into print"*: Spiderline press release, quoted in John Metcalf, "A Collector's Notes on the House of Anansi," *CNQ* 61 (2002).

 *"without compromising"*: Godfrey to Lee, March 29, 1969, Lee Papers, box 17, folder 14.

160 *"House of Atreus"*: James Polk, "Anansi at Fifteen," *Canadian Forum*, June/July 1982.

 *Macmillan offered a dollar*: ibid.

 *reduce their publishing schedule*: "A State-of-Anansi Letter," Feb. 15, 1971, Lee Papers, box 17, folder 32; Marilyn Beker, "Canadian Publishing Is in Real Trouble," *Montreal Gazette*, April 17, 1971.

 *warehouse fire*: Anansi press release, March 18, 1971, Lee Papers, box 17, folder 33.

 *killed by a train*: Brian Johnson, "The Lonely Life and Death of Russell Marois," *Montreal Gazette*, Nov. 27, 1971.

 *Gibson replaced Lee*: after Lee resigned as president in March (Lee to the Anansi board, March 29, 1972, Lee Papers, box 17, folder 41).

 *detailed timesheets*: Anansi memo, July 15, 1972, Lee Papers, box 17, folder 44.

 *"top banana"*: quoted in MacSkimming, "Perilous Trade Conversations Four."

 *resigned altogether*: Lee to Ann Wall, Nov. 22, 1972, Lee Papers, box 17, folder 48.

161 *"CanLit for Dummies"*: Atwood interview, Dec. 15, 2010.

 *Poets 67*: Nick Drumbolis, *10four Between the* TWENY/20 *Lines: Extenuating Impressions of a Back Lane Community of Mindless Acid Freaks* (Letters Press, 1991); *changed the title*: Souster to George Jonas, Dec. 1, 1965, Jonas Papers, Fisher Library, uncatalogued correspondence.

 *throw around a ball*: Coleman interview.

 *Dudek hated it*: Dudek to Souster, Nov. 5, 1966, in Frank Davey, *Louis Dudek and Raymond Souster* (Douglas & McIntyre, 1980), 29–30; *Miller quit*: Miller, "Contact Press."

161–162 *"cornerstone of the press"*: Bevington interview.

162 *"unrecognizable"*: MacSkimming, *Perilous Trade*, 245.

## Chapter 11: The Boat Who Wouldn't Float

163–166    *Laurence*: James King, *The Life of Margaret Laurence* (Knopf, 1997); Laurence, *Dance on the Earth: A Memoir* (M&S, 1989).

163    *"generous and warm"*: Lee in *A Very Large Soul: Selected Letters from Margaret Laurence to Canadian Writers*, ed. J. A. Wainwright (Cormorant, 1995), 109.

*"anybody else"*: Findley, ibid., 79.

163–164    *"filling scribblers"*: Laurence, *Dance on the Earth*, 68.

164    *"two sweaters"*: ibid., 92–93.

*Somalia*: Laurence, *The Prophet's Camel Bell* (M&S, 1963).

*June 1955*: Lyall Powers, *Alien Heart: The Life and Work of Margaret Laurence* (U of Manitoba P, 2003), 147; *"first real story"*: Laurence, *Dance on the Earth*, 95.

165    *"where I imagined"*: ibid., 157–58.

166    *"It was home"*: ibid., 174.

*Canada Council grant*: Laurence to Al Purdy, Jan. 16, 1967, *Yours, Al: The Collected Letters of Al Purdy*, ed. Sam Solecki (Harbour, 2004), 124.

*Two of every three books*: Ernst & Ernst, *The Book Publishing and Manufacturing Industry in Canada* (Department of Industry, Trade and Commerce, 1970), 1.

*children's books*: Abraham Rotstein and Gary Lax, eds., *Getting It Back: A Program for Canadian Independence* (Clarke, Irwin, 1974), 202–3.

166–167    *legally pirate*: "The Manufacturing Clause," *Columbia Law Review* 50.5 (1950).

167    *Canadian publishers' sales*: Delores Broten, *The Lumber Jack Report* (CANLIT, 1975), 3–4.

*American subsidiaries*: Dennis Lee's figures, cited in Donald Cameron, "Jack McClelland," *Saturday Night*, June 1971.

*"l'affaire Hachette"*: Frédéric Brisson, "L'implantation de la Librairie Hachette au Québec," *Revue de BAnQ* 2 (2010); Jacques Michon, ed., *Histoire de l'édition littéraire au Québec au XXe siècle*, vol. 3 (Fides, 2010), 348–50.

167*    *After 1965*: Marilyn Beker, "Canadian Publishing," *Montreal Gazette*, April 17, 1971.

168    *"singlehandedly"*: Laurence, March 16, 1982, *Selected Letters of Jack McClelland*, ed. Sam Solecki (Key Porter, 1998), 282.

168–176    *McClelland*: James King, *Jack: A Life with Writers* (Knopf, 1999); Elspeth Cameron, "Adventures in the Book Trade," *Saturday Night*, Nov. 1983.

169    *"slay the fair sex"*: quoted in King, *Jack*, 12.

170      *leaky schooner*: Mowat, *The Boat Who Wouldn't Float* (M&S, 2009), 4–6.

"*large amount of vodka*": King, *Jack*, 121.

"*buyer-friendly*": Roy MacSkimming, *The Perilous Trade: Book Publishing in Canada, 1946–2006* (M&S, 2007), 124–25.

171      "*instantly in love*": quoted in King, *Jack*, 31; "greatest writer": ibid., 274.

171–172   *The Double Hook*: F. T. Flahiff, *A Life of Sheila Watson* (NeWest, 2005), 195–99; Jordan Rendell Smith, "How *The Double Hook* Caught On," Historical Perspectives on Canadian Publishing, http://hpcanpub.mcmaster.ca.

171      "*We all steal from Sheila*": Ondaatje at "Celebrating Sheila," University of St. Michael's College, Toronto, Oct. 24, 2009.

172      "*didn't try them all*": quoted in Marika Robert, "What Jack McClelland Has Done to Book Publishing," *Maclean's*, Sep. 7, 1963.

172–173   *Richler jumped ship*: Charles Foran, *Mordecai: The Life and Times* (Knopf, 2010), 270.

173      *Purdy signed*: S. J. Totton to Purdy, July 25 and Sep. 13, 1963, Purdy Papers, University of Saskatchewan, box 21, folder IX, F.

"*author is king*": "Editorial Policy at M&S" [ca. 1968–69], quoted in King, *Jack*, 174.

"*Once he decided*": Fulford interview, July 4, 2012.

"*kick in the ass*": McClelland to Austin Clarke, Sep. 23, 1965, quoted in King, *Jack*, 126.

173–174   "*I haven't read it*": Cohen, *Typing* (Vintage Canada, 2001), 124.

174      *Atwood helped spread the story*: e.g. in her introduction to the 1981 Virago edition of *The Edible Woman*, reprinted in *Second Words* (Anansi, 1982).

"*publish this guy*": quoted in Ira B. Nadel, *Various Positions: A Life of Leonard Cohen* (Vintage, 1997), 68.

*main innovation*: Janet B. Friskney, *New Canadian Library: The Ross-McClelland Years, 1952–1978* (UTP, 2007), 30.

"*He Roams Afar*": cited in Carl Spadoni and Judy Donnelly, *A Bibliography of McClelland and Stewart Imprints* (ECW, 1994), 37n2.

175      "*most ambitious event*": Berton, *My Times* (Doubleday, 1995), 283.

"*Great publicity*": quoted in Sandra Martin, "Jack McClelland," *Globe and Mail*, June 16, 2004.

176      *didn't believe in grants*: Beker, "Canadian Publishing," *Montreal Gazette*, April 17, 1971.

176    *"Jack cared a great deal"*: Newman, "The Man Who Made CanLit Sexy," *Maclean's*, July 1, 2004.

      *"only businessman"*: Mowat quoted in Martin, "Jack McClelland."

      *"cared for books more than profit"*: Berton quoted in "Writers Lift Glasses," *Toronto Star*, June 23, 2004.

176–177    *"laugh bitterly"*: Laurence to McClelland, May 5, 1967, quoted in King, *Margaret Laurence*, 242–43.

177    *"No visitors allowed"*: Laurence, *Dance on the Earth*, 199.

178    *Hutchinson winning*: ibid., 211; *another account*: Cameron, "Adventures in the Book Trade"; *Porter's purse*: MacSkimming, "Perilous Trade Conversations Seven," *CNQ* 81 (2011).

      *"I did my books"*: quoted in King, *Margaret Laurence*, 379.

## Chapter 12: The New Romans

179–181    *Gallant: A Writer's Life: The Margaret Laurence Lectures* (M&S, 2011); "The Four Seasons of Mavis Gallant," *Ideas*, CBC Radio, Feb. 15, 2012; Sandra Martin, "Gallant Dies," *Globe and Mail*, Feb. 18, 2014.

179    *Until recently*: Stephen Henighan, "Jimmy the Romanian Cross-Dresser," *CNQ* 92 (2015).

179–180    *"only thing I remember"*: quoted in Deborah Treisman, "Mavis Gallant," *New Yorker*, March 3, 2014.

181    *"a life I liked"*: introduction, *Selected Stories of Mavis Gallant* (M&S, 1996), xiv.

      *"no friends"*: ibid., xiii.

      *boyfriend at Air Canada*: interview by Geoff Hancock, *Canadian Fiction Magazine* 28 (1978).

      *hell of a nice purse*: Judith Knelman, "Mavis Gallant, On Going It Alone," *The Graduate*, Jan./Feb. 1984, clipping, Gallant Papers, Fisher Library, MS COLL 189, box 4A.

181*    *Besides the RCMP*: The RCMP's interest in Gallant and McConnell's subsequent payment to her of a year's salary has been uncovered in as yet unpublished research by Terry Rigelhof, as reported by John Metcalf in "My Heart Is Broken," *CNQ* 94 (2016).

182    *they began to leave*: Nick Mount, *When Canadian Literature Moved to New York* (UTP, 2005).

      *"wheat, railroads"*: Walter Blackburn Harte, quoted in *Toronto Week*, Feb. 12, 1892.

      *"Kamschatka"*: John Richardson, introduction to *Wacousta* (M&S/NCL, 2008), 583.

182      *tried to interest American publishers*: Margaret Laurence, *Dance on the Earth: A Memoir* (M&S, 1989), 154.

     *Atwood tried*: for the unpublished "Up in the Air So Blue." Atwood denied this in our interview, but her biographer Rosemary Sullivan cites a rejection letter of Aug. 26, 1964, from Kay Grant at Abelard-Schuman (*The Red Shoes*, 142).

     *"pathetic provincial"*: Richler, *Hunting Tigers under Glass* (M&S, 1968), 8.

183      *Maclean's made him a nationalist*: Berton in *A Writer's Life: The Margaret Laurence Lectures* (M&S, 2011), 116.

     *Levine left Montreal*: Levine, "The Girl in the Drugstore," *The Sixties: Writers and Writing of the Decade*, ed. George Woodcock (UBC, 1969).

     *"regarded as freaks"*: Richler in *Canadians Abroad* (NFB, 1956), quoted in Charles Foran, *Mordecai: The Life and Times* (Knopf, 2010), 202.

     *"flee home and family"*: "Why I Left Canada," *Chatelaine*, March 1961.

     *"Canadian writing"*: "Why Are Canadians So Dull?" *The Standard*, March 30, 1946, quoted in Janice Kulyk Keefer, *Reading Mavis Gallant* (OUP, 1989), 204.

     *"been to Paris?"*: Marianne Ackerman, "When Mavis Gallant's in Town," *Montreal Gazette*, Oct. 6, 1984.

183–184      *"désert littéraire"*: Anne Hébert quoted in Jean Royer, "Anne Hébert," *Le Devoir*, April 26, 1980; *"condemned to damnation"*: Hébert, *Le Jour*, Oct. 31, 1975, quoted in Neil B. Bishop, *Anne Hébert* (Presses universitaires de Bordeaux, 1993), 84, trans. Myra Bloom.

184      *"not happy here"*: Blais quoted in Byron Riggan, "Lightning on the Literary Landscape," *Saturday Night*, March 19, 1960.

     *Wilson and Blais*: Barry Callaghan, "An Interview with Marie-Claire Blais," *Tamarack* 37 (1965); *"a class by herself"*: Wilson, *O Canada: An American's Notes on Canadian Culture* (FSG, 1965), 147.

     *"genius scouting"*: Philip Marchand, *Marshall McLuhan: The Medium and the Messenger* (Random House, 1989), 172.

184–185      *"most important thinker"*: Tom Wolfe, "What If He Is Right?" *New York*, Nov. 1965.

185      *greatest audience response*: William Kloman, "'I've Been on the Outlaw Scene Since 15,'" *New York Times*, Jan. 28, 1968.

     *sold out its first printing*: Stephen Chesley, "Cohen!" Toronto *Telegram*, Oct. 12, 1968.

     *"best-selling poet"*: McClelland to Malcolm Ross, Sep. 9, 1968, *Selected Letters of Jack McClelland*, ed. Sam Solecki (Key Porter, 1998), 127.

186    *Wiebe learned*: Wiebe in *A Writer's Life: The Margaret Laurence Lectures* (M&S, 2011), 292–93.

*Tremblay's early influences*: Tremblay, Avant-propos, *Contes pour buveurs attardés* (Bibliothèque Québécoise, 1996).

*writers she most admired*: Laurence to Ernest Buckler, Nov. 24, 1976, *Selected Letters from Margaret Laurence*, ed. J. A. Wainwright (Cormorant, 1995), 40.

*"writers who have influenced me"*: John Metcalf, "A Conversation with Alice Munro," *Journal of Canadian Fiction* 1.4 (1972).

*"only Mazo de la Roche"*: Richler, "Why I Left Canada."

*"blank sheet of paper"*: Atwood in Elaine Kalman Naves, *Robert Weaver* (Véhicule, 2007), 103.

*William Carlos Williams*: Bowering, *A Magpie Life* (Key Porter, 2001), 56, 192; *Duncan*: Bowering, "Al and Me," *Walrus*, April 2010.

*creative writing programs*: George McWhirter, "Creative Writing at UBC," *University of the Fraser Valley Research Review* 3 (2010); Clark Blaise, *I Had a Father: A Post-Modern Autobiography* (HarperCollins, 1993), 120.

187    *"more from Alfred"*: McClelland quoted in MacSkimming, *The Perilous Trade* (M&S, 2007), 126.

*Ken Gass*: quoted in Denis W. Johnston, *Up the Mainstream: The Rise of Toronto's Alternative Theatres, 1968–1975* (UTP, 1991), 83.

*Canadian faculty plummeted*: 1951 Census, Table 12, "Labour Force"; 1971 Census, Table 4, "Labour Force."

*foreign born*: Abraham Rotstein and Gary Lax, eds., *Getting It Back: A Program for Canadian Independence* (Clarke, Irwin, 1974), 195–96.

188    *usual guess*: John Hagan, *Northern Passage: American Vietnam War Resisters in Canada* (Harvard UP, 2001), 3.

*"major patron"*: Brison, *Rockefeller, Carnegie, and Canada: American Philanthropy and the Arts and Letters in Canada* (MQUP, 2005), 202.

188*    *Manual for Draft-Age Immigrants*: Joseph Jones, "Anansi's Singular Bestseller," CNQ 61 (2002); *Coleman's statement*: interview, July 13, 2010; *"I will admit"*: Bevington interview, Aug. 25, 2010.

189    *"No other Western nation"*: Berton, *1967* (Doubleday, 1997), 59.

*nobody knew*: see also Ian Macdonald, "Foreign Ownership: Villain or Scapegoat?" *Nationalism in Canada*, ed. Peter Russell (McGraw-Hill, 1966).

*"branch-plant cultures"*: *Lament for a Nation* (Carleton UP, 1997), 56.

190    *"a challenge"*: Cohen, *Typing* (Vintage Canada, 2001), 75.

*"Americanism"*: Fetherling, *Travels by Night* (Lester, 1994), 113, 129.

190   *Acorn refused royalties*: ibid., 193; *MacEwen wished*: undated clipping, MacEwen Papers, Fisher Library, MS COLL 00121, box 31; *Purdy told the Globe*: "Will Risk Suit," *Globe and Mail*, Nov. 6, 1970; *Gibson led a protest*: Gibson interview, Oct. 26, 2010.

191   *"a political sense"*: Marlatt interview, July 17, 2012.

      *Gallant arrived in Paris*: interview with Jhumpa Lahiri, *Granta* 106 (2009).

      *"my hands get numb"*: quoted in Sandra Martin, "Gallant Dies," *Globe and Mail*, Feb. 18, 2014.

192   *"the edge of hunger"*: Gallant, "The Hunger Diaries," *New Yorker*, July 9, 2012.

193   *first-reading agreement*: Fulford, "Gallant's Best Fiction Yet," *Maclean's*, Sep. 5, 1964.

      *Gallant in the New Yorker*: based on the *New Yorker* Fiction Index at www.newyorkerfiction.com, and a best guess by *New Yorker* fiction editor Deborah Treisman.

      *"all the Canadian culture I can stand"*: cartoon seen by Megan Williams framed on a wall in Gallant's apartment in Paris, ca. 2011 ("The Four Seasons of Mavis Gallant," *Ideas*, CBC Radio, Feb. 15, 2012). *New Yorker* staff could not find this cartoon in their database and suspect that it was made just for her (Colin Stokes, email, June 10, 2015).

      *documentary*: "A Canadian in Paris," *Telescope*, CBC TV, Jan. 22, 1965.

      *"never heard of the New Yorker"*: Hancock interview.

## Chapter 13: Cocksure

195–199  *Layton*: Elspeth Cameron, *Irving Layton: A Portrait* (Stoddart, 1985); Layton, *Waiting for the Messiah* (M&S, 1985); *Wild Gooseberries: The Selected Letters of Irving Layton*, ed. Francis Mansbridge (Macmillan, 1989).

195   *"vast reservoirs"*: David O'Rourke, "Interview with Irving Layton," CNQ 72 (2007), 51.

196   *"best scrapper"*: Layton, *Waiting for the Messiah*, 56; *atheist*: Alexander Ross, "The Man Who Copyrighted Passion," *Maclean's*, Nov. 15, 1965.

      *"grow out of it"*: quoted in Cameron, *Irving Layton*, 55.

198   *"voice of God"*: Layton, *Waiting for the Messiah*, 229.

      *Purdy wrote a fan letter*: Purdy, *Reaching for the Beaufort Sea* (Harbour, 1993), 143.

      *"Cheers"*: quoted in Cameron, *Irving Layton*, 222.

      *"black panties"*: *A Red Carpet for the Sun* (M&S, 1959), no. 141.

198     *"Now you're married"*: as told by Aviva Layton to Sylvie Simmons in *I'm Your Man: The Life of Leonard Cohen* (M&S, 2012), 66.

199     *"long gravy slide"*: Layton to Jonathan Williams, Jan. 11, 1957, *Wild Gooseberries*, 80.

        *Globe story*: Lotta Dempsey, *Globe and Mail*, Jan. 14, 1957.

199*     *"You've got it"*: "The Private World of Raymond Souster," *Time* (Canada), June 12, 1964, reprinted in Louis Dudek and Michael Gnarowski, ed., *The Making of Modern Poetry in Canada* (Ryerson, 1967), 242.

199–200 *"inhibited sexually"*: quoted in Cameron, *Irving Layton*, 261.

200     *"respectably unrespectable"*: McClelland to Layton, March 22, 1968, quoted in James King, *Jack: A Life with Writers* (Knopf, 1999), 179.

        *"ice-breaking role"*: Lacey, "Canadian Bards and South American Reviewers," *Northern Journey* 4 (1974), reprinted in *Canadian Poetry* 60 (2007).

        *"gave us fire"*: Hertz quoted by a contributor to leonardcohenforum. com, Feb 17, 2006.

        *"Without his influence"*: MacEwen, "Praise Be Guts and Bombast," *Globe and Mail*, April 12, 1975.

        *"converted a whole generation"*: quoted in Cameron, *Irving Layton*, 367.

        *"Beauty and the Beast"*: James King, *Jack* (Knopf, 1999), 79.

        *"my great entry"*: Layton to Desmond Pacey, Sep. 25, 1959, *Wild Gooseberries*, 109.

201     *Star Weekly profile*: "The Lusty Laureate from the Slums," *Star Weekly Magazine*, Feb. 6, 1960.

        *"Take away the socialites"*: Joan Finnigan, "Canadian Poetry Finds Its Voice," *Globe and Mail*, Jan. 20, 1962.

202     *Le Hibou*: "Coffee House Has Arrived," *Globe and Mail*, Dec. 16, 1961; *"like masturbation"*: Roy MacSkimming, liner notes, *Irving Layton at Le Hibou* (Postcrity, 1963).

        *poets outselling novelists*: McClelland to Robertson Davies, April 19, 1963, *Selected Letters of Jack McClelland*, ed. Sam Solecki (Key Porter, 1998), 72.

        *"Golden Age"*: "Canadian Poetry Finds Its Voice in a Golden Age," *Globe and Mail*, Jan. 20, 1962.

202–206 *Cohen*: Sylvie Simmons, *I'm Your Man: The Life of Leonard Cohen* (M&S, 2012); Ira B. Nadel, *Various Positions: A Life of Leonard Cohen* (Random House, 1996).

203     *"a time is coming"*: MacLennan to Cohen, Feb. 13, 1955, Cohen Papers, Fisher Library, MS COLL 122, box 10A, folder 55.

        *"new poet"*: Avison, "Poetry Chronicle," *Tamarack* 1 (1956).

203     *Publishers rejected*: Knopf to Cohen, Aug. 8, 1957, Cohen Papers, box 10A, folder 70; Macmillan to Cohen, Sep. 17, 1957, ibid., folder 67.

203–204 *sold poems to Anthology*: CBC Radio to Cohen, Oct. 23, 1957, Cohen Papers, box 10B, folder 10.

204     *$400 advance*: McClelland to Cohen, Aug. 29, 1961, ibid., folder 45.

        *little choice but to reject*: McClelland to Cohen, Nov. 12, 1960, ibid.

        *"best young poet in Canada"*: Arnold Edinborough, *Saturday Night*, Oct. 14, 1961; Robert Weaver, *Toronto Daily Star*, June 10, 1961, 29.

        *"anything but poetry"*: Webb, *Critically Speaking*, CBC Radio, July 30, 1961, from transcript in Cohen Papers, box 3, folder 38.

        *Cavalier magazine*: Marian McNamara to Cohen, June 4, 1963, Cohen Papers, box 5, folder 34.

        *"readings have been packed"*: Ralph Thomas, "Poets Prove Vaudeville Humour Still Gets Laughs," *Toronto Daily Star*, Oct. 28, 1964.

205     *"Canada's answer to the Beatles"*: quoted in Joel Deshaye, "Irving Layton's Televised 'Public Poetry,'" *Canadian Poetry* 73 (2013).

        *"most talented"*: letter to the editor, *Montreal Star*, Nov. 4, 1964.

        *twenty hours a day*: Jon Ruddy, "Is the World Ready for Leonard Cohen?" *Maclean's*, Oct. 1, 1966.

        *didn't want to write for academics*: e.g. interview with Michael Harris, *Saturday Night*, June 1969, 27.

        *"most revolting"*: Fulford, "Cohen's Nightmare Novel," *Toronto Daily Star*, April 26, 1966; *bill bissett*: "!!!!!," *Alphabet* 13 (June 1967).

206     *likely to be censored*: William French, "Books & Bookmen," *Globe and Mail*, Feb. 26, 1966.

        *found twenty-four books*: Frank Davey, *From There to Here: A Guide to English-Canadian Literature Since 1960* (Porcépic, 1974), 17–18.

        *almost six hundred poets*: Chaviva Hošek, "Poetry in English: 1950 to 1982," *The Oxford Companion to Canadian Literature*, 2nd ed. (OUP, 1997), 933.

        *"highest per capita consumers"*: Margaret Atwood, "Poetry in the Buffer Zone," *TLS* Oct. 26, 1973.

207     *Star Weekly called Purdy*: Purdy to George Jonas, Feb. 14, 1970, Jonas Papers, Fisher Library, uncatalogued correspondence, folder P. The resulting poem was "Lament for Robert Kennedy."

        *Hudson's Bay Company*: Lorraine York, "Viticultural Verse," *Canadian Poetry* 69 (2011).

        *poets on television*: e.g. on *Modern Canadian Poetry*, prod. John Kennedy, CBC TV, April 30–July 23, 1967. Atwood's reading was in the final episode.

207     *"time of starvation"*: quoted in Bruce Lawson, "A New Religious Age for Leonard Cohen," *Globe and Mail*, July 23, 1966.

208     *"poetry of the future"*: Layton to A. J. M. Smith, Nov. 30, 1956, *Wild Gooseberries*, 72.

      *"placed my hand"*: "Misunderstanding," *Red Carpet for the Sun*, no. 68.

      *twelve hundred people*: King, *Jack*, 241.

209     *"most over-rated poet"*: Dudek in *Delta*, quoted in Robert Fulford, "War Among the Poets," *Toronto Daily Star*, Dec. 22, 1959.

      *"popular buffoonery"*: Dudek, "Peripatetic Poets," *Montreal Star*, Oct. 1964, clipping, Cohen Papers, box 7, folder 28.

      *"degeneration of poetry"*: Dudek, "Poetry in English," *The Sixties*, ed. George Woodcock (UBC, 1969).

      *poems wouldn't permit it*: William French, "Leonard Cohen Wants to Be Governor-General?" *Globe and Mail*, May 17, 1969.

## Chapter 14: George, Vancouver

211–214   *Bowering*: Bowering, *A Magpie Life: Growing a Writer* (Key Porter, 2001); Roy Miki, *A Record of Writing: An Annotated and Illustrated Bibliography of George Bowering* (Talonbooks, 1990).

212     *"guard was lowered by books"*: Bowering, *Magpie Life*, 23.

      *first poem*: Judith Fitzgerald, "George Bowering: 'Bullshit Artist,'" *Globe and Mail*, Aug. 17, 2010.

      *"best minds of this campus"*: "Growl," *Ubyssey*, March 20, 1959.

213     *"a real sucker"*: notebook, Dec. 10, 1961, quoted in Miki, *Record of Writing*, viii.

213–214   *"After ten beers"*: Barry Lord, "Swinging London (Ontario)," *Star Weekly*, Jan. 13, 1968.

214     *"fuckin' Easterners"*: Bowering interview, July 17, 2012.

      *Donald Duck tie*: Atwood, "George Bowering," *Capilano Review* 3.24 (2014).

      *"until 1971"*: Peter Sypnowich, "Poet Wins Award," *Globe and Mail*, April 14, 1970; *velvet suit*: Sypnowich, "Literary Prize-Givers," *Toronto Daily Star*, May 12, 1970.

215     *"enchantment of words"*: Angela and George Bowering, David Bromige, and Michael Matthews, *Piccolo Mondo: A Novel of Youth in 1961* (Coach House, 1998), 12, 153–54, 221.

215–216   *"moment in The Wizard of Oz"*: "The New American Poetry Revisited—Again," Aug. 20, 2013, DooneysCafe.com.

216     *Tallman attributed*: Tallman, *In the Midst: Writings, 1962–1992* (Talonbooks, 1992), 123.

216    *"gave us everything"*: Bowering, *Magpie Life*, 216.

*study group*: Tallman, "Wonder Merchants," *boundary* 2 3.1 (1974); cf. Frank Davey, *When Tish Happens* (ECW, 2011), 103.

*Wah proposed*: Pauline Butling and Susan Rudy, *Writing in Our Time* (WLUP, 2005), 58n2.

217    *"literary activity"*: quoted in Ken Norris, *The Little Magazine in Canada* (ECW, 1984), 110.

*Tish movement*: see Davey's editorial in *Tish* 1, which works the joke mercilessly.

217–218    *no women*: Davey, *When Tish Happens*, 198.

218    *"muse figure"*: Marlatt interview, July 17, 2012; *"welcoming dance"*: Tallman, "Wonder Merchants," 77.

*"on the edge"*: Marlatt quoted in Davey, *When Tish Happens*, 196.

*New Design Gallery*: Stan Persky to Michael Boughn, email, Oct. 9, 2015, my copy.

218–219    *Blaser*: Stan Persky and Brian Fawcett, *Robin Blaser* (New Star, 2010); *"enormous force"*: Sharon Thesen to Michael Boughn, email, ca. 2012, my copy.

219    *"Poetry in the morning"*: Tallman, *In the Midst*, 205. See also *The Line Has Shattered: Vancouver's Landmark 1963 Poetry Conference*, directed by Robert McTavish (Non-Inferno Media, 2013).

*father's death*: Avison to Aaron Vidaver, Aug. 2, 1999, *Minutes of the Charles Olson Society* 30 (1999).

220    *"electrified"*: Bowering, *Magpie Life*, 71–72.

*leaving Dawson*: Bowering, "The Most Remarkable Thing about *Tish*," *Tish* 20 (Aug. 1963).

221    *Hindmarch*: "Quiet Wedding," *Ladysmith-Chemainus Chronicle*, March 2, 1967.

*Lang*: Claudia Cornwall, *At the World's Edge: Curt Lang's Vancouver* (Mother Tongue, 2011).

*"a real Ginsberg"*: Jamie Reid, "Th Erlee Daze of Blewointment," *bill bissett*, ed. Linda Rogers (Guernica, 2002), 15.

*Copithorne dropped out*: Copithorne, "Personal and Informal Introduction," *Making Waves*, ed. Trevor Carolan (Anvil, 2010).

*"never melted"*: Alan Twigg, "Bissett Interview #1," 1978, www.abc-bookworld.com.

222    *tasted like tar*: Bowering, "Wild Grapes & Chlorine," *Flycatcher and Other Stories* (Oberon, 1974).

222      *Black Spot*: Nichol, *Organ Music* (Black Moss, 2012), 45; Davey, *When Tish Happens*, 100; bissett interview, Jan. 27, 2015.

222–223  *Kiyooka's reading series*: Marlatt interview.

223      *Acorn's series*: bissett interview; "An Evening of Poetry," advertisement, *The Ubyssey*, Nov. 6, 1964, 12.

         *"many other Trips"*: list of Fourth Avenue businesses tipped into *blew ointment*, Jan. 1967.

223–224  *Advance Mattress*: Chris Gudgeon, *Out of This World* (Arsenal Pulp, 1996), 125; *first chant poem*: bissett interview, Jan. 27, 2015.

224      *carrying a guitar*: Stephen Scobie, "God Is Alive," *Canadian Poetry* 76 (2015).

         *"unofficially replaced"*: Davey, "Tish," *Oxford Companion to Canadian Literature*, 2nd ed. (OUP, 1997), 1119.

         *"directly to a large audience"*: quoted in Michael Barnholden, "The Radical Impulse in Poetry and Poetics," *Making Waves*, 109.

         *thirty-sixth book*: *The World, I Guess* (New Star, 2015).

225      *"nitrous fog"*: Bowering, preface, *The Concrete Island* (Véhicule, 1977).

         *"pay attention"*: Marlatt in McTavish, *The Line Has Shattered*.

## Chapter 15: Next Episode

227      *"a Cuban"*: trans. Malcolm Reid in *The Shouting Signpainters* (M&S, 1972), 122–23.

227–230  *Tremblay*: Gilbert David and Pierre Lavoie, eds., *Le monde de Michel Tremblay* (Cahiers de théâtre Jeu, 1993); Marie-Lyne Piccione, *Michel Tremblay* (Presses universitaires de Bordeaux, 1999).

227      *"a right to exist"*: Bélair, *Michel Tremblay* (Presses de l'université du Québec, 1972), 57, trans. Myra Bloom.

         *"three families"*: *La Presse*, Aug. 16, 1969, quoted in David and Lavoie, *Le monde de Tremblay*, 7, trans. Myra Bloom.

228      *"I started to write"*: Ann Barr, "A Taste of Canadian Controversy," *Evening Standard* (London), May 18, 2000.

         *kept his writing to himself*: Luc Boulanger, "Noces d'art," *Voir Montréal*, July 29, 1998.

         *$167 a week*: "Playwright and Novelist," *Montreal Gazette*, Nov. 1, 1978.

         *sometime lover*: Benoît Aubin, "André Brassard," *Journal de Montréal*, March 13, 2010.

         *travel grant*: Canada Council, *11th Annual Report, 1967–1968*, 44.

         *began Les belles-soeurs*: Luc Boulanger, *Pièces à conviction* (Leméac, 2001), 9.

228–229   *during Expo*: "André Durand présente Michel Tremblay," Nov. 2014, www.comptoirlitteraire.com.

229   *"first vision"*: Tremblay quoted in Boulanger, *Pièces*, 9, trans. Myra Bloom.

*"speak joual"*: trans. in Reid, *Shouting Signpainters*, 18.

*"proud to write badly" ("Je suis fier de mal écrire")*: ibid., 99.

*"astheure"*: ibid., 70.

230   *"cries of all kinds"*: Benoit Gignac, *Québec 68: L'année révolution* (La Presse, 2008), 190, trans. Myra Bloom; *"so many curses"*: ibid.

*"first real critical gazes"*: Jean Basile, "Les Belles-soeurs de Michel Tremblay," *Le Devoir*, Aug. 30, 1968, trans. Myra Bloom.

*"permits a drama" ("joual permet au drame d'en être un")*: André Major, "Un exorcisme par le joual!" *Le Devoir*, Sep. 21, 1968, trans. Myra Bloom.

231   *"Young people"*: Vallières, *White Niggers of America*, trans. Joan Pinkham (M&S, 1971), 42.

*"use our words"*: Reid, *Shouting Signpainters*, 39.

*"name everything"*: *Blackout*, trans. Alan Brown (Anansi, 1974), 40.

*more than any other province*: Peter H. Aykroyd, *The Anniversary Compulsion* (Dundurn, 1992), Appendix C.

231–232   *"tried very hard"*: Roberts in William Kilbourn et al., "The Canada Council and the Theatre," *Theatre Research in Canada* 3.2 (1982).

232   *Chaput-Rolland*: Pierre Berton, *1967* (Doubleday, 1997), 325.

*"entertaining" bits*: Hubert Aquin, "The Cultural Fatigue of French Canada," trans. Larry Shouldice, *Writing Quebec: Selected Essays by Hubert Aquin*, ed. Anthony Purdy (U of Alberta, 1988), 31.

*$1.2 million*: Robin M. Farr, "Sources of Financial Assistance," Ontario Royal Commission on Publishing, *Background Papers* (Queen's Printer, 1972), 103.

*literary-prize capital of Canada*: Marie-Pier Luneau and Ruth Panofsky, "Prizes and Distinctions," *History of the Book in Canada: Vol. III*, 121.

232*   *"exaggerated importance"*: Aquin, "Occupation: Writer," trans. Paul Gibson, Reva Joshee, and Anthony Purdy, ibid., 51.

232–233   *Miron accepted*: Canada Council, *Second Annual Report, to March 31, 1959*, 77; *said no to Expo*: Reid, *Shouting Signpainters*, 188.

233   *Godin at CBC*: ibid., 232.

*French-Canadian publishers*: Jacques Michon, ed., *Histoire de l'édition littéraire au Québec au XXe siècle*, vol. 3 (Fides, 2010), and "Book Publishing in Quebec," *History of the Book in Canada, Vol. III*, 202–5.

234–237   *Aquin*: Gilles de La Fontaine, *Hubert Aquin et le Québec* (Parti pris, 1977); André Durand, "Hubert Aquin," Dec. 2014, www.comptoirlit-teraire.com; Gordon Sheppard, *HA! A Self-Murder Mystery* (MQUP, 2003).

234   *"a few curses"*: Aquin, "Cultural Fatigue," *Writing Quebec*, 41.

*"defective" language*: Aquin, *"Joual*: Haven or Hell?" (1974), trans. Paul Gibson, Reva Joshee, and Anthony Purdy, *Writing Quebec*, 101.

236   *"flaming bordello"*: Aquin, "Occupation: Writer," trans. Paul Gibson, Reva Joshee, and Anthony Purdy, ibid., 50, 53.

*"total war"*: quoted in *Deux episodes dans la vie d'Hubert Aquin*, directed by Jacques Godbout (NFB, 1979), trans. Myra Bloom.

*a revolutionary*: "Mental Test Set for Accused 'Revolutionary,'" *Globe and Mail*, July 8, 1964.

*"learned to write small"*: quoted in Ted Ferguson, "The Mental Inmate Who Had to Write," *Maclean's*, April 2, 1966.

*released on bail*: "Aquin to Be Tried on Two Charges," *Montreal Gazette*, Sep. 23, 1964.

237   *book accepted*: Tisseyre to Aquin, Feb. 10, 1965, Fonds Hubert Aquin, Université du Québec à Montréal.

*$1,000 help*: Canada Council, *Annual Report, 1965–66*, 55.

*"truly inspired"*: Gilles Vadeboncoeur in *Le Devoir*, trans. in Louis Dudek, "Aquin's *Prochain*," *Montreal Gazette*, Feb. 5, 1966, Fonds Aquin.

*"literary bomb"*: quoted in Dominic Marcil, "Champ littéraire et para-doxe de la Révolution tranquille," *Postures* 6 (2004), trans. Myra Bloom.

*"our great writer"*: trans. in Dudek, "Aquin's *Prochain*."

*four thousand copies*: Rapport de Droit d'auteur, Jan 31, 1971, Fonds Aquin.

*Chambres de bois*: André Vanasse, "L'exportation de notre littérature: un échec?" *Lettres québécoises* 58 (1990).

238   *L'Avalée des avalés*: Pascal Millot, "Réjean Ducharme, enquête sur un fantôme," *L'actualité*, April 15, 2000; Myrianne Pavlovic, "L'affaire Ducharme," *Voix et images* 6.1 (1980).

238*   *"My novel is public"*: quoted in Gérald Godin, "Gallimard publie un Québécois de 24 ans, inconnu," *Le magazine Maclean*, Sep. 1966, trans. Myra Bloom; *suggested Cendrars*: Normand Lassonde, "Réjean Ducharme? OUI, c'est MOI!" *Le Nouvelliste*, Aug. 10, 1968, trans. Myra Bloom.

238–239   *Harvest House*: Alan Hustak, "Maynard Gertler," *Métropolitan*, April 27, 2011.

239     *bilingual literary community*: Michael Benazon, "Athens of the North," *Language Acts*, ed. Jason Camlot and Todd Swift (Véhicule, 2007); Sheila Fischman, "Postcard Village," *Montreal Gazette*, March 16, 1979.

240     *"us anglais novelists"*: Ludwig, "Wild Talent," *Globe and Mail*, April 18, 1970.

     *"curtain scene"*: Woodcock, "Comedy of Coffins," *Toronto Daily Star*, April 11, 1970.

     *blue suede coat*: Fischman, "A Life in Translation," CNQ 73 (2008).

     *some forty*: Ronald Sutherland, "The Literature of Québec in Translation," *Read Canadian*, ed. Robert Fulford, David Godfrey, and Abraham Rotstein (Lewis & Samuel, 1972), 238.

     *only six*: Sutherland, *Second Image* (New Press, 1971), 181. The other three were Robert Goulet's *The Violent Season*, Gwethalyn Graham's *Earth and High Heaven*, and Margaret Laurence's *The Fire-Dwellers* (Éditions HMH, 1971), which Sutherland missed.

     *bilingual anthology*: Jacques Godbout and John Robert Colombo, eds., *Poésie/Poetry 64* (1963).

     *sympathetic reviews*: Gilles Henault, "*The Favourite Game*," *La Presse*, Dec. [?] 1963, clipping, Cohen Papers, Fisher Library, MS COLL 122, box 6, folder 1.

241     *no French-Canadian literature*: Laurent Girouard in *Parti pris* 3, trans. in Reid, *Shouting Signpainters*, 52.

     *"enterprise of mystification"*: Major trans. ibid., 148.

     *"most celebrated"*: Denis W. Johnston, *Up the Mainstream: The Rise of Toronto's Alternative Theatres* (UTP, 1991), 162; cf. Jane Koustas, "Quebec Theatre in Toronto," *Studies in Canadian Literature* 17.2 (1992).

     *standard French*: Paul Malone, "Translating and Transplanting the Joual in *Les Belles-Soeurs*," *Theatre Research in Canada* 24.1/2 (2003).

242     *residency permit rejected*: "Swiss Deny Residence to Aquin," *Montreal Gazette*, Dec. 19, 1966.

     *"political commitment"*: Aquin to Governor General, April 15, 1969, Fonds Aquin, trans. Myra Bloom.

     *he'd be happy*: William French, "Leonard Cohen Wants to Be Governor-General?" *Globe and Mail*, May 17, 1969.

243     *"a last chance"*: Yanacopoulo in Sheppard, *HA!*, 36.

     *"I have lived intensely"*: quoted in introduction, *Writing Quebec*, xxiii–xxiv. Sheppard's massive *HA!*—the weirdest book in or about Canadian literature that I have yet encountered—includes a facsimile of the letter, along with pretty much everything else about Aquin's death.

## Chapter 16: In Hardy Country

245–248  *MacLeod*: Holly Rubinsky, "Interview with Alistair MacLeod," *The Brick Reader*, ed. Linda Spalding and Michael Ondaatje (Coach House, 1991); Shelagh Rogers, "Interview with Alistair MacLeod," *Alistair MacLeod: Essays on His Works*, ed. Irene Guilford (Guernica, 2001); William Baer, "Interview with Alistair MacLeod," *Michigan Quarterly Review* 44.2 (2005).

245  *ancestors*: Catherine Lockerbie, "The Literary Tortoise," *The Scotsman* (Edinburgh), Aug. 5, 2000.

"*just like the dog*": quoted in John Laycock, "Carefully Chosen Words," *Windsor Star*, May 10, 2002.

246  *hitchhiked to Elliot Lake*: Charles Taylor, "MacLeod's Own Odyssey," *Globe and Mail*, Dec. 10, 1977.

"*a big mistake*": quoted in Curtis Gillespie, "If Only I Had More Time," *Edmonton Journal*, Jan. 2, 2000.

"*the very best he can*": "Five Questions," *Ottawa Citizen*, Jan. 30, 2005.

246*  *same story*: Rogers interview, 15.

247  "*my native landscape*": Baer interview.

248  "*most effective story*": Patrick A. Brooks, *North American Review* (Spring 1970), 76.

248–252  *Nowlan*: Patrick Toner, *If I Could Turn and Meet Myself: The Life of Alden Nowlan* (Goose Lane, 2000); Gregory M. Cook, *One Heart, One Way: Alden Nowlan, A Writer's Life* (Pottersfield, 2003).

248  "*nose in a book*": quoted in Toner, *If I Could Turn*, 50.

"*few North American writers*": Nowlan to Anne Greer, quoted in Cook, *One Heart*, 193.

249  "*seen me wear lipstick*": Nowlan, "Something to Write About," *Canadian Literature* 68/69 (1976).

"*knapsack crammed with books*": ibid.

251  "*drink vodka*": Nowlan to Cogswell, May 27, 1962, quoted in Cook, *One Heart*, 138.

251–252  "*going to die*": quoted in Gary Geddes and Phyllis Bruce, *Fifteen Canadian Poets* (OUP, 1970), 286.

252  "*half-wit*": Nowlan to Sylvia Pride, April 30, 1968, quoted in Cook, *One Heart*, 198.

"*Newfcult*": Sandra Gwyn, "The Newfoundland Renaissance," *Saturday Night*, April 1976.

253  "*power-house*": Smallwood quoted in Roger Bill, "The Evolution of Cultural Policy in Newfoundland and Labrador," *Newfoundland and Labrador Studies* 24.1 (2009).

253      *provincial archive*: Melvin Baker, "Memorial University's Role in the Establishment of a Provincial Archive," *Newfoundland Studies* 9.1 (1993).

           *Mummers Troupe*: Alan Filewod, "The Mummers Troupe, the Canada Council, and the Production of Theatre History," *Theatre Research in Canada* 19.1 (1998).

254      *"worth writing about"*: Clyde Rose, foreword, *Baffles of Wind and Tide: A Selection of Newfoundland Writings* (Breakwater, 1973).

           *"what they were losing"*: Cook quoted in Gwyn, "Newfoundland Renaissance."

255      *"masters in our own house"*: Moores quoted in Harry H. Hiller, "Emergent Nationalism in Newfoundland," *Ethnic and Racial Studies* 10.3 (1987).

256–257  *Dawe*: interview, June 16, 2008.

257      *Atlantic expatriate community*: Martin Ware, introduction, *An Island in the Sky: Selected Poetry of Al Pittman* (Breakwater, 2003), 18.

258      *"Let Jack top that"*: William French, "Newfoundland on the Coffee Table," *Globe and Mail*, Aug. 16, 1977. See also Patrick O'Flaherty, "Like a Beached Whale?", ibid., Oct. 4, 1975.

           *"got poverty right"*: "Picquefort's Column," *Canadian Forum*, Sep. 1968; *"Don't get funny"*: Nowlan, letter to the editor, *Canadian Forum*, Jan. 1969.

258–259  *"typical scene"*: quoted in Cook, *One Heart*, 309.

259      *"confidence to writers"*: ibid., 286–87.

           *"since pre-birth"*: quoted in Sandra Martin, "'You Carry a Landscape with You,'" *Globe and Mail*, April 29, 2000.

260      *"best piece of Canadian writing"*: McClelland to MacLeod, Nov. 26, 1973, M&S Fonds, McMaster University, Hamilton, box 2Ca40. See also Rick Stapleton, "The Publication of *The Lost Salt Gift of Blood*," Historical Perspectives on Canadian Publishing, http://hpcanpub.mcmaster.ca.

           *writing shack*: Frank Macdonald, "MacLeod Mourned," *Inverness Oran* [2014].

           *richest literary prize*: "MacLeod Wins Ireland's IMPAC Award," Canadian Press NewsWire, May 14, 2001.

           *"in No Hurry"*: Margalit Fox, *New York Times*, April 23, 2014.

## Chapter 17: Lives of Girls and Women

261      *"In the shadows"*: Marie-Clair Blais, "The Sleepers," *Veiled Countries/ Lives* (1964), trans. Michael Harris (Véhicule, 1984), 81.

261–265  *Munro*: Robert Thacker, *Alice Munro: Writing Her Lives* (M&S, 2005); Sheila Munro, *Lives of Mothers and Daughters* (M&S, 2001).

262    *"a private activity"*: quoted in Thacker, *Alice Munro*, 68.

*"My mother"*: ibid., 60.

*in the cafeteria*: Munro interview by Kim Jernigan and Anita Lahey, *New Quarterly* 119 (2011).

*"overly modest"*: quoted in Thacker, *Alice Munro*, 92.

263    *"without housework"*: ibid., 94.

*"most of the writers"*: ibid., 116.

264    *story about a woman*: "The Office," first published in the *Montrealer*, Sep. 1962, collected in *Dance of the Happy Shades* (Ryerson, 1967).

*"very poor"*: quoted in Thacker, *Alice Munro*, 180.

265    *"I can write better books"*: Jim Munro quoted in William French, "In Alice Land," *Globe and Mail*, June 19, 1973.

*"astounded"*: quoted in Thacker, *Alice Munro*, 198.

*first prime minister to attend*: William French, "Leonard Cohen Wants to Be Governor-General?" *Globe and Mail*, May 17, 1969.

266    *"bedroom and kitchen"*: Betty Friedan, *The Feminine Mystique* (Norton, 2013), 27.

*not as rare*: Joanne Meyerowitz, "Beyond the Feminine Mystique," *Journal of American History* 79.4 (1993).

267    *de Beauvoir*: Rosemary Sullivan, *The Red Shoes: Margaret Atwood Starting Out* (HarperFlamingo, 1998), 106.

CTV *pulled Brown*: Berton, *My Times* (Doubleday, 1995), 241–48.

*"Nice girls don't say no"*: Trina Robbins quoted in Susan Kuchinskas, "'That's Ms. Hippie Chick to You," Salon.com, Nov. 17, 1997.

*"a guy thing"*: Atwood, introduction, *Ground Works*, ed. Christian Bök (Anansi, 2002).

*"much of a piss"*: Atwood interview, Dec. 15, 2010.

267–268  *"only good for screwing"*: Atwood quoted in Roy MacGregor, "Mother Oracle," *Canadian Magazine*, Sep. 25, 1976.

268    *based on Bowering*: so thinks Frank Davey in *When Tish Happens* (ECW, 2011), 294.

*"potential muses"*: Marlatt interview, July 17, 2012.

*"Quebec is a woman"*: quoted in Malcolm Reid, *The Shouting Signpainters* (M&S, 1972), 136.

*studying Portuguese*: Joseph Blake, "Interview with P. K. Page," *Making Waves*, ed. Trevor Carolan (Anvil, 2010); cf. Laura Cameron, "Page's Poetic Silence," *Canadian Poetry* 75 (2014).

268    *frustrated housewife*: Gallant quoted in Janice Kulyk Keefer, *Reading Mavis Gallant* (OUP, 1989), 3.

       *"typical housewife"*: Sheila Munro, *Lives of Mothers*, 191.

268*   *"the canon is not male-centered"*: bissett interview, Jan. 27, 2015.

268–269  *"Writing by women"*: Laurence, *Dance on the Earth: A Memoir* (M&S, 1989), 5.

269    *Atwood asked the students*: "Sexual Bias in Canadian Reviewing" (1971), printed as Atwood et al., "A Question of Bias," *LRC*, Nov. 2015.

270    *juvenile parody*: "The Lady of the Lake," *Canadian Forum*, May/June 1974.

       *"snaky-haired Medusa"*: "A Skeletal Novella in Plain Diction," *Globe and Mail*, Sep. 28, 1974.

       *"grab my ass"*: quoted in Sullivan, *Red Shoes*, 245.

270*   *"best piece of fiction"*: "*Surfacing* and the Critics," *Canadian Forum*, ibid.; *"rampant sexism"*: Atwood to Lee, Aug. 5, 1974, Lee Papers, Fisher Library, MS COLL 271, box 1, folder 1. Lee's and Macpherson's letters both appeared in the September *Forum*.

270–274 *Blais*: Mary Jean Green, *Marie-Claire Blais* (Twayne, 1995); Blais, *American Notebooks*, trans. Linda Gaboriau (Talonbooks, 1996).

270    *"I write about monsters"*: Byron Riggan, "Lightning on the Literary Landscape," *Saturday Night*, March 19, 1960. Subsequent Blais quotes are from Riggan's article unless otherwise noted.

272    *woman of the year*: "Editors Pick Dr. Whitton," *Toronto Daily Star*, Dec. 28, 1960.

273–274 *"I'll feel less alone"*: Blais, *American Notebooks*, 73–74.

274    *invited a fan*: Rosemary Sullivan, *Shadow Maker: The Life of Gwendolyn MacEwen* (HarperCollins, 1995), 230; *schoolgirl French*: MacEwen to Blais, ca. 1964, Fonds Marie-Claire Blais, Bibliothèque et Archives nationales du Québec, MSS 266 S5 SS5 D1, trans. Myra Bloom.

275    *Laurence told Gibson*: *Eleven Canadian Novelists Interviewed by Graeme Gibson* (Anansi, 1973), 199.

       *"male, female, or an elephant"*: ibid., 19.

       *"horribly wrong"*: Phyllis Brett Young, *The Torontonians* (MQUP, 2007), 222.

275–276 *Friedan's survey*: *Feminine Mystique*, 431, 433.

276    *"classified as housewife"*: MacLennan, "The Future of the Novel," *Scotchman's Return* (Macmillan, 1960).

       *wasn't a "joiner"*: Laurence quoted in Sullivan, *Red Shoes*, 243.

       *"not a feminist in sight"*: Atwood interview.

276     *"proper path"*: "The Woman as Writer," *Women in the Canadian Mosaic*, ed. Gwen Matheson (Peter Martin, 1976).

*Vancouver Women's Bookstore*: "New Book Store," *Vancouver Sun*, July 19, 1973.

*Toronto Women's Bookstore*: Carol Zavitz, "The Toronto Women's Bookstore," *Canadian Women's Studies* 1.3 (1979).

276*     *"a feminist all my life"*: MacEwen quoted in Sullivan, *Shadow Maker*, 369.

276–277     *"going to be read"*: Atwood interview.

277     *a talk she gave*: "A Writer's Life," trans. Nigel Spencer, *A Writer's Life: The Margaret Laurence Lectures* (M&S, 2011).

*"does not like labels"*: Meigs quoted in Danielle Laurin, "Marie-Claire Blais," *L'actualité*, April 15, 2001, trans. Myra Bloom.

*"fifty people"*: William French, "Coming Home," *Globe and Mail*, Sep. 5, 1974.

279     *"This time it's real"*: quoted in Thacker, *Alice Munro*, 289.

## Chapter 18: Civil Elegies

281     *"selling like shit"*: undated postscript to letter of Nov. 14, 1972, Lee Papers, Thomas Fisher Rare Book Library, MS COLL 271, box 6.

*second Canada Council grant*: Grant Maxwell, "Body Found in Trinidad Drain," *Toronto Sun*, Aug. 24, 1973, clipping, Lee Papers, box 6.

*near Couva*: "Probe Set for Writer's Death," *Baltimore Afro-American*, Dec. 1, 1973.

282     *drafts of about ten novels*: Dennis Lee to Robert Fulford, Aug. 27, 1973, Lee Papers, box 6.

*"die young"*: Robert Fulford, "Death Cut Short 'Ferocious' Energy of Harold Ladoo," *Toronto Star*, Sep. 8, 1973.

*Saturday Night*: "The Short Life and Sudden Death of Harold Ladoo," May 1974.

*"Your dying"*: *The Death of Harold Ladoo* (San Francisco: Kanchenjungas, 1976), 9.

*"my totem"*: Findley to Lee, n.d., Lee Papers, box 5, Findley folder.

*"The artist is strong"*: Ladoo to Lee, Sep. 25, 1972, Lee Papers, box 6.

*"creating myths about myself"*: quoted in Stephen Kimber, "The People's Poet," *The Canadian*, Dec. 18, 1976.

*"a demon possesses me"*: quoted in Elspeth Cameron, *Irving Layton: A Portrait* (Stoddart, 1985), 456.

282    *"I am Lilith"*: quoted in Rosemary Sullivan, *Shadow Maker: The Life of Gwendolyn MacEwen* (HarperCollins, 1995), 201.

       *"I'm your man"*: Leonard Cohen, *I'm Your Man* (Columbia, 1988).

283    *"still disappointingly low"*: W. J. Keith, *Canadian Literature in English*, revised edition, vol. 1 (Porcupine's Quill, 2006), 181.

       *more sympathetic*: e.g. D. A. Hadfield, *Re: Producing Women's Dramatic History* (Talonbooks, 2007).

284    *"no recognizable names"*: Moscovitch quoted in "From Stage to Page," *Quill & Quire*, Jan./Feb. 2015.

       *Davey's survey: From There to Here: A Guide to English-Canadian Literature Since 1960* (Porcépic, 1974).

       *BookThug*: Coleman interview, July 13, 2010.

       *"enduring pleasure"*: Sheard, "Heady Fumes of Ink and Ideas," *Toronto Life*, April 1997.

285    *"scarcely existed"*: Atwood, introduction, *Ground Works*, ed. Christian Bök (Anansi, 2002).

       *"the structure exists"*: Fulford, "Flowers from the Compost," *Books in Canada*, May 1976.

286    *Coutts*: Jamie Reid, "Th Erlee Daze of Blewointment," *bill bissett*, ed. Linda Rogers (Guernica, 2002), 29.

       *Marois*: Elizabeth Gill, "Crossing over Russell Marois," CNQ 89 (2014).

       *Lowther*: Christine Wiesenthal, *The Half-Lives of Pat Lowther* (UTP, 2005).

       *Butler*: Charles Butler Mackay, "Juan Antonio Butler," *Cabbagetown Diary* (WLUP, 2012).

       *"Don't snow me"*: Booth to Lee, Nov. 18, 1969, Lee Papers, box 2.

287    *fifteenth novel: The Heart Goes Last*, on Dec. 26, 2015; *documentary: Al Purdy Was Here*, directed by Brian D. Johnson (Purdy Pictures, 2015).

       *wasn't literary quality*: Heather Jackson, *Those Who Write for Immortality: Romantic Reputations and the Dream of Lasting Fame* (Yale UP, 2015).

287–288  *"Those years were crucial"*: *Typing* (Vintage Canada, 2001), 82.

288    *"verbal explosion"*: *Literary History of Canada*, 2nd ed., vol. 3 (UTP, 1976), 318.

       *"heroic age"*: Marchand, "The Heroic Age of Canadian Literature," *Toronto Star*, Dec. 4, 2004.

       *"golden age"*: Romanow, "A House Half Built," *Walrus*, June 2006.

       *"literary renaissance"*: Berton, *1967* (Doubleday, 1967), 362.

288*  *"CanLit boom"*: "The Well-Read Mr. Weaver," *Radio Guide*, Nov. 1986, 67; *"boomlet"*: Lownsbrough, *The Best Place to Be* (Penguin, 2012), 237.

289  *"naissance"*: Govier quoted in Noah Richler, *This Is My Country: What's Yours?* (M&S, 2007), 433.

*"Perhaps we should rejoice"*: Grant, *Lament for a Nation* (Carleton UP, 1997), 99.

290  *"why so much chatter?"*: Lacey, "Poetry Chronicle IV," *Edge* 9 (1969), reprinted in *Canadian Poetry* 60 (2007), 103–4.

*"much more inspiring"*: Richler, *This Is My Country*, 385.

291  *life after death*: Hood, "Author's Commentary," *Sixteen by Twelve*, ed. John Metcalf (McGraw-Hill Ryerson, 1970), 87.

*absolute despair*: Grant, *Lament for a Nation*, 24.

292  *"opening a floodgate"*: "'How Beautiful We All Were,'" *Walrus*, Oct. 2004.

*CanLit in high schools*: see also Susan Swan, "Why Aren't We Teaching More of These Books?" *Globe and Mail*, Dec. 3, 2010; Michael LaPointe, "What's Happened to CanLit?" *Literary Review of Canada*, May 2013.

*Canada's largest universities*: from data compiled by Sean Allingham (for English Canada) and Myra Bloom (for French Canada).

*"like macramé"*: Stephen Marche, "What Was Canadian Literature?" *Partisan* 1 (April 13, 2015).

*"get on with their art"*: Richler, *This Is My Country*, 387.

293  *as early as 1967*: Frye, *The Modern Century* (OUP, 1967), 17.

*"Can. Lit."*: Birney, *Ice Cod Bell or Stone: A Collection of New Poems* (M&S, 1962), 18. Written in 1959, the poem wasn't titled "Can. Lit." until published in *Delta* in January 1962 (Elspeth Cameron, *Earle Birney* [Penguin, 1994], 408; Peter Noel-Bentley, *Earle Birney: An Annotated Bibliography* [ECW, 1983], B108).

*"coming out of our ears"*: French, *Globe and Mail*, March 22, 1969, A14.

*declared CanLit dead*: "The Rise and Fall of Serious CanLit," *Saturday Night*, May 1979.

294  *inevitable maturing*: Frye and Robert Fulford, "From Nationalism to Regionalism: The Maturing of Canadian Culture," *The Anthology Anthology* (Macmillan, 1984).

*"opened the box"*: Gibson interview, Oct. 26, 2010.

# Sidebar Notes

Acorn, Milton. *I've Tasted My Blood: Poems 1956 to 1968*. Selected by     90
Al Purdy. Toronto: Ryerson Press, 1969.

Aquin, Hubert. *Prochain épisode*. Montréal: Cercle du livre de     237
France, 1965. Translated by Sheila Fischman as *Next Episode*.
Toronto: McClelland & Stewart/NCL, 2001.

———. *Trou de mémoire*. Montréal: Cercle du livre de France, 1968.     242
Translated by Alan Brown as *Blackout*. Toronto: House of
Anansi, 1974.

Atwood, Margaret. *The Animals in That Country*. Toronto: Oxford     125
University Press, 1968.

———. *The Circle Game*. Toronto: Contact Press, 1966.     94

———. *The Edible Woman*. Toronto: McClelland & Stewart, 1969.     95

> *"anti-comedy"*: Atwood quoted in *Eleven Canadian Novelists
> Interviewed by Graeme Gibson* (Anansi, 1973), 20.

———. *The Journals of Susanna Moodie*. Toronto: Oxford University     21
Press, 1970.

———. *Power Politics*. Toronto: House of Anansi, 1971.     59

> *"whole man-woman thing"*: quoted in Rosemary
> Sullivan, *The Red Shoes: Margaret Atwood Starting Out*
> (HarperFlamingo, 1998), 252.

———. *Procedures for Underground*. Toronto: Oxford University     133
Press, 1970.

> *"Don't be alarmed"*: copy signed for Daryl Hine, for sale on
> AbeBooks, Oct. 2014.

> *Frye's notion*: "Canada and Its Poetry," *Canadian Forum*,
> Dec. 1943.

———. *Surfacing*. Toronto: McClelland & Stewart, 1972.  269

———. *Survival: A Thematic Guide to Canadian Literature*. Toronto:  70
House of Anansi, 1972.

Blais, Marie-Claire. *La Belle Bête*. Québec: Institut Littéraire du  272
Québec, 1959. Translated by Merloyd Lawrence as *Mad
Shadows*. Toronto: McClelland & Stewart; London: Jonathan
Cape; Boston: Little, Brown, 1960.

———. *David Sterne*. Montréal: Éditions du Jour, 1967. Translated by  273
David Lobdell. Toronto: McClelland & Stewart, 1973.

"*friends live again*": Blais, *American Notebooks*, trans. Linda
Gaboriau (Talonbooks, 1996), 106.

———. *Un Joualonais sa Joualonie*. Montréal: Éditions du Jour, 1973.  234
Translated by Ralph Manheim as *St. Lawrence Blues*. New
York: Farrar, Straus & Giroux; Toronto: Doubleday Canada,
1974.

———. *Manuscrits de Pauline Archange*. Montréal: Éditions du Jour,  278
1968. Translated by Derek Coltman as *The Manuscripts of
Pauline Archange*. New York: Farrar, Straus & Giroux;
Toronto: Doubleday Canada, 1970.

———. *Une saison dans la vie d'Emmanuel*. Montréal: Éditions du  274
Jour, 1965. Translated by Derek Coltman as *A Season in
the Life of Emmanuel*. New York: Farrar, Straus & Giroux;
Toronto: McGraw-Hill Ryerson, 1966.

"*a kind of gothic tale*": Wendy Smith, "Interview: Marie-
Claire Blais," *World Literature Written in English* 29.1 (1989).

———. *Tête Blanche*. Québec: Institut Littéraire du Québec, 1960.  66
Translated by Charles Fullman. Toronto: McClelland &
Stewart, 1961.

Blaise, Clark. *A North American Education: A Book of Short Fiction*.  72
Garden City, NY: Doubleday; Toronto: Doubleday Canada,
1973.

Bowering, George. *Baseball: A Poem in the Magic Number 9*. Toronto:  155
Coach House, 1967.

*about poetry*: Bowering quoted in Roy Miki, *A Record of
Writing* (Talonbooks, 1990), A6.

"*outlive us*": Davey, *When Tish Happens* (ECW, 2011), 248.

———. *George, Vancouver: A Discovery Poem*. Toronto: Weed/Flower  225
Press, 1970 [1971].

*found a journal*: Bowering interview, July 17, 2012.

———. *Mirror on the Floor*. Toronto: McClelland & Stewart, 1967.  169

————. *Rocky Mountain Foot: A Lyric, a Memoir*. Toronto: McClelland & Stewart, 1968 [1969].                                                  213

Brown, Cassie. *Death on the Ice: The Great Newfoundland Sealing Disaster of 1914*. Toronto: Doubleday Canada; Garden City, NY: Doubleday, 1972.                                                          255

Butler, Juan. *Cabbagetown Diary: A Documentary*. Toronto: Peter Martin, 1970.                                                              101

Campbell, Maria. *Halfbreed*. Toronto: McClelland & Stewart, 1973.          266

  *"biography with a purpose"*: Brendan Frederick R. Edwards, "Maria Campbell's *Halfbreed*," Historical Perspectives on Canadian Publishing, McMaster University, http://hpcan-pub.mcmaster.ca.

Carrier, Roch. *La guerre, yes sir!* Montréal: Éditions du Jour, 1968. Translated by Sheila Fischman. Toronto: House of Anansi, 1970.                                                                     240

Clarke, Austin C. *The Meeting Point*. London: Heinemann; Toronto, Macmillan, 1967.                                                           106

  *some reviewers objected*: e.g. Chicago *Tribune*, May 21, 1972, J5, and Miriam Waddington, "No Meeting Points," *Canadian Literature* 35 (1968).

Cohen, Leonard. *Beautiful Losers*. Toronto: McClelland & Stewart; New York: Viking, 1966.                                                    30

  *"most vivid"*: quoted in Stan Dragland, Afterword, *Beautiful Losers* (M&S/NCL, 1991), 268.

————. *The Favourite Game*. New York: Viking; London: Secker & Warburg, 1963.                                                               205

  *"says it well"*: Lorne Parton, "The Written Word," *Vancouver Province*, Sep. 21, 1963, photocopy, Cohen Papers, box 6, folder 1.

————. *Flowers for Hitler*. Toronto: McClelland & Stewart, 1964.          206

————. *Let Us Compare Mythologies*. McGill Poetry Series. Montreal: Contact Press, 1956.                                                      150

————. *The Spice-Box of Earth*. Toronto: McClelland & Stewart, 1961.       174

  *"I want an audience"*: quoted in Sylvie Simmons, *I'm Your Man: The Life of Leonard Cohen* (M&S, 2012), 77.

Coleman, Victor. *One/Eye/Love*. Toronto: Coach House, 1967.               153

Davey, Frank. *D-Day and After*. Oliver, BC: Rattlesnake Press for Tishbooks, 1962.                                                          217

Davies, Robertson. *Fifth Business*. Toronto: Macmillan; New York: Viking, 1970.                                                             37

Dawe, Tom. *Hemlock Cove and After*. Portugal Cove, NF: Breakwater   257
Books, 1975.

Ducharme, Réjean. *L'avalée des avalés*. Paris: Gallimard, 1966.   238
Translated by Barbara Bray as *The Swallower Swallowed*.
London: Hamish Hamilton, 1968.

Engel, Marian. *No Clouds of Glory*. Toronto: Longmans Canada, 1968.   100

Findley, Timothy. *The Last of the Crazy People*. New York: Meredith   99
Press; London: Macdonald; Toronto: General Publishing,
1967.

> *reviewers wondered*: e.g. John Clute, "Mom's Mad, Dad's
> Depressed, Sonny's Silly," *Globe and Mail*, June 3, 1967.

Frye, Northrop. *The Educated Imagination*. Toronto: Canadian   121
Broadcasting Corporation, 1963.

> *seventh printing*: John Ayre, *Northrop Frye* (Random
> House), 286.

———. *The Modern Century*. Toronto: Oxford University Press, 1967.   55

Gallant, Mavis. *Green Water, Green Sky*. Boston: Houghton Mifflin,   182
1959.

———. *My Heart Is Broken: Eight Stories and a Short Novel*. New   117
York: Random House, 1964.

———. *The Other Paris*. Boston: Houghton Mifflin, 1956.   181

> *"doesn't get better"*: Keefer, *Reading Mavis Gallant* (OUP,
> 1989), 12.

———. *The Pegnitz Junction: A Novella and Five Short Stories*. New   192
York: Random House, 1973.

> *"where fascism came from"*: interview with Geoff Hancock,
> *Canadian Fiction Magazine* 28 (1978), 41.

Gibson, Graeme. *Five Legs*. Toronto: House of Anansi, 1969.   159

> *"most sophisticated"*: quoted on back cover of third printing.

Glassco, John. *Memoirs of Montparnasse*. Toronto: Oxford University   139
Press, 1970.

> *"Nous voici encore"*: Arthur Marshall, "Well-Spent Youths,"
> *New Statesman*, May 29, 1970.

Godfrey, Dave. *Death Goes Better with Coca-Cola*. Toronto: House   144
of Anansi, 1967.

> *"first-rate work," etc.*: quoted on back cover of first edition.

———. *The New Ancestors*. Toronto: New Press, 1970.   38

Hébert, Anne. *Kamouraska*. Paris: Éditions du Seuil, 1970. Translated   233
by Norman Shapiro. Toronto: Musson, 1973.

Hood, Hugh. *Flying a Red Kite*. Toronto: Ryerson Press, 1962.  141

    *Metcalf called*: *Freedom from Culture* (ECW, 1994), 160.

Janes, Percy. *House of Hate*. Toronto: McClelland & Stewart, 1970.  253

Johnston, George. *The Cruising Auk*. Toronto: Oxford University Press, 1959.  28

    *"not so much a poet"*: The Essential George Johnston (Porcupine's Quill, 2007), 61.

Jonas, George. *The Happy Hungry Man*. Toronto: House of Anansi, 1970.  114

Kroetsch, Robert. *The Studhorse Man*. Toronto: Macmillan; London: MacDonald, 1969; New York: Simon and Schuster, 1970.  208

    *"Horny books"*: Paul West, "The Studhorse Man," *New York Times*, April 26, 1970.

Ladoo, Harold Sonny. *No Pain Like This Body*. Toronto: House of Anansi, 1972.  160

Lane, Patrick. *Letters from the Savage Mind*. Vancouver: Very Stone House, 1966.  223

    *"poetry saved me"*: Lane, *There Is a Season* (M&S, 2004), 51.

Laurence, Margaret. *A Bird in the House*. Toronto: McClelland & Stewart; New York: Knopf; London: Macmillan, 1970.  167

    *"women's magazine standards"*: Honor Tracy, "Growing Up in Manawaka," *New York Times*, April 19, 1970.

———. *The Diviners*. Toronto: McClelland & Stewart; New York: Knopf; London: Macmillan, 1974.  177

    *"extraordinary gift"*: Phyllis Grosskurth, "Sexually Uninhibited Laurence," *Globe and Mail*, May 4, 1974.

———. *The Fire-Dwellers*. Toronto: McClelland & Stewart, 1969.  29

———. *A Jest of God*. London: Macmillan; New York: Knopf; Toronto: McClelland & Stewart, 1966.  275

    *several reviewers*: according to Robert Fulford, "A Painful Life," *Toronto Daily Star*, Sep. 30, 1966.

———. *The Stone Angel*. London: Macmillan; Toronto: McClelland & Stewart; New York: Knopf, 1964.  166

———. *This Side Jordan*. Toronto: McClelland & Stewart; London: Macmillan; New York: St. Martin's, 1960.  165

    *"easiest novel"*: Laurence, *Dance on the Earth: A Memoir* (M&S, 1989), 152.

    *"suspiciously sunny"*: Gerda Charles, "New Novels," *New Statesman*, Nov. 19, 1960.

    *adaptation for CBS*: "Show Shows Problems Now Facing Africa," *New York Amsterdam News*, March 4, 1961.

Layton, Irving. *Balls for a One-Armed Juggler*. Toronto: McClelland & Stewart, 1963.   198

    *"nasty bore"*: C.J. Vincent, "Layton's Labor Lost," *Globe and Mail*, Feb. 23, 1963.

———. *The Laughing Rooster*. Toronto: McClelland & Stewart, 1964.   209

    *"Poems in Poor Taste"*: preface, *The Laughing Rooster*, 25. *"affirming life"*: "The Tragic Poet," ibid., 57.

———. *A Red Carpet for the Sun*. Toronto: McClelland & Stewart, 1959.   172

    *"any word!"*: quoted in Elspeth Cameron, *Irving Layton* (Stoddart, 1985), 63.

———. *The Swinging Flesh*. Toronto: McClelland & Stewart, 1961.   197

    *"best thing since Dubliners"*: Layton to Pacey, May 13, 1961, quoted in Cameron, *Irving Layton*, 325.

Lee, Dennis. *Civil Elegies and Other Poems*. Toronto: House of Anansi, 1972.   105

———. *Kingdom of Absence*. Toronto: House of Ananse, 1967.   149

    *"For five years"*: "Interview with Dennis Lee," *Canadian Fiction Magazine* 6 (1972).

    *"enact in words"*: Lee, "Cadence, Country, Silence," *Body Music* (Anansi, 1998), 24.

Levine, Norman. *One-Way Ticket*. London: Secker & Warburg; London [*sic*]: McClelland & Stewart, 1961.   183

MacEwen, Gwendolyn. *Julian the Magician*. New York: Corinth Books, 1963.   79

———. *The Rising Fire*. Toronto: Contact Press, 1963.   81

———. *The Shadow Maker*. Toronto: Macmillan of Canada, 1969.   82

MacLennan, Hugh. *The Watch That Ends the Night*. Toronto: Macmillan; New York: Scribner's; London: Heinemann, 1959.   19

    *18,000 copies*: Elspeth Cameron, *A Writer's Life* (UTP, 1981), 287.

MacLeod, Alistair. *The Lost Salt Gift of Blood*. Toronto: McClelland & Stewart, 1976.   247

    *"finest book"*: Hugh MacLennan to Jack McClelland, March 26, 1976, quoted in Rick Stapleton, "The Publication of *The Lost Salt Gift of Blood*," Historical Perspectives on Canadian Publishing, McMaster University.

Marlatt, Daphne. *Steveston*. Photographs by Robert Minden. Vancouver: Talonbooks, 1974.   221

    *oral-history project*: Fred Wah, introduction, *Selected Writing*, by Daphne Marlatt (Talonbooks, 1980), 12.

———. *Vancouver Poems.* Toronto: Coach House, 1972.　218

　"*thru the poems*": Marlatt, Aug. 10, 1970, *What Matters:
　Writing 1968-70* (Coach House, 1980), 154.

Marois, Russell. *The Telephone Pole.* Toronto: House of Anansi/　239
　Spiderline, 1969.

McLuhan, Marshall. *Understanding Media: The Extensions of Man.*　63
　New York: McGraw-Hill, 1964.

McLuhan, Marshall, and Quentin Fiore. *The Medium is the Massage:*　185
　*An Inventory of Effects.* New York: Bantam, 1967.

　*seventeen publishers*: Philip Marchand, *Marshall McLuhan:
　The Medium and the Messenger* (Random House, 1989),
　192-93.

　"*didn't have the time*": Agel quoted in Marvin Kitman, "Get
　the Message?" *New York Times*, March 26, 1967.

Metcalf, John. *Going Down Slow.* Toronto: McClelland & Stewart,　67
　1972.

Mowat, Farley. *The Boat Who Wouldn't Float.* Toronto: McClelland　254
　& Stewart, 1969.

Munro, Alice. *Dance of the Happy Shades.* Toronto: Ryerson Press,　' 263
　1968.

———. *Lives of Girls and Women: A Novel.* Toronto: McGraw-Hill　264
　Ryerson, 1971.

　"*young girl*": J.R. Struthers, "Interview with Alice Munro,"
　*Probable Fictions: Alice Munro's Narrative Acts*, ed. Louis
　K. MacKendrick (ECW, 1983), 25.

———. *Something I've Been Meaning to Tell You.* Toronto: McGraw-　83
　Hill Ryerson; New York: McGraw-Hill, 1974.

Nichol, bp. *bp.* Toronto: Coach House Press, 1967.　131

　"*poetry kit*": Marilyn Beker, "Concrete Poetry," *Toronto
　Daily Star*, Aug. 12, 1967.

———. *The Captain Poetry Poems.* Vancouver: Blewointment Press,　200
　1971.

　"*macho male bullshit*": Nichol, "Some Words on All
　These Words" (1986), *The Captain Poetry Poems Complete*
　(BookThug, 2011).

———. *The Martyrology: Books 1 & 2.* Toronto: Coach House Press,　24
　1972.

———. *The True Eventual Story of Billy the Kid.* Toronto: Weed/　52
　Flower Press,1970.

　"*affront to decency*": *Hansard*, June 10, 1971, 6554.

Nowlan, Alden. *Bread, Wine and Salt*. Toronto and Vancouver: Clarke, Irwin, 1967. 252

Ondaatje, Michael. *The Collected Works of Billy the Kid*. Toronto: House of Anansi, 1970. 137

*"what's-his-name"*: "Who Needs Davy Crockett?" *Toronto Star*, Nov. 30, 1971.

———. *The Dainty Monsters*. Toronto: Coach House, 1967. 156

Purdy, Al. *The Cariboo Horses*. Toronto: McClelland & Stewart, 1965. 119

*on a map*: D.G. Jones, "Al Purdy's Contemporary Pastoral," *Canadian Poetry* 10 (1982).

*"telephone booth"*: Purdy, *Reaching for the Beaufort Sea* (Harbour, 1993), 52.

———. *Love in a Burning Building*. Toronto: McClelland & Stewart, 1970. 207

*"leftovers"*: Atwood, "Love Is Ambiguous," *Canadian Literature* 49 (1971).

———, ed. *The New Romans: Candid Canadian Opinions of the U.S.* Edmonton: Hurtig, 1968. 189

*30,000 copies*: Marci McDonald, "Editor Purdy," *Toronto Daily Star*, Sep. 10, 1968.

*prompted a sequel*: Wainwright interview, June 5, 2008.

———. *North of Summer: Poems from Baffin Island*. Toronto: McClelland & Stewart, 1967. 44

*old Inuk*: Purdy to George Woodcock, Aug. 21, 1965, *Collected Letters of Al Purdy*, ed. Sam Solecki (Harbour, 2004), 113.

*"geriatric vomit"*: Purdy to Laurence, April 20, 1967, ibid., 129.

———. *Poems for All the Annettes*. Toronto: Contact Press, 1962. 111

———. *Selected Poems*. Toronto: McClelland & Stewart, 1972. 170

*another poet*: Purdy to Brian McCarthy, May 12, 1973, *Collected Letters of Al Purdy*, 224.

Richler, Mordecai. *The Apprenticeship of Duddy Kravitz*. London: André Deutsch, 1959. 36

———. *Cocksure*. London: Weidenfeld & Nicolson; Toronto: McClelland & Stewart; New York: Simon and Schuster, 1968. 87

*"staggeringly filthy"*: quoted in Charles Foran, *Mordecai: The Life and Times* (Knopf, 2010), 336.

*"wish I'd written it"*: quoted in Simon & Schuster ad, *New York Times*, April 9, 1968, 45.

————. *The Incomparable Atuk*. London: André Deutsch; Toronto:    49
McClelland & Stewart; New York, Simon & Schuster, 1963.

*Twentyman Fur Company*: Reinhold Kramer, *Mordecai Richler* (MQUP, 2008), 163.

*"worst work"*: quoted in James King, *Jack: A Life with Writers* (Knopf, 1999), 131.

————. *St. Urbain's Horseman*. Toronto: McClelland & Stewart; New    45
York, Knopf; London: Weidenfeld & Nicolson, 1971.

*"rich pleasure"*: Jonathan Yardley, *New York Times*, June 27, 1971, BR7.

Thomas, Audrey Callahan. *Ten Green Bottles*. Indianapolis: Bobbs-    187
Merrill, 1967.

*her experiences*: *A Writer's Life: The Margaret Laurence Lectures* (M&S, 2011).

Vallières, Pierre. *Nègres blancs d'Amèrique: Autobiographie pré-*    231
*coce d'un "terroriste québécois."* Montréal: Éditions Parti
pris, 1968. Translated by Joan Pinkham as *White Niggers of America*. Toronto: McClelland & Stewart, 1971.

Watson, Sheila. *The Double Hook*. Toronto: McClelland & Stewart,    89
1959.

*western that wasn't a western*: Watson, "What I'm Going to Do," *Sheila Watson and The Double Hook*, ed. George Bowering (Golden Dog, 1985), 14.

*obscure*: Isabelle Hughes, "Left Hook, Right Hook, KO!" *Globe and Mail*, May 16, 1959.

Webb, Phyllis. *Naked Poems*. Vancouver: Periwinkle Press, 1965.    219

*"private achievement"*: Colombo, "Energetic and Exciting," *Globe and Mail*, Feb. 12, 1966.

————. *The Sea Is Also a Garden*. Toronto: Ryerson, 1962.    115

Wiebe, Rudy. *The Temptations of Big Bear*. Toronto: McClelland &    71
Stewart, 1973.

Young, Phyllis Brett. *The Torontonians*. Toronto: Longmans, Green,    97
1960.

# Index

Page numbers in *italics* refer to text in sidebars.

**NICK MOUNT** is a professor of English literature at the University of Toronto, an award-winning critic, and former fiction editor at *The Walrus*. He regularly gives public talks on the arts in Canada, and has appeared on TVO's *Big Ideas* and CBC Radio's *Sunday Edition*. In 2011, he was awarded a 3M National Teaching Fellowship, the country's highest teaching award. He lives in Toronto.

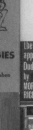

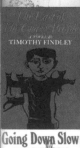